*computer–aided*

*design of digital systems*

# Computer Systems Engineering Series

DOUGLAS LEWIN, *Editor*

# Computer-Aided Design of Digital Systems

## Douglas Lewin

Crane Russak • *New York*
Edward Arnold • *London*

Computer-Aided Design of Digital Systems

*Published in the United States by*

Crane, Russak & Company, Inc.
347 Madison Avenue
New York, N.Y. 10017

*First published in Great Britain in 1977 by*

Edward Arnold (Publishers) Ltd.
25 Hill Street
London, W1X 8LL

Crane, Russak ISBN 0-8448-0918-7
Edward Arnold ISBN 0-7131-2633-7

LC 76-250

*Printed in the United States of America*

# Contents

In Memory

of my Mother, Rose Ann,

without whom...

# Editor's Foreword

The continuing expansion of knowledge in the computer sciences means that it is now more important than ever for the professional computer engineer to keep abreast of the latest developments in his field. Moreover, due to the rapid assimilation of computer techniques into all areas of science and engineering, non-specialists are also finding it essential to acquire expertise in these disciplines. Thus, there exists a need for readable, up-to-date texts on relevant specialist topics of computer engineering which can form authoritative source books for both the practicing engineer and the academic.

This series is an attempt to fulfill such a requirement and is directed primarily at the professional engineer and graduate student in computer technology; in many cases the books will also meet the needs of specialist options offered in undergraduate courses.

The texts will embrace all aspects of computer systems design with an overall emphasis on the engineering of integrated hardware–software systems. In general the series will present established theory and techniques which have found direct application in systems design. However, promising new theoretical methods will also be covered.

All the books will follow a similar basic pattern of a review of the fundamental aspects of the subject, followed by a survey of the current state of the art, and, where applicable, design examples. An important feature will be the associated bibliography and references, which will select the more important and fundamental publications. The objective is to bring the reader up to a level in the subject where he can read current technical papers and apply the results to his own research and design activities. In the main, authors will be chosen from specialists in their field, drawn from both industrial and academic environments, and experienced in communicating technical ideas.

New books will be regularly added to the series to provide an up-to-date source of specialist texts in Computer Systems Engineering.

DOUGLAS LEWIN
*Brunel University*

vii

# Preface

At Least One of the Pregnant Mysteries is Brought to Bed,
With Full Measure of Travail, but Not as Yet Delivered to
the Light.

*The Sot-Weed Factor* – John Barth

The use of digital computers as an aid to the engineering of digital systems is not a recent innovation. Indeed, design automation (DA) schemes have been in existence since the time of first-generation computers. These earlier systems, and the majority of subsequent ones, were principally concerned with production logistics such as printed circuit board layout and the generation of wiring schedules etc. The system and logic-design phases were performed manually, using experience and intuition, based on the theory of gate-level switching circuits. With the introduction of LSI logic components, however, the situation has radically changed. Digital systems have now reached such a high level of sophistication that conventional engineering design practice is proving inadequate. The major problem is the sheer complexity of the systems which are possible using

LSI subsystem modules such as arithmetic units, shift registers, and microprocessor chips. In order to handle and control this complexity it has become essential to enlist the aid of computers in the initial specification and design stages of digital systems engineering. Moreover, the major problem of digital-system design, that of ensuring reliable and secure operation, may only be soluble using more formal design techniques which must of necessity be implemented on a computer. It has thus become essential for designers to be fully conversant with existing software tools for digital-system design, such as logic simulators, fault-test generators, hardware description languages, etc., and to prepare themselves for the new design techniques which must inevitably emerge if digital systems are to be fully exploited in the future.

The objective of this book is to review the current state of computer-assisted design and to attempt to present the fundamental principles which have so far emerged. In addition the subject matter is presented in such a way that the book should be of interest both to the user and designer of design automation schemes. The book commences with an introductory chapter covering the philosophyof computer-aided design and the relevant programming techniques. This is followed by chapters on specifying and evaluating the system, simulation techniques both at systems and gate level, system synthesis methods, and finally logic-circuit testing and fault-tolerant design. Each chapter contains an extensive list of references and bibliography to enable the work described (much of which has never before been published in book form) to be pursued further.

The book is intended primarily for use as a specialized text for post-graduate students in Computer Science and Engineering, and as an introduction to the subject for practicing engineers. However, in certain cases it would also be suitable as a course text for final-year options in undergraduate courses; a basic knowledge of switching theory, logic design, and programming is assumed on the part of the reader.

In conclusion I would like to thank all my ex-research students and colleagues who have contributed, often unwittingly, to the ideas expressed in this book. Lastly, but certainly not least, my sincerest thanks to Audrey Witham who translated my scrawl into interpretable text and managed at the same time to keep my spirits high.

# Basic Principles

## 1.1. INTRODUCTION

*Computer-Aided Design (CAD)* is concerned with the application of digital computers and computer-based techniques to the design of engineering systems. The use of digital computers to assist in the engineering design process is not novel; in fact the numerical solution of design equations was one of the earliest applications of computers. Thus, the term CAD was used initially to describe the application of computers to any design calculation; it has now taken on a more specific meaning referring to interactive systems where the designer and computer are working together in an intimate partnership. Note that it is not intended that the engineer becomes redundant, but should in fact be the senior partner in the relationship, providing the overall control and creative inspiration. Using CAD systems the engineer is able to explore new ideas and techniques, with design results being rapidly communicated back to him in a graphical or typewritten form. In this way the experienced designer can quickly acquire a fundamental understanding of the problems involved, whilst at the same time gaining valuable experience of different design procedures. As well as providing analysis and synthesis procedures, the use of CAD also enables the engineer to document his designs and generate checking facilities.

Owing to the logistics problems peculiar to the engineering of digital systems, such as the generation of wiring schedules, cabinet and printed circuit board (PCB) layout, etc., the computer industry was one of the first major users of CAD methods. Manufacturers of MOS and LSI components were also quick to appreciate the advantages of CAD, particularly for chip layout and artwork design. Subsequently, systems have become more sophisticated, and include gate-level simulation, logic synthesis and testing facilities, and automatic mask generation, as well as the initial applications of component placement, logic partitioning, and wire routing. Thus, complete *Design Automation* schemes are now available which assist the designer through all stages of development and production, providing automatic documentation, wiring and maintenance schedules, etc. In many cases a common *data base* is used to store all relevant information, including design and production data, component libraries, management information, etc., to provide a fully *integrated CAD scheme.*

Why was it that the computer industry in particular found it necessary to adopt and develop CAD techniques? Present-day computer systems, comprising both hardware and software processes, represent one of the most sophisticated technological advances of modern society. Consequently, it has been essential to employ CAD methods in order to achieve the required reliability and performance. However, CAD has in the main been applied to the production engineering stages, and the initial systems and logic-design processes are still performed in the traditional manner. For example, most CAD systems require a logic diagram, suitably digitized, as the primary input source. Actual design programs (for example, logic synthesis packages) are still not generally available. The only software design tool which has so far met with general acceptance is the logic simulator, which enables the engineer to model (and evaluate) his circuits at the basic gate (or register transfer) level.

Unfortunately, the existing techniques are still inadequate to cope with the ever-increasing requirements of present-day digital systems. Computer-systems manufacturers are slowly, but inevitably, reaching a stage where the sheer physical and intellectual complexity of the systems they are attempting to design are establishing barriers to further progress. The phrase "complexity barrier" was coined by Glazer (1) as early as 1969 to describe this situation, which unfortunately is even more apparent at the present time. That this situation still exists is evidenced by the current state of the industry, where, for example computer systems are often late in delivery and in many cases still contain logical faults even after final installation has taken place. (For similar reasons CAD plays a smaller part than it should do in MOS/LSI circuit design. This is due, in the main, to uneconomical implementation techniques and a heavy reliance on error-prone manual operations.)

The objective of this book is to introduce digital engineers to computer-design techniques that are rapidly becoming required practice for the development of large digital systems and to outline some of the inherent problems involved. In so doing it is hoped that progress in this field will be accelerated so that the necessary software tools, essential to design the complex systems of the future, will emerge.

We shall commence by describing a typical design automation scheme and then, after considering some of the basic difficulties involved in developing such a system, carry on to examine the individual techniques, such as simulation, synthesis, testing, etc., in more detail. We shall not, however, consider the more production-oriented methods, such as component placement and interconnection, since it is felt that the major problems exist in the initial design phases.

## 1.2. DESIGN AUTOMATION SYSTEMS (2, 3)

Design automation (DA) is primarily concerned with reducing the cost and development time normally required in engineering complex digital systems. In general, design automation is restricted to those aspects of design which are involved with translating the initial systems specification into a viable logic design, complete with packaging and fabrication details. Though a complete DA scheme comprises many varied functions, as can be seen from Fig. 1.1 they all have the common objective of eliminating the repetitive manual and computational procedures.

There are many advantages in using a design automation system.

(a) Allows formal design algorithms to be adopted without requiring tedious hand computation, and in many cases expert theoretical knowledge.

(b) Fast and error-free (providing the initial specification is correctly formulated) design of large variable systems.

(c) Alternative designs may be evaluated by restating the problems or by changing implementation parameters such as minimization criteria, logic modules, board sizes, layout, etc.

(d) The establishment of a common data base, storing library, and derived design information allows detailed documentation to be provided for all stages of the design process.

(e) Wiring schedules, cable lists, cabinet and board layouts, and other manufacturing data can be prepared automatically, or extracted from the data-base and modified as required.

(f) Modification and editing of design data is easily accomplished without the risk of introducing errors.

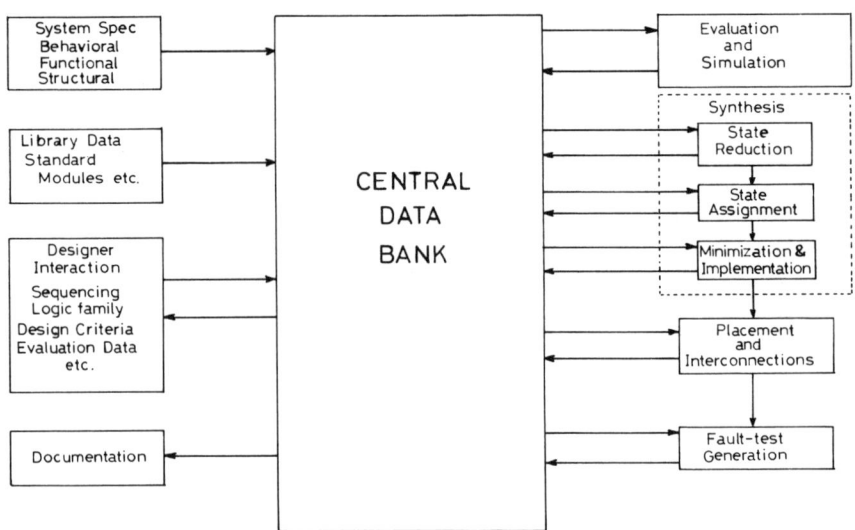

**Figure 1.1.** Design automation system.

(g) Simulation packages allow logic designs to be evaluated, and errors corrected, before proceeding to final implementation.

(h) Automatic generation of fault-test schedules, or manual generation using simulation techniques, can be provided.

A generalized scheme for a design automation system is shown in Fig. 1.1. This is centered around a shared data base (typically a disk-based information-retrieval system) which communicates directly with each functional package of the CAD system; communication is also possible between selected individual design packages. In operation, design packages can either access the data base for relevant input data or obtain it directly from other packages; output results are always returned to the data-base.

External inputs to the DA system arise principally from the designers who would initially compile the standards library consisting of a catalog of subsystem modules, fan-in–fan-out constraints, costs, and any other relevant design parameters. Other inputs from the designer, ideally in a real-time terminal based interactive mode, would include the initial system description (both conceptual and functional levels), requests for documentation, library updating, modifications and amendments, selection of design criteria, etc. All these input operations would be executed under the command of the CAD operating system which has overall control of all DA system functions, for example, sequencing and selection of CAD packages, input–output transfers, etc. Computer-aided design packages are available for most of the digital engineering functions, from logic synthesis and analysis through implementation, placement and interconnections to fault-test generation. Documentation is available at all stages, providing feedback to the designer and information for manufacturing and maintenance personnel.

Existing design automation schemes are, in the main, batch-processing rather than interactive systems. However, the essential designer involvement can be obtained by allowing the designer to change the parameters in the DA programs or input new data, etc., depending on the results of previous trial runs. The disadvantage of this mode of working is obviously the time required to develop a design. This depends virtually on the turn-round time of the computer installation, that is, the overall operational and organizational time required to produce results. In some cases it has been found necessary to have computers entirely dedicated to the CAD function; this is of course out of the question for many smaller companies.

There is no doubt that interactive schemes, based on teletype or graphics terminals, are far superior to batch-processing systems. Moreover, the facility of having immediate access to CAD programs is essential for many design functions, for example, logic design and simulation, LSI circuit design, component layout, etc.

The inclusion of synthesis packages (in conjunction with a suitable method of system specification and evaluation) in the DA scheme vastly increases its usefulness, particularly when coupled with interactive techniques. Such a system, for example, would allow the designer to specify and evaluate a systems proposal and then proceed directly to implementation (using either hardware or software modules), thus producing a viable engineering design. The main advantage of a "front-end" of this type is the reduced costs and time involved in producing reliable designs (including quotations), and the facility to perform system evaluation and optimization. Moreover, the creative ability of the designer continually increases as he learns through man–machine interaction. Unfortunately, systems of this type have not, as yet, been fully developed (4, 5).

One reason for the lack of progress in DA [the first papers on design automation were published as early as 1956 (6)] is that manufacturers tend to develop DA systems which are peculiar to their own computer and engineering requirements. Moreover, since there are considerable technical and economic advantages to be gained in using DA techniques (and also a considerable investment in manpower and computing), manufacturers are understandably reluctant to make their systems freely available.

## 1.3. THE PROBLEMS OF COMPLEXITY

At this point it is necessary to define more specifically what is meant by complexity in order to appreciate the difficulties associated with designing digital systems and also in developing CAD software tools. A complex logical system can be considered as being comprised of a large number of functional subsystems that interact in a non-trivial manner to determine the information flow through the total system. In such systems the whole is greater than the sum of the individual components in the sense that, given the transfer functions of the components and the laws of their interaction, it is a complex and difficult process to infer the characteristics of the total system. Moreover, in order to describe and design sophisticated digital systems it seems inherently necessary to decompose the total system into suitable subsystem functions which in many cases conform to a hierarchical structure.

Currently, digital engineering is still in the main performed intuitively, with the system being designed, generally from the lowest level upwards, using MSI and LSI logic subsystems. Though a partitioning of the system can be achieved in this manner, a true hierarchical structure is not necessarily obtained. This demands that the partitioning is performed taking into consideration the specified relationships that are required between the subsystem components. This can only be done by designing from the top down, that is from a functional specification to actual operational components. Note that there are a number of differing criteria that may be used to partition the system, for example, logical operation, ease of manufacture (size of board, number of pins, etc.), diagnostic testing, use of existing subsystems, hardware–software implementation, etc. Ideally it should be possible to partition the system in a number of different ways, attempting to optimize globally about certain system-design parameters, for instance, trade-offs between development and manufacturing costs and reliability and maintainability. Unfortunately, at the present time the lack of suitable design aids normally means that an inspired guess as to the correct partitioning must be made at the initial design stages. Once the design has been commenced it is then far too time consuming and costly to attempt to re-configure the system. This "do or die" method of working also applies to a limited extent at the lower levels of subsystem design.

Thus, we have a situation where complex systems are being developed without any fundamental basis of design, except that of hard-won experience. It is essential to partition the system to handle the complexity involved. However, the partitioning should be done in a logical manner so as to achieve a heirarchical structure capable of providing a viable engineering design; to date no technique or methodology exists which provides the digital engineer with the necessary tools to perform this function.

The use of CAD techniques can improve the situation by systems-level simulation and automated design and testing procedures, etc., but until a suitable means of representing, and evaluating, systems is developed (and there is a sad lack of mathematical formalism in this area) no real improvements will be obtained. The current state of the art in this area, and some indications as to future trends, are reviewed in Chapter 2 which is concerned with system specification.

At another level a more fundamental difficulty associated with the automatic design of logic systems, and also encountered in the artificial intelligence area, is the vast amount of computation and storage required to solve practical (that is, large-variable) problems. For example, it is comparatively simple to program a computer to effect a Boolean minimization based on the Quine–McCluskey algorithm (7). However, the computational time rapidly increases with the number of switching variables until the process becomes impracticable. The actual amount of computation time that can be tolerated varies with the application. In one-off batch-design processes it is simply a matter of economics, but in interactive design schemes the computation time can impose a real constraint on system performances.

This rapid expansion of computational time, known as a "combinatorial explosion", is a limiting factor in all areas of information processing and prohibits the use of formal algorithmic methods which derive an exact optimum solution to a problem. Computer algorithms based on these methods work well for a limited universe of discourse, but in a real environment, involving many degrees of freedom, existing computing facilities are just not adequate enough to effect a solution.

In order to understand fully this basic limitation it is necessary to be more explicit in the definition of the term algorithm (8). An algorithm is generally defined as a finite set of rules which gives a sequence of operations for solving a specific class of problem. In general the difficulties outlined above are due to the *finiteness* property of the algorithm. An algorithm must, of course, always terminate after a finite number of steps, but the *number* of steps involved is a critical parameter which determines the efficacy of the algorithm for computer usage. Many problems can be solved algorithmically, but the time required to compute the answer can be so large that to all intents and purposes the problem remains insoluble. Thus, a practical (computable) algorithm must have a reasonable number of finite steps which are executed in a realistic time (dependent on the application and the number of variables involved).

In many areas of non-numerical data processing, particularly those involved with engineering design, it is not possible (or even desirable) to generate an exact unique answer (in the majority of cases a unique answer does not exist). The engineering design process can be described as a selective "trial and error" procedure which optimizes about given parameters and constraints—in fact a compromise or "trade-off" solution is generally required. The theoretical optimum is usually impossible (or uneconomical) to obtain and it is therefore necessary to be content with a satisfactory solution in terms of engineering viability. The term "satisficing" has been coined by Simon (9) to describe problem-solving procedures where some ideal properties are sacrificed for a satisfactory solution.

This problem is fundamental to any information-processing function, for example pattern recognition; in order to achieve an optimum result it is necessary to have available all the basic and derived data about the system; in most practical cases this is an impossibility. The answer lies in the selection of the important and characteristic parameters for the system in the hope that this will lead to a satisfactory result. The design of logic circuits is an easier problem in some respects since, providing the original switching requirements are satisfied, a functional correct but non-optimal circuit can always be obtained.

Since the techniques of human design (and problem solving in general) have the characteristic of searching for a satisfactory solution rather than an exact one, methods of emulating this approach on the computer, known as *heuristic* programming, have been evolved. In general a heuristic is a set of rules which, if followed, may achieve a solution but cannot guarantee doing so. In practice a heuristic is an approximate (in the solution sense) form of algorithm which relaxes the constraints imposed by the problem parameters to allow a satisfactory (according to some predetermined criteria) rather than an exact solution to be obtained. In so doing the amount of computing time (and storage space) is considerably reduced, thus providing an economic solution. Moreover, many problems (especially in the artificial-intelligence area) are impossible to formulate using standard algorithmic methods, for example parking a motor car, and a heuristic approach which indicates possible actions (based on previous experiment) is the only way to emulate the situation and obtain a satisfactory solution.

All these concepts apply equally to the design of digital systems and to CAD systems themselves, which are of course all typical examples of complex logical systems. Consequently, the underlying philosophy in the design of CAD procedures is to produce a satisfactory solution in terms of a good computable algorithm (economical in machine time and storage) based on heuristic-programming principles. For example, in the minimization of Boolean equations, rather than employ the Quine–McCluskey algorithm which derives an optimum solution by the exhaustive search of a minterm list and the subsequent generation of the prime implicants on an iterative step-by-step basis, it is better practice to devise a heuristic routine which generates and tests for the presence of the largest prime implicants first and if unsuccessful tries in turn the next largest prime implicant and so on. This type of procedure does not guarantee to find the optimum solution but has the advantage of quickly converging to a satisfactory minimal result. Chapter 4, which deals with the synthesis of logic circuits, covers this aspect of CAD in more detail.

Another more formal approach to the design of complex engineering systems is the concept of *fuzziness* first postulated by Zadeh (10). Basically, fuzziness is a form of imprecision which results from a grouping of objects into classes which do not possess well-defined characteristics and consequently are impossible to classify exclusively into specific classes. Such classes, called *fuzzy sets*, arise when adjectives such as large, small, approximate, substantial, sufficient, etc., are used to describe sets of objects. For example, the names used to describe colors, such as red, green, blue, etc., are all names of fuzzy sets, for instance, "the class of green objects".

Fuzziness is intimately concerned with complexity, in the sense that the human brain has a limited capacity to handle classes having a large number of members and must inevitably partition the classes into subclasses in order to reduce the complexity. In this process the boundary between the subclasses necessarily becomes imprecise and fuzziness naturally results. Thus, one can argue that as the complexity of a task, or system performing that task, exceeds a certain threshold limit, then the nature of the system becomes fuzzy.

Based on these principles a formal algebraic method (employing *fuzzy algorithms*) has been evolved (11) for describing systems which cannot, or need not be, precisely specified. Essentially, a fuzzy algorithm is an ordered set of instructions some of which are fuzzy in nature, that is containing names of fuzzy sets. The instruction "Decrease $y$ *slightly* at each step until $X$ becomes *substantially* greater than 10" is a typical example where the adjectives "slightly" and "substantially" characterize fuzzy sets. In essence this approach is very similar to heuristic programming described earlier, since a heuristic program may be regarded as a non-fuzzy approximation to a fuzzy algorithm. The basic difference is that fuzzy algorithms contain fuzzy instructions which cannot as yet (12) be implemented *directly* on a conventional machine and consequently must be represented as heuristic procedures. Thus, the concept of fuzziness allows a more formal derivation of heuristic programs.

It will be obvious that these techniques are particularly well suited to CAD problems involving wiring, component placement, logic design, etc. However, though fuzzy algorithms portend great promise for the design of complex systems, much work remains to be done before they could become a practical technique.

As we have seen the problem of complexity presents a considerable challenge to the future of digital systems. The inevitable demands placed by the user on digital systems will undoubtedly further increase their complexity. Though CAD techniques can go a long way in providing design tools, nevertheless it might well be necessary completely to re-evaluate the basic tenets of design. Is it really necessary to design a system that functions correctly for all conceivable logical conditions? (Assuming of course that the system can be *completely* specified in the first place!) It is the author's contention that systems in the future could well be designed on a statistical basis with a designed probability of success or failure. This approach would still necessitate formal methods of design and evaluation, but would enable the complexity to be controlled.

## 1.4. SWITCHING THEORY AND ITS APPLICATION TO CAD

Considerable work has been published over the last two decades on switching and automata theory and its application to the design of logical circuits. In fact it could be argued that switching theory provides a complete design technique for implementing logic systems using basic components such as NAND/NOR gates and bistables. Unfortunately, these techniques have not gained favor with the majority of designers owing mainly to the reason that practical problems with large numbers of switching variables are difficult to specify, and the associated computation, if done by hand, is prohibitively excessive. The obvious remedy would seem to be in the use of computers to eliminate the drudgery of hand computation, but this regretfully does not provide the complete answer.

The theoretical design procedures described in published research papers are in general not good computable algorithms, and even when powerful modern computers are used take an exorbitant amount of machine time to effect a design. In addition most of the work refers specifically to circuits implemented using basic NOR/NAND gates, whereas current design employs complex MSI circuits such as read-only memories (ROM's), shift registers, arithmetic and logic modules, etc.

Another, more fundamental, problem is the specification of logic circuits. The established methods of finite-state machine theory, whereby logic systems are specified in terms of state diagrams or state tables, are far too cumbersome for large-variable systems. Even the task of defining combinational logic using truth tables becomes impractical with large circuits (say in the order of 15 variables).

In view of the above remarks, is switching theory of any use in CAD? The answer is quite definitely yes. Though at the present time the theory seems inadequate when dealing with many practical problems, it is nevertheless the only theory we have! Any breakthrough in this field must inevitably come about via existing automata and switching theory, and as such the theory forms an essential basis to CAD work. Moreover, as we shall see in later chapters, much of the work already performed in CAD, for example, logic-circuit synthesis and testing, is based on these principles. However, it is necessary to exercise caution in the use of switching-theoretic techniques. It seems necessary at the present time to treat much of the published work as a starting point for deriving computable heuristics for CAD, rather than as an end in itself.

Another important aspect, which we shall return to later, is the man–machine interface. Experience to date has shown that, unless CAD systems are easy to use, exploitation of the system by designers rapidly diminishes after the initial novelty value has passed and the difficulties involved in using the system become all too apparent. It is essential that any theoretical concepts employed in a CAD scheme should, if possible, be invisible to the user. The input–output transfer characteristic of the system must relate as far as possible to accepted design practice, and the operating procedure should be simple and efficient to use.

There is, however, an alternative school of though which holds the view that, in order to provide the necessary design tools for complex logic systems, designers must inevitably learn new techniques. Any realistic solution must of course be a compromise, but it is prudent to realize that novel techniques are only acceptable if the advantages to be accrued far outweigh any difficulties encountered in accommodating to the new disciplines.

The major problems still to be solved in switching theory (as far as CAD is concerned) are all concerned with the design of complex systems; they are as follows.

(a) The need to *formally* represent and specify logic circuits at a high systems level rather than, as at present, in terms of individual binary variables at the gate level. This might possibly be achieved using a form of Boolean vector algebra.

(b) Implementation techniques based on subsystem modules such as ROM's, counters, shift-registers, etc., need to be devised.

(c) A suitable methodology for designing and evaluating complex systems (particularly logic validation and diagnostic testing) must be developed.

Though some research has taken place in these areas, mainly in the application of graph-theoretic methods, no suitable systems theory has yet been evolved and much fundamental work still remains to be done.

## 1.5. PROGRAMMING CAD SYSTEMS

Though in practice engineers will seldom, if ever, need to implement their own CAD packages it is nevertheless instructional to consider some of the problems associated with this task. The majority of digital design procedures, for example, logic synthesis and simulation, are essentially non-numerical in nature. Numbers can, and do, occasionally occur in such problems, but generally only as a very minor part of the overall computation. It is the comparison and decision capabilities of the computer that are required rather than its arithmetic facilities. The data presented to a CAD program is also non-numeric in so far as it is the *structure* of the data (and the interrelations between data elements) which contain the required information rather than any numerical properties. For example, in generating fault-test sequences or in logic-circuit simulation it is necessary to set up and analyze the characteristics of a topological model of the circuit under examination.

Another important consideration is that the amount of storage required varies considerably according to the parameters of the problem. Consequently, if the program working space is not to be excessively large it is necessary for data storage to be made available as the computation proceeds, and any storage that becomes redundant must be retrievable for use later in the program.

When implementing CAD algorithms the following requirements must be satisfied.

(a) *Symbol Manipulation*—the ability to structure and manipulate non-numeric data.

(b) *Dynamic Storage Allocation*—means must be provided for the allocation of storage to different parts of the program as dictated by circumstance during program run-time, because it is normally impossible to determine *a priori* the required distribution. Any storage that becomes redundant during the execution of the program must be retrieved for possible use later.

(c) *Minimized Program Overheads*—the cost of implementing and running CAD programs must be kept to an absolute minimum.

(d) *Easily Modifiable*—must be possible to transfer programs to other machines (portability) and to modify and add new design packages (modularity).

(e) *Arithmetic Facilities*—basic functions like add and subtract should be available, but more complex operations such as multiplication, division, and floating-point operation are generally not required.

(f) *Input–Output Facilities*—the input and output of data, particularly internal disk transfers, must be easy to accomplish. The system must also be correctly interfaced to the user via graphics or teletype terminals.

A further requirement, and a major design consideration in any CAD system, is the organization and storage of the primary and derived data—that is, the *data structure*. A distinction must be drawn between data structure and data representation, the latter being the actual methods used to represent the data in the computer store. Data storage must be arranged in such a way as to allow efficient retrieval and processing, including such operations as the creation of data stores, modification, deletion, searching, and comparison routines. Moreover, the data storage must be able to grow and contract as the designer proceeds with his work.

Data is usually stored in a tabular or list format which is then operated upon by the computer program. This tabular representation can in practice take many forms, from simple linear lists of elements and two-dimensional arrays to tree structures (representing hierarchical relationships) and complex multi-linked ring structures (13).

The requirements outlined above determine to a vary large extent the type of programming languages employed in writing CAD systems. Most standard high-level languages, such as FORTRAN, BASIC, etc., are oriented to numerical computation, and consequently are extremely inefficient when used for data-processing operations. At tht other extreme, and certainly the most efficient, are machine-dictated assembly languages. This alternative, however, has the major disadvantage of being specific to one type of computer (thereby prohibiting portability) as well as being difficult to use and document. What is required is a high-level language capable of setting up data structures (normally in the form of lists) and manipulating the items on the lists. This type of high-level language is known generally as a *list-processing language* (14, 15). In practice it is convenient to retain a conventional high-level language structure (say FORTRAN or ALGOL) for ease of communication and programming, with the list-processing function being embedded in the language as machine-language macros which are then called as standard procedures. The basic concept in implementing list structures is the idea of *linking* (or *chaining*) the items in a list. Normally a list consists of data elements (items) stored in contiguous memory locations. This mode of organization gives rise to many problems; for example, when adding or deleting items on a list it is necessary to reorganize the store layout completely. In a linked list each data element contains the actual data (the item) *and* the address in store (called a *pointer*) of the next element on the list. Thus, items may be located anywhere in the store, and modification of the list simply entails changing pointer values in the data elements; Fig. 1.2 shows the symbolic representation and store layout for a simple linked list.

It is also possible to store *two* pointers in a data element (in practice this is the more usual procedure); that is, the item field of the data element is replaced by a pointer to the store address of the item, or a pointer to another list (called a *sublist*). List-processing structures are normally represented in a computer by splitting the available storage into two sections, with stores containing the items to be manipulated, and list stores which contain addresses pointing to other lists or to the items themselves; the items, which do not have the two-pointer nature, are called *atoms* since they cannot be divided. Figure 1.3 shows a typical storage structure, and the corresponding representation of sublists.

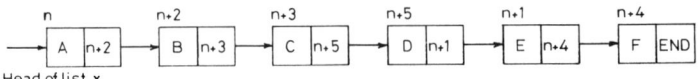

a) List representation  x = (A,B,C,D,E,F)

| Address | Data Elements Item | Pointer |
|---------|------|---------|
| n | A | n+2 |
| n+1 | E | n+4 |
| n+2 | B | n+3 |
| n+3 | C | n+5 |
| n+4 | F | END |
| n+5 | D | n+1 |

b)  Store contents

**Figure 1.2.**  Linked list structure.

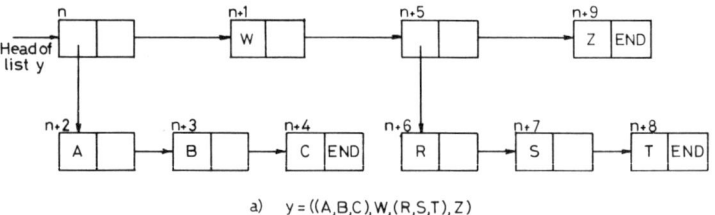

a)    y = ((A,B,C),W,(R,S,T),Z)

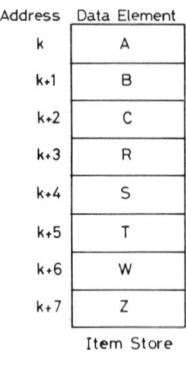

| Address | Data Element |
|---------|--------------|
| k | A |
| k+1 | B |
| k+2 | C |
| k+3 | R |
| k+4 | S |
| k+5 | T |
| k+6 | W |
| k+7 | Z |

Item Store

| Address | Data Element | |
|---------|------|------|
| n | n+2 | n+1 |
| n+1 | k+6 | n+5 |
| n+2 | k | n+3 |
| n+3 | k+1 | n+4 |
| n+4 | k+2 | END |
| n+5 | n+6 | n+9 |
| n+6 | k+3 | n+7 |
| n+7 | k+4 | n+8 |
| n+8 | k+5 | END |
| n+9 | k+7 | END |

List Store

b)  Store Contents

**Figure 1.3.**  Sublist structures.

14

Typical operations which are required to be performed on a linked list are as follows.

(a) To access a specified element on the list in order to insert new data elements and delete old ones, or to examine and change its contents.

(b) Combine linear lists into two or more new lists; this is known as *concatenation*.

(c) Search the list for the occurrence of specified data.

(d) Split a linear list into two or more new lists.

(e) Make a copy of a linear list.

In general these, and many other operations, can be obtained by the use of five basic primitives which are fundamental to most list-processing languages (16); these are as follows.

(a) *Head (x)*—obtains the first element of a list $x$.

(b) *Tail (x)*—obtains all the elements of a list $x$ occurring after the head element. For example, let us suppose a linear list is defined by

$$x = (A,B,C,D,E,F)$$

then

$$\text{Head } (x) = (A)$$

and

$$\text{Tail } (x) = (B,C,D,E,F).$$

Again, let us suppose

$$x = ((A,B,C),(D,E),(F,G))$$

then

$$\text{Head } (x) = (A,B,C)$$

and

$$\text{Tail } (x) = ((D,E),(F,G))$$

(c) *Cons (x,y)*—joins two lists together as the head and tail of a new list. For example, let us suppose

$$x = (A,B,C,D)$$

and

$$y = (W,X,Y,Z)$$

then

$$\text{Cons } (x,y) = (A,B,C,D,W,X,Y,Z)$$

(d) *Atom (x)*—assumes the value true if $x$ is an atom and is false otherwise.

(e) *Equ (x,y)*—assumes the value true if the two atoms $x$ and $y$ are identical and is false otherwise (both arguments must be atoms). These last two procedures are effectively conditional tests which allow iterative and recursive programs to be written.

(f) *Null (x)*—has the value true if $x$ is END (that is the termination of a list), otherwise false.

Using these basic primitives it is possible to develop many more sophisticated routines for specialized functions, for instance, procedures for copying lists and searching for specific items on a list.

It is often necessary when using list processing to rethink the original problem so that it can be solved in terms of list structures (caution must always be exercised, however, to ensure that the use of simple structures, such as two-dimensional arrays, etc., would not offer a better solution). The Quine–McCluskey tabulator method of minimization is an obvious example of a problem which is very well suited to list processing, involving the setting up of lists, searching the lists for specific factors, and generating new lists from the results. More complicated data structures can be generated from the fundamental linked list by incorporating additional pointer linkages. For example, a *circular list* (see Fig. 1.4a) can be formed by simply arranging that the last data element in a list store points back to the head element instead of terminating in the END symbol. A basic disadvantage of the simple linked list is that in order to find any particular item it is necessary to start at the head of the list and work progressively through it—a very time-consuming process. This disadvantage can be overcome by the use of multi-linked data elements with pointers to the left and right successors of items in the list, (see Fig. 1.4b). Using this form of list processor the data may be represented in the form of tree structures which allow more economical searches to be performed.

The importance of data structures in CAD is that it is essential to be able to represent faithfully in the computer the relationships that exist between physical and conceptual objects in a system model. For example, in logic simulation the networks are modeled as a topological gate structure. This

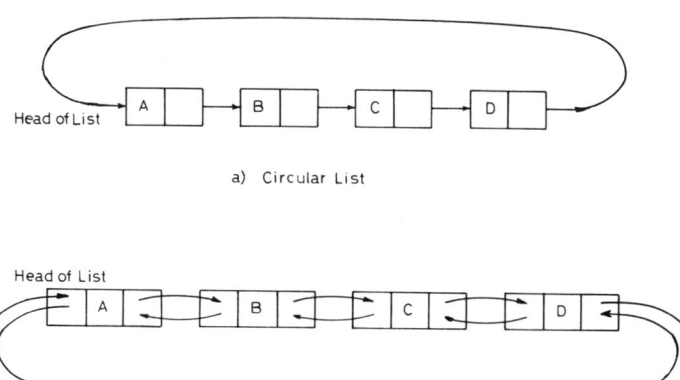

a) Circular List

b) Doubly Linked List

**Figure 1.4.** Multi-linked lists.

requires a description of the logic module in terms of logical action, propagation delay, fan-out, etc., and a complete record of the interconnection paths. Note that the item can, if required, consist of more than one data element; in practice the item description would have a number of computer words allocated to it depending on the application. The same techniques are used in computer graphics to provide the internal storage structures required to represent pictorial and network data for CRT displays.

The most generally used data structure in CAD is the *ring-processing system* (17, 18, 19). The term *ring structure* (basically a multi-linked circular list) originates from the fact that sets of item blocks can be linked through pointers into closed rings, thus permitting any item block to be reached from any other involved in the same relation (see Fig. 1.5). An item block may contain any number of pointers to other rings, and hence can be simultaneously involved in several relationships with specified sets of other item blocks. It is generally necessary to select one item on each ring to be the *ring start*, which is analogous to the head, that is the first member, of a simple linked list. Note that the ring processor allows a complex tree structure to be represented (see Fig. 1.5*b*) with provision for traversing the tree in all directions.

List- or ring-processing structures are normally held completely in core in order to facilitate fast access and manipulation. However, when representing large systems this is impractical, and facilities must be available in the language to communicate directly with a suitable backing store (usually a disk store). This allows the appropriate parts of the data structure to be fetched from the disk store as and when required.

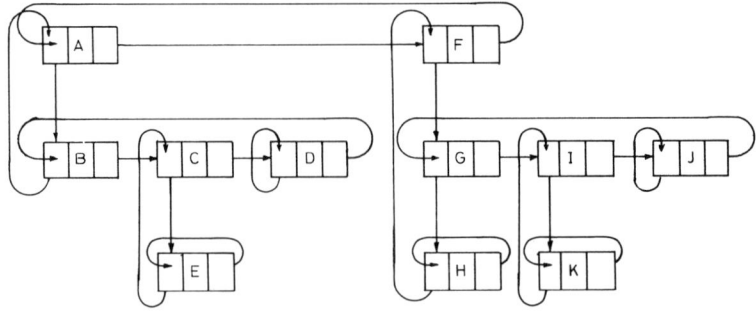

a)   x = (A(B,C(E),D), F(G(H), I(K), J))

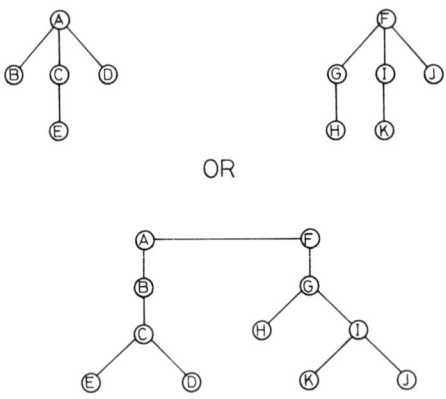

OR

b) Equivalent Tree Representation

**Figure 1.5.** Ring structures.

## 1.6. INTERACTIVE SYSTEMS

Essentially the problem is that of establishing direct communication between man and machine in such a way that their inherent incompatibilities are matched as efficiently as possible. The basic requirements of an interactive CAD system are as follows.

(a) A problem-orentated conversational language which is *easy to use and understand*.

(b) Fast feedback of results and operational messages so that the designer's imaginative and creative abilities are not inhibited.

(c) A satisfactory compromise must be made between the vastly differing volumes of data obtainable from man and machine in order to achieve maximum mutual comprehension.

(d) Input devices should require the minimal amount of manual intervention, and output data must be suitably displayed and capable of being edited as required.

(e) Automatic error detection and guidance through the operating procedures.

(f) The technicalities of the software and design procedures should be "invisible" to the user.

These principles should always be borne in mind when designing the input (and output) procedures for a CAD package. Many CAD systems have fallen into disuse because insufficient attention has been paid to the interface problem. In many cases the use of CAD techniques (for instance, logic-circuit analysis) is intermittent, and the designer should not be required to relearn the operational procedures each time he wishes to use a CAD procedure. Ideally the CAD input routines themselves should provide sufficient instructional feedback to enable the designer to input his problem, and obtain a solution, with the minimum of prior knowledge.

Care should also be exercised to ensure that the designer is not bored or frustrated by input procedures which demand excessive typing or graphical maneuvers on a CRT display. Where possible input requirements should be kept to a minimum. This philosophy also applies to output data; facilities should be provided to allow the output (or irrelevant sections) to be suppressed when not required.

As well as problem-orientated languages for use with design algorithms, it is also necessary to provide a conversational *system command language* to control the organizational and "housekeeping" functions associated with the CAD software packages. Various time-sharing commands must be provided (assuming multi-user operation); typical commands are as follows.

(a) Logging in and out of the system.

(b) Creating, deleting, and manipulating data files.

(c) Accessing CAD packages (including the problem-oriented languages) and sequencing their operation.

(d) Determining current system status.

(e) Controlling input–output devices.

Many of these functions can be provided by standard operating systems, where they exist; otherwise it is necessary to implement them as part of the total CAD system.

The choice of input–output devices is also critical, since this can often be the determining factor in achieving an effective CAD system. The principal input devices used in CAD systems are the teletypewriter and CRT displays (20). In particular, interactive graphic displays, which can be used for both input and output operations, have great advantages when performing design processes requiring the monitoring and editing of topographical systems such as circuit layout, routing and placement, etc. Manual intervention can be provided by the use of light-pens, tracker-balls, and simple cursor-following devices in conjunction with a simple function keyboard. However, the cost of graphic terminals can be substantial, and it is better practice to develop systems using teletype terminals (which are more freely available) unless the problem is such that graphic displays are essential. It is bad practice to use graphic terminals to input basic design data, such as logic-circuit configuration. This operation can best be done off-line by using a digitizing system based on a movable cursor which is manually tracked round a circuit diagram (drawn on grid paper) generating digital $XY$ coordinates (on paper tape or cards) at operator-specified places. In many cases when graphical output is required standard peripheral equipment, such as line-printers and incremental $XY$ plotters etc., can be employed. [In some instances, however, special output devices are required, such as automatic drafting equipment in the case of LSI manufacture (21)].

There is a popular misconception that CAD inevitably means the application of computer graphics; in fact to some people the two terms are almost synonymous. It is certainly true that CAD systems should be inter-active, and that the graphics terminal is the prime interactive device, but the resemblance stops there. Too many CAD systems have been designed from the viewpoint of "let's see what sort of CAD system we can design using computer graphics", with dire results!

### 1.7. SUMMARY

The design of a CAD system involves the solution of three basic problems.

(a) The selection and implementation of a suitable data structure for the representation of system models and design parameters.

(b) The development of design algorithms which operate on the data structure, together with an appropriate design methodology.

(c) The provision of a viable man–machine interface, with realistic interactive problem specification and editing facilities.

There are still many basic problems to be solved before the sophisticated CAD systems that are urgently required can be designed. However, as we shall see in the following chapters, there is a good fund of knowledge, particularly on design techniques, which can usefully be employed at the present time.

## REFERENCES AND BIBLIOGRAPHY

1. Glazer, E. L. Computer aided design for computing systems. *IEEE Conference on Computer Science and Technology*, Publ. No. *55*, pp. 13–19, 1969.
2. *Design Automation.* Special issue, *IEEE Comp.*, pp. 18–52, May/June 1972.
3. Breuer, M. A. Recent developments in the automated design and analysis of digital systems. Proc. IEEE **60**, 12–27, 1972.
4. Lewin, D. W., Purslow, E., and Bennetts, R. G. Computer assisted logic design–The CALD system. *IEE Conference on CAD*, Publ. No. 86, pp. 343–350, 1972.
5. Heath, F. G. The LOGOS system. *IEE Conference on CAD*, Publ. No. 86, pp. 225–230, 1972.
6. Cray, S. R., and Kisch, R. N. A progress report on computer applications in computer design. *Proc. WJCC* **14**, 82–85, 1956.
7. Lewin, D. W. *Logical Design of Switching Circuits* (2nd edn). Nelson, London, 1973.
8. Knuth, D. W. *The Art of Computer Programming, Vol. 1, Fundamental Algorithms*, Chap. 1. Addison-Wesley, Reading, Mass., 1972.
9. Simon, H. A. *The Sciences of the Artificial.* MIT Press, Cambridge, Mass., 1969.
10. Zadeh, L. A. Fuzzy sets. *Inf. Control* 8, 338–353, 1965.
11. Zadeh, L. A. Fuzzy algorithms. *Inf. Control* 12, 94–102, 1968.
12. Chiang, S. On the execution of fuzzy programs using finite state machines. *IEEE Trans. Computers* C21, 241–253, 1972.
13. Knuth, D. E. *The Art of Computer Programming, Vol. 1, Fundamental Algorithms*, Chap. 2. Addison-Wesley Reading, Mass., 1972.
14. Foster, J. M. *List Processing.* Macdonald Computer Monographs, London, 1967.
15. Green, B. F. Computer language for symbol manipulation. *IRE Trans. Electron. Computers* **EC10**, 729–735, 1961.
16. Bobrow, D. G., and Raphael, B. A comparison of list-processing languages. *Comm. ACM* 7, 231–240, 1964.
17. Gray, J. C. Compound data structures for computer-aided design; a survey. *Proceedings of ACM 20th National Conference*, p. 355. Thompson Books, Washington, D.C.
18. Lang, C. A., and Gray, J. C. ASP–A ring implemented associative structure package. *Comm. ACM* 11, 550–555, 1968.
19. Wiseman, N. E., and Hiles, J. O. A ring structure processor for a small computer. *Computer J.* 10, 338–346, 1968.
20. Lewin, M. H. An introduction to computer graphic terminals. *Proc. IEEE* 55, 1544–1552, 1967.
21. Canell, D. A. *Introduction to Computer-Aided Manufacturing in Electronics.* John Wiley–Interscience, New York, 1972.
22. Beck, H. W. Computer-aided design of MOS/LSI circuits. *AFIPS SJCC* **40**, 1059–1063, 1972.
23. Date, C. J. *An Introduction to Database Systems.* Addison-Wesley, Reading, Mass., 1975.

# System Specification

## 2.1. INTRODUCTION

The most important prerequisite of any computer-aided logic-design scheme is to be able to specify the problem under consideration using a suitable representation. Moreover, in order to handle complex systems it must be possible to describe the system at several levels, that is on a *hierarchical* basis. At the top level is the *behavioral* (information flow) description which treats the system as an interconnection of functional modules specified by their input–output (transfer function) characteristics. The next level down is the *functional* (data flow) description; this partitions the system into subsystem components and details the logical algorithms (or microprograms) to be performed by the components together with their corresponding highway transfers. At this level it should be possible to represent the algorithms in a variety of ways, for example, in terms of Boolean equations, state tables, timing diagrams, flow-charts, etc. Finally, at the lowest level, is the *structural* (implementation) representation, which describes in detail the actual gates, bistables, MSI chips, software procedures, etc., used to realize the subsystem functions physically.

Ideally a methodology for representing and evaluating logical structures in a CAD environment should have the following characteristics.

**(a)** Hierarchical, block-oriented structure, capable of including predefined subsystem components held in a data base.

**(b)** Able to represent both hardware and software processes.

**(c)** Easily assimilated by the designer; description should be simple to modify and edit.

**(d)** Unambiguous and concise descriptions capable of serving as a means of communication between designers, implementers, and users.

**(e)** Possible to proceed from description to system realization using either hardware or software processes.

**(f)** Facility to represent the information flow in large-variable systems, that is at the macro or subsystem level. Insight should also be provided into the best methods of partitioning and implementation.

**(g)** System evaluation and checking should be possible at all levels. At the behavioral level evaluation should preferably be performed by formal analysis rather than step-by-step simulation.

**(h)** Ability to handle parallel, that is concurrent, processes in both synchronous and asynchronous modes.

**(i)** Easily machinable (as a software implementation) on a computer system.

Numerous techniques have been described in the literature for the description and design of digital systems; these methods may be generally classified into three basic areas, which are as follows.

**(i)** *Functional descriptive programming languages*, such as register-transfer languages (RTL), simulation languages, and some general-purpose high-level languages such as APL (the Iverson language).

**(ii)** *Finite-state machine (FSM) techniques*, such as state tables, regular expressions, flow charts, etc.

**(iii)** *Graph-theoretic methods*, employing transition graphs, Petri nets, occurrence graphs, state diagrams, etc.

Many of the necessary characteristics listed earlier for a specification system are present in one or other of these techniques, but in general all the methods described to date fall short of the ideal methodology. For instance, problem-oriented programming languages suffer from the inherent disadvantage that they have no formal mathematical structure. Consequently, system behavior must be interpreted indirectly from program performance whilst operating on certain specified data types. Simulation languages in particular suffer from this disadvantage. A simulator language usually describes a logic system in terms of simulated components (that is gates, bistables, etc.) and their interconnections. In order to evaluate or analyze a logic network represented in this manner it is necessary to perform an exhaustive, sequential examination of all possible logic conditions; that is, the circuit model must be driven (by providing specified input conditions) and then "exercised" step by step to determine the resultant outputs. It will be obvious that this is a time-consuming process and that large amounts of storage will be required to represent the circuit model. Moreover, since a logical system is described as a topological circuit network, rather than by specifying system functions, the simulation description is difficult to follow and of little use for documentation and communication purposes.

A useful comparison between formal and simulation methods may be drawn by contrasting the functional description of a binary counter circuit, using a state table showing the present and next-state transitions, as against a simulation-language description detailing bistables, logic gates, etc. and their interconnections. An important difference is that the formal specification describes a logical algorithm which could be implemented in either software or hardware form. Problem-oriented design languages, because they are constrained to operate on well-defined data types, are normally restricted to hardware representation. (However, in some cases, for instance the generation of test sequences for logic circuits, it is often essential to use an implemented hardware version of the circuit.) Note that procedural programming languages must still be employed even with a formal methodology, since the notational system must be represented in some way in order to input a description to the computer. The difference is, however, that the programming language is simply acting as a vehicle to describe the variables (represented as data structures) and to control the execution of the associated functional operations, not as an end in itself, as, for example, in a general-purpose programming language used to represent graphical structures and their manipulation.

The major problem to be overcome in any specification language for CAD is how complex systems containing a very large number of binary variables may be represented and analyzed. In the general case the system variables will be both primary inputs and internal state conditions. Finite-state theory, though theoretically capable of representing any digital system (which must of course in its engineered form be deterministic) is not viable in practice owing to the considerable difficulties involved in expressing the problem and the inordinate amount of computation required for manipulating the resultant structures.

There are also some more fundamental disadvantages of the FSM concept (1). In general the FSM accepts a serial input (or inputs) and progresses from state to state producing an output sequence in the process. Owing to its finite memory capacity (i.e. the number of internal states) the FSM is best suited to describing systems where the amount of memory required to record past events (that is the effect of earlier inputs) is *small* and *finite*, for example, serial adder–subtractor circuits and pattern detectors where the computation can proceed as a step-by-step operation on the input and the amount of information required to be "carried" or "remembered" is very small (1 bit in the case of the adder–subtractor).

Serial multiplication, however, is very different. In this case it is necessary to have *all* the input data available before the computation can proceed; moreover, large amounts of information need to be stored during the course of the multiplication (for instance, to accumulate partial sums). It follows logically from this constraint that it is impossible to specify a finite-state machine that can multiply together *arbitrarily large* pairs of numbers. Note also that the FSM does not have the ability to refer back to earlier inputs unless the entire input sequence is initially stored; this implies that the input sequence of interest is of known *finite* length.

These limitations can of course be overcome by using an infinite-machine model [derived from the Turing machine (2)] where the amount of available storage is unlimited. (Some of the more promising formal methods of specification to be described later, such as Petri nets etc., are in essence infinite models.) Using this type of model the designer is unconstrained in his thinking, allowing general system concepts to be specified without reference to a particular implementation. It is important to remember, however, that all machine models must eventually be implemented as a finite memory machine. (The digital computer can, for example, be considered as an infinite memory machine for a restricted range of problems, dependent of course on the total storage available.) Unfortunately the transformation from a conceptual infinite model to a practical realization as a finite-state machine can, and does, present serious difficulties.

Another inherent difficulty is encountered in the analysis of large systems. It would appear inevitable that, if a detailed analysis of a logic algorithm is required, there is no other choice but to examine all possible alternatives in an iterative manner. In general, particularly if an infinite-machine model is adopted, it is necessary to determine the system operation by specifying a restricted set of input and state conditions. This technique, which corresponds to examining particular paths through the algorithmic structure (for example, a particular state sequence in a state table) results in a loss of information and can affect the accuracy of the analysis. However, there seems no alternative but to adopt this method for complex systems.

As we have seen in § 1.3, in order to design complex systems it is necessary to partition the system into suitable subsystem functions. This fact has been extensively used to alleviate some of the problems of implementing large systems. In particular the approach of dividing the system into a *control function* and a *data structure* has been widely adopted. Using this technique a data structure may be specified in terms of registers, processing units, etc. and their interconnections; the control algorithms, specifying the required processing operations and their timing, are then defined separately. Note that the data structure also includes processing operations and is not restricted to data storage. Thus, the complexity of the system is reduced by partitioning the principal components into comprehensible subsystems—the usual human heuristic for handling any complex situation.

In the remainder of this chapter we review the work done so far in the specification and evaluation of complex systems. However, the reader should be aware that many of the techniques to be described are still in the development stages and that a viable system meeting the requirements outlined above remains to be developed.

## 2.2. DIRECTED GRAPHS (3)

One mathematical tool which is being increasingly applied to computer systems design and analysis is *graph theory*, and many of the specification methods to be discussed later are formally defined using graph-theoretic concepts. A *directed graph* is simply a mathematical model of a system showing the relationships that exist between members of a set. The elements of the set are usually called *vertices* or *nodes*, with the relationships between them being indicated by directed *lines* or *edges*. An example of a directed graph is shown in Fig. 2.1*a* where the set of nodes is given by

$$N = (n_1, n_2, n_3, n_4, n_5)$$

and the set of edges by

$$E = (e_1, e_2, e_3, e_4, e_5, e_6).$$

Directed graphs have been used, for instance, to represent information flow in control and data structures, scheduling operations in multiprocessor systems, diagnostic procedures in logic systems, parallel programming schemata, etc. The major advantage of using graph theory is that formal methods exist for the manipulation (for example reduction) of graphic structures, which can be represented using matrices for computer processing.

Graphs may be classified into various types depending on their properties. For example, a *net* shown in Fig. 2.1*b* is a directed graph consisting of a finite non-empty set of nodes and a finite set of edges; thus a single node

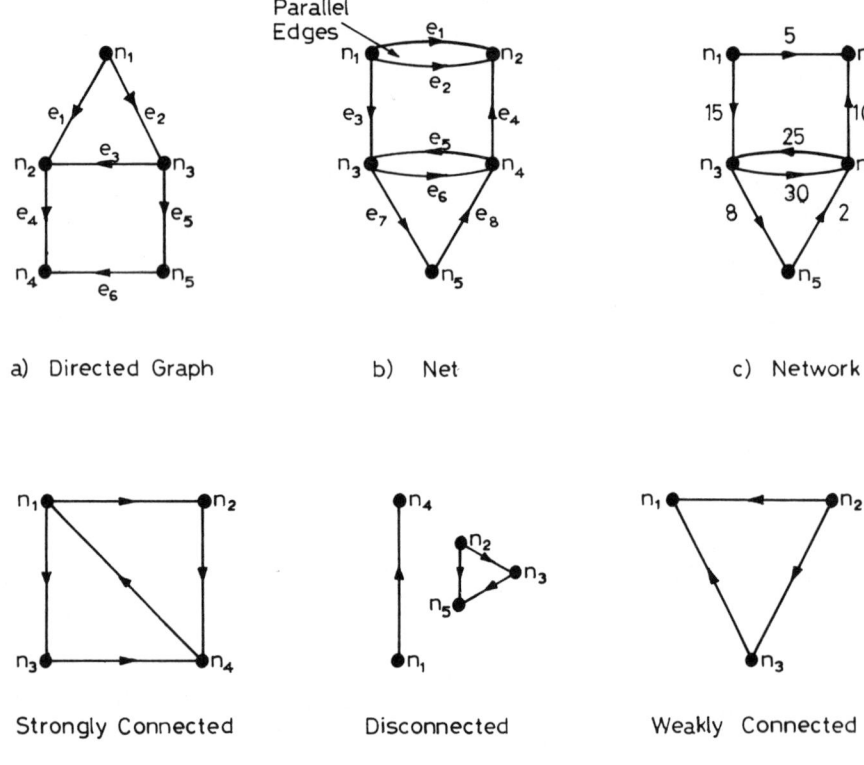

a)  Directed Graph              b)   Net              c)  Network

Strongly Connected        Disconnected        Weakly  Connected

d)  Connectedness of  Graphs

**Figure 2.1.**  Directed graphs.

could constitute a trivial net. The concept of a net is used in the Petri-net
representation to be discussed later in § 2.3. A net may have *parallel edges*,
that is two nodes connected by two different edges but both acting in the
same direction. A graph which satisfies the criteria for a net but does not
contain any parallel edges is called a *relation*. If the edges of a relation are
assigned values the graph is called a *network*; this is shown in Fig. 2.1c. The
concept of a network is an important one, since it can be used to describe the
quantized parameters of a system such as flow, frequency, probability, etc.

One very important property of a graph is the degree of *connectedness*
exhibited by the components of the graph. A *strongly connected* graph is one
in which every node is reachable (along directed edges) by every other node.
A *disconnected graph* implies that there exists at least one node that neither
reaches nor is reached from any other node. In a *weakly connected* graph
there exists a sequence of edges between any two nodes but not necessarily in

continuous directions. These connectedness conditions are shown in Fig. 2.1$d$.

Graphs may be represented by matrices in which one row and one column are assigned for each node in the graph, thus generating a square matrix. Many different typs of matrix, each illustrating a particular property of a graph, may be formed. For example, the *adjacency* or *connectivity* matrix $A$ is formed by inserting a 1 in element $a_{ij}$ if there is a connecting edge between node $i$ and node $j$; otherwise 0 is inserted (this matrix is equivalent to the primitive connection matrix encountered in switching theory). Thus, for the strongly connected graph of Fig. 2.1$d$ we have

$$A = \begin{array}{c} \\ n_1 \\ n_2 \\ n_3 \\ n_4 \end{array} \begin{array}{cccc} n_1 & n_2 & n_3 & n_4 \\ \left[\begin{array}{cccc} 0 & 1 & 1 & 0 \\ 0 & 0 & 0 & 1 \\ 0 & 0 & 0 & 1 \\ 1 & 0 & 0 & 0 \end{array}\right] \end{array}$$

where the non-zero elements of $A$ indicate the number of paths of unit length that exist between corresponding nodes; the method may be extended, using normal matrix multiplication, to form $A^n$ which gives the number of paths of length $n$. Another useful matrix, which has found wide application in the realization of graphs, is the *reachability matrix R*. In this matrix the element $r_{ij} = 1$ if node $i$ can reach node $j$ irrespective of path length; obviously for $i = j$, $r_{ij} = 1$. If there are no possible paths between nodes $i$ and $j$, $r_{ij} = 0$. For the weakly connected graph of Fig. 2.1$d$ we have

$$A = \begin{array}{c} \\ n_1 \\ n_2 \\ n_3 \end{array} \begin{array}{ccc} n_1 & n_2 & n_3 \\ \left[\begin{array}{ccc} 1 & 0 & 0 \\ 1 & 1 & 1 \\ 1 & 0 & 1 \end{array}\right] \end{array}$$

Note that for a strongly connected graph all the entries would be 1, indicating that any node is reachable from any other node.

Though graph theory is being extensively researched and applied to computer system design considerable work still remains to be done before a unified approach can be developed. Currently, graph theory provides an ideal method of expressing and evaluating a problem area, but some doubt remains as to whether or not the technique can generate practical solutions.

## 2.3. TRANSITION GRAPHS (4)

The major drawback when using state diagrams to describe logical systems, particularly when handling large numbers of variables, is that *all* state transitions must be specified and each next state must be *uniquely* defined in terms of the present state and the current values of the input variables. This inherent difficulty may be overcome when designing synchronous sequential machines (for example, pattern recognizers etc., as shown in Fig. 2.2) by using *transition graphs.* The main difference is that, whereas the state diagram represents the behavior of a deterministic finite-state machine which is fully specified, the transition graph is non-deterministic allowing alternative behavior to occur. (Note that the state diagram is a special case of the transition graphs.) Though the transition graph is useful for specifying certain classes of automata, it should not be confused with a model for a realizable machine.

The transition graph is a directed graph consisting of a set of labeled vertices connected by various directed arcs. In every graph there is at least one *starting vertex* and at least one accepting or *terminal vertex* (denoted by a double circle). The terminal vertex is usually assigned the output value 1, to indicate when a particular input sequence has been recognized, that is, accepted. Each directed arc is labeled with symbols from the *input alphabet* of the graph; in the case of binary systems the input alphabet $I = \{0,1\}$. A sequence of directed arcs through the graph is referred to as a *path* and describes the input sequence consisting of the symbols assigned to the arcs in the path. An input sequence is said to be accepted (or recognized) by the graph if a path exists between a starting and terminal vertex, otherwise it will be rejected. Figure 2.3 compares the state-diagram and transition-graph representation for a 4-bit synchronous odd-parity check circuit. Note for example that the input sequence 1000 is recognized by both schemata; in the case of the transition graph a path may be traced through the graph from the starting vertex 1 via vertices 5, 9, and 12 to the terminal vertex 16. The sequence 1010 is rejected by the transition graph since it traverses round the path 1,2,3,4 and never reaches a terminal vertex. (Note the non-determinancy in the transition graph, since the sequence 1000 can also travel the path 1,2,3,4.)

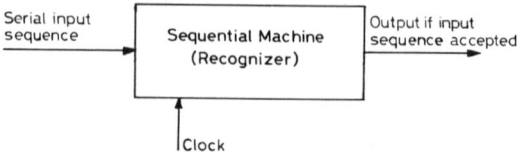

Figure 2.2. Sequential-machine model.

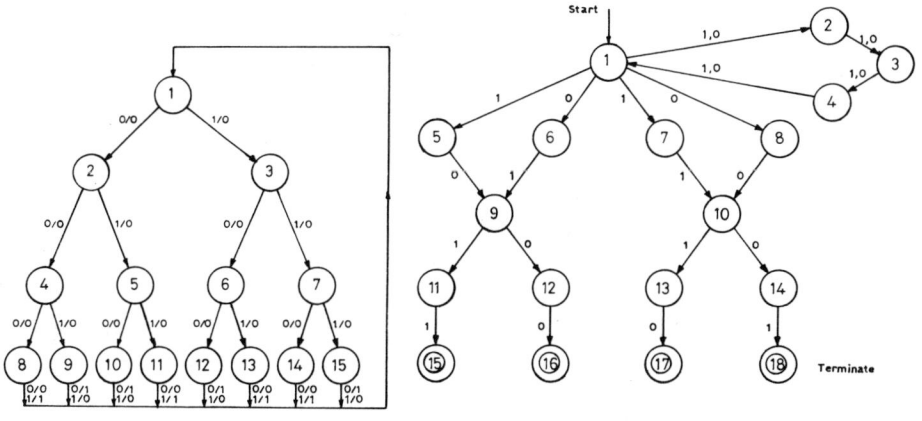

a)  State Diagram                              b)  Transition  Graph

**Figure 2.3.**  Four-bit odd-parity check circuit.

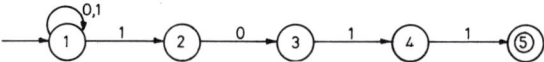

**Figure 2.4.**  Transition graph for Recognizer.

Though more vertices occurred in the transition graph than states in the state table, the construction is nevertheless simpler since it is only necessary to define the actual input sequences of interest, alternative input transitions being omitted from the graph. This is more apparent from the example in Fig. 2.4 which shows the transition graph for a sequential machine which gives an output if and only if the last four input symbols correspond to 1011.

At this point it is relevant to consider whether the non-deterministic transition graph has greater computational power than the deterministic state diagram? That is, can the transition graph represent machines which are beyond the power of the state diagram? In fact this is not so since it is always possible to convert a transition graph into an equivalent state diagram (5, 6). The transition graph then is simply a convenient "shorthand" notation for representing deterministic machines. However, in general it is not easy to derive a transition graph which faithfully represents a required machine specification.

## 2.4.  REGULAR EXPRESSIONS

Regular expressions constitute a language which can be used to characterize the external (input–output) behavior of sequential circuits (combinational logic can be treated as a special case). The approach is a mathematical one derived from the formal automata theory of finite-state machines. Kleene (7) showed in 1956 that any finite-state, deterministic, synchronous automaton can be described by a regular expression and, inversely, that every regular expression can be realized as a deterministic machine. Later work by a number of authors studied the conversion between regular expressions, transition graphs, and finite-state machines, and their use in logic design (8), but Brzozowski's work (9) using the derivative of a regular expression appears to be the most natural and systematic method of going from a regular expression to a state diagram or table.

Regular expressions are used to describe the valid (or required) set of input sequences to a finite-state machine in order to generate an output. Thus, the usual word (or behavioral) description can be reduced to an algebraic formula. For example, let us consider the machine shown in Fig. 2.5; the set of $n$ binary variables constitute the *input signals,* and the ordered $n$-tuples of 0's and 1's $(x_{n-1}, x_{n-2}, \ldots, x_0)$ an *input combination.* Each of the $K = 2^n$ different input combinations are *symbols* of the *input alphabet* $A_K$, which comprises the set of all symbols. Only synchronous machines are considered; the values assumed by the input signals at successive clock times is called an *input sequence* or *word.* It will be shown that the sets of input sequences which are of interest can be described using regular expressions.

Let us assume the regular operators + (disjunction), . (concatenation), * (star), and parenthesis acting on the alphabet $A_K = (0, 1, 2, \ldots, K-1)$. Then, regular expressions can be defined recursively in the following manner.

(a) Sequences of length $l$, consisting of the symbols of the input set $A_K$; the element $\lambda$ corresponding to a sequence of zero length and the empty set $\phi$ are regular expressions.

(b) If $A$ and $B$ are any regular expressions, so are $(AB)$, $A^*$, and any Boolean function of $A$ and $B$, i.e. f$(A, B)$, where the *star operation* * is defined as $A^* = U_{n=0}^{n=\infty} A_n$, that is "any number of occurrences of $A$". Note also that $(AB)$ implies concatenation and the use of parenthesis; the expression can be read as "$A$ followed by $B$". (The star operation can be considered as the iteration of concatenation.)

(c) Only expressions satisfying, or derived from a finite application of, rules (a) and (b) can be considered as regular expressions. For example, $A * B$, $(A + BC + D) * E$, $(ABC)(DB) * FG$ are all regular expressions.

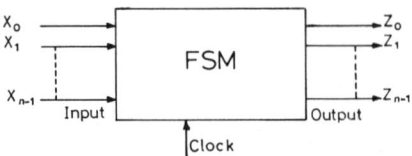

Figure 2.5. Machine model for regular expressions.

As an example consider the regular expression $11(01)^*$; this describes the set of input sequences whose members are made up of the symbols 11 followed by any number of occurrences of 01 (including zero). Thus we have

$$S = \{11, 1101, 110101, 11010101, \ldots \}.$$

Similarly the expression $(01)^*(10+01)$ describes the set of sequences consisting of any number of occurrences of 01 followed by either 10 or 01, or both 10 and 01. Consequently the set contains, among others, the sequences

10, 01, 0110, 0101, 010101, 0101010110, etc.

Some words of explanation are required to distinguish between $\lambda$ and $\phi$. Consider a word comprised of two symbols, i.e. of length 2. Now if one symbol is deleted the result is a word of length 1; deleting the last remaining symbol results in a word of zero length, the null word. For instance, the regular expression $(01)^*$ has the set of sequences

$$S = \{\lambda, 01, 0101, 010101, \ldots \}.$$

In connection with input sequences we may interpret $\lambda$ as a special starting signal occuring only at time 0. Since by convention all input sequences begin at time 1, the occurrence of $\lambda$ means that the machine is ready to receive signals. The concept of the null word is also important because of its concatenation properties; thus for any set of sequences $S$, $\lambda S = S\lambda = S$. The empty set $\phi$, on the other hand, is a set-theoretic concept meaning a set with no members and has the property $S\phi = \phi S = \phi$. (It is necessary to be able to describe a set with no members to cover the case of machines which accept no sequences at all.) Note that the null word $\lambda$ could also be considered in set-theoretic terms as an identity element.

The regular-expression language defined above can be modified to include the operations of intersection and complementation, but this extended form presents difficulties when manipulating expressions and the restricted language is normally used. The major application areas suggested for regular expressions have been in the fields of programming, to clarify compilation procedures etc., and the logical design of synchronous machines. The advantages claimed for regular expressions when used as a specification language for logic design (5) are as follows.

(a) In contrast to a state-graph approach descriptions can be written out in a line from left to right.

**(b)** It is precise and formal as opposed to the ambiguities inherent in natural languages.

**(c)** Once the designer is conversant with the language, ideas can readily be expressed without undue computation or excessive reflection. (This advantage particularly applies to the extended form of the language.)

For example, consider the specification of a machine which is required to recognize the particular sequence 1011 in a 4-bit serial input sequence; note each operational cycle consists of examining four bits and generating an output if the pattern 1011 is recognized. The equivalent regular expression is obtained by concatenating two strings, the string which describes the set of all inputs and the required input string, that is

$$[(0 + 1)(0 + 1)(0 + 1)(0 + 1)] * (1011).$$

Similarly, to recognize the occurrence of 1011 (once only) anywhere in a continuous input sequence one may write the expression

$$(0 + 1) * 1011 (0 + 1)*$$

where $(0 + 1)* = \lambda + (0 + 1) + (0 + 1)(0 + 1) + (0 + 1)(0 + 1)(0 + 1) \ldots$ etc.

It is possible to show that to every regular expression there corresponds a transition graph (6) and hence a deterministic finite-state machine. For example, consider the regular expression $(0 * 11 * 01)*$ which describes a machine which will recognize occurrences of the string 101 in a continuous input sequence; the transition graph may be formed directly as shown in Fig. 2.6. In many cases, however, the translation from regular expressions to transition graph is not so obvious and algorithmic procedures have to be adopted.

From the logic-design point of view, however, since it is easier to generate regular expressions than transition graphs, a better technique would be to go directly from regular expressions to state diagrams. The best method described to date is that due to Brzozowski (9) which uses the concept of the derivative of a regular expression to obtain near-minimal state diagrams (other approaches tend to produce highly redundant state diagrams which need to be further reduced before machine implementations can take place).

The derivative Ds of a regular expression $F$ (used in the set-theoretic sense of *deriving* a new expression rather than the more usual calculus concept) is defined in the following way:

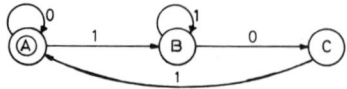

Figure 2.6. Pattern recognizer for string 101.

$\mathrm{D}sF = \{x \mid sx \in F\}$.

Thus for a set of sequences

$\quad F = \{0111, 10111, 010111, 01010111\}$

$\quad D_{10}F = \{111\}, \quad D_{01}F = \{11, 0111, 010111\}$.

Brzozowski has investigated the algebraic properties of derivatives and propounded an algebra sufficient to derive the derivation of any set of regular expressions.

The technique normally adopted in converting regular expressions to state diagrams is to number all the 0's and 1's in the expression from left to right, and then consider all possible input sequences and their allowable transitions to a terminal state. It will be obvious that this procedure can involve an excessive amount of computation and generally results in a redundant machine. The derivative forms of regular expressions indicate whether or not a particular sequence is contained in the expression; thus they may be used to identify the states of an equivalent machine. In so doing it is also necessary to realize the fact that two derivatives can describe the same set of sequences. In order to obtain a state diagram from a regular expression all possible derivatives are formed and used to define a state diagram for the machine. The final step is to eliminate all redundant equivalent states; this may be performed using standard state-reduction techniques.

It would appear from the above that regular expressions have many of the properties required of a specification language for logical systems, for example, a formal structure capable of analysis, direct implementation, etc. However, there are two major disadvantages when using regular expressions to design logical systems. The first is that, contrary to what has been written, the method is not easy to use. In practice designers find the formalism very difficult to accept and considerable experience must be acquired before becoming fluent in the language. The second basic snag is that the language is really only suitable for describing machines with a single output terminal, where the output value is set to logic 1 whenever the specified input sequence is accepted by the machine. The only method to adopt with multiple-output circuits is to assume that there are $n$ binary outputs and to derive a separate regular expression for each.

Thus, owing mainly to the difficulties encountered in converting from a verbal description to a set of regular expressions (even for small systems), the method has not found practical use in any CAD system to date. However, it is conceivable that regular expressions could be employed as a form of meta-language for system use in defining the modes of expression within a higher-level specification language.

### 2.5. PETRI NETS (10)

Another graph-theoretic approach which has found considerable application in the description of digital systems is the *Petri net*, also called a *transition net* (11, 12, 13). The Petri net is basically a directed graph consisting of nodes and arcs (directed lines) which may be used to describe the control structure in a logical system, that is it can represent conceptually either hardware or software processes. As illustrated in Fig. 2.7, the Petri net has two kinds of node: *places* drawn as circles, and *transitions* drawn as bars. Each directed line or arc connects a place to a transition, or vice versa; in the former case the place is called an *input place* and in the latter an *output place* of the transition. The places correspond to system conditions which must be fulfilled in order for a transition, that is an event, to occur.

The behavior of the Petri net, and consequently the system it represents, may be visualized by thinking of the net as a form of board game involving *tokens* which are moved from place to place (this analogy was first suggested by Holt). Thus, any condition in the system may be represented by the presence or absence of a token in a particular place in the net: if the condition holds the place contains a token; if the place is empty the corresponding condition does not hold. A Petri-net *marking* is an assignment of tokens to some or all of the places in the net; the distribution of tokens may be considered in this simplified model as representing some state of the system. For example, in Fig. 2.7, the marking which makes the places B and C full and all others empty defines the state where the conditions B and C hold and no others. Note that the Petri net allows *concurrent* or independent operations to be described.

Progress through the net from one marking to another, corresponding to state changes, is determined by the *firing* of transitions according to the following rules.

(a) A transition is enabled if all of its input places hold a token.
(b) Any enabled transmission may be fired.
(c) A transition is fired by transferring tokens from input places to output places; thus firing means that instantaneously all of the transition's inputs are emptied and its outputs filled.

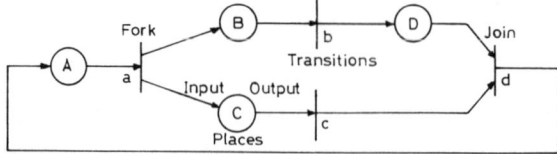

**Figure 2.7.** Petri net.

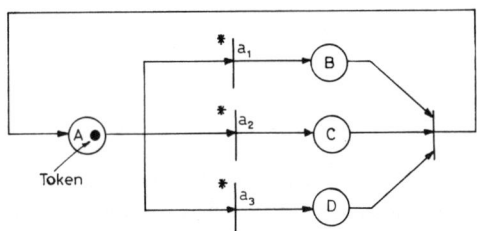

* denotes  enabled  transitions, $a_1$, $a_2$, $a_3$ are in conflict

**Figure 2.8.** Petri net with conflicts.

A Petri net is said to be *safe* when each place is restricted to containing only one token at the same time. Thus it follows that the application of the firing rule must never lead to a net marking with places containing more than one token. This restriction gives rise to another constraint on the model; that is the net should be *conflict free*. A conflict arises when two transitions share at least one input place (see Fig. 2.8); if the common input place has only one token the firing of any one of the transitions will disable the other transition. Thus conflict-free nets are nets in which transitions are allowed to share input places, but the initial marking distribution is such that the conflict situation never arises during the operation of the system.

A *live* Petri net is defined as one in which it is possible to fire any transition of the net by some firing sequence, irrespective of the marking that has been reached. Note that a live net still remains live after firing.

The system model described above is really a subclass of the general Petri-net concept in that only one token is allowed to traverse the network at a time and conflict situations are prohibited. Moreover, since conflict in a network can be interpreted as a state of indeterminacy, that is at certain transition times there is uncertainty about which of several possible mutually exclusive events will occur, the model is less powerful. It is interesting to note that every finite-state machine has an equivalent Petri net, but the reverse does not hold true except for the restricted model. (As we have seen earlier, and demonstrated with transition graphs, the ability of a specification system to represent indeterminate behavior is of paramount importance.) Nevertheless it seems necessary to apply constraints of this type in order to allow the system model to be physically realized in terms of hardware or software processes. This is essential in the case of hardware implementation, since in general the presence or absence of a token will be realized by a binary variable taking the values 0 or 1. In addition conflict-free nets also have the property of *persistence*, that is a transition which is enabled is not disabled until it fires, thus accounting for circuit delays and processing times. The use of the simplified Petri net also allows more freedom in developing evaluation and analysis algorithms on a formal basis.

One of the major uses of Petri nets is to represent the control structure of a logical system. When used to specify hardware systems, transitions in the Petri net are assumed to correspond to the operators (that is processing or conditional elements) of a data-flow structure and the places to the control links between the two structures. This is because, in order to deal with concurrent processes, fully asynchronous operation must be assumed, which requires control signals to be provided between the control and data structures. Thus, a ready signal must be sent from the control structure (that is from a place) to initiate operations in the data structure (such as addition, multiplication, etc.) When the required operation has been completed the data-processing unit must respond by transmitting an acknowledge signal back to the control structure (this in fact corresponds to the "handshake" principle used in most interface units). In the case of a conditional element a decision link is required to the data structure. This consists as before of a ready signal from the control structure but this time the data structure replies with either a true or false signal. For example, Fig. 2.9 shows the control Petri net and its associated data structure for processing the function $(x + y)(x^2 + y)/z^2$. Note that the data structure contains registers ($x, y, z, a, b, c$, etc.) and processing elements for the operations of addition, multiplication, etc. In order to operate this procedure (and to allow for the subsequent implementation of the control structure in hardware) the transition firing rules for the Petri net must be modified to the following basic steps.

(a) Remove token from input places.
(b) Send a ready signal to the processing unit.
(c) Wait for acknowledge signal.
(d) Put token in output places.

The expression shown in Fig. 2.9 is evaluated in the following manner. Initiation of the process is accomplished by placing a token in place $Q$ which corresponds to sending a ready signal to the data structure to signify that the operation of loading the registers $x, y,$ and $z$ should commence. When the registers are loaded the data structure responds with an acknowledge signal. Applying the firing rules to the Petri net this procedure may be stated as follows.

(a) A token is placed in place $Q$ which sets up transition $a$ ready for firing.
(b) Remove token from $Q$ and send ready signal to register circuits.
(c) Wait for acknowledge signal; when it is received place tokens in places $R, S,$ and $T$.

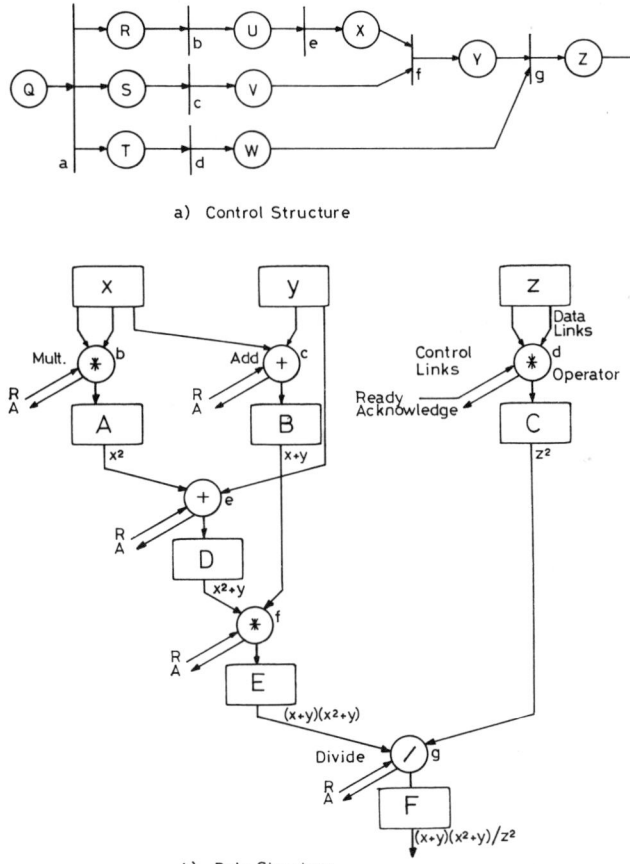

a) Control Structure

b) Data Structure

**Figure 2.9.** Petri-net structures.

Application of the transition firing rules to transitions $b$, $c$, and $d$ initiate the next stages of the process; this procedure is continued until the evaluation is complete, as indicated by a token in place $z$. Note that each processing element contains its own registers and that concurrent or parallel processing is easily handled. For example, transition $f$ cannot be fired until places $X$ and $Y$ are filled, that is the separate operations of addition and multiplication and addition are completed.

It has been shown (14, 15, 16) that it is possible to replace the individual components of a Petri net for a control structure by a hardware circuit. For example there are direct hardware equivalents of a place, with or without a token, a branch, a join, etc. In the hardware implementation the presence, or absence, of tokens is represented by changes in signal level; for example, a 0-1

change corresponds to a place being marked with a token. The basic
circuit-block replacements (on a one-to-one basis) for transitions and places in
a conflict-free Petri net are shown in Fig. 2.10. In the case of a place circuit
the fundamental component is essentially one exclusive OR gate. The function
of the additional exclusive OR gates is to provide fan-in facilities for the case
where more than one transition goes to a single place and to allow for the
situation where a place feeds more than one transition. Transitions may be
represented by the circuit shown in Fig. 2.10*b*, which is similar in action to a
master–slave bistable. The inputs from the places go to a logic unit called a
*concensus* circuit which has the characteristic that its output goes to logic 1 if,
and only if, all the inputs are 1, the output value being retained until all the
inputs become logic 0. Thus, it is only the concensus of the input values
which effects a change in the circuit output. In operation, when the output of
the concensus gate goes to 1, indicating that all the associated input places
contain a token, a transition is initiated. This causes the first bistable circuit
to change state, which generates a canceling signal back to the places
(equivalent to removing the tokens from the input places and satisfying the
persistence condition in the process). The effect of removing all the tokens
causes the concensus gate to operate again; this sets the second bistable which
then sends a ready signal to the operator module.

It is possible to overcome the conflict limitation by including an *arbiter
circuit* in the transition block. In the case where transitions share a common
place only one transition is permissible; consequently it is necessary to be able
to decide which transition should fire. The function of the arbiter then is to

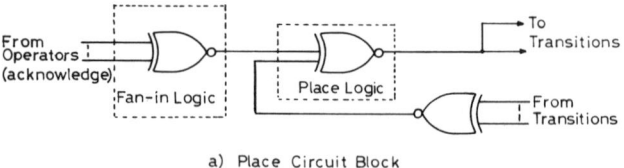

a) Place Circuit Block

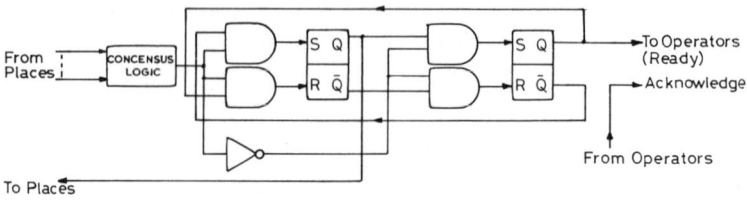

b) Transition Circuit Block

**Figure 2.10.** Petri-net circuits.

resolve conflicts between transitions, allowing only the chosen transition (or that with the highest priority) to proceed whilst blocking all other transitions. It should be noted that the arbiter principle is particularly useful for dealing with the allocation of common resources, for instance, shared processing elements.

One of the major advantages of the directed-graph approach to system representation is that, owing to its formal structure, it is amenable to mathematical analysis. Various authors have described algorithmic methods for the analysis of directed graphs [in particular marked groups (12)]. Notable among the work has been that of Holt (11) and particularly Karp and Miller (17, 18). The use of the theory provides the designer with methods of analyzing system performance and algorithm consistency, and is specially useful when dealing with parallel or concurrent processing.

In the main the analysis techniques apply to the control-graph function only. This is known as an *uninterpreted* analysis because no allowance is made for the operations performed by the data structure. However, in certain cases the methods can be extended to include the data-structure functions, in which case an *interpreted* analysis is said to be performed.

An important characteristic of a control graph is whether or not the implied algorithm is *determinate*. In general, determinate systems have the property that for any two inputs which have the same values the system gives identical outputs. Acquiring a knowledge of this property is extremely important when analyzing parallel processes, since it is necessary to ascertain if multiple accesses to a common resource, with a given initial control state and data value, always results in the same set of final values. In essence this corresponds to eliminating "race" conditions in the control structure; that is, the following conditions must always be satisfied.

(a) No two data operations can simultaneously write into the same data location.

(b) Data operations must not be allowed to read and write simultaneously into the same location.

This leads of course in hardware terms to the usual precautions, such as "handshaking" circuits, which must be taken when working with asynchronous systems.

The problem of determinacy (and also algorithmic termination) has been extensively studied by Karp and Miller, who have defined the necessary conditions on a parallel control algorithm which allows determinacy analysis to be conducted. Further work has been done by Holt, who has investigated the problems of resource management and system deadlocks using a derived form of directed-graph model known as an *occurrence graph*.

The obvious advantage of the Petri-net method of design is that it is possible to generate a control graph, to evaluate it, and then to proceed immediately to direct implementation. Moreover, the general Petri net has the considerable advantage over other methods of specification (for example, state diagrams) that it can handle complex systems. The major disadvantages are as follows.

(a) The evaluation procedures, unless considerably constrained, are very laborious.

(b) In general the design method must be used in conjunction with a predefined and restricted data structure.

In addition, the hardware realization of the control-graph components leads to non-standard circuitry (for instance, ROM's are normally used for micro-program control stores) accompanied by a considerable redundancy of system components.

## 2.6. THE LOGOS SYSTEM

The Petri-net concept forms the basis of a CAD system called LOGOS (19, 20, 21) which is currently completing development at Case Western Reserve University. The aim of project LOGOS is to provide the computer systems designer with a CAD environment which enables highly parallel complex systems to be defined, evaluated at all levels, and finally implemented in either hardware or software form. Inherent in the overall design philosophy is the hierarchical handling of complexity which was discussed in § 1.3. The chief influence in this area appears to be the work of Dijkstra (22) on structured programming which formalized the concepts of "layered" systems. In structured programming a sequential program is viewed as a hierarchy of layers (processes) in which each layer (or process) is executed on a "virtual" processor existing on the next level down. Each virtual processor has a "machine language" which can execute the primitives of the process at the level immediately above it.

Thus, in LOGOS a digital system is considered as a partially ordered hierarchy of layers, the highest layer being the interface with the user and the lowest the system primitives. The system primitives (which can be considered as subsystem components) may, in the case of software, be machine code, macros, library subroutines, etc., whilst the hardware equivalent would be NAND/NOR gates, MSI chips, $\mu$-processors, etc. A system *facility*, that is a processing or storage operation that may be shared by more than one user, may be activated by a facility at a higher level, and can in turn activate lower-order facilities. A facility is considered to be comprised of the following elements.

(a) Local resources (such as logical units and storage) which may be required by the facility suboperations.

(b) A control unit which governs resource allocation and sequencing of suboperations.

(c) A set of algorithms (called *activities*) which define the suboperations (the activation of an algorithm is called a process).

(d) An interpreter which translates user directives.


Inherent in the system is the ability to handle asynchronous concurrent operations and the existence of an interface discipline between control and data paths. Compatibility is achieved at all levels, in that it is possible to consider the interconnection and analysis of subsystem blocks and facilities without being concerned with their detailed composition; similarly it is also possible to analyze independently the component parts which constitute a facility.

The LOGOS representational system uses two directed graphs, one for data flow and the other for control flow, to describe an algorithm (activity). The data graph (DG) defines the algorithmic data structure and the transformations upon it, whilst the associated control graph (CG) sequences the transformation and defines its control flow. The control graph, shown in Fig. 2.11, consists of two types of nodes: c-cells containing control variables (i.e. state variables) represented by squares, and control operators represented by circles. Directed lines are used to connect cells to operations or vice versa. The DG consists of data cells, which represent the information structures of the activity, and data operators, which perform the required transformations such as ADD, SHIFT, MULTIPLY, etc.; data operators can only be connected to data cells and vice versa. Each data operator is associated with a unique control operator (represented by linkages between the CG and DG) which determines when the data-processing operations may take place (analogous to the Petri-net approach).

The initiation of a control operation (A in Fig. 2.11) triggers the associated data operator (a), which then reads its input cells and performs the data-processing operation, writing the result into its output cells. After the operation is completed the data operator communicates back to the termination control operator (A′), and the control operator terminates by altering its c-cells appropriately.

The flow of control in the CG is determined by the values in the control cells and the enabling functions defined for the control operators. The control operator stores a binary vector (called the *domain*, equal in length to the number of input cells) which, in conjunction with the value of the output c-cells, is used to control the initiation and termination of events in the corresponding data operator. The enabling function is specified as a transfer

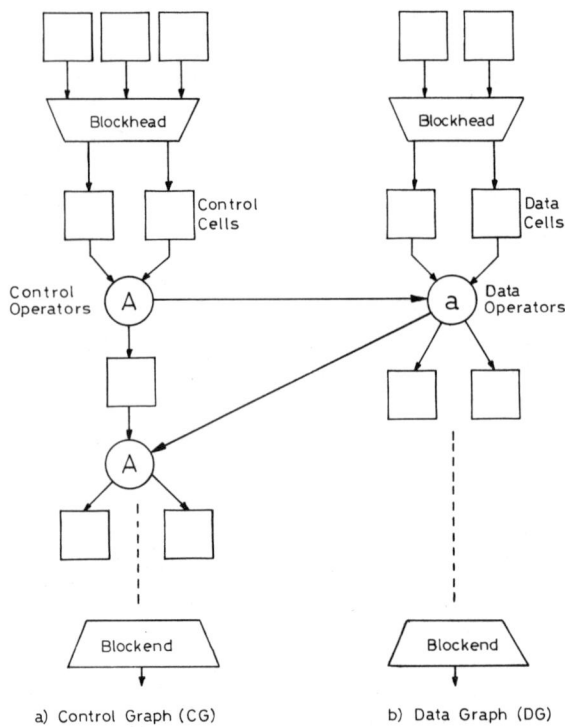

a) Control Graph (CG)                    b) Data Graph (DG)

**Figure 2.11.** LOGOS representation of an activity.

function on this total state vector. Thus, the control operator can only initiate a data operation when its input and output c-cells have the values specified by the enabling function. Upon termination the control operator will change the values of the input and output c-cells to the values specified by the transfer function. Thus the control operator must read its output cells before initiating an action and write into its input cells upon termination. This "backward" flow of control information provides the necessary synchronization between control operators; note that the control operators function in an essentially asynchronous mode, using the "handshaking" principle, though synchronous control can also be represented.

The *blockhead* and *blockend* operators (analogous to the **ALGOL** "begin-end" block) are paired to delineate an activity and form the enclosing control for the task being represented. This facility allows a simple operator at one level of design to be replaced by another self-contained structure. This ALGOL-like block structure also allows nesting of activities and the use of global and local parameters.

The control operators in the directed graphs may all be realized in a hardware form, and work has been performed in this area by Rose (23) and Howard (24). Unfortunately there are as yet no formal semantics in the LOGOS system for data operators (which are defined in terms of input-output data structures) and functional definition is therefore not possible.

Though the LOGOS system is probably the most advanced specification and design environment described to date, it nevertheless still requires considerable further development; in fact the designers of the system view it as open ended, with the users themselves participating in its eventual development. In common with the Petri-net approach there are many outstanding problems in the evaluation of the total activity of a complex system, that is including the data structures. Further problems arise in the implementation of the system. Although it seems possible to implement the control graphs using rather specialized logic (the problem of merging control graphs to produce one overall control unit remains to be solved), it is still unclear how data structures can best be realized.

One approach has been to generate specific data structures (in terms of software or hardware) from the initial data graphs using a textural string language based on ALGOL 68 semantics. For example, a data-cell representation for a computer word would be declared as

T word = PDP10 word ($\langle 0 \rangle$ [6] : S1, $\langle 6 \rangle$ [30] : S2)

which represents a word in the PDP10 computer with a field S1 of 6 bits commencing at bit 0 and a field S2 of 30 bits. (Note that this representation could equally be used to define data buses etc. in hardware systems. In the case of software the data primitive is 1 bit, whereas in hardware it is an attachment point for a wire.) Though it seems possible to parse linear non-parallel CG-DG pairs (for a known structure defined as above) and generate code using an intermediate meta-language, no actual code has as yet been compiled. Moreover, many major problems still remain: for instance how to generate code for a sequential computer from parallel control graphs, the generation of code for a computer defined semantically in LOGOS, dynamic storage allocation etc.

Another descriptive graph model based on Petri nets is the E (for *evaluation*) net, due to Noe and Nutt (25, 26). E-nets are hierarchical in concept and are primarily intended for the evaluation (and simulation) of hardware-software resources and their process interactions, for example, the analysis of the interaction in a system between hardware modules (stores, processors, input-output devices, etc.) and utility software modules (compilers, service routines, etc.). This would include, for instance, such parameters

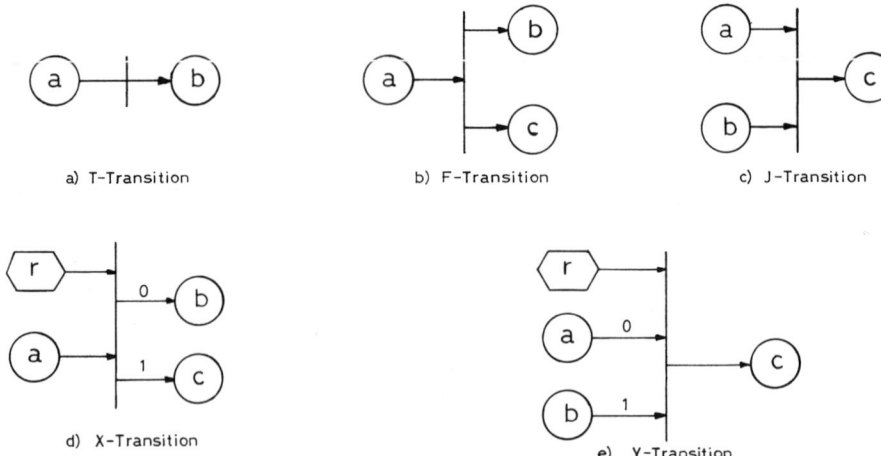

a) T-Transition                    b) F-Transition                    c) J-Transition

d) X-Transition

e)  Y-Transition

**Figure 2.12.** E-net primitives.

as resource allocation, queueing, throughput, turn-round time, etc. Thus, the structure of the system can be investigated, and in particular the control function required to be performed by the operating system. The method has been used to represent systems such as the IBM/360 under the OS/MFT operating system and the CDC 6400 under SCOPE.

The primitive operators used in the model are shown in Fig. 2.12; the close similarity with the Petri nets shown in Fig. 2.7 should be noted. The T-transition primitive is the identity operation, and the F and J transitions correspond to the Petri-net FORK (branch) and JOIN respectively. The X and Y transitions do not appear as such in Petri nets and allow conditional decisions in the E-net, for example, to resolve conflicts. The transitions depend on the outcome of a resolution procedure r, which determines which transition is permissible. Another important difference between E-nets and conventional Petri nets is that, in addition to the tokens indicating control flow, they can also carry attributes such as timing data.

The representation has been successfully used (off line) to describe small digital systems, including the PDP-8 computer, and there is no doubt that the system shows considerable promise of providing the required overall CAD environment.

## 2.7. THE PMS AND ISP DESCRIPTIVE SYSTEM (27)

This work represents an attempt to develop a notational system to describe computer architecture at the information-flow level, called the PMS level (Processor–Memory–Switch) and the register-transfer level, called ISP

(Instruction–Set–Processor). It arose originally out of a need to describe the physical structure of computer systems in terms of a small number of elementary components in order to undertake a comparison of computer architectures for textbook purposes (28). The methodology has been successfully employed to describe and compare complex computer systems (such as System/360, CDC 6500, etc.) and also for the design of the PDP11 computer (29). Unfortunately, there is no supporting software for the PMS notation, and analytical and synthesis procedures are still to be developed. (It is highly doubtful if the notational system could in fact support formal analysis or even simulation procedures.) However, software interpreters and compilers have been written for the ISP language, but in practice ISP seems to have relatively little advantage over other types of register-transfer languages (see § 2.8).

The PMS system consists of a number of structural primitives connected together in such a way as to form a network of components, each performing data-processing operations on the information flow through the network. Information is assumed to occur in packets called *i-units* and is measured in bits, or equivalent units such as bytes, etc. There are seven basic primitives, each distinguished by the function it performs; they are as follows.

*Memory, M.* A read–write storage component for i-units, including an addressing scheme.

*Link, L.* A component that transfers i-units from one component to another.

*Control, K.* A component that initiates the operation of other components, analogous to the control structure of a program or a microprogram unit. All components, except for control, consist of a set of discrete operations which must be individually evoked.

*Switch, S.* This component is used to construct a link between other components and functions essentially either as a multiplexer or demultiplexer circuit.

*Transducer, T.* Used to change i-units from one form to another whilst at the same time preserving its meaning (but not necessarily its information content, that is the number of bits in the representation), for instance, parallel to serial conversion, voltage levels to magnetic flux or holes in punched paper tape, etc.

*Data operation, D.* Used to change the meaning of i-units, for example, the component would perform arithmetic functions, logical and shifting operations, etc.

*Processor, P.* A component capable of interpreting a program in order to execute a sequence of operations. It consists of a set of operations of the type described above, that is, M, L, K, S, T, and D primitives.

These components can be connected together to form a structure representing a stored-program digital computer (or any other digital system). For example, the basic configuration for a computer C is defined by:

$$C := M_p - P_c - T - X$$

where $P_c$ represents a central processing unit (CPU) and $M_p$ a primary memory (that is, one which is directly accessible from $P_c$) which holds the program. The input–output devices are represented by T which are connected to the external environment X. An alternative arrangement at a more detailed level would be

$$M_p - D - T - X$$

where $P_c$ is split into a control and arithmetic unit; the full lines represent data and the broken lines control paths. The diagram can be further expanded by associating local control with each component, rather than combining all the control functions into the component K. For example, K may be decomposed into $K(M_p)$, $K(P)$, and $K(T)$ to represent the control of the memory, processor/data-operations, and transducer components respectively.

Using this notation computer systems can be described at various detailed levels. For instance, in the above descriptions the links were not written in as separate entities; this would only become necessary if the transmission details were relevant to system performance, etc. Note that components are themselves decomposable into other component; for example memories can be considered as a set of addressing switches and submemories, a processor may be partitioned into a data-operation component plus control, etc. Thus it will be seen that the PMS notational system embodies the principle of layering described in the last section.

As well as using component suffixes to denote particular properties (for example $M_p$ to indicate that the function of M is that of a primary store) a detailed specification may be associated with each component. This takes the general form

$$X(a_1 : v_1; a_2 : v_2; \ldots a_k : v_k)$$

where X is the component and $a$ is an attribute having the value $v$. Each component parameter, that is the pair $(a_i : v_i)$ can be defined independently and thus there is no significance in the order in which they are written. The parameters may take various forms, for example, costs, memory capacities, information flow rates, power, etc. There are in general a very large number of parameters that can be associated with each component; this is one of the major difficulties in specifying a viable descriptive system. The technique adopted is to abbreviate where possible, using only pertinent parameters. For example, a processor may be defined in terms of operation times, thus

$P_c$ (operation times: add: 2 $\mu$s; store: 2 $\mu$s; multiply: 18 $\mu$s; ...)

In which the times for each operation are listed independently. Alternatively, it is possible to give an abbreviated description by simply stating a range of operating times, i.e.

$P_c$ (operation time: 2 $\sim$ 18 $\mu$s).

Again, a core store may be defined as:

M (function: primary; technology: core; operation time: 1.5 $\mu$s;

size: 4096 W; word: 16 bits)

but is is also possible to convey the same information to an informed reader by the expression

M core (1.5 $\mu$s; 4 kW: 16 bits).

The PMS notation allows complex digital computer systems to be specified at many levels, from a complete detailed description to a highly simplified schematic. Though the notation is somewhat fluid, it is sufficiently standardized to enhance the communication of ideas and systems. However, it is unsuitable in its present form for CAD purposes, since it is essentially a descriptive, rather than formal, notation which prohibits the development of analysis and synthesis procedures.

The function of the ISP notation is to describe the programming level (that is register-transfer level) of a computer in terms of memory, instruction format, data types, data operations, etc. Thus ISP allows the specification of an instruction set and the rules for its interpretation to be precisely defined. In effect ISP is an ALGOL-based register-transfer language with facilities for defining an instruction set in terms of basic operations, registers, and data types. Concurrent operations and the sequencing of activities can also be handled in a limited manner.

Using ISP the memory structure of a machine may be specified by declaring a name and the number of storage bits associated with it. For example, an accumulator register may be defined as

AC $\langle 0:11 \rangle$

which signifies a 12-bit register, with bits 0–11 labeled from left to right, and called AC. Similarly a core store would be specified as

M $[0:7777_8]$ $\langle 0:11 \rangle$

which is a primary memory consisting of 7777 octal words of 12 bits each. The basic data operators include the following classes:

Concatenation $\square$

Boolean (AND/OR/EXOR/INV/EQIV)

Arithmetic $(+, -, *, \div)$

Relational $(=, \neq, <, \leqslant, >, \geqslant)$

Transfer $\leftarrow$

These classes are used to specify data-processing operations between registers. For instance, the conventional fetch operation in a digital computer could be expressed as

Instruction $\leftarrow$ M [PC] ; PC $\leftarrow$ PC + 1; next

which signifies that the primary memory M is addressed with the contents of the program counter PC and the result placed in the instruction register; the contents of PC are then incremented by 1.

The main function of ISP would appear to be that of hardware description, and serious consideration is being given to its adoption by the US armed forces as a standard language for specifying computer structures.

### 2.7.1. The Register-Transfer Module Design Concept (30, 31)

The basic concepts of the PMS/ISP descriptive system have been developed into a complete digital-design philosphy called the *register-transfer module* system (RTM), currently manufactured by the Digital Equipment Corporation under the name PDP-16. The RTM procedure allows specific high-level hardware to be used for the design of digital systems, that is, design at the subsystem, rather than basic gate, level. In order to design a system the engineer need only be conversant with the use of registers, data-processing operations between registers, and conventional flow-charting technique. Using these concepts logical algorithms may be represented by a flow chart, specifying the control flow, coupled to a data structure that stores and carries out the processing functions. Thus a designer can flow chart a logic process, in an analogous way to programming a computer, which can then be translated (using off-line software packages) into a hardware realization employing RTM's.

The RTM system consists of about 20 different hardware modules based on a modified form of the PMS primitive-structure types. The method of interconnecting modules is via a common bus that carries timing and data signals for the register transfers; operation is essentially asynchronous, requiring interlock signals between control and data structures. Register-transfer operations can be described using the ISP language discussed above.

There are four main classes of module, these are as follows.

(a) *DM type* (data-processing operations with memory). This unit normally comprises two registers, A and B, transfer gates, and processing logic. It can be considered as a programmable arithmetic and logic unit which evaluates the right-hand side of a transfer equation; that is the result of data operations performed on the two internal registers can be written to other external registers via the data bus. Typical operations would be:

$$\leftarrow A + B, \leftarrow A \oplus B, \leftarrow A - B, \leftarrow A \vee B, \leftarrow A \wedge B, \text{ etc.}$$

(It should be noted that the expression $C \leftarrow A + B$ is used to indicate that the integer or Boolean value of the right-hand side is placed in the register on the left-hand side.)

(b) *M type* (memory). These units consist of bistable registers, flag bistables (single-bit stores), ROM and conventional random-access stores.

(c) *K type* (control). These modules control the transfer of data between registers (via the data bus) by initiating operations in DM- and M-type modules; in effect they perform the control functions of a computer program. Various types of K modules are available (including clocks, delays, and manual-operation units); however, the three most important modules are as follows.

   *K (evoke)*. This unit is used to evoke a function consisting of a data operation and a register transfer, that is an arithmetic or logic operation. When a Ke unit is evoked it in turn evokes an operation in a DM unit, say, and when that function is complete (determined by a control line back from the evoked unit) the Ke unit then evokes the next K type in the control sequence. (Note the asynchronous operation based on the "handshaking" principle.) Figure 2.13*a* shows the flow-chart representation for the module. In essence the action is analogous to that of an FSM in that Ke represents an internal state with the ability to initiate an output operation (on receipt of an evoke signal) and then make a transition to another state.

   *K (branch)*. This module provides for the routing and sequencing of the control operations based on the condition of selected Boolean variables in the data structure, etc.; the equivalent flow chart is shown in Fig. 2.13*b*.

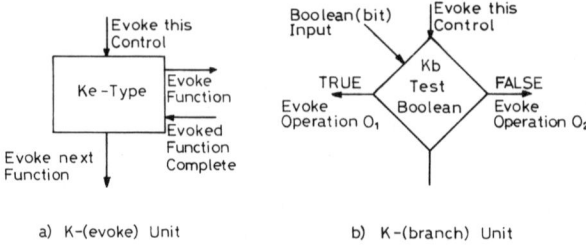

a) K-(evoke) Unit                    b) K-(branch) Unit

**Figure 2.13.** K-type control modules.

*K (bus).* This unit controls all transfer operations on the data highways, including monitoring all register transfers and supplying the evoke-function completion signals. Other functions include power-on initialization, manual operation, and bus termination.

**(d)** *T types* (transducers). These units provide an interface between the common data bus and peripheral equipment such as teletypes, paper-tape reader, light switches, etc.

A typical example of an **RTM** flow-chart–wiring-diagram description is shown in Fig. 2.14 for a circuit that determines whether or not the contents of register C are greater or equal to the sum of registers A and B. Note that the system can be split into two basic parts, the K modules showing the control flow and the **DM/M** modules to form and hold the result. At the present time RTM modules are implemented in terms of printed-circuit boards containing TTL and MSI packages; however, there is no reason why LSI technology should not be used eventually.

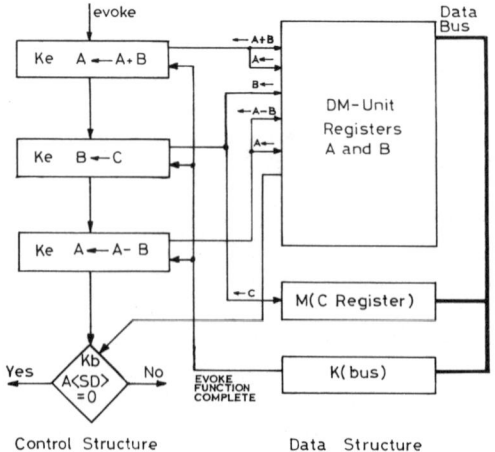

Control Structure                    Data  Structure

**Figure 2.14.** RTM system for C ⩾ A + B.

It is interesting to observe the similarity between this exclusively hardware-oriented system-design technique and the directed-graph methods described earlier. In both cases the system structure is partitioned into control and data paths, and special hardware modules used to implement the control algorithm. Though the RTM flow chart is not amenable to formal analysis (except in a restricted way using ISP as a simulation language), it does have the advantage over directed-graph methods in that the data structures can be systematically realized and interpreted.

Though this method has many practical limitations from the computer designer's point of view (particularly the constraint to use special modules, for instance, control stores are normally implemented using ROM's), it nevertheless represents an important contribution to evolving a design methodology applicable at the subsystem level.

## 2.8. REGISTER-TRANSFER LANGUAGES

The intuitive design procedures used in computer systems engineering are normally centered around a predefined register configuration (this is also true, to a large extent, in any digital system). The execution of a machine-code instruction set for a computer is then interpreted in terms of micro-order sequences [a set of which is called a microprogram (32)] which control the required transfers and data-processing operations between registers. These heuristic design procedures have been semi-automated using problem-oriented *register-transfer languages* (RTL) to declare a proposed register structure and the required logical operations between them. In all register-transfer languages it is assumed that the logical functions of a machine can be completely defined by its register structure, the information flow between them, and the operations (micro-orders) it has to perform. Note once again the necessity to partition the system into control and data structures; in this case, however, the data structure contains only storage elements, the processing functions being specified in the RTL statements together with the control requirements. The declarative section of the language in essence forms a linguistic description of the block diagram of a machine. Using this technique microprograms for a particular machine-code instruction set may be specified in a register-transfer language as operational procedures which can then be used for documentation and simulation purposes; it is also possible in many cases to generate Boolean design equations directly from the RTL description.

Register-transfer languages are normally *non-procedural* languages in that no meaning is attached to the lexographical ordering of statements describing the operation of the system. Statements are associated with some sort of "label" detailing the conditions for executing the operations described by the register-transfer statements. *Procedural* languages, on the other hand, impose an explicit ordering on the statements, with each operation conditioned by the completion of the preceding ones.

The first register-transfer language was proposed by Reed (33); this was non-procedural in nature with a small vocabulary (and thus easily learned) and had the advantage that its statements could be directly associated with hardware elements. However, it was not possible to specify a complex system using this language, since no provision existed for partitioning into subsystem blocks and the small vocabulary necessitated the use of an inordinate number of symbols. Nevertheless, the Reed language forms a good starting point for any discussion of register-transfer languages. For the purpose of a register-transfer language a register A is defined as an ordered sequence of cells (bistable elements) each capable of storing 1 bit of data, that is

$$A_{(i)} \text{ where } i = 1, 2, 3 \ldots n.$$

Note that each cell of the register can be indexed separately, which allows identification of individual cells and variable-length working. Registers are identified by using a defined character string, and can generally be considered as a vector with $n$ components.

Operations between registers are normally specified between the entire arrays, but individual stages can be selected if required. For example

$$A_{(i)} \vee B_{(i)} \rightarrow C_{(i)}, i = 1, 2, 3, \ldots 16$$

or simply

$$A \vee B \rightarrow C$$

indicates that the contents of the 16-bit register A is OR'ed with the contents of register B and the result placed in register C, whereas

$$A_{(1)} \vee B_{(3)} \rightarrow C_{(5)}$$

indicates that bit 1 of register A is OR'ed with bit 3 of register B and the result placed in bit 5 of register C.

It is assumed that all operations between registers can be accomplished within some finite interval of time; however, the interval need not necessarily depend upon the completion of the operations involved. For instance, the time period may be defined as the period between two successive clock pulses, where the generation of the clock pulses may be either independent of, or dependent upon, the operations to be performed during the time interval. Consequently the RTL notation may be used to specify both synchronous and asynchronous systems. Thus it is possible in the language to specify the following:

$$|f| : A + C \rightarrow B$$

where the "label" $|f|$ represents a function which goes to logic 1 for the duration of the time interval, and can be either the period of a regularly occurring machine clock or, alternatively, a compound conditional statement. For example

$$|C_1| : A + C \rightarrow B$$

implies that the register operations take place when clock pulse $C_1$ occurs. Again

$$|\bar{A}_1 B_3| : A + C \rightarrow B$$

means that the operations take place only when the conditions of bit 1 in register A equals zero and bit 3 in register B equals 1 are satisfied. Various logical and arithmetic functions such as AND, OR, complementation, shifting, addition, subtraction, etc. can be performed between registers, the operations being applied component by component in the transfer operations. A further useful function in the Reed language was an addressing facility which allowed a location in the main core store, or any set of registers, to be individually addressed. The notation used is to let M⟨C⟩ represent a register or storage location contained within a store M, the address of the register being given by the contents of register C; thus M⟨C⟩ may be considered as a register of M selected by C.

Reed's language is essentially an algorithmic descriptive language for defining microprograms. For example, Table 2.1 shows how a sequence of register-transfer operations (micro-orders) for executing the computer instruction "Add the contents of the location whose address is specified in the instruction to the Accumulator" might be expressed in the Reed language. Note that the sequencing of the operations is implied by the order in which the transfer statements are written, and any timing delays must be allowed for directly. Alternative choice of operations, that is simple program branching, may be handled by prefacing the register transfers with conditional statements based on logical 0 or 1 tests on register contents and flag bits. (In essence this corresponds to the "conditions" circuits in a conventional microprogram control unit.) Owing to these inherent restrictions the language is severely limited if concurrent processing or branching operations are required to be specified. For instance, repetitive operations, such as shifting the contents of a

**Table 2.1. Reed RTL Descriptions of the Add Instruction**

| TIME INTERVAL | OPERATION | COMMENT |
|---|---|---|
| $n$ : | $I \rightarrow SA$ | Transfer contents of Instruction register to Store Address register |
| $n + 1$ : | $M \langle SA \rangle \rightarrow SB$ | Access store; place next instruction in Store Buffer register |
| $n + 2$ : | $SB \rightarrow C$ | Buffer register to Control register |
| $n + 3$ : | $I \rightarrow I + 1$ | Increment Instruction register by $+ 1$ |
| $n + 4$ : | $C \rightarrow DR$ | Control register to Decode unit |
| $n + 5$ : | $CA \rightarrow SA$ | Address bits of Control register to Store Address register |
| $n + 6$ : | $M \langle SA \rangle \rightarrow SB$ | Access store; place operand in Store Buffer register |
| $n + 7$ : | $SB \rightarrow X$ | Store Buffer register to Auxiliary register X |
| $n + 8$ : | $AC + X \rightarrow AC$ | Add contents of register X to Accumulator |

register a given number of places, are best performed by counting round a loop; this requires a test-and-jump facility. In general determining the sequence of events which are required to take place from a Reed-language description is not an easy task. As we shall see later the question of timing is a fundamental problem with all register-transfer languages which to date has only been partially overcome.

### 2.8.1. Formal Language Systems

Schorr (34) extended the language by including timing pulses as an integral part of the conditional statements, and also included a form of "GOTO" transfer. For example, it is possible to write statements in the form

$$|t_1 \bar{s}_3| : A \wedge B \rightarrow D; 1 \rightarrow t_5$$

$$|t_1 s_3| : A \rightarrow A - 1; 1 \rightarrow t_2$$

where, if $\bar{s}_3$ is 1 when $t_1 = 1$, the operation $A \wedge B \rightarrow D$ is performed and the next statement to be executed occurs in $t_5$, that is a jump to $t_5$ takes place; if $s_3 = 1$ the alternative operation takes place. Table 2.2 illustrates how the obey part of the computer instruction "shift contents of Accumulator left $n$ places" would be programmed. In the example register K contains the number of places ($j$) to be shifted and $T_0$ is a flag bistable. The left shift operation takes the general form

$$L_j AC \rightarrow D, X$$

which is an abbreviation for the three simultaneous transfers

$$AC_{(i)} \rightarrow D_{(i-n+j)} \qquad i = n - j + 1, n - j + 2, \ldots, n$$
$$AC_{(i-j)} \rightarrow X_{(i)} \qquad i = j + 1, j + 2, \ldots, n$$
$$0 \rightarrow X_{(i)} \qquad i = 1, 2, 3, \ldots, j.$$

It should be noted that a double-length shift is allowed for, the contents of the accumulator being shifted through into register D, and that X is an auxiliary register. It will also be apparent that a parallel shifting operation is assumed, this being performed in the usual way by gated transfers between registers; that is, the contents of the accumulator are transferred to X shifted $j$ places and then X is transferred back to the accumulator to complete the operation.

Schorr's language not only provided a more practical means of documenting microprograms but also had the fundamental advantage of being fully implemented in software using a syntax-directed compiler based on ALGOL 60. Moreover, it was also possible to perform both logic synthesis and analysis functions using algorithmic routines. Microprograms, expressed in RTL statements with registers formally identified and dimensioned by declaration statements, could be translated automatically by the software routines into sets of Boolean input equations for the bistable registers, which could then be implemented as hardware circuits using set and reset bistable elements. The translation process is in two steps; these are as follows.

(a) Each separate RTL statement is expressed in a form showing the necessary bistable set and reset conditions for individual register transfers.

(b) The equations are examined for common terms which are then collated and OR'ed together.

**Table 2.2. Schorr RTL Description of the Shift Instruction**

| TIMING | OPERATION | COMMENT |
|---|---|---|
| $|t_1 \text{ Start}|$ : | $1 \rightarrow t_2$ | |
| $|t_2|$ : | $V(K) \rightarrow T_0$; $1 \rightarrow t_3$ | Contents of K register OR'ed and placed in $T_0$ |
| $|t_3 \ \bar{T}|$ : | END | |
| $|t_3 \ T|$ : | $L_1 (AC) \rightarrow X$; $1 \rightarrow t_4$ | Shift Accumulator left one place into X |
| $|t_4|$ : | $X \rightarrow AC$; $1 \rightarrow t_5$ | |
| $|t_5|$ : | $K \rightarrow K - 1$; $1 \rightarrow t_2$ | Decrement K register |

An example will make this clear; let us consider the following program statements:

(1)  $|t_1 \overline{A}_2| : A \wedge B \rightarrow C; 1 \rightarrow t_2$

(2)  $|t_1 A_2| : A + B \rightarrow C; 1 \rightarrow t_3$.

It should be noted that registers A, B, and C would have been declared as 8-bit registers earlier in the program. Implementing these operations in terms of set–reset bistables we have, for the first stage,

(1)  $C_{(i)}/1 = t_1 \overline{A}_2 (A_{(i)} \wedge B_{(i)})$     $i = 1, 2, \ldots, 8$

$C_{(i)}/0 = t_1 \overline{A}_2 (\overline{A_{(i)} \wedge B_{(i)}})$     $i = 1, 2, \ldots, 8$

(2)  $C_{(i)}/1 = t_1 A_2 (A_{(i)} + B_{(i)})$     $i = 1, 2, \ldots, 8$

$C_{(i)}/0 = t_1 A_2 (\overline{A_{(i)} + B_{(i)}})$     $i = 1, 2, \ldots, 8$

where the terms on the right-hand side are those which cause bistable stage $C_{(i)}$ to be set to logic 1 (or logic 0), that is the input conditions for the set–reset terminals. Collecting these terms together produce the following results:

$$C_{(i)}/1 = t_1 \overline{A}_2 (A_{(i)} \wedge B_{(i)}) + t_1 A_2 (A_{(i)} + B_{(i)})$$

and

$$C_{(i)}/0 = t_1 \overline{A}_2 (\overline{A_{(i)} \wedge B_{(i)}}) + t_1 \overline{A}_2 (\overline{A_{(i)} + B_{(i)}}).$$

The timing-control equations for the circuits generating $t_1$, $t_2$, etc. must be extracted separately. This is done by relating the timing conditions and jump orders, which give the required sequence, to the coded states of a program counter, and then deriving the bistable input equations in the usual way. For instance, in our example the program counter must go from state $t_1 \rightarrow t_2$ for the condition $t_1 \overline{A}_2$ and state $t_1 \rightarrow t_3$ for the condition $t_1 A_2$. In this simple case the design of the control circuitry is trivial; however, with complex microprograms involving multiple branching etc. the evaluation of the control sequence can become extremely difficult.

Facilities also exist in the language for the analysis of digital systems, that is to check that the requirements of the original specification have been satisfied. The analysis procedures are basically the reverse of the synthesis process and require the system to be specified in terms of Boolean set–reset bistable equations, expressed in sum-of-product form, which are then translated into register transfers. However, the method is impracticable since for a large system considerable human effort is required to generate the required sets of Boolean equations.

Reed's language was also used as a model for the LDT language developed by Gorman and Anderson (35) and Proctor (36). The LDT language being of the procedural type was more formally defined and included high-level ALGOL-type operators such as IF, THEN, ELSE, GOTO, etc. More important, however, was the introduction of subroutine facilities which allowed system components, such as adders, counters, shift registers, etc., to be declared as high-level blocks, thus enabling a digital system to be described in terms of subsystem modules.

The software system, written in Burroughs ALGOL 58 language, consists of three main sections: (a) a translator for the RTL descriptions, (b) a timing analyzer for register-transfer operations, and (c) a logic-equation generator. The translation process commences by generating from the RTL descriptions a comprehensive table specifying the registers, operations, and transfers between registers and timing conditions. This table is additionally modified and extended by the designer, particularly with regard to timing operations. When the table is complete it is then analyzed and optimized where possible to achieve the shortest execution times; finally the Boolean equations are extracted for the bistable circuits.

Designing the software to realize a register-transfer language (which is in effect a problem-oriented computer language) is essentially a compiler writing operation (37). In order to input an RTL description into a computer it is essential to define precisely the syntactic rules (or grammar) used by the language in constructing the register structures and specifying their operation. The compiler is used in the conventional sense to translate from the source language (the RTL description) into a lower-level object language (the Boolean equations) with reference to the predefined syntax table. In fact the LDT software can be regarded as a three-pass special-purpose compiler with logic equations, rather than machine code, as the final output. The number of actual passes required by any translator, that is compiler, will depend on the type and speed of the computer, the storage media, the size of the problem being handled, the final form of the output, etc.

It is common practice to define the syntax of a computer language recursively using the *Backus Naur form* (BNF) (38) and register-transfer languages are no exception. For example, Table 2.3 shows the BNF description of a register and the information flow for the LDT language. It should be noted that ::= means "is defined as", the vertical slash | separates alternative definitions, and items enclosed by the diamond brackets ⟨⟩ represent variables which will be similarly defined in their due turn. Symbols outside the diamond brackets denote themselves, while the concatenation of

### Table 2.3. BNF Definitions of LDT Syntax

(a) *Machine register*

⟨register⟩ ::= ⟨identifier⟩ | ⟨identifier⟩(⟨size⟩) | ⟨register⟩(⟨structure list⟩)

⟨size⟩ ::= ⟨unsigned integer⟩ | ⟨unsigned integer⟩, ⟨unsigned integer⟩

⟨structure list⟩ ::= ⟨register⟩ | ⟨structure list⟩, ⟨register⟩

(b) *Information flow*

⟨transfer⟩ ::= ⟨destination register⟩ = (⟨source register set⟩)

⟨destination register⟩ ::= ⟨register⟩

⟨source register set⟩ ::= ⟨register⟩ | ⟨source register set⟩, ⟨register⟩

---

symbols or variables represents the order of the actual sequences they represent. Thus, a register may be declared, for example, as

$$A\,(1,48)\,[A_1(1,12),\,A_2(13,24),\,A_3(25,36),\,A_4(37,48)]$$

which is a complete specification including the field description, or simply as AC(1,48). Information flow between registers can be represented as

$$A = B;\, A1 = B9;\, A(1,3) = B(8,10)\ \text{etc.}$$

The normal practice in LDT is to specify the registers first, followed by the information flow (the connection data) and finally the algorithms for the operation codes.

Various software aids have been devised to assist in compiler writing, and these may of course be used for developing RTL compilers. The most important of these is the syntax-directed compiler (39), which takes the BNF definitions of a language, together with appropriate semantic information, and generates the required machine language and compiler compilers (40) which produce a compiler for any language expressed in a phrase-structured notation.

Another design concept which has been used, particularly in the work on LDT, is the use of a sequence chart (41) to display timing and sequencing information in a graphical manner. The format of the sequence chart is basically a square grid, with the horizontal axis scaled in units of time and the individual transfer operations arranged along the vertical axis. Transfer operations are shown on the chart as a horizontal bar the length of which is proportional to the execution time; the transfer operation being performed is normally written over the bar. Conditional operations are indicated by writing the conditions immediately to the left of the bar; branching is represented by broken lines and arrows. The sequence chart is essentially a method of presenting a completed design and has limited application in the initial design stages. Moreover, the graphic layout of the chart is difficult to reproduce unless fairly complex input-output equipment is employed.

Another ALGOL-based language called CDL, again modeled on the Reed notation (42), was described by Chu. The language had the advantages of being able to describe special operators, predetermined sequences, branching and controlled transfers, as well as the basic RTL operations. However, CDL has the limitation that all transfer operations are synchronous, thereby necessitating that any simultaneous operations must be performed in the same clock period; thus, it is not possible to describe independent concurrent operations. Though an ALGOL-like structure is employed, unfortunately no advantage is taken of the inherent block structure to describe hierarchical systems (it is in fact a non-procedural language). Most of the features of the CDL language have been successfully implemented in software (43) using FORTRAN IV. The CDL description takes the usual form of an initial declaration statement of registers and control functions followed by the microprogram statements. Table 2.4 shows a typical input description for the FETCH instruction of a microprogrammed parallel computer (Note the use of the IF THEN ELSE operations).

CDL is primarily a simulation language, though Boolean translators have been described (44) for the generation of bistable equations. The simulator is

**Table 2.4. CDL Description for FETCH Instruction**

| Register | R (0 — 17) | Buffer register memory M |
|---|---|---|
| | A (0 — 17) | Arithmetic register |
| | C (0 — 11) | Address register for memory M |
| | D (0 — 11) | Program register |
| | F (1 — 18) | Buffer register for control memory CM |
| | G | Stop/start control register |
| | H (1 — 5) | Address register memory CM |
| Subregister | R(OP) = R(0 — 5) | Operation code part of register R |
| | R(ADDR) = R(6 — 17) | Address part of register R |
| | F(ADDR) = F(1 — 5) | Address part of register F |
| Memory | M (C) = M(0 — 4095, 0 — 17) | Main Memory |
| | CM (H) = CM(0 — 31, 1 — 18) | Control register |
| Switch | Power (ON) | Power switch |
| | Start (ON) | Start switch |
| | Stop (ON) | Stop switch |
| Clock | P (1 — 3) | Three-phase clock |

```
       |F (6) * P (1)|    R ← M (C)
       |F (7) * P (2)|    H ← R (OP), C ← R(ADDR), D ← count up D
       |F (8) * P (3)|    IF (G) THEN [F ← CM(H)] ELSE (H ← O, C ← O, D ← O, R ← O)
       END
```

in two sections, a translator program (which establishes a polish string data structure from the CDL description) and the simulator proper. The simulation program consists of five parts: loader, output, switch, simulate, and reset routines. The loader accepts test data (that is initial register values, etc.) and stores them into the simulated registers held in the data structure; manual switches are set by the switch routine. The simulate routine executes the polish string representation of the registers in an interpretive mode (with output of selected registers, switches, memory words, etc. as dictated by the output routine). The reset routine re-initializes the simulator program for the next simulation run.

The CDL language is used primarily for the specification and simulation of digital systems, and has also been extensively used for teaching purposes. It is also possible to use the language for both hardware and software development, and as such forms a useful means of communication between designers.

Many implementations of the language exist, often including considerable modification. One such language is the ERES system (45) which includes the following additional features.

(a) The declaration of operators defining the function and duration of micro-operations; this overcomes the synchronous nature of CDL and makes it possible, in conjunction with control labels, to specify accurate microprogram timing.

(b) Block declarations which allow hardware procedures to be specified and called later in the same way as micro-operations.

Various other design languages have been described (46–49) which are basically very similar in concept to those described above, differing only in details of timing, subroutine facilities, and notation.

### 2.8.2. System Design Languages

Though some of the languages considered so far are capable of describing subsystem components, none of them have the ability of representing a partitioned system consisting of interconnected autonomous modules. In the Digital Design Language (DDL) described by Duley and Dietmeyer (50) a system is viewed as a collection of several subsystems, or *automatons*, each containing "private" facilities and having access to "public" facilities (common highways) which are used for intercommunication between automatons.

In DDL a system is specified using a layered-block structured description, where the outermost block defines the whole system in terms of subsystem blocks (automata), global variables, input–output requirements, etc., and the inner blocks specify the automata in terms of their state and signal behavior. The description itself is in Reed-like statements and contains the usual transfers, including Boolean and arithmetic operators, as well as special operators and declarations necessary for the system-level specification. Table 2.5 shows a selection of the more unusual declarations and operators available in the language. For example, since the subsystem components communicate with each other via the common highway, activity in one component may influence activity in another; consequently it is necessary to provide an activation operator of the form

$\Rightarrow$ AVID (CSOP)

where AVID is the name of a subsystem component and CSOP a set of operations $OP_i$ (including conditionals and transfers) which may be executed simultaneously by previously declared hardware; thus

$$CSOP = OP_1, OP_2, \ldots, OP_n \quad \text{for} \quad n \geqslant 1.$$

For instance, let us consider the statement

$\Rightarrow$ ACC (A $=$ B $\vee$ D, C $=$ E, F $\leftarrow$ G, $\rightarrow$ STATE 4).

This indicates that signals B $\vee$ D and E are to be connected to the common highway terminals A and C and the contents of register G transferred to register F; the symbol $\Rightarrow$ ACC signifies that the automaton ACC will also be influenced by these signals. Note that the order in which $OP_i$ is specified is immaterial, since it is assumed that all the processes will be performed in parallel.

Conditional operations are handled in two basic ways, corresponding to the IF THEN ELSE and IF THEN statements of conventional high-level languages. For example:

|BE| $CSOP_1$ ; $CSOP_0$

defines the syntax of the IF THEN ELSE conditional, where BE is a single-output Boolean expression which has the value 1 if $CSOP_1$ is to be executed and 0 for $CSOP_0$. Similarly the IF THEN structure is given by

|BE| $CSOP_1$

which executes $CSOP_1$ when BE $= 1$.

Timing control is accomplished by declaring state identifiers and the CSOP's that are to be performed when the automaton is in each of its states, or by using the TIme declaration which specifies a periodic clock generator. Thus, the state declaration

# Table 2.5. Declarations and Operators in the DDL Language

(a) *Declaration*

| TYPE | HARDWARE |
|---|---|
| MEmory or REgister | $n$ — or one-dimensional arrays of bistables |
| TErminal | $n$ — dimensional set of wires, terminals, or buses |
| BOolean | Logic network defined by Boolean equations |
| OPerator | Combinational circuitry shared among facilities |
| ELement | Input–output terminals of standard module |
| STate | Defines states of an automation |
| AUtomation | Defines an automaton composed of FSM and facilities |
| SEgment | Defines portion of the automaton which contains the declaration |
| SYstem | Defines a system with K automata and the system's public facilities |
| IDentifier | Assigns identifiers to previously defined operands |
| TIme | Periodic clock or signal generator |

(b) *Operators*

| OPERATION | SYNTAX | SEMANTICS |
|---|---|---|
| Activation | $\Rightarrow$AVID (CSOP) | CSOP is a set of operations that effect automaton AVID |
| Connection | ID = BE | The terminals ID are connected to the network defined by Boolean expression |
| Transfer | ID $\leftarrow$ BE | Memory elements ID are loaded from network defined by Boolean expression |
| Transition type 1 | $\rightarrow$ SID | Execute a transition to state SID (in the same block) |
| Transition type 2 | $\Rightarrow$ SEGID($\rightarrow$ NID, $\Rightarrow$ RID) | Execute a transition to state NID in segment SEG and return to state RID upon execution of a return operation |
| Return transition | $\Rightarrow$ | Return to the state specified by a transition type 2 |
| IF – THEN | \|BE\| CSOP$_1$ | If BE = 1, execute CSOP$_1$ |
| IF – THEN – ELSE | \|BE\| CSOP$_1$ ; CSOP$_0$ | If BE = 1, execute CSOP$_1$ ; if BE = 0 execute CSOP$_0$ |

$\langle ST \rangle$ T0 : GO : A ← B, → T1

   T1 :      B ← C ∧ D, → T5

specifies the situation where the automaton waits in state T0 until the signal GO is received, when the transfer A ← B is executed and a transition to state T1 is effected, etc. Each state identifier SID can be regarded as naming a condition or terminal which goes to 1 when the automaton is in state SID; for instance, T0 and GO must be satisfied before the transfer A ← B can take place. It is possible to express both synchronous and asynchronous designs using these techniques.

The main advantage of the DDL language is that it allows large digital systems to be dealt with in an organized manner. As a result of the language being based on established design procedures, system descriptions can parallel the block structure of the anticipated hardware, hence facilitating design and documentation. Moreover, it is also possible to translate a DDL specification into sets of Boolean and next-state equations which describe a hardware realization of the system (51). The translation process is accomplished by a series of transformations (in effect a multi-pass compiler) each of which generates another DDL description, but in a simpler format using less sophisticated features of the language. The control section of the description is translated by converting the state-declaration statements into register-transfer statements, and defining a state-sequencing register which is assigned either by the designer or the translator (note the similarity with the procedure used in the Schorr language). Thus, control is effected by using a finite-state machine model where the state registers are used to store information about the state of the machine, their value being modified by the state identifiers.

Other system-design languages have been described in the literature. A similar language to DDL, called CASSANDRE, with much the same facilities was proposed by Mermet and Lustman (52); CASSANDRE was based on ALGOL, and used the inherent block structure of that language to achieve the required system partitioning. The language is hierarchical in structure and is based upon recursively defined subsystem elements called *units*, which can represent existing hardware or some specified partitioning. A CASSANDRE description consists of defined units and their interconnections; each unit may itself comprise a network of units. The associated compiler accepts a CASSANDRE description, checks the syntax and compatibility of operations (for instance, the dimension of register transfers), and then generates a data base. Units may be extracted from the data base and compiled into either a simulation model or a logical description of a hardware circuit; microprogram generation has yet to be developed. The system has been implemented on an IBM360/67 computer at the University of Grenoble and is used primarily for simulation of logic and microprograms. A similar language with the same objectives, also developed in France, is the CRISMAS system (53). Once again this consists of a hierarchical block-structured definition language, but as yet no implementation has been reported.

The Computer-Aided System Design (CASD) system (54) encompassed high-level system descriptions, simulation at both systems and logic-gate level, and automatic translation to detailed hardware. CASD was based on the PL/1 language and utilized its block-structured facilities to develop a hierarchical specification. Timing in the CASD system was based on the use of asynchronous design as first proposed by Metze and Seshu (48). The work originated at IBM and was intended as a feasibility study of the problem; though prototype programs were developed, the project was eventually abandoned.

More recently a language for automated logic design (LALD) has been proposed (55), which allows a multi-level description of a system in terms of subsystem components which can then be interconnected to form an integral assembly. The data and control structure are required to be specified separately, and the control structure can be implemented using either software or hardware processes. Two versions of LALD translators have been written, one in SNOBAL for the CDC 6400 and the second in PL/1 for the IBM model 91.

### 2.8.3. Hardware-Independent Languages

All the design languages considered so far have been based on a predetermined register or hardware structure, and the translation process generated the Boolean equations for the input–output logic associated with the bistable components of the registers.

The hardware structure usually employed in RTL languages is that of a set of registers suitably interconnected via common highways with transfers being effected in a parallel mode of operation. Gerace (56) proposed a more general structure for digital systems consisting of cascaded finite-state machines; this model is shown in Fig. 2.15. In this method digital systems are considered as being comprised of two interconnected subsystems called the *operation part* (O) and the *control part* (C). The function of the control part is to provide the sequence of micro-instructions which controls the execution of elementary operations in subsystem O. The operation part includes the cascaded sequential networks which perform the basic operations and conditions the performance of subsystem C. A conventional register-transfer language is used to describe the required machine operations (thereby still retaining the same conceptual design procedures), but with the difference that the RTL statements were then transformed into state tables specifying the control and operational functions of the system. As an example of the method let us

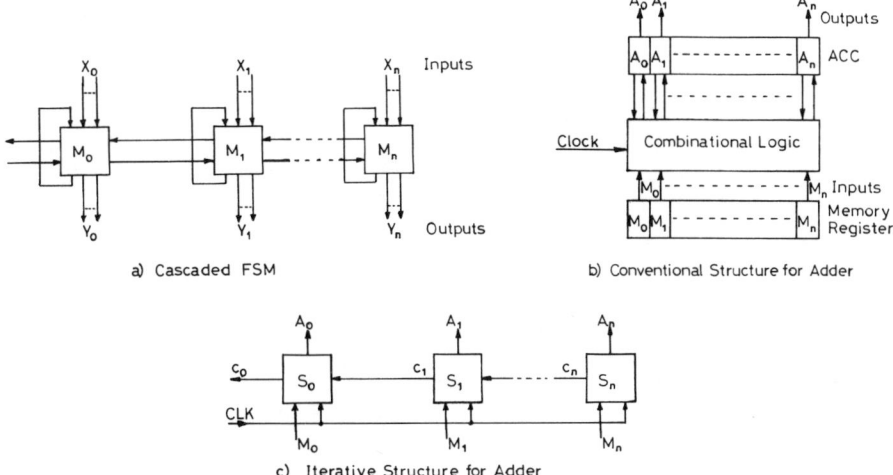

a) Cascaded FSM

b) Conventional Structure for Adder

c) Iterative Structure for Adder

**Figure 2.15.** Structure due to Gerace

consider the design of a simple adder circuit; this can be described in the following way, assuming a standard parallel-register structure:

Registers: $A(0-3), M(0-3)$

Inputs: $M_i$

Outputs: $A_i, C_i$

Functions: $C_i = [C_{i+1}]$ described by a truth table since $i = 0, 1, 2, 3$

The microprogram for addition may then be written as follows:

$|t_1|$ $A_i \oplus M_i \oplus [C_{i+1}] \rightarrow A_i$

$\qquad A_n \oplus M_n \oplus [C_{n+1} = 0] \rightarrow A_n$

where the square brackets denote a function specified by a truth table (shown in Table 2.6) which in this case is the carry function

$$C_i = M_i C_{i+1} + M_i A_i + C_{i+1} A_i.$$

Basically, the method used for deriving the state table is similar to that used for translation into Boolean equations and relies on the fact that the transfer statements describe the way the memory cells are modified (that is the state-variable behavior) and the Boolean equations define the outputs. Thus in

**Table 2.6. Truth Table for Carry Logic**

| $x$ | $y$ | $C_{i+1}$ | $C_i$ |
|---|---|---|---|
| 0 | 0 | 0 | 0 |
| 0 | 0 | 1 | 0 |
| 0 | 1 | 0 | 0 |
| 0 | 1 | 1 | 1 |
| 1 | 0 | 0 | 0 |
| 1 | 0 | 1 | 1 |
| 1 | 1 | 0 | 1 |
| 1 | 1 | 1 | 1 |

$A_i$ replaces $x$

$M_i$ replaces $y$

$C_i = M_i C_{i+1} + M_i A_i + C_{i+1} A_i$

Gerace's procedure the variables on the right-hand side of all transfer statements are taken to be state variables and the left-hand side variables as inputs to the memory cell. The outputs are assumed to be defined by some Boolean function of the input and state variables, that is a Mealey machine is generally realized. In our example the next state variable is given by $Y = A_i$ and the present state by $y = A_i$, the inputs are $M_i$ and $C_{i+1}$, and $A_i$ and $C_i$ are the required outputs. We may now write the application and output equations for the circuit as

$$Y = y \oplus M_i \oplus C_{i+1}$$

$$C_i = M_i C_{i+1} + M_i y + C_{i+1} y.$$

Note that this specifies the function for one basic stage of the adder, and a number of these must be cascaded to give the structure shown in Fig. 2.15. It follows that for the circuit to function satisfactorily the carry outputs $C_i$ must be propagated through the entire circuit before the operation is completed. This is a general requirement for any cascaded system, and Gerace imposed the following two conditions to ensure correct operation.

(a) The system is clocked in such a way that when a clock pulse is absent no changes in internal states can occur; output values may change, however, with input, as defined by the Boolean equations, but the internal states cannot be affected by these changes in the absence of a clock pulse.

(b) Changes in internal state (and hence output values assuming the circuit has settled out) can only occur on the negative-going edge of the clock pulse, that is no change occurs during the actual presence of the pulse.

These conditions correspond to a sequential circuit (called the LLC circuit by Gerace) with voltage levels representing the input–output signals and storage and timing provided by edge-triggered clocked bistable circuits (alternatively, the circuits may be considered as pulse-mode asynchronous logic). Note, however, that with a single-clocked system the propagation time through the cascaded circuit (the carry settling time for the adder) must be less than the repetition rate of the clock pulses.

The simplest way of implementing these circuits is to use clocked JK bistables (which meet the LLC-circuit conditions) deriving the input equations in the usual way. As an example let us continue the design of the adder circuit; the state table may be derived directly from the basic application equation by substituting into a K-map format representing the input variables $M_iC_{i+1}$ and the state variable $y$. This is shown in Table 2.7a. The transition table for the equivalent LLC circuit is shown in Table 2.7c; the transition table may be considered as an asynchronous flow table with the state entries for the condition clock $= 0$ representing the stable states of the circuit. Input and output conditions for the JK bistable are shown plotted on K-maps in Table 2.7b, while Fig. 2.16 shows the logic diagram for a single stage of the adder circuit.

The register-transfer language used for this design method is relatively simple and based on conventional notation. Gerace has defined any register-transfer relation specifying an elementary operation which is executed in the operation part of the system as an *operation word* (OW) of the language. A state-transfer relation indicating a jump from one micro-instruction to another is similarly called a *control word* (CW). A list of words separated by commas and formed by one CW and a set of OW's is said to be a *sentence*. The execution of transfers in a sentence (or word) may be conditioned by a *conditional expression* (Ce) which precedes the sentence or word. A list of OW's is said to be *convertible* if all the OW's in the list have the same index values. Gerace has shown that any convertible OW list can be transformed into the transition table and output table of a corresponding LCC circuit.

The main advantage of this method is that complex systems may be conveniently described by a set of micro-programs written in a register-transfer language which may then be converted into state tables. (In general most systems are far too complex to allow a direct description in terms of state tables.) Once formed the state tables can be manipulated using conventional switching theory, thereby reducing the logical complexity of the system and allowing formal synthesis algorithms to be applied. A similar procedure has been described by Stabler (57), which defines the control processes in terms of state tables and uses RTL statements for the operational logic; transformations between the two representations, indicating speed and hardware trade-offs, are also possible with this method. One criticism of the Gerace method could be that the cascaded system structure is unrealistic in terms of present-day technology. For example, microprogram control units are seldom, if ever, hard wired and normally employ some form of control store. However, it is possible to realize a state-table representation in terms of

# Table 2.7. State Table and K-maps for Adder Stage

(a) *State table*

| PRESENT STATE $y$ | INPUTS $M_i, C_{i+1}$ | | | |
|---|---|---|---|---|
| | NEXT STATE | | | |
| | 00 | 01 | 11 | 10 |
| 0 | 0 | 1 | 0 | 1 |
| 1 | 1 | 0 | 1 | 0 |

(b) *K-maps*

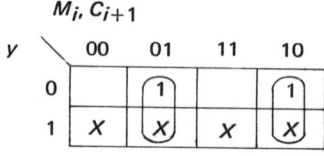

$$J = \bar{M}_i C_{i+1} + M_i \bar{C}_{i+1}$$

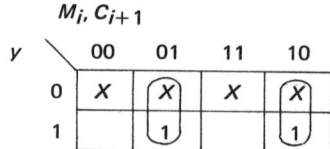

$$K = \bar{M}_i C_{i+1} + M_i \bar{C}_{i+1}$$

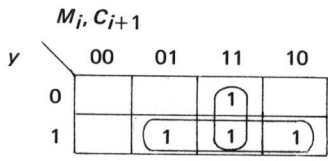

$$C_i = M_i C_{i+1} + M_i y + C_{i+1} y$$

(c) *Transition tables*

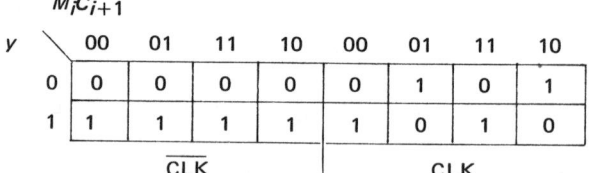

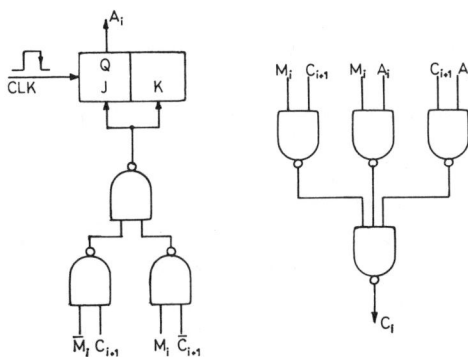

**Figure 2.16.** Single register stage.

read-only memory (ROM) by a simple rearrangement of the table (58). In order to implement the state table for the control unit in terms of ROM's the assigned (that is binary-coded) state table must be organized into two columns representing present and next-state values (the normal transition-table format). Since the next state of an FSM is a function of the input values and present states, the address inputs to the ROM are composed of the primary (external) inputs and the present-state values obtained from the output word of the ROM (thereby providing the required feedback loop). Each word in the ROM contains the coded address of the next state and the required output values. The size of the ROM is determined by the fact that the sum of the number of bits used for the external input and the state codes must be less than or equal to the address bits of the ROM. The word-length of the ROM is dictated by the total number of bits required for the state code and output functions.

### 2.8.4. A Programming Language (APL)

One of the most important developments in programming languages over the recent years has been that due to Iverson (59) called A Programming Language (APL). This procedural programming language has been used extensively by IBM to define computer systems at both hardware and software levels (60), its principal characteristic being the ability to provide a succinct description of algorithms. The language is intended to be universal in the sense that it can express functions which are hardware oriented as easily as the more usual software processes. This is in direct contrast to other programming languages, since either they are at too high a level to have sufficient resolution for, say, bit operations or at too low a level and consequently strongly machine dependent. The Iverson notation is mathematically oriented and contains a comprehensive set of operators which allows operation to be expressed at the bit, array, and matrix level with ease and clarity. Thus, one of the major advantages of the language is that manipulations on *entire arrays* of operands can be concisely expressed. Moreover, operands can be introduced and defined directly in the program, thereby eliminating the need for formal declaration statements at the start of the program. The variables (operands) in the language are defined as either scalars or arrays, which can be either one dimensional (vectors) or two dimensional (matrices). Scalar and vector operands are represented by both lower, and upper-case characters, with vector quantities being printed in bold text face (x or X). Upper-case characters only are used for matrix operands and these are printed in, for example, bold sans serif (**X**). (In the handwritten version of the language vector quantities are usually represented by underlined lower-case roman characters only, with upper case roman being reserved exclusively for matrix operands; we shall adopt this format in the text.)

Each element of a vector may be identified by the use of a subscript, that is the index, for example

$$\underline{a} \equiv a_0, a_1, a_2, \ldots, a_{\nu(a)-1}.$$

The number of elements in a vector is called the *dimension* of a vector and is denoted by $\nu(\underline{a})$. Matrices are represented as a two-dimensional array of operands in which each row must have the same number of elements as every other row. Elements of the matrix may also be specified by subscripts, for example, $A_j^i$, where $i = 1, 2, 3 \ldots, \nu(A)$ and $j = 1, 2, 3 \ldots, \mu(A)$, where $\nu(A)$ and $\mu(A)$ are respectively the column and row dimensions of the matrix. Thus the entire matrix may be referenced by, say, A, individual rows (vectors) by $A^i$, columns (again vectors) by $A_j$, and individual elements (scalars) by $A_j^i$.

Scalar operations are expressed in much the same way as in other programming languages; array operations are handled in a similar manner but extended on an element-by-element basis. The assignment symbol ($\leftarrow$) denotes specification in the same sense as the symbol " = " in FORTRAN, " := " in ALGOL, and " $\rightarrow$ " in other languages. For example, if $\odot$ is any binary operator or relation, then

$$a \leftarrow b \odot c$$

is a scalar operation with scalar variables, whereas

$$\underline{a} \leftarrow \underline{b} \odot \underline{c}$$

refers to one-dimensional vectors as defined earlier, and

$$A \leftarrow B \odot C$$

is the matrix operation of the same form. (Note the right to left precedence of the operators.)

The elements of the vector or matrix can be any numeric or logical parameter, including alphanumeric characters. The one-dimensional vector operations are particularly relevant to digital systems design since they can be used to indicate register-transfer operations directly. The two-dimensional (matrix) array can be used to represent computer storage modules and any associated processing function.

The language comprises all the usual arithmetic functions plus a powerful and comprehensive set of logical and relational operators. These include AND, OR, negate, $<$, $\leqslant$, $>$, $\geqslant$, $=$, $\neq$, shifting, selection and masking operations, etc. Moreover, any operation defined on a scalar operand can be extended, component by component, to dimensionally compatible vectors; if one of the operands is a scalar it is treated as a vector of the appropriate dimension. The shifting operations, or *rotations*, defined on a vector $\underline{a}$ correspond to normal logical shifts of $K$ places left or right; for example the left shift is defined by

$$\underline{y} \leftarrow K \uparrow \underline{a}.$$

For a right shift the arrow head points downwards; the notation $\overset{\uparrow}{\circ}$ is used to indicate that zeros are shifted into vacated positions. A rather unusual logical function is the residue modulo $m$ operator defined by

$$K \leftarrow m \mid n$$

where $K$ is the remainder after dividing $n$ by $m$.

However, the power of the language is derived primarily from the set of special operators used for the reduction, masking, expansion, and compression of arrays. When an operation such as addition is applied to all the components of a vector to produce a simpler structure (usually a scalar), it is called a *reduction*. Thus the $\odot$ reduction of a vector $\underline{a}$ is defined as:

$$y \leftarrow \odot / \underline{a}$$

which is equivalent to

$$y = \underline{a}_1 \odot \underline{a}_2 \odot \underline{a}_3 \ldots \odot \underline{a}_{\nu(\underline{a})-1}.$$

In order to make effective use of structured operands the facility to specify and select certain elements or groups of elements must be provided. Consequently *selection* operators are available in the language which can be used to form new arrays. The operation of *compression* forms a vector $\underline{y}$ from a vector $\underline{a}$ by deleting certain elements of $\underline{a}$ as determined by a logical vector $\underline{u}$ (called a selection map). The elements specified by a 1 in the selection vector are extracted to form a new vector; it should be noted that $\nu(\underline{a})$ must be the same as $\nu(\underline{u})$. Thus we have

$$\underline{y} \leftarrow \underline{u} / \underline{a}$$

Let us suppose, for example, that

$$\underline{a} = \text{F,U,N,C,A,D,D,R,E,S,S,I}$$
$$\underline{u} = 1,1,1,1,0,0,0,0,0,0,0,1$$

then

$$\underline{y} \leftarrow \underline{u} / \underline{a} = \text{F,U,N,C,I.}$$

It will be obvious that the vector $\underline{a}$ could have represented the instruction word of a computer, the operator being used to extract the function and indirect address bits.

A more complex operation is that of *masking*. In this case the selection vector $\underline{u}$ is used to select elements from a vector $\underline{a}$ while its inverse $\bar{\underline{u}}$ is used to select elements from another vector $\underline{b}$. This operation is expressed as

$$\underline{y} \leftarrow /\underline{b}; \underline{u}; \underline{a}/$$

where $\bar{\underline{u}}/\underline{y} \equiv \bar{\underline{u}}/\underline{b}$ and $\underline{u}/\underline{y} \equiv \underline{u}/\underline{a}$ and obviously

$$\nu(\underline{u}) = \nu(\underline{a}) = \nu(\underline{b}) = \nu(\underline{y}).$$

Another useful operator is the *base value function*, which derives a number $y$ from a specification of a radix $r$ and a digit string $\underline{s}$ representing the number; in general we have the expression

$$y \leftarrow r \perp \underline{s}$$

which means that $y$ is specified as the value obtained by treating the elements of the vector $\underline{s}$ as digits in the number system of radix $r$. This operator is particularly useful in digital systems design when base-2 values are required. Suppose, for example, that $\underline{r}$ is a register and contains the address of a word in the main memory $M$, and that it is necessary to extract this word and place it into a register $\underline{a}$. This may be written simply as

$$\underline{a} \leftarrow M^{\perp \underline{r}}.$$

Certain types of vectors can be referred to directly in the program statement instead of being specifically declared at the start of the program (note that Iverson has no formal declaration statements). This is an extremely useful feature, both for general programming use and digital systems specification. These special vectors are listed below.

Full vector $\quad \underline{\epsilon}(n)$—vector of $n$ 1's.

Unit vector $\quad \underline{e}^{j}(n)$—$j$th element is 1, all others 0.

Prefix vector $\quad \underline{\alpha}^{j}(n)$—first $j$ elements are 1, the rest 0.

Interval vector $\quad \underline{i}^{j}(n)$—elements are numerically consecutive beginning with $j$.

Suffix vector $\quad \underline{\omega}^{j}(n)$—the last $j$ elements are 1, the rest 0.

These vectors, in conjunction with the special selection operators mentioned earlier, provide a very powerful means of concisely specifying binary operations both at bit and word levels.

Before concluding this very brief description of the Iverson language it is necessary to discuss the *branching* facilities. The simplest form of branching operation is the unconditional jump to another statement, which may be used by itself or appended to the right of any statement using a semicolon as a separator. This form of branching instruction may also be extended to a specified jump to any one of a number of statements selected by the value of a parameter. These instructions correspond to the GOTO statement in FORTRAN; for instance

GOTO 6     corresponds to     $\rightarrow (6)$

GOTO (6,15,31),I     corresponds to     $\rightarrow (6,15,31);$

The general conditional branching statement takes the form

$$s:y; R \rightarrow (n)$$

which denotes a jump to statement $n$ of the program if the relationship $sRy$ holds good; the parameters $R$ and $n$ may themselves be defined in other parts of the program. This form of instruction is equivalent to the FORTRAN IF statement; for example:

IF $(X - Y)4,7,59$     corresponds to     $(x - y):0;(<,=,>) \rightarrow 4,7,59.$

At the present time a full compiler for the Iverson language is not available; however, a restricted subset of the language has been implemented in the APL interpreter (61, 62, 63) written for the IBM 360 and 1130 machines. APL is rapidly gaining acceptance as a general-purpose programming language, and specifically for teaching and the computer-aided design of analog and digital systems. The full power and advantages of the language can readily be seen if we apply it to non-numerical problems, particularly those involved in logical-systems design. For instance, the operation of checking a vector $\underline{a}$ for even parity can be expressed in the one-line statement

$$2 \mid ({}^{+}/\underline{a}):0;(=) \rightarrow n.$$

The operation is such that the individual elements of the vector $\underline{a}$ are added together; if the residue modulo 2 of the sum is equal to zero a jump to $n$ is executed indicating correct parity. Similarly, the function of checking a 7-bit Hamming code ($\underline{h}$) may be expressed as

$$\perp [2 \mid ({}^{+}/(\underline{\epsilon}^{0,2,4,6}(7)/\underline{h})), 2 \mid ({}^{+}/(\underline{\epsilon}^{1,2,5,6}(7)/\underline{h})), [2 \mid ({}^{+}/(\underline{\omega}^{4}(7)/\underline{h}))] :0;]$$
$$(=) \rightarrow (n).$$

Though it would be simpler perhaps in practice to express the operation in separate statements, the example demonstrates the highly parallel structure of the language (this compact encoding of algorithms, "one liners", can sometimes be a drawback when reading programs). It will be obvious by now that Iverson is ideal for describing microprograms, since the vector operations allow it to be used as a versatile register-transfer language. Table 2.8 shows how a microprogram for converting BCD numbers to pure binary may be written in the Iverson notation. This example uses the "represent base 2" operator, that is

$$\underline{y} \leftarrow (n) \top j$$

where $n = \nu(\underline{y})$ and $j$ may be a positive or negative decimal integer, to set binary values directly into the counter. Note that, owing to the machine-independent nature of the Iverson notation, the realization of the micro-program could be accomplished using either hardware or software processes.

Though the basic Iverson notation (and APL) is extremely effective at defining algorithms and can be used to express register transfers, it has inherent limitations which make it difficult to use for digital systems design. For example, it is not possible to declare specific hardware structures, or to express control and timing functions adequately; also concurrent activities cannot be specified. Moreover, the language is at too low a level and does not

**Table 2.8. Microprogram for BCD to Binary Conversion**

| Step no. | Statement | Comment |
|---|---|---|
| 0 | $\underline{m} \leftarrow \underline{a}$ | Transfer accumulator to M-register |
| 1 | $\underline{a} \leftarrow \bar{\varepsilon}\,(18)$ | Clear accumulator |
| 2 | $\underline{k} \leftarrow 5\,\top\,(-3)$ | Set k-counter to $-3$ |
| 3 | $\underline{a} \leftarrow 18\,\top\,(\bot\underline{a}) + \bot\,2 \downarrow \underline{\alpha}^4 /\underline{m}$ | Add binary value of MS BCD digit to binary value of $\underline{a}$ |
| 4 | $\underline{k} \leftarrow 5\,\top\,(1) + \bot\,\underline{k}$ | Add $+1$ to k-counter |
| 5 | $\nu/\underline{k}:0; (=) \rightarrow (5)$ | Check $\underline{k} = 0$, stop |
| 6 | $\underline{a} \leftarrow 1 \updownarrow (18\,\top\,(\bot\underline{a}) + \bot\,2 \updownarrow \underline{a})$ | Effective multiplication by binary 10 |
| 7 | $\underline{m} \leftarrow 4 \updownarrow \underline{m}$ | Shift BCD in M-register 4 places left |
| 8 | $\rightarrow (3)$ | |

allow functional description at the higher, conceptual levels to be represented. Nevertheless, the language provides an ideal descriptive subset for a systems design language, being simple in nature and using a small number of constructs. [The language has also found considerable acclaim in the teaching of digital systems design and at least two textbooks have been based on APL (64, 65).] In particular AHPL (A Hardware Programming Language) described by Hill and Peterson has been adopted for teaching purposes and a number of compilers are in existence.

The Iverson notation has also been used in the ALERT (Automatic Logic Design Generator) system (66) as the basis of a high-level language to depict the architecture of a proposed machine. ALERT was developed by IBM and has been programmed for the IBM 7094 machine. It is basically an RTL system of the type described in § 2.8, the Iverson description being "compiled" into logic equations which can be implemented in terms of basic gate and bistable elements. The form of Boolean equations produced by ALERT can be accepted directly by the IBM logic automation system (67, 41). This system performs a simple Boolean minimization and then implements the resulting logic in terms of IBM solid logic technology with the output expressed as logic diagrams.

In order to use Iverson as a design language it was necessary to develop additional conventions. Since the variables used in the description of the data structure represent physical devices such as bistables, registers, signal lines, etc., declaration statements were included to enable the categories and dimensions of the variables to be fixed. Because of this convention Iverson operators which serve to modify operand dimension or rank, such as compression, must be excluded. In addition, since Iverson uses a number of non-standard symbols, it was necessary to modify the APL symbol set to allow a standard keyboard to be used (the input was required on punched cards). For example, the base-2 value ⊥ was transliterated to VALUE, the suffix and prefix vectors ($\alpha$ and $\omega$) to PREFIX AND SUFFIX, etc. (It is now possible to obtain APL keyboards for both teletype and graphics terminals.) The architectural description takes the usual form of declaring the data structure in terms of registers, storage, highways, etc., and can include subsystem modules, such as adders, decoders, etc., as macrofunctions. Data flow paths are represented using register transfers, with control functions and instruction sets specified by microprogram statements. Since APL does not allow block structures and parallel processes to be represented, additional conventions were added to ALERT to handle this situation.

In ALERT the design process was separated into eight major steps; these are as follows.

*Translation.* This converts the modified Iverson notation into a more restrained format for use in the design file; it also checks the input for format syntax and consistency errors. The translation is a parsing analysis and decomposition of the input statements into a simpler, more design-oriented form. For example, intermediate variables implied by Iverson expressions, but not explicitly represented in the microprograms, are generated and filed along with the declared statements.

*Selection decoding.* Variable subscripts on arrays provide a convenient shorthand notation for representing complex logic structures. In a design compiler these must be expanded to allow the selection of an element in an array and provide the necessary input and output gating logic. The selection-decoding programs scan the design file, and, when a variable subscript is discovered, it is replaced by the appropriate selection logic.

*Macrogeneration.* In addition to the basic logic operators it is also possible in the input language to specify higher-order subsystem functions; these must be replaced in the design file by the combinational logic necessary to accomplish the required operations. The logic may be obtained directly from a library file or specifically generated.

*Sequence analysis.* This step determines the control and sequencing requirements for the specified architecture. As with most RTL systems the timing may be either explicitly stated or implied by the inherent sequencing of operations (for example, in a microprogram). The sequence-analysis routine scans the microprogram in the design file and partitions the microprogram statements into groups of operations which can occur concurrently in the same time period; particular account is taken of GOTO and IF statements which signify partition points where new sequences can occur. The partition points are recorded in a sequence-of-events table which is later used to provide control logic [this procedure is almost identical with the method used by Gorman and Anderson (35)].

*Bistable identification.* In this routine the microprograms are scanned for any variable which serves as a signal source during a *later event* period than when it acquired its value, and is thus identified as a bistable output. In addition to bistables defined in this way (usually control and flag bits) the registers and bistables formally declared in the structure are also processed. Bistables are assumed to be of the set/reset type and corresponding set and reset statements are generated. For example, the statements A ← B would be automatically rewritten in the design file as:

A = SET B

and

A = RESET NOT B

which signifies that the output from bit B is connected to the SET input line of bistable A, and that $\overline{B}$ is connected to the RESET input line.

*Control provision.* This routine generates a sequence control counter for every microprogram with implicit timing in the sequence of events table. The number of stages needed for each counter is automatically determined using the formula:

$$S = \overline{\lceil \log_2 \rceil} \, n$$

where S denotes the number of counter stages required and *n* is the greatest event number for that micro-program, and $\overline{\lceil x}$ signifies the least integer not less than *x*.

*Consolidation.* The function of this step in the process is to reorganize and optimize the design file so that duplicated logic blocks are eliminated, associated elements and signal lines are commoned together and any inefficiencies incurred in connecting together arrays are reduced by rearranging the logic.

*Expansion.* The purpose of this final step in the process is to examine each statement in the design file and expand them into sets of Boolean equations.

Though ALERT has been successfully implemented and the results found to correspond reasonably well with intuitive designs (68) the system produces rather uneconomical results. The design system has been used to process a major part of the IBM 1800 computer, but the resulting design required some

160% more gates than the original system; however, modifications have been proposed for ALERT which would produce designs with only 33% redundancy.

## 2.9. CONSLUSIONS

There are many problems to be solved before an ideal specification and evaluation language for digital design automation systems can be developed. The register-transfer language technique is adequate for the design of register-structured systems, but it is specifically computer-hardware oriented and analysis (as against simulation) algorithms have yet to be developed. However, some work has been done at the University of Dortmund on applying Karp and Miller algorithms to register-transfer language descriptions. In general the main application of RTL's is in microprogram evaluation and their direct translation into ROM bit patterns, and most current work seems to be directed towards this area. Another disadvantage is that the languages tend to generate very simple constructs. This is due to the fact that the languages provide only simple elements and the users themselves perpetuate the situation by designing at a low level.

Of all the methods described in this chapter the directed-graph methods such as Petri nets, used for example in the LOGOS system, seem to be the most promising. There is, however, a fundamental problem to be solved before any of these systems can become operational: that is, the analysis and evaluation of large systems. It would appear inevitable that, if a detailed analysis of a logic algorithm is required, there is no alternative but to examine all possibilities in an iterative manner. For example, the overall system operation can be determined (for a restricted set of input combinations) by allowing only particular paths through a Petri net or state table; this technique amounts to a loss of information and affects the accuracy of the analysis. If exact information about a system is sought (for example to evolve detailed test schedules) the Petri net must be examined for all possible "firing" sequences and the state table for all state transitions. In both cases this could prove to be prohibitive in computer time; however, it could still be more efficient than direct simulation.

Another problem occurs in the use of library routines for components used to represent complex MSI circuits and other data structures. There are two distinct cases when subsystem blocks are required.

(a) To represent a component or subroutine which will be used by the system many times over, but not actually implemented each time, for example, an arithmetic unit or any complex data-processing structure.

(b) The insertion of a standard hardware component (similar to a software macro), such as a multiplexer unit, which needs to be implemented as such in various places in the system.

The major difficulty here is that of isolating identical functions and, if necessary, merging them together.

Further problems occur in the physical realization of the logic descriptions. At the moment hardware implementations seem feasible for all the systems described (though in the case of the LOGOS system it is not completely clear how to implement the data graphs). Recent work by Patil (69) has indicated that control Petri nets can be implemented directly using asynchronous programmable logic arrays (70). Software implementation, however, is another matter, and considerable work remains to be done, particularly in the realization of data-processing structures (program-control structures can be handled by Petri nets and state tables).

It is worthwhile considering in more detail the place of state tables in systems specification languages. Some workers in this field have castigated state-table techniques on the grounds that they are impracticable for large systems involving many variables, owing mainly to the problem involved in setting up and manipulating the tables. This is undoubtedly true, particularly if data and control structures are represented in the same table. However, large systems must inevitably be partitioned by the designer into subsystem components in order to comprehend their complexity, and in general if the concept of separate data and control structures is adhered to there is no reason why state tables should not be employed. There are many good reasons for retaining the state-table approach.

(a) It provides a formal and compact description of a logical process which can be analyzed and implemented using existing FSM theory.

(b) The use of decomposition techniques, either formally or heuristically, can be employed to describe large systems.

(c) It is independent of hardware structures and can be realized in either hardware or software form (in the case of the control logic).

(d) The use of state diagrams affords a graph-theoretic approach directly analogous, for example, to the Petri net.

Moreover, a new method of logical design based on algorithmic state machine (ASM) charts (71), and used extensively by Hewlett Packard for the design of calculators, draws heavily on FSM theory. The technique allows the specification and design of the control circuitry of a logic system to be performed using a flow-chart technique; unfortunately, no computer realization of the ASM chart currently exists. There would seem very sound reasons for continuing with the state-table approach, providing of course engineers can be offered computer assistance in specifying subsystem components in terms of state tables. We shall conclude this chapter with a summary of the essential characteristics required by a digital system design language; these are as follows.

(a) *Multilevel structure.* It must be able to support a system specification capable of handling varying degrees of detail, for instance, a concise behavioral description at the top level, progressing downwards to an exact, detailed realization.

(b) *General application.* It must be possible to describe a wide range of systems, including digital control, message switching, etc., as well as computer systems. The organization of the description should reflect the structure of the system, allowing easy communication between engineers and designers.

(c) *Technology independent.* The modeling primitives must be independent of any particular technology and capable of realization in either hardware or software.

(d) *Evaluation capability.* The representation should be such that the system behavior can be thoroughly evaluated, and if necessary optimized, before progressing to the detailed design stages.

(e) *Interactive.* It must be possible to involve the designer in the design process, with appropriate feedback of errors and intermediate results including editing facilities. The design language must be simple and convenient to use.

(f) *Extendable.* The system must be capable of being modified to embrace new component technology and design procedures.

(g) *Self-documentation.* It must be able to provide a readily understandable means of communicating ideas and detailed design information.

(h) *Parallel representation.* Since most systems are essentially parallel in nature, concurrent operations must be easily handled.

Thus it will be apparent that at the present time there is no ideal specification, evaluation, and design scheme available for logical systems. The specification systems described in this chapter only partially fulfil the above requirements or are still in the early stages of development. Nevertheless, it is essential for the future development of complex logical systems that a suitable methodology be quickly established.

## REFERENCES AND BIBLIOGRAPHY

1. Minksy, M. L. *Computation–Finite and Infinite Machines*, Chap. 2. Prentice Hall, Englewood Cliffs, N. J., 1967.
2. Minsky, M. L. *Computation–Finite and Infinite Machines*, Chap. 6. Prentice Hall, Englewood Cliffs, N. J., 1967.
3. Stigall, P. O., and Tasar, O. A review of directed graphs as applied to computers. *IEEE Computer* 7(10), 39–47, 1974.
4. Myhill, J. *Finite Automata and the Representation of Events.* WADC Tech. Rep. No. 57-624, pp. 112–137, 1957.

5. McNaughton, R., and Yamada, H. Regular expressions and state graphs for automata. *IRE Trans. Electron. Computers* **EC9**, 39–47, 1960.
6. Ott, G. H., and Feinstein, N. H. Design of sequential machines from their regular expression. *J.Assoc. Computing Machinery* **8**, 585–600, 1961.
7. Kleene, S. C. *Representation of Events in Nerve Nets and Finite Automata, Automata Studies Annals of Mathematical Studies No. 34*, pp. 3–41. Princeton University Press, Princeton, N. J., 1956.
8. Brzozowski, J. A. A survey of regular expressions and their applications. *IRE Trans. Electron. Computers* **EC11**, 324–335, 1962.
9. Brzozowski, J. A. Derivatives of regular expressions. *J.Assoc. Computing Machinery* **11**, 481–494, 1964.
10. Petri, C. A. Communication with automata. *Schriften des Rheinisch-Westerälischen Institutes für Instrumentelle Mathematik an der Universität Bonn*, Vol. 2, Bonn, 1962.
11. Holt, A. W. *Information System Theory Project*. Applied Data Research Test Rep. No. RADC-TR-68-305, 1968.
12. Commoner, F., Holt, A. W., Even, S., and Pnueli, A. Marked directed graphs. *J. Comp. System Sci.* **5**, 511–523, 1971.
13. Holt, A. W. *Introduction to Occurrence Systems, Associative Information Techniques* (Ed. E. L. Jacks), pp. 175–203. Elsevier, New York, 1971.
14. Patil, S. S., and Dennis, J. B. The description and realisation of digital systems. *Proceedings of 6th Annual IEEE Computer Society International Conference, 1972*, pp. 223–226.
15. Patil, S. S. *Co-ordination of Asynchronous Events*. Rep. MAC-TR-72, Project MAC, MIT, Cambridge, Mass., June 1970.
16. Patil, S. S. *Circuit Implementation of Petri Nets* Rep. MAC Computation Structures Group Memo 73. MIT, Cambridge, Mass., Dec. 1972.
17. Karp, R. M., and Miller, R. E. Properties of a model for parallel computation: determinacy, terminations, queuing. *J. Appl. Math.* **14**, 1300–1411, 1966.
18. Karp, R. M., and Miller, R. E. Parallel program schemata. *J. Computer System Sci.* **3**, 147–195, 1969.
19. Rose, C. W. LOGOS and the software engineer. *AFIPS FJCC* **41**(1), 311–323, 1972.
20. Heath, F. G., and Rose, C. W. The case for integrated hardware/software design with CAD implication. *IEEE Computer Conference Digest*, September 1972.
21. Heath, F. G. The LOGOS System *IEE Conference on CAD*, pp. 225–230. IEE Publ. No. 86, 1972.
22. Dijkstra, E. W. *EWD 249 Notes on Structured Programming*. T.H.Rep. 70-WSK-03, Technical University, Eindhoven, Netherlands, April 1970.
23. Rose, C. W. *A System of Representation for General Purpose Digital Computer Systems*. PhD Thesis, Case Western Reserve University, Cleveland, Ohio, Sept. 1970.
24. Howard, B. V. Parallel computation schemata and their hardware implementation. *Digital Processes* **1**, 183–206, 1975.

25. Nutt, G. J. Evaluation nets for computer system performance analysis. *AFIPS FJCC* **41**, 279–286, 1972.

26. Noe, J. D., and Nutt, G. J. Macro E-nets for representation of parallel systems. *IEEE Trans. Computers* **C-22**, 718–727, 1973.

27. Bell, C. G., and Newell, A. The PMS and ISP descriptive system for computer structures. *AFIPS SJCC* **36**, 351–374, 1970.

28. Bell, C. G., and Newell, A. *Computer Structures: Reading and Examples* McGraw-Hill, New York, 1971.

29. Bell, C. G., and Cody, R. A new architecture for mini computers—The DEC PDP11. *AFIPS SJCC* **36**, 657–675, 1970.

30. Bell, C. G., Eggert, J. L., Grason, J., and Williams, P. The description and use of register transfer modules (RTM's). *IEEE Trans. Computers* **C22**, 495–500, 1972.

31. Bell, C. G., and Grason, J. The register transfer module design concept. *Computer Des.* May 1971, pp. 87–94.

32. Lewin, D. W. *Theory and Design of Digital Computers*, Chap. 4. Nelson, London, 1972.

33. Reed, I. S. Symbolic synthesis of digital computers. *Proc. ACM* Sept. 1952, pp. 90–94.

34. Schorr, H. Computer-aided digital systems design and analysis using a register transfer language. *IEEE Trans. Electron. Computers* **EC13**, 730–737, 1964.

35. Gorman, D. F., and Anderson, J. P. A logic design translator. *AFIPS FJCC* **22**, 251–261, 1962.

36. Proctor, R. M. A logic design translator experiment demonstrating relationships of language to systems and logic design. *IEEE Trans. Electron. Computers* **EC13**, 422–430, 1964.

37. Gries, D. *Compiler Construction for Digital Computers*. John Wiley, New York, 1971.

38. Backus, J. W. The syntax and semantics of the proposed international algebraic language of the Zurich ACM-GAMM conference. *Proceedings of International Conference on Information Processes*, pp. 125–132. UNESCO, June 1959.

39. Irons, E. T. A syntax directed compiler for ALGOL 60. *Comm. ACM* **4**, 51–55, 1961.

40. McKeeman, W. M., Horning, J. J., and Wortman, D. B. *A Compiler Generator*. Prentice Hall, Englewood Cliffs, N. J., 1970.

41. Roth, J. P. Systematic design of automata. *AFIPS FJCC* **27**, 1093–1100, 1965.

42. Chu, Y. An Algol-like computer design language. *Comm. ACM* **8**, 607–615, 1965.

43. Chu, Y. *A Higher-Order Language for Describing Micro-programmed Computers.* Tech. Rep. 68-78, Computer Science Center, University of Maryland, Sept. 1968.

44. Mesztenyi, C. K. *Computer Design Language, Simulation and Boolean Translation* Tech. Rep. 68-72, Computer Science Center, University of Maryland, June 1968.

45. Becker, M., Klar, R., and Spies, P. P. Informatik III and Informatic IV (lecture notes). *Arbeit. Inst. Math. Maschinen Datenverarbeit.* 5(5), Oct. 1972.
46. Schlaeppi, H. P. A formal language for describing logic, timing and sequencing (LOTIS). *IEEE Trans Electron. Computers* **EC13**, 439–448, 1964.
47. Parnas, D. L. A language for describing the functions of synchronous systems. *Comm. ACM* **9**, 72–76, 79, 1966.
48. Metze, G., and Seshu, S. A proposal for a computer compiler. *AFIPS SJCC* **28**, 253–263, 1966.
49. Okada, Y., and Motooka, T. Logical design language. *Electron. Comm. Japan* **50**, 109–117, 1967.
50. Duley, J. R., and Dietmeyer, D. L. A digital system design language (DDL). *IEEE Trans. Computers* **C17**, 850–861, 1968.
51. Duley, J. R., and Dietmeyer, D. L. Translation of a DDL digital system specification to Boolean equations. *IEEE Trans. Computers* **C18**, 305–313, 1969.
52. Mermet, J., and Lustman, F. CASSANDRE: Un language of description of machines digitales. *Rev. Fr. Inf. Rech. Operationelle* No. 15-B3-13F, pp. 3–35, 2$^e$ année Dec. 1968.
53. Leraillez, F., Sarre, A., and Waterlot, B. CRISMASS: A tool for conception, realisation, implementation and simulation of sequential synchronous circuits. *IEE Conference on CAD*, pp. 59–71. IEE Publ. No. 51, 1969.
54. Crockett, E. D., Copp, D. H., Frandeen, J. W., Isberg, C. A., Bryant, P., Dickinson, W. E., and Paige, M. R. Computer aided system design. *AFIPS SJCC* **36**, 287–296, 1970.
55. Baray, M. B., and Su, S. Y. H. A digital system modelling philosophy and design language. *Proceedings of 8th Annual Design Automation Workshop*, Atlantic City, June 1971, pp. 1–22.
56. Gerace, G. B. Digital system design automation—a method for designing a digital system as a sequential network system. *IEEE Trans. Computers* **C17**, 1044–1061, 1968.
57. Stabler, E. P. Micro-program transformations. *IEEE Trans. Computers* **C19**, 908–916, 1970.
58. Lewin, D. W. *Logical Design of Switching Circuits* (2nd edn), Chap. 10. Nelson, London, 1974.
59. Iverson, K. E. *A Programming Language*, Chap. 2. John Wiley, New York, 1962.
60. Falkoff, A. D., Iverson, K. E., and Sussenguth, E. H. Formal description of system/360. *IBM Systems J.* **3**, 198–262, 1964.
61. Falkoff, A. D., and Iverson, K. E. *APL/360 User's Manual.* IBM Watson Research Center, Yorktown Heights, N. Y., 1968.
62. Corberry, R. S., *et al. APL/1130.* IBM Contributed Library 1130 03.3.001, 1968.
63. Katzan, H. *APL Programming and Computer Techniques.* Van Nostrand, New York, 1970.

64. Hellerman, H. *Digital Computer System Principles.* McGraw-Hill, New York, 1967.
65. Hill, F. J., and Peterson, G. R. *Digital Systems: Hardware Organisation and Design.* John Wiley, New York, 1973.
66. Friedman, T. D., and Yang, S. C. Methods used in an automatic logic design generator (ALERT). *IEEE Trans. Computers* **C18**, 593–614, 1969.
67. Case, P. W., Graff, H. H., Griffith, L. E., Leclercq, A. R., Murley, W. B., and Spence, T. M. Solid logic design automation for IBM system 360. *IBM J. Res. Dev.* **8**, 127–140, 1964.
68. Friedman, T. D., and Yang, S. C. *Quality of Designs from an Automatic Logic Generator* IBM Res. Rep. RC 2068, 25 April, 1968.
69. Patil, S. S. On structured digital systems. *Proceedings of International Symposium on Computer Hardware Description Languages and their Applications, New York, 1975,* pp. 1–6.
70. Patil, S. S. *An Asynchronous Logic Array.* Tech. Mem. 62 Project MAC, MIT, Cambridge, Mass., May 1975.
71. Clare, C. R. *Designing Logic Machines using State Machines.* McGraw-Hill, New York, 1973.
72. Baer, J. L. Models for the design, simulation and performance of distributed function architecture. *IEEE Computer*, March 1974, pp. 25–30.
73. Stabler, E. P. System description languages. *IEEE Trans. Computers* **C19**, 1160–1173, 1970.
74. Barbacci, M. R. A comparison of register transfer languages for describing computers and digital systems. *IEEE Trans. Computers* **C24**, 137–150, 1975.
75. Hardware Description Languages. *IEEE Computer* 7, Dec. 1974 (special issue).
76. Breuer, M. A. (ed.) *Digital System Design Automation: Languages, Simulation and Data Base* Computer Science Press, Calif., 1975.
77. Foo, S. Y., and Musgrave, G. An engineering approach to a model for specification and evaluation of parallel digital systems. *Proceedings of Conference on Simulation 75, Geneva, June 1975.*
78. Bednar, M. G., and Tracey, J. H. An asynchronous circuit design language (ACDL). *IEEE Trans. Computers* **C23**, 971–976, 1974.
79. Stucki, M. J., An approach for synthesizing transition logic circuits. *11th Allerton Conference on Circuits and Systems, Oct. 1973*, pp. 418–427.

# Simulation Techniques

## 3.1. INTRODUCTION

Simulation is a process whereby it is possible to model, either mathematically or functionally, the behavior of a real system; experiments can then be conducted on the model and related back to the actual system. It is important to realize, however, that the simulated system is just a model, and not necessarily an exact representation of the physical system, owing to the constraints and necessary approximations inherent in constructing the model.

Though the digital computer can handle both mathematical and functional models, in the majority of cases the system to be modeled is so complex that exact mathematical definition is usually impossible (the normal case in digital systems design) and functional methods have to be employed. For example, consider how a combinational logic circuit implemented in terms of logic gates may be modeled. It is possible to describe formally the *logical* operation of the circuit using Boolean equations; however, though this model will enable the input–output transfer function (that is the truth table) to be verified, it cannot provide any information about the performance of the actual circuits;

this information would be essential, for example, for the generation of test schedules and the verification of intuitive designs. Since it is very difficult to produce mathematical equations describing both the logical and circuit properties of a logic network, a functional model would normally be used. In the case of functional modeling there is usually some direct correspondence between the real system and the model. For example, a logic circuit could be represented by a topological model, with specific words in the computer memory being allocated to represent each logic gate and its interconnections.

Care must also be taken in devising the experiments which are required to be run on the model. In the case of mathematical models this involves changing the initial conditions, constants, parameters, etc., in the equations, and then allowing the computer to *compute* the results. Functional models must be exercised, that is required to emulate the actions of the real system, again starting from specified initial conditions and system parameters. The information derived from such a model depends on the way the experiments are run and the *interpretation* placed upon the results.

System models may be classified into *deterministic* or *stochastic* depending on the system variables. A system which has completely predictable variables (i.e. deterministic) may usually be represented by a mathematical model and evaluated using classical methods. However, if it is impossible to define the system variables precisely (the usual case in the modeling of discrete systems), then probabilistic methods must be used and a simulation approach adopted. Random-number generators are often used to generate the random values of the variables.

The major use of simulation in digital system design is to verify and check designs, both at systems (1) and logic-gate levels (2), prior to actual manufacture. Another important use, as we shall see in Chapter 5, is to generate test schedules for manufacturing and operational testing procedures. Owing to the limitations mentioned earlier, and the methods used in exercising the model, simulation does not entirely eliminate the need for debugging the actual equipment, but it does considerably reduce the problems involved.

Digital systems may be simulated at basically three different levels, these are as follows.

(1) *Systems level.* This consists at the moment of using high-level general-purpose simulation languages, such as GPSS (3) and SIMSCRIPT (4), and deals mainly with a timing analysis of the system modeled in terms of subsystem components such as arithmetic and logic units, memory modules, peripherals, etc.

(2) *Register-transfer level.* In this case data flow at the register level is modeled, thereby enabling microprograms etc. to be evaluated. This form of

language was dealt with in the last chapter and would of course include APL, DDL, etc.

(3) *Gate or logic level.* Here the actual logic gates, or modules, and their interconnections are functionally modeled in the computer. Each signal line is restricted to binary values, and time is usually quantized to gate-propagation delays.

Other forms of simulation are sometimes used, predominantly at the device and circuit levels, but these are more in the realm of circuit-design techniques and will not be dealt with in this book.

The major benefits to be accrued by using simulation techniques are savings in time and cost caused by eliminating fundamental design errors. Some of the more specific advantages of using simulation in digital systems design are as follows.

(a)  Operational specifications can be validated.

(b)  Corrections and modifications can be made during the early design stages.

(c)  Alternative procedures and designs may be evaluated.

(d)  The simulation description can serve as design documentation.

Simulation at the logic level is currently the most frequently employed technique, and has become a valuable tool for logic designers. In particular the technique is used to generate and verify fault-test procedures and to discover the presence of circuit races and hazards. It is essential, however, that the simulator should accurately model the timing of the circuit devices, to allow prediction of hazards and races, in order for it to be effective in design verification. It is also possible to obtain detailed operational and maintenance data, for example the logical state of all elements for every bit time, which is not always feasible on the actual hardware. The major disadvantages of simulation is that it can be very time consuming, particularly if detailed results about large systems are required. For example, in order to test completely a complex LSI logic circuit it may be necessary to simulate the system under all possible input conditions. This often proves prohibitive in time and cost, and generally a more intuitive approach must be adopted. In this chapter the main emphasis will be on gate-level simulation, and the following sections will survey the techniques and languages available; the chapter is concluded with an appreciation of system simulation techniques.

## 3.2. LOGIC LEVEL SIMULATION

The process of simulation at the logic-gate level, shown in Fig. 3.1, requires the logic diagram to be described in terms of logic modules and their

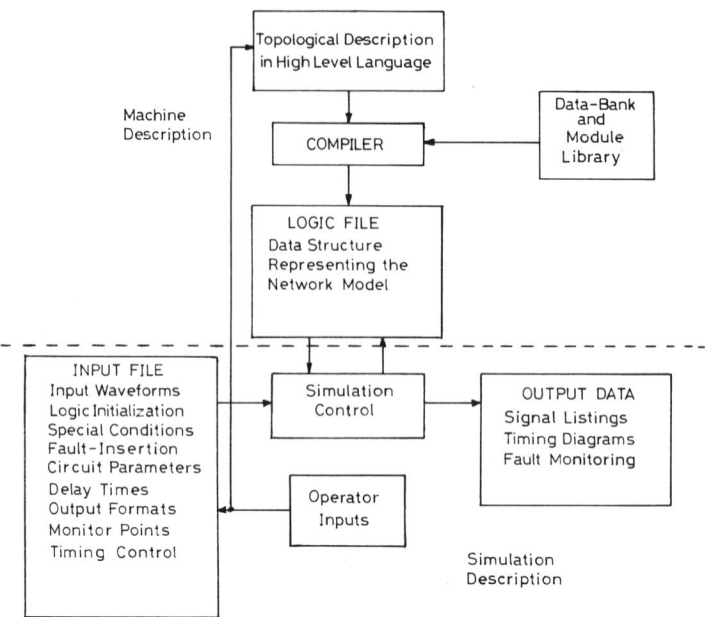

**Figure 3.1.** Simulation system.

interconnections using some form of problem-oriented language. (In some cases the logic diagram may be prepared on a specially formated blank chart which is then digitized off-line to produce the required computer input.) This description is then compiled into a suitable data structure, such as a list or ring structure, which represents a topological network model of the logic circuit; where necessary library descriptions of logic modules are obtained from a data base. Once the model is established it must be exercised; this is done via the simulation control program which requires inputs from the user defining such parameters as initial logic states, input values and sequences, gate delays, timing steps, monitoring points, output formats, etc. Once the parameters are set the simulation may be run; note that the parameters require to be changed for each simulation run, which can be done using static or dynamic modes of operation.

The simulation process proceeds by tracing changes in logic values through the network, on a discrete-time-interval basis, to generate the signal-time behavior of the circuit. That is, the computer program computes the output status of the logic elements at each basic machine-time interval (usually measured as a function of gate propagation delays, in the simplest case one time interval corresponding to the worst-case gate delay) and continues to advance in simulated time until the logic comes permanently to rest (a stable

**Table 3.1. Simulator Input Description**

| | Code | Logic type | Input 1 | Input 2 | Output |
|---|---|---|---|---|---|
| 1. | G1 | NAND | A | B | C |
| 2. | G2 | NAND | A | C | D |
| 3. | G3 | NAND | C | B | E |
| 4. | G4 | NAND | D | E | SUM |
| 5. | G5 | INV | C | | CARRY |

condition) or reaches some previously specified state. Thus, by gate-level simulation we mean the generation of a state–time map (truth or transition table) for the logic system, given the initial states and input sequences. In order to illustrate the technique let us consider a simple example which is typical of many gate-level simulators (5, 6, 7). Table 3.1 shows a common type of input format, using a simple logic-description language, for the half-adder circuit shown in Fig. 3.2.

A typical example of the type of output obtained after running the simulator is shown in Table 3.2a. In this case the initial circuit conditions have been specified as A = 0, B = 0 and the inputs allowed to change from $AB = 00 \rightarrow 10$ and $00 \rightarrow 11$. The timing has been assumed to be one gate delay per clock, that is, with the duration of the clock pulses being set equal to the propagation delay of the logic gates. In the case of the input change $00 \rightarrow 11$ a dynamic circuit hazard is indicated in the SUM output, since the output value should remain at zero during the input change. The "spike" on the SUM output is caused by the two different signal paths between the inputs A and B and the output, that is G1G2G4 and G2G4 respectively, which differ in length by one gate delay.

Note that the output routine prints the logic-1 outputs slightly displaced to the right of the logic 0 outputs, thus producing a form of waveform diagram which highlights any circuit transitions. It is of course possible to

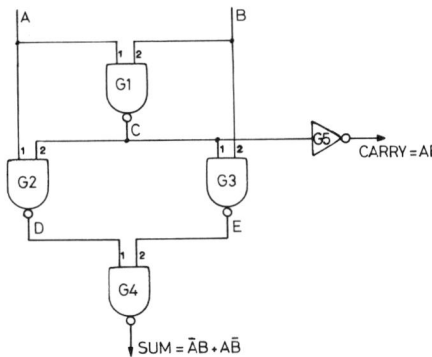

**Figure 3.2. Half-adder circuit.**

**Table 3.2. Output Timing Diagram**

(a)  Initial conditions   A = 0   B = 0
     Input                A = 1   B = 0

| Clock | Outputs | C | D | E | SUM | CARRY |
|-------|---------|-----|-----|-----|-----|-------|
| 0 | | . 1 | . 1 | . 1 | 0 | 0 |
| 1 | | . 1 | 0 | . 1 | 0 | 0 |
| 2 | | . 1 | 0 | . 1 | . 1 | 0 |
| 3 | | . 1 | 0 | . 1 | . 1 | 0 |

(b)  Initial conditions   A = 0   B = 0
     Input                A = 1   B = 1

| Clock | Outputs | C | D | E | SUM | CARRY |
|-------|---------|-----|-----|-----|-----|-------|
| 0 | | . 1 | . 1 | . 1 | 0 | 0 |
| 1 | | 0 | 0 | 0 | 0 | 0 |
| 2 | | 0 | . 1 | . 1 | . 1 | . 1 |
| 3 | | 0 | . 1 | . 1 | 0 | . 1 |
| 4 | | 0 | 1 | 1 | 0 | 1 |

obtain more sophisticated waveform diagrams using graphics or incremental graph plotters. Other information is often required to be printed out; this could include, for example, loading (fan-out) statistics and tables showing the maximum number of gate levels a signal has to pass through for each particular clock-time.

As well as providing a descriptive language for inputing logic circuits, simulator packages must also include facilities for the user to input data and control the timing, that is to drive the simulation. (In our simple example we assumed initial values only and basic clock timing.) This is normally done by adding program instructions which are obeyed during the simulation run and operate on the circuit model. In some early simulators, which effectively just produced a logical truth table, the simulation was completely automatic, utilizing all possible input values and starting from present initial conditions and gate delays. This form of simulator is of very limited value in a design environment.

Most logic-level simulators are designed to operate in terms of basic logic gates, such as NAND/NOR modules, and are thus inherently combinational in nature. Higher-level modules, however, can be simulated in terms of these basic units, and then referred to in later simulations as a separate compound element (block-structured simulators). A sequential circuit would be simulated by first representing the bistable elements in terms of asynchronous pulse-mode NAND/NOR circuits, and then substituting these complex elements into the circuit description and data structure wherever a bistable unit was specified. Compound elements of this type could of course be permanently stored in the data-base library and inserted as macros when compiling the program. A major difficulty, however, is encountered when simulating asynchronous networks comprising NAND/NOR gates with feedback paths. In this case the technique is to identify the essential feedback loops (that is those generating the internal state variables), which are then "cut" and the circuit considered as a pure combinational network. That is, the modified circuit is exercised as if it were a combinational circuit, with the secondary outputs after one clock period being used as inputs in the next period. The identification of feedback loops is usually done manually (not an easy task!) though computer algorithms do exist (8).

We shall now consider some of the necessary properties and techniques of gate-level simulation in more detail.

### 3.2.1. Input Language Requirements

Though it is feasible to define a logic circuit in terms of Boolean equations, and some early simulators have adopted this form of input (9), it is not the best method to employ in practice with large complex circuits. There are two main reasons for this. Firstly, in order to reflect the implemented configuration the equations must be derived directly from the actual logic circuit; this can be a time-consuming and error-prone procedure. For instance, the logical action of the circuit shown in Fig. 3.3 could be represented by

$$Z = \overline{A}\overline{B}D + ABD + ACD + \overline{A}\overline{B}E + A\overline{D}\overline{E}$$

but this would not indicate the manner in which the circuit was connected. (In the very early stages of design, prior to implementation, this may not present a problem.) The actual Boolean circuit description is rather cumbersome:

$$Z = \overline{\overline{(A\overline{B} + \overline{C}D)} + \overline{(\overline{A}B \cdot \overline{D}\overline{E})}}$$

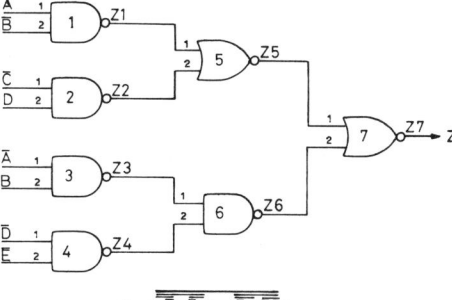

**Figure 3.3.** Boolean input forms.           $Z = \overline{\overline{(A\overline{B} \cdot \overline{C}D)} + \overline{(\overline{A}B\,\overline{D}\overline{E})}}$

and though it is possible to reduce this to a FORTRAN-like description, for example

$$Z = \text{NOR}(\text{NOR}(\text{NAND}(A,\bar{B}),\text{NAND}(\bar{C},D)),\text{NAND}(\text{NAND}(\bar{A},B),\text{NAND}(\bar{D},\bar{E})))$$

where the gates are named directly and the argument specifies the inputs, the description is still very complicated. Moreover, this form of input description is difficult to use for other CAD functions, such as module placement, etc. The second reason, though of less importance than the first, is that the computation techniques required are rather time consuming and involve fairly complex manipulations, since the connection network must be derived from the input equations [though some ingenious solutions have been suggested in the literature (10, 11)].

Much the best form of input language is the one based on a module description, with the inputs and outputs of each unit being explicitly defined. For example, the circuit elements in Fig. 3.3 could be coded using the input format

gate type/gate number : inputs; outputs

This yields the following description:

NAND / 1 : $\bar{A}, \bar{B}$; Z1

NAND / 2 : $\bar{C}, D$; Z2

NOR / 5 : $Z_1, Z_2$; Z5      etc.

Note that it is essential to be able to identify uniquely each input and output of the circuit module; in some cases the gate number can be used to identify the output. This form of description is easily adapted to allow the definition of compound modules and their subsequent use in more complex circuits. Consider, for example, the D-type bistable circuit shown in Fig. 3.4; this consists of three d.c. SR bistables (latches) suitably interconnected to give the required edge-triggered characteristic. The basic SR bistable may be defined as a compound element; thus

COMP − SRFF : $\bar{S}_1, \bar{S}_2, \bar{R}_1, \bar{R}_2$; Q, $\bar{Q}$

NAND / 1 : $\bar{S}_1, \bar{S}_2, \bar{Q}$; Q

NAND / 2 : $\bar{R}_1, \bar{R}_2, Q$; $\bar{Q}$

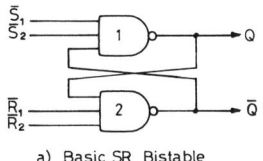

a) Basic SR Bistable

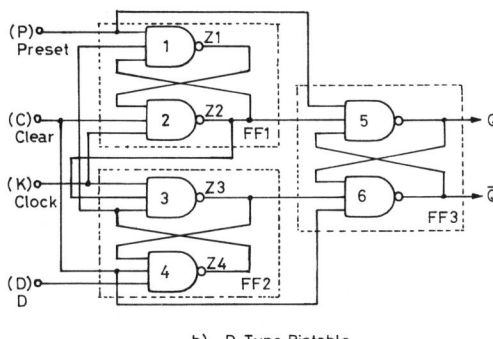

b)  D-Type Bistable

**Figure 3.4.**  D-type bistable circuits.

The connection of the three SR bistables to form the D-type bistable may now be specified as

$$\text{SRFF} \, / \, 1 : P, Z_4, C, K; Z_1, Z_2$$
$$\text{SRFF} \, / \, 2 : K, Z_2, D, C; Z_3, Z_4$$
$$\text{SRFF} \, / \, 3 : P, Z_2, C, Z_3; Q, \bar{Q}$$

It is also possible to specify compound elements using Boolean notation; the process can become complicated, however, when handling bistable circuits. For example the SR bistable in Fig. 3.4*a* would be represented as

$$Q = \overline{\bar{S}_1 \bar{S}_2 \bar{Q}} \quad \text{and} \quad \bar{Q} = \overline{\bar{R}_1 \bar{R}_2 Q}$$

giving

$$Q = \overline{(\bar{S}_1 \bar{S}_2)(\bar{R}_1 \bar{R}_2 Q)}$$
$$= \overline{\bar{S}_1 \bar{S}_2} + \bar{R}_1 \bar{R}_2 Q$$

that is

$$Q_+ = (S_1 + S_2) + \overline{(R_1 + R_2)}Q$$

where $Q_+$ is the output of the bistable in the next clock pulse. That is, the characteristic equation of the bistable must be used to obtain a Boolean definition of the circuit, which in some cases can prove unrealistic

Alternative forms of Boolean input, which are also used internally in the software procedures for defining compound elements, are the truth table and, in the case of sequential circuits, the state table. This form of specification allows an element to be defined as a 'black box' with a given input–output transfer function. The same result can of course be achieved using a programmed macro, which may be substituted in the simulated model as and when required.

Most current simulators provide a library of simple compound elements which may be referred to directly in the input language; these could include, for example, exclusive OR gates, $n$-bit full adders, bistables, decoders, etc. The main advantage of using compound elements of this type is that it economizes in the amount of storage required to support the simulated model. The alternative of course is to generate compound elements from basic NAND/ NOR gates; this is both inconvenient for the user and wasteful of storage space.

As well as defining circuit topology there are two other important conditions which need to be specified before the model is complete. These are the initialization of circuit nodes, such as counter and bistable outputs, and the specification of element delays.

The basic delay requirement is to be able to assign a propagation time, usually in terms of integer units of the machine clock, to each gate or compound element in the circuit (either individually or for a given module type). In the simplest case this may be done with an assignment statement of the form

⟨list⟩ = ⟨delay time⟩

where

⟨list⟩ ::= ⟨output identifier⟩ | ⟨logic function⟩ |

⟨output identifier⟩, ⟨logic function⟩

which would normally be proceeded by some directive such as DELAY, for instance:

DELAY

OUT 1, OR = 2

implies that all OR gates and the output function OUT 1 have a delay of 2 units.

In many cases a constant value, usually either the nominal propagation delay obtained from the manufacturer or the worst-case delay, is used. However, for some applications simple delay values of this type are insufficient to model and check out a circuit fully, for instance when checking race conditions etc., and a more sophisticated range of delay parameters must be used. In fact up to five parameters may be required as defined below (12):

$t_{1 \to 0}$      propagation delay for $1 \to 0$ change in state

$t_{0 \to 1}$      propagation delay for $0 \to 1$ change in state

$t_{min}$      minimum time allowable between edges of input pulse that operate a device

$t_{hold}$      minimum time input pulse must maintain its state after a clock pulse

$t_{set}$      minimum time input pulse must maintain its state before a clock pulse

The delay parameters are shown in Fig. 3.5 for the NAND gate; note that it is assumed that, when the overlap time for the input pulses is less than $t_2$, the

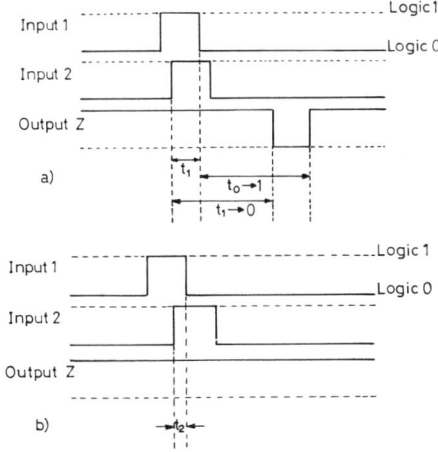

**Figure 3.5.** Delay parameters.

output state does not change. If $t_2 <$ overlap time $> t_1$, then the output state is uncertain; in practice the parameter $t_{min}$ is often assumed to be $t_{min} = t_1 = t_2$. The parameters $t_{set}$ and $t_{hold}$ are only required for certain clocked devices such as bistable circuits; the very minimum delay parameters that are required in a logic simulator are $t_{0 \rightarrow 1}$ and $t_{1 \rightarrow 0}$. Using these parameters the assignment statement would be modified to

$$\langle List \rangle = \langle t_{1 \rightarrow 0} \rangle \langle t_{0 \rightarrow 1} \rangle \langle t_{min} \rangle \langle t_{hold} \rangle \langle t_{set} \rangle.$$

In some cases the delay times are incorporated with the element descriptions. Thus, a NAND gate might be described as

$$NAND - G1 - t_{1 \rightarrow 0}, t_{0 \rightarrow 1} - IP_1, IP_2, IP_3 - OUT \ Z1$$

and for an edge-triggered JK bistable:

$$JKFF - MEM1 - t_{1 \rightarrow 0}, t_{0 \rightarrow 1}, t_{set}, t_{hold} - J,K,CLK,C,D - Q,\bar{Q}$$

where the symbol – stands for delimiter symbols used to separate data of a different type.

In order to analyze fully circuit race conditions both the shortest and longest delay times (as stated by the manufacturer) are of concern, and in some cases a statistical distribution of the delay values is used. The best and safest approach, however, is to determine the critical delay paths in the circuit [using a form of critical-path analysis (13)] and assign the worst-case values to the components in the path.

Note that the detection of circuit hazards is generally only required when asynchronous circuits are being analyzed. The use of a clock in synchronous circuits ensures that the circuit perturbations have all settled out by the time the outputs etc. are sampled. However, it is still necessary to ensure that the maximum delay through the circuits (which in general will be multilevel) is less than the minimum specified clock period.

The specification of initial conditions requires that the logical states of a network at the start of a simulation be defined. That is the user must be able to specify the states of any, or all, of the circuit nodes before the simulation begins. This may be done as before by using a simple assignment statement, preceded by a suitable directive; thus we have

$$\langle output \ variable \rangle = \langle state \rangle$$

where state specifies the logical state or states, usually in binary, of an output mode, for example

INITIAL

$G1 = 0, G5 = 1, Z2 = 0.$

In some simulators certain devices, such as counters and shift registers, can be set by quoting the decimal or octal equivalent of the number required to be stored. Monitor points may be specified in a similar way by using a directive to introduce a list of monitor-point statements of the form

⟨identifier⟩ = MP⟨n⟩

where identifier can be any function output in the block, or a block input, and ⟨n⟩ is a monitor-point number within a specified range. Thus

MONITOR

$G3 = MP1; Z4 = MP2; Z5 = MP3.$

### 3.2.2. Command Statements

In order to operate and control the simulation run a number of command codes must be provided in the language. These commands are generally concerned with the setting up of input data signals and their timing, including the provision for waveform generation, monitor points, output listings, and conditional controls. In addition basic directives such as START, FINISH, PRINT (state of monitor points), etc. are also required, including file-handling routines for large systems.

During the simulation of a network specified waveforms must be applied to the inputs. The simulator waveforms are normally read by the simulator from a compiled waveform file or inputted directly, using an interpreted mode, from user-originated declarations. Input waveforms are generally represented in idealized form, with zero rise and fall times, and specified in time order. One method of achieving this, used in the HILO system (14) is to list the new state of all those output nodes that change state at a given time using the instruction

@ ⟨time⟩ : ⟨list⟩

where ⟨time⟩ is an integer specifying the simulation time (in machine units) at which the list is to be evaluated, and

⟨list⟩ := ⟨identifier⟩ = ⟨state⟩

where ⟨identifier⟩ is the name of a network input and ⟨state⟩ is its logical value. For example, the waveform shown in Fig. 3.6a would be coded as follows:

@  0 : A = 0

@  5 : A = 1

@ 10 : A = 1

@ 15 : A = 0      etc.

It will be obvious that this technique can become laborious, and a CHANGE statement is often employed which takes the form

⟨identifier⟩ = CHANGE @ (⟨list of times⟩).

This statement assumes a particular starting value which must be set initially; for instance

@ 0 : A = 0

A = CHANGE @ (5,10,20,35).

The value of ⟨time⟩ is normally given as an integer with an upper limit determined by the characteristics of the particular simulation program.

An alternative but similar approach is to use a waveform generator whose behavior can be described by a series of "events" representing changes of output state. The first event is the state of the generator at time zero, and the remaining events refer to times at which the generator changes state, for example

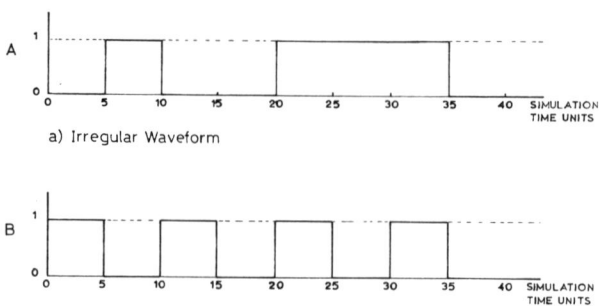

a) Irregular Waveform

b) Cyclic Waveform

**Figure 3.6.** Waveform generation.

GEN := ⟨identifier⟩, ⟨event time⟩ | ⟨identifier⟩, ⟨trip⟩.

The ⟨trip⟩ facility allows the event time to be a function of either a postive- or negative-going edge in any circuit node after a certain number of changes of state on that node. For instance a typical trip event would be ⟨−4, Z2, +2⟩ which signifies a change of state on the fourth negative-going edge of node Z2 after the second positive edge has occurred. Cyclic generation can be obtained by using a character as an event, for example C. The cycle starts at some time preceding the character C and continues until the last time in the event list (that is after C). The waveform in Fig. 3.6*a* may be coded as

GEN = A( 0, 5, 10, 20, 35 )

and the cyclic waveform in Fig. 3.6*b* as

GEN = A( 1, C, 5, 10 ).

Instead of using complex waveform generators a simple time scale or interval may often suffice. Facilities normally exist for defining a repetitive clock of the form

OP = CLOCK ($\langle t_i \rangle$, $\langle t_2 \rangle$, $\langle t_3 \rangle$)

where, assuming a zero start, OP goes to 1 after time $t_1$, stays there for a time $t_2$, and then goes to 0 and stays there for time $t_3$, the cycle repeating continuously.

In some cases an equal mark–space ratio clock is implicit in the program and the only requirement is to specify the period of the clock and the total number of pulses required; quite often specific values are obtained automatically by default, that is if no declaration is made.

Output commands are required to specify the identity and number of circuit nodes required to be monitored and their output formats. For example, it may be required to print out the state of each node and the time taken to reach that node or, alternatively, a simple truth table. A graphical output, however, is more useful, and this may be obtained in the usual way using digital plotters or outputting a page format on a line printer arranged to resemble a waveform diagram. The time scale represented may be either in the form of linear time increments or a non-linear scale where the value of monitored points are printed (together with the time) only when a change of state occurs. Table 3.3 shows typical output formats—note that in Table 3.3*a* the effect of a waveform diagram may be obtained by rotating the page 90° anticlockwise. In addition to the waveform and state print-outs fault

### Table 3.3.  Simulator Outputs

(a)  Graphical Output with Non-linear Scale

| Time machine units | Z1 | Z2 | Z3 | Z4 | Z5 | Z6 | Output nodes |
|:---:|:---:|:---:|:---:|:---:|:---:|:---:|:---|
| | O1 | O1 | O1 | O1 | O1 | O1 | Binary output values |
| 0 | 1 | 1 | 1 | 1 | 1 | 1 | |
| 2 | 1 | 1 | 1 | 1 | 1 | 1 | |
| 150 | 1 | 1 | 1 | 1 | 1 | 1 | |
| 160 | 1 | 1 | 1 | 1 | 1 | 1 | |
| 200 | 1 | 1 | 1 | 1 | 1 | 1 | |

(b)  Truth-Table Output with Linear Time Scale

| | Inputs | | Outputs | |
|:---:|:---:|:---:|:---:|:---:|
| Time | I1 | I2 | Z1 | Z2 |
| 0 | 0 | 0 | 0 | 0 |
| 5 | 0 | 0 | 0 | 0 |
| 10 | 0 | 1 | 1 | 0 |
| 15 | 0 | 1 | 1 | 0 |
| 20 | 1 | 1 | 0 | 1 |

conditions may also be indicated. For example, circuit conditions such as signals which change state together, and are thus likely to give rise to a circuit hazard, simultaneously setting and resetting of bistables, and the propagation of unacceptable narrow pulses would be indicated on the print-out. Facilities also normally exist for printing out the specified network configuration in the form of a list giving the component (or subsystem module) identity, type, input–output connections, propagation delay, and initial logical states.

For instance, in order to output a circuit configuration a command of the type

LIST = ⟨module numbers⟩

would be given; similarly a command

PRINT = ⟨module numbers⟩ | ⟨monitor point⟩

would be used to print the logical values of the output nodes of the modules or monitor points specified. In both cases omitting the argument list would result in data on all modules being outputted. In order to obtain a print-out of those modules which change state in a designated time interval, a command such as

$$\text{TRACE} = \langle t_1 \rangle \mid \langle t_2 - t_3 \rangle, \langle t_4 - t_5 \rangle \dots$$

where $t_1$ is the time limit of the desired run, and $t_2 - t_3$ etc. are the time intervals of the runs would be given. It is also possible to express timing and print commands in a single statement, for example:

@ 20 : PRINT MP1, MP4

would print out the value of monitor pairs MP1 and MP4 at simulated time 20.

In some cases the state of the monitor points are automatically printed out as the simulation proceeds (from time 0), and special commands are needed to stop and start the printing routines. As well as controlling the output, commands are also needed to start and stop the simulation run itself. The start command is often combined with a time limit specifying the required duration (in simulated time) of the run. Thus, the commands

RUN

and

$$\text{RUN} = \langle t_1 \rangle$$

would, respectively, cause the simulator to run until a STOP is encountered or for a time period $t_1$. More sophisticated simulators would also contain conditional commands of the form

IF ⟨condition⟩ THEN ⟨command⟩

which allows the command to be executed only if the specified condition (such as an output node being equal to 0 or 1) is satisfied. These commands are normally used in conjunction with JUMP instructions which transfer control to other sections of the simulator program.

Commands of the type described above are normally inserted at the start of a simulation program or alternatively mixed with waveform declarations and obeyed when they occur in the program. [This latter procedure is normally adopted in conversational systems (15).] Most simulators also include some form of editor for checking syntax and other errors (indicated to the user in the form of error messages) which can occur during program preparation.

Finally, many simulators, in particular those employed in time-shared systems, require file-handling routines. In this case special commands are provided which allow files to be created, erased, copied, dumped from, and read into main store, etc. Thus, library files, including input–output waveform data, may be created and used as input for subsequent simulator runs etc. In this way it is possible to simulate circuit blocks held on file using a library file containing waveform data as input, with the output results being stored away on an output file.

## 3.3. SIMULATION TECHNIQUES

Various methods have been described for setting up and manipulating a computer model of a logical network. The model must of course be formed from the source-language input statements describing the network. In general the statements can either be interpreted directly and executed, or compiled into machine-code instructions to be executed later. Alternatively, the statements may be used to set up a data structure representing the network configuration.

In the case of *compiled-code simulators* the usual practice is to generate a set of subroutines (macros) which perform the logical functions required by each specific element type. For example, a three-input NAND gate could be programmed as

| Inputs | A, B, C | |
|--------|---------|---|
| FETCH | A | (Fetch input A to Accumulator) |
| COLLATE | B | (AND with B giving AB) |
| COLLATE | C | (AND with C giving ABC) |
| INVERT | | (Invert giving $\overline{ABC}$) |
| STORE | Z | (Store $\overline{ABC}$ in Z) |

It should be noted that using this approach all the logic elements are represented in an identical form with zero propagation delays.

The logical network to be simulated is represented in the computer as a series of interconnected macros which evaluate the logical functions of the element in the order in which they appear in the circuit, that is, as specified by the logic levels, starting at the input gates and progressing through the circuit (outputs of one gate being considered as inputs to the succeeding gates) until the final output gate is reached. The ordering of the circuit (and hence the ensuing computation) is performed at compile time by assigning logic levels to each gate in the network and then performing a logic-level sort. Using the compiled-code technique combinational circuits can be simulated in one pass through the network; sequential circuits, however, must be iterated (performing several simulations in one clock period) until a stable condition is realized. Timing is performed by using an internally generated clock and is normally synchronous, that is the gate outputs are sampled (and used as inputs) only at definite time intervals. In some cases asynchronous timing can be used; in this case the gate outputs can be applied as inputs immediately a state change occurs.

One disadvantage often encountered in the above technique (and others if adequate precaution is not taken) is the risk of modeling a circuit that can oscillate indefinitely. This can occur, for example, in sequential systems when two gates feed each other (as in a NAND/NOR d.c. bistable). The difference between a real and modeled bistable is that a race condition produces a race in the first, but triggers a synchronous but endless oscillation in the second. The reason is that both halves of the modeled bistable have identical delays and thus do not allow the race to settle out, which it will do in practice owing to the unequal delays. Another characteristic of the cross-coupled bistable which can set up oscillatory conditions is the fact that *both* outputs go to one when the inputs $S = R = 1$ occur. One method of detecting this condition is to count the number of iterations and automatically terminate the simulation after a specified time has elapsed.

The major disadvantage of the compiled-code technique is that if any changes are required to be made to the logic configuration a new network description must be recompiled. Moreover, since all logic elements are evaluated in sequence by the program (even if a signal path is unactivated) the time required to simulate a large system can become excessive. It also follows that it is not possible to evaluate selectively part of the network.

Similar in principle is the use of Boolean equations to describe the logical functions of a network; in this case, however, computer algorithms must be developed to evaluate the Boolean expressions (16). The same basic ideas are employed in the *Table-look-up* method in which the truth table for each logic element are stored in the model (analogous to the use of a macro) and accessed using the input values to determine the resultant output.

Most of the early simulators were either interpretive or executed compiled code; current simulators, however, usually employ some form of data structure and are essentially *table-driven*. In the table-driven method the parameters of individual logic elements in a network are stored in a tabular form with each entry comprising such data as logic function, propagation delay, output values, input sources, output destination, etc. Thus, the source-language statements are translated into a data structure representing the circuit; Table 3.4 shows a typical set of such data tables for the circuit shown in Fig. 3.7. (Note that in practice the tables would be stored as a list structure; in the example pointers refer to the address of the first cell in the sublist.) During simulation the data structure is operated on by a control program which interprets the information in the lists in accordance with the simulator command statements to determine the data flow and logical values in the network. The interpreter program operates by following the linkages (pointers) from one circuit element to the next, evaluating the outputs from

## Table 3.4. Data Structures for Table-Driven Simulation

Element List

| Cell address | Type | Name | Delay | I-O pointers Input | I-O pointers Output | Output value |
|---|---|---|---|---|---|---|
| 100 | NAND | G1 | 5 | 200 | 203 | |
| 101 | NOR | G2 | 3 | 204 | 206 | |
| 102 | NAND | G3 | 5 | 207 | 210 | |
| 103 | NOR | G4 | 3 | 212 | 214 | |

Interconnection List

| Cell address | Preceding elements pointer/ pin no. | Destination elements |
|---|---|---|
| 200 | PI | — |
| 201 | PI | — |
| 202 | PI | — |
| 203 | — | 400 |
| 204 | 100/4 | — |
| 205 | 102/3 | — |
| 206 | — | OP |
| 207 | PI | — |
| 208 | PI | — |
| 209 | PI | — |
| 210 | — | 401 |
| 211 | — | 402 |
| 212 | 102/3 | — |
| 213 | PI | — |
| 214 | — | OP |
| 215 | | |

Output Connection List

| Cell address | Pin No. | Element pointer |
|---|---|---|
| 400 | 1 | 101 |
| 401 | 2 | 101 |
| 402 | 1 | 103 |
| 403 | | |

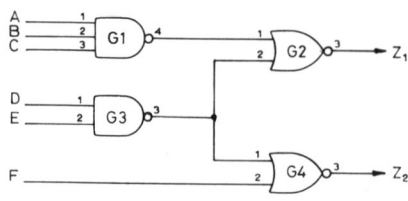

**Figure 3.7.** Network for table-driven simulation.

each element from the input–output values as it proceeds. Each logic function is evaluated by a specific subroutine which is accessed as required rather than using individual macros. From Table 3.4 the circuit could be simulated by starting at gate G1 and obtaining the input from the interconnection list (as determined by the input pointer); in this case they are the primary inputs (PI) to the circuit, and in practice further pointers to a waveform or signal list would be required. Using the appropriate NAND subroutine the output of G1 would be generated and the result stored in the element list (or in some cases temporary program storage). The next step would be to determine, from the interconnection list, those elements which accept this output as their input; in this case a pointer to the output connection list specifies the NOR gate G2. The other inputs to G2 are obtained from the element list (in this example the output from NAND gate G3 would be the only one), which, if not already available, must be computed and the results used in conjunction with the output of G1 to generate the new output of G2. In so doing it would be apparent from the interconnection list that G3 also feeds the input to NOR gate G4, the output of which would also be computed.

Note that in this technique the circuit topology, such as the connection between logic levels etc., is inherent in the data structure rather than the control program. Thus, the course of the simulation is determined by the data structure rather than the program, hence the name table-driven. A very important advantage accrues from this property, namely that it is no longer necessary to simulate the entire circuit to obtain the result of an input change. As one would expect, the realization of the data structure is a crucial factor in the design of an efficient simulator.

When large logic circuits containing many thousands of gates are simulated the running time of the simulator can become a significant factor owing to the sequential nature of the program and the large number of instructions to be executed. These limitations can be overcome, however, if *significant events* only are simulated, as and where they occur in the circuit. For any given input change only a small number of logic elements will change state (termed a significant event), and an appreciable reduction in computation time can be achieved if only those elements which change value are evaluated. As we have seen the simulation model of a network consists of a number of interrelated tables with pointers representing the circuit interconnections. Thus, the table-driven simulator has the advantage that it allows the effect of an input change to be traced through the circuit so that only the active element need be simulated.

Next-event simulation can be implemented by representing current and future events by two push-down stacks (that is a list-storage structure such that the last item placed on the list is the first one out). Logic elements whose states are due to change at a particular time are placed on a *current-activity* stack. At clock-period intervals each element on the stack is examined, and if necessary (owing to the progress of time and new inputs) a new output value is computed. Where an output state has changed all the succeeding elements which accept this signal are placed on a *future-activity* stack; the examination of the current-activity stack proceeds until the stack is exhausted. Note that at this stage the future-activity stack contains a list of elements whose output values could change as a result of new input values.

When all the elements in the current-activity list have been processed, the future-activity list is examined in the same way (in effect the roles of the two stacks have been interchanged); the procedure continues until both stacks are simultaneously empty. In this way a signal may be propagated through a network and only those elements which are activated need be processed; the method also allows oscillatory conditions to be handled. The method can also be extended (17) to handle asynchronous simulation, where each event has a different completion time. (The basic simulator operates in a synchronous mode where events are modeled as if they were executed and completed at the *same* time.)

An alternative method is to use a time-ordered event list in conjunction with a data structure representing the logical connections between gate outputs and the inputs to succeeding gates (the fan-out). Entries in the event list indicate that, as a result of a change of state on the inputs to a gate, a new output stage has been predicted. When an entry is removed from the time-ordered list, the predicted signal change is generated and the simulator control program proceeds to examine any other gates, at a higher logic level, which have this output as their input.

As well as the advantages of reduced computation time the table-driven event simulator allows easy modification to the circuit topology by simply changing the appropriate pointers in the list structure.

### 3.3.1. Parallel Simulation

Most simulators operate in a serial mode with *single* changes in the input state being traced through a circuit level by level, the intermediate outputs being applied successively to obtain the final output. Normally an entire computer word is used to store each input variable, and only one set of inputs can be applied to the network for a particular simulation. This procedure involves a considerable amount of storage space and, more important, computation time. In general the time required to simulate a circuit is linearly related to its complexity (M) which is determined by the number of elements and their interconnections. For a single simulation run the computation time can be represented by machine time $= M2^N$

where $N$ is the number of input variables.

A simple way to increase the efficiency of logic simulation (16, 18) is to use each bit position in the computer word to represent an input variable. Each word, and hence the multiple inputs represented, would be processed simultaneously in the computer, since the COLLATE instruction, for example, is executed in such a way that the AND operation is performed independently on each bit position. Thus, the NAND macro described in § 3.3 would process multiple inputs in the same time as it takes for a single input variable. In this way it is possible to increase the efficiency of a simulation run by a factor approaching the number of bits in the computer word. This process is called *parallel simulation* and allows a logic network to be exercised using several different input patterns in the same clock period. The parallel-word mode of representing signals is best suited for use in compiled-code simulators; however, the technique has been employed with table-driven models. The method must not be confused with parallel error simulation, which is described in § 3.3.3.

### 3.3.2. Three-Value Simulation (19)

The presence of hazards and races in combinational and sequential logic circuits may be detected using the concepts of ternary algebra (20, 21). In this method a third value, $X$, which may assume the value of either 0 or 1, is used to represent unspecified initial conditions, unpredictable oscillations, and "don't-care" states. Basic logic gates, such as AND/OR etc., may be redefined in terms of ternary functions using the values 0, 1, and $X$. Table 3.5 gives the truth table for the functions AND, OR, and NAND; note that there are now $3^2 = 9$ possible input combinations. In general, the ternary function of a logic

**Table 3.5. Ternary Logic Functions**

| Inputs | | Outputs | | |
|---|---|---|---|---|
| A | B | $Z = A \cdot B$ | $Z = A + B$ | $Z = \overline{AB}$ |
| 0 | 0 | 0 | 0 | 1 |
| 0 | 1 | 0 | 1 | 1 |
| 1 | 0 | 0 | 1 | 1 |
| 1 | 1 | 1 | 1 | 0 |
| $X$ | 0 | 0 | $X$ | 1 |
| 0 | $X$ | 0 | $X$ | 1 |
| $X$ | 1 | $X$ | 1 | $X$ |
| 1 | $X$ | $X$ | 1 | $X$ |
| $X$ | $X$ | $X$ | $X$ | $X$ |

gate may be determined by putting the $X$ inputs to the gate alternately at 0 and 1, and noting whether the gate output $(Z)$ changes $(Z = X)$ or remains at 0 or 1 $(Z = 0, 1)$.

In order to detect hazards using three-valued simulation the unknown value $X$ is included in the primary inputs between every 0 to 1 and 1 to 0 transition. The simulation then proceeds in the normal way, except that the ternary function of the logic elements is used to generate the output values. The presence of an $X$ in an output value indicates the presence of a hazard, which may be propagated, through the circuit, to the final output; Fig. 3.8 shows the method applied to single logic circuits. In practice (22) the three-valued simulation is performed in two stages. The first part, the $X$-pass, consists of setting each primary input (as specified in the command language) in turn to $X$ and propagating this value through the network until no more changes occur; this sequence is repeated until all the primary inputs have been examined. The second stage, called the value-pass, is performed by setting the primary inputs to their specified values and then allowing them to propagate through the circuit. Any $X$ values which remain after this pass indicate a circuit hazard, since the network must contain stable values which can be either 0 or 1.

The use of the three-valued method allows hazards to be detected that would normally go unnoticed in a two-value simulation. For example (see Fig. 3.8*a*, *b*) when the inputs to an AND or OR gate both change state

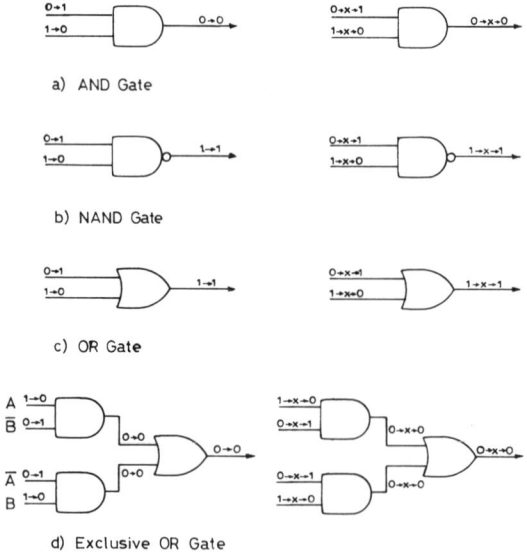

a) AND Gate

b) NAND Gate

c) OR Gate

d) Exclusive OR Gate

**Figure 3.8.** Hazard detection using three-valued logic.

simultaneously a temporary erroneous output (spikes) may be produced; this condition would not be detected in a two-value simulator. It is important to realize, however, that the indicated hazard may or may not occur in the actual hardware implementation, depending on the duration of the spike and the logic delays in the circuit. This comes about because the three-valued simulator is essentially a zero-delay simulator and takes no account of signal propagation times; however, it is possible to simulate relative delays through signal paths.

In addition to hazard detection the three-value method may also be used to represent "don't-care" input conditions to the circuit. This enables the amount of test data required to check a given circuit to be considerably reduced. For example, suppose it is required to simulate the reset logic of a machine; normally this would have to be performed by applying the reset input repetitively and checking that, for every possible combination of bits in the registers, latches, etc., the output value always goes to zero, requiring some $2^n$ simulation runs where $n$ is the number of bistable stores. By initially setting all the registers etc. to the value $X$ and then simulating the reset it is possible to determine in *one pass* those stages which have not been reset to a known value, since their bistable outputs will stay unchanged at the $X$ value.

Three-valued logic has also been used for the functional partitioning of digital systems (23). The $X$ value is used to trace out the logical paths followed when a particular algorithm, say binary addition, is executed. The information flow may be identified by signal lines which have a value of $X$, indicating those elements in the circuit which, when activated, give rise to the next stable state of the system. Both the data-structure elements and control logic can be isolated in this way and automatically extracted from the rest of the circuit. The advantage of this procedure is that only the active parts of the circuit need to be simulated for any particular set of test conditions; thus simulation times can be reduced.

### 3.3.3. Fault Simulation

The problem of automatically generating a set of input sequences for testing combinational and sequential logic circuits is discussed in a later chapter. Here we shall consider the place of simulation in test-sequence generation, and in particular some of the techniques available. The major objective of digital fault simulation is to generate a set of tests for a logical circuit which can be applied to the fabricated design to detect if a physical defect exists in the circuit. Fault simulation can also be used to validate fault detection or diagnostic tests, create fault dictionaries, and assist in the design of diagnosable logic. Ideally the basic simulator used in the fault-simulation process should be capable of analyzing circuit races and hazards as well as performing the normal logic-simulation functions.

In order to constrain the problems to a tractable form, single logical faults emanating at input–output terminals permanetly stuck at either 0 or 1 are assumed (these faults are normally abbreviated to s-a-0 and s-a-1 respectively). Though it has been found that this class of fault covers a high percentage of the physical defects which occur in production boards, it should be stressed, however, that it is not inclusive. Note that the prime concern is with faults that can arise during manufacture, such as bad connections, faulty components, etc., which normally manifest themselves as logical faults; the circuit is considered to be free of design errors. Any logical network can of course be completely tested by applying all possible input combinations and comparing the output values with the correct result. This procedure becomes impossible for large networks, and consequently it is necessary to search for the minimal set of input sequences that will detect all faults.

Gate-level simulation is generally used to evolve a set of input patterns which will detect the presence of single logical faults introduced into a network. The procedure is first to simulate the fault-free circuit, and then to repeat the simulation with all possible faults inserted into the network. Comparison of the outputs obtained with the faulty and fault-free circuit yields a list of identifiable faults.

A serious disadvantage of this method is that large networks require an excessive amount of computation time. In order to ensure that all faults (s-a-0 and s-a-1 on all connections) are covered test simulations must be performed many times over, and, in the limit, all possible input combinations may be required. Consequently, most fault simulators compromise by producing an effective covering of faults (hopefully a large percentage of all possible faults) rather than the complete optimum cover. Alternatively, statistical procedures are used where the circuit is driven by random input sequences.

In order to evaluate the fault-mode characteristics of a network it is necessary to be able to introduce the effect of, say, a component failure into the circuit—this is known as *fault injection* (24). The manner in which this is done depends on the type of simulator. For example, in the compiled-code type the logically correct macro can be modified to emulate the faulty behavior of the element. It will be obvious that the compiled-code simulator is very inefficient when used as a fault simulator, since it may be necessary to update the macro (remember it is an integral part of the network model) after each fault-simulation run.

For the table-driven model it is simply a case of modifying the pointers in the data structure to allow a conditional choice to be made between input and output values. In some cases a special data structure is used to contain the signal faults which must be inserted. Using a table-driven simulator normal and faulty conditions are treated as different cases of the same model, and the fault parameters can be set and reset by suitable command-language statements which operate on the data structures. For example (14), s-a-0 and s-a-1 faults may be introduced into a network (for the duration of a simulation) by using the directive FAULT followed by a list of fault statements of the form

⟨identifier⟩ = ⟨1 or 0⟩ for output faults

and

⟨identifier⟩ = ⟨1 or 0⟩ ⟨list⟩ for input faults

where ⟨identifier⟩ is the name of the connection point, usually an output, and ⟨list⟩ a list of identifiers which are outputs of the elements whose inputs are s-a-0 or s-a-1. Thus

Fault

A = 1 (Z1, Z2)

would represent s-a-1 faults on the inputs of the elements whose outputs are Z1 and Z2, the fault emanating at output A. Note that there is a distinct difference between input signal and output pin faults. In the case of an output pin fault the fault affects the *entire* signal, which is normally distributed to other units. An input fault is restricted to a single input on a particular element. By a suitable construction of these fault modes it becomes possible to emulate the effect of physical breaks in the connecting tracks of a fanned-out signal.

It is also common to provide some form of comparison command which enables waveforms or output sequences to be compared automatically. For instance, the output sequences of successive fault simulations (or runs with different propagation times) could be stored on an output file and compared with a previously compiled file of correct sequences. In this case a command of the form

COMPARE ⟨Waveform 1⟩, ⟨Waveform 2⟩

would be used, followed by a list of identifiers specifying specific waveforms, or output nodes, required to be compared. The effect of this command statement is that the contents of the two specified waveform files would be compared; should a difference occur the time and states of the waveforms at that instant would be printed out.

Manual insertion of faults can become a laborious process; consequently many simulators are able to generate certain classes of faults automatically. One technique is to use independent subroutines, controlled by suitable command statements, to generate fault classes specified by the user.

Normally a testing sequence would be checked out by performing separate simulation runs for each possible fault. This can be a time-consuming process; consequently methods of speeding up the fault-simulation procedure have been sought. One method that has been used extensively is *parallel error simulation* (25, 26). This technique is based on a compiled-code simulator and uses each bit position in the computer word to represent the binary value of the specified faults. Individual input-signal values are contained in separate words, but the value is repeated through all bits. The signal word used for normal (fault-free) simulation is modified during fault simulation by the contents of masking words; this is achieved by appropriate assembly language routines in the control program.

The parallel-simulation procedure is best illustrated by way of an actual example. Consider a three-input NAND gate and the simulation of the circuit under fault conditions such that input 1 is s-a-0 and input 2 is s-a-1. (Note that single faults only are being considered, and hence the simulation represents two *different* fault models.) Let us also assume that the three inputs to the gate would have the binary values 101 in the normal, unfailed condition. Table 3.6a shows the contents of the computer words representing the input-signal values and masks; note that an 8-bit word has been used, and that the first three most significant digits are reserved for the normal unfailed machine. The normal compiled-code simulation is shown in Table 3.6b with the fault version in Table 3.6c. Faults are introduced into the input signals by OR'ing or AND'ing the signal word with the mask words. Thus a gate signal may be forced to s-a-0 by AND'ing, for instance the signal word IN1 with the mask MA. Similarly by OR'ing the signal IN2 with mask MB the gate signal may be forced to s-a-1. The final result in the Accumulator (Table 3.6c) gives the correct output for the NAND gate (repeated in the first three digits) followed by the two fault outputs.

*Multiple faults*, that is a group of faults that exist at the *same* time, can also be modeled by this method. The difference is that in this case a group of faults is forced to affect only one bit position in the computer word (but at different levels in the circuit) rather than a unique bit position for each fault. Note that the maximum number of faults that can be simulated during a single simulation pass is dependent on the word-length of the host machine.

Parallel fault simulation can also be used in a table-driven simulation (24); in this case the same technique of masking the signal word is employed, but the faults are specified by appropriate command-language statements incorporated in the control program. At the beginning of a simulation pass a table is

### Table 3.6. Parallel Fault Simulation

*(a)* Data Words

| | | |
|---|---|---|
| Input 1 | IN1 | 1 1 1 1 1 1 1 1 |
| Input 2 | IN2 | 0 0 0 0 0 0 0 0 |
| Input 3 | IN3 | 1 1 1 1 1 1 1 1 |
| Mask A | MA | 1 1 1 0 1 1 1 1 |
| Mask B | MB | 0 0 0 0 1 0 0 0 |

*(b)* Normal Simulation Program

| Instruction | | Comment | Accumulator |
|---|---|---|---|
| LOAD | IN1 | Load Accumulator with IN1 | 1 1 1 1 1 1 1 1 |
| AND | IN2 | AND Accumulator with IN2 | 0 0 0 0 0 0 0 0 |
| AND | IN3 | AND Accumulator with IN3 | 0 0 0 0 0 0 0 0 |
| INV | | Invert contents of Accumulator | 1 1 1 1 1 1 1 1 |

*(c)* Fault Simulation Program

| Instruction | | Comment | Accumulator |
|---|---|---|---|
| LOAD | IN1 | Load with IN1 | 1 1 1 1 1 1 1 1 |
| AND | MA | AND with Mask A | 1 1 1 0 1 1 1 1 |
| STORE | TEMP | Store Accumulator in TEMP | 1 1 1 0 1 1 1 1 |
| LOAD | IN2 | Load with IN2 | 0 0 0 0 0 0 0 0 |
| OR | MB | OR with Mask B | 0 0 0 0 1 0 0 0 |
| AND | IN3 | AND with IN3 | 0 0 0 0 1 0 0 0 |
| AND | TEMP | AND with TEMP | 0 0 0 0 1 0 0 0 |
| INV | | Invert | 1 1 1 1 0 1 1 1 |

constructed which contains all the signal faults; the contents of this table are then used to modify the signal words contained in the data structure under the direction of the command-language statements.

As well as the solid s-a-0 and s-a-1 faults it is also possible to simulate complex faults arising from physical defects such as shorted signal lines, NAND gates that operate as AND gates, open-circuited diodes, etc. This may be done by using a special software routine which models the complex fault. For example, let us consider an invertor which no longer inverts; in this case the simulation would be performed with the normal invertor routine, followed by the fault routine which simply passes the input signal through the circuit. If the simulator is time based, intermittent faults may also be modeled by specifying a fault condition and arranging that the fault signal changes periodically. This is normally achieved by internal timing circuits (in some cases a random-number generator is employed) which control the signal changes.

Though parallel signal representation greatly enhances the efficiency of the system, the compiled-code simulator requires that the entire code is evaluated each simulated clock period. Moreover the advantages of parallel fault simulation are to a large extent lost when event-driven simulators are used. In an event-driven simulation only those elements in the network which are activated are processed. Thus, faults will give rise to several different paths through the network, each of which must be traced through to an output point. The procedure usually adopted is to simulate the circuit until the first divergent path is encountered; each path must then be examined in turn, which necessitates back-tracking each time to the initial point of divergence and resetting all the elements to their original conditions.

Another common method of speeding up the fault-computation process is to use *collapsed fault sets* as input to the fault simulator. It is possible for different fault conditions to generate identical output values; these *indistinguishable faults* (forming an equivalence class) can all be simulated by one fault signal. For example, an s-a-0 on the input pins of an AND gate and an s-a-0 on the output of the AND gate cannot be distinguished. If this group of faults is collapsed into one representative fault, it is considered to be a single-gate collapse. This procedure is relatively simple to perform and may be extended to larger circuits with considerable reduction in simulation time.

Most methods of improving the efficiency of fault simulation depend on the assumption that, on average, a fault only activates a small part of the network under test. Moreover, when the same input is applied to a good circuit and a bad version containing a single fault, the *activity sequences* are rarely substantially different from each other. Theoretical work by Armstrong (27) has established that the concurrent simulation of a large number of nearly identical single faults is a practicable proposition. Armstrong's *deductive* method is based on generating a dynamic list of faults for each circuit node which can effect the output at that instant of time; the *fault lists* are up-dated as the simulation proceeds. The fault list contains one entry for each fault which is detectable on the output of that gate, plus an entry containing the number of faults in the list; the fault list for a gate output is computed from the fault lists associated with its inputs. All faults are considered in one simulation pass and the fault lists are propagated from the site of the failures to the circuit outputs.

An extension to this work which allows the concurrent simulation of nearly identical networks has been described by Ulrich and Baker (28). Though conceptually related to the deductive approach the method differs in that bad gates rather than fault effects are represented, including the classification of bad inputs as bad gates. The method consists of simulating the activity of a good circuit concurrently with a bad network, but *only* if the activity of the bad network differs from that of the good one. The technique has been implemented using an event-scheduled simulator, and includes three-value simulation for the detection of hazards and races. The simulator gives a considerable saving in computation time (especially for large circuits) but the storage required is extremely large and unpredictable.

All the fault simulators described so far have worked on the principle of applying known inputs to the network being modeled and then proceeding to calculate the resultant outputs. An alternative approach is to perform a *backwards simulation* in which, given the output of a network (or node), the necessary inputs to produce this output are determined. This technique is based on the D-algorithm due to Roth (29), which is described later in Chapter 5. The algorithm is used to perform a backwards trace from a fault in the network to the input conditions required to detect the fault.

## 3.4. SYSTEM LEVEL SIMULATION

As we have seen in Chapter 2, a major problem in digital systems design is specification and evaluation at the systems level. Simulation has been the principal tool in the practical solution to this problem, employing either general-purpose simulation languages or special high-level descriptive languages, a variation of the latter being the RTL languages described in Chapter 2. In general, high-level simulation languages specify the *behavior* of the system rather than its detailed structure, which is often, however, implicit in the system desription. In contrast, gate-level simulators give a complete *structural* description of the circuit, with register-transfer languages falling somewhere between the two approaches and providing a *functional* description of the data and control processes. System simulations have of course been performed using all three techniques; however, none of the methods are completely satisfactory by themselves, since it seems necessary that both the behavioral and structural properties of the system are represented in the same model. Moreover, the independent use of a structural simulator to model an entire system is often precluded by the prohibitive amounts of storage (and computation time) required.

An ideal system simulator should have the following basic properties.

(a) Capable of specifying the system in an hierarchical, modular fashion.
(b) Able to describe the function of each module by independently specifying the structure and control functions.
(c) Facility to construct complex structures and control functions by interconnecting blocks specified as macro-like definitions.
(d) Handle the specification and control of concurrent operations.

These characteristics imply that modules can be specified formally as Boolean equations, truth tables, etc., or algorithmically as macros. Furthermore, it must also be possible to insert these modules into a higher-level structure and specify the control at this level.

The majority of existing design and simulation languages fail to meet this specification. For example, basic register-transfer languages such as Schorr's RTL and Gorman and Anderson's LDT do not allow the system to be partitioned or for concurrent operations to be specified; structural representation is normally restricted to the register level. Languages such as Chu's, which are algorithmically based, are satisfactory when describing system behavior, but are imprecise when specifying system structure and control. Most of the requirements are contained in the DDL language and CASSANDRA, but they are unfortunately rather complex to use and require multiple passes to effect a translation, thus restricting their use in a time-shared environment.

One extremely promising systems-modeling language, which satisfies all the above criteria, is that proposed by Baray and Su (30) (called the LALD system). This language allows a systems model to be specified and evaluated (31); moreover, a translator is also available (32) which effects a realization in term of the control structures (deriving a finite-state machine) and the Boolean logic for the structural functions. However, there are no facilities for fault insertion or simulation of faulty networks either at the system or module level.

In use the specification language allows a large system to be partitioned into modules called *units*, which must be capable of operating independently or with the minimum amount of intra-system communication. Each unit of the system is considered to consist of a *structural part*, where the unit operations take place, and a *control part*, which sequences the operations. The structural part of each unit is comprised of two main elements called *generators* and *links*. Operators may be *basic*, consisting of combinational switching circuits described by Boolean functions, or *complex*, which can be any function specified by its terminal characteristics, that is a "black-box" transfer-function description. Complex operators are used during the early design stages where the user specification is known but the detailed design is still incomplete. More important, the complex operator can be used in the simulation of large systems where a detailed description of the units would not be a viable proposition from the viewpoint of computation efficiency. Links are used to connect operators to each other, and in essence to define a highway bus system. They may be of two types, *terminal* or *register*, depending on whether or not memory elements are included in the connecting paths; register links allow register-transfer operations to be specified.

The control part of the unit executes the necessary sequencing of the operations, normally performed using a number of control variables, and may comprise up to four elements; these are as follows.

(a) The *activity element*, which initiates operators in the structural part of the unit. In the asynchronous mode the "hand-shake" principle is employed; that is, after initiating the operator the activity element waits for a completion signal before transferring control to the next element in the sequence. In the alternative synchronous mode the end of the operator function is determined by the elapse of a fixed time interval indicated by a clock pulse.

(b) *Selector elements*, which perform conditional (or unconditional) branches in the control sequence based on the value of a parameter in the structural part of the unit.

(c) The *branch element* allows parallel operations to be controlled separately by causing the control sequence to fork into two or more independent paths.

(d) The *junction element* enables two or more parallel branches to join together.

The description of a system begins with a definition of the operators which are common to two or more units, followed by a description of each unit in terms of the structural and control parts. The structural description is specified in two parts, firstly a definition of the operators and links, and secondly the connections between operators and links. The language has a hierarchical block structure, shown in Fig. 3.9; note that the operators and links associated with a given unit are local to that unit. The language has been implemented on the basis of a significant-event simulator, using the high-level

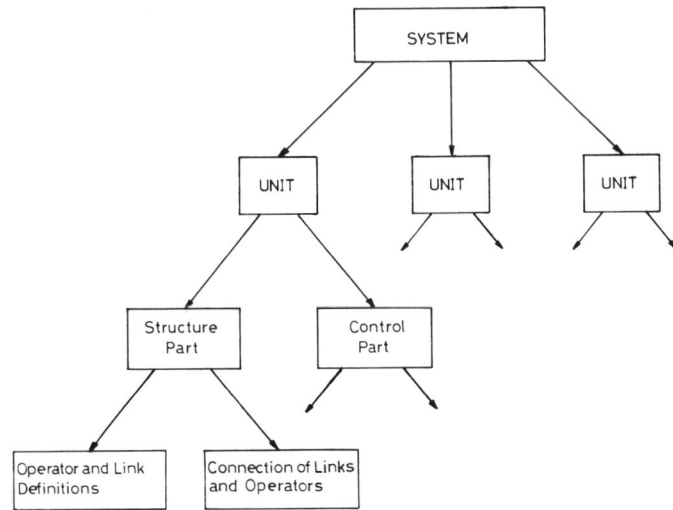

**Figure 3.9.** LALD system hierarchy.

language PL1 on a CDC 6400 computer. The system model is stored as a list structure, the data base being generated algorithmically from the design-language specification. Since it is not possible to simulate parallel processes concurrently in a single machine, parallel operations must be converted to a series of sequential events. In order to obtain a correct representation of parallel events it is necessary to ensure that the states reached by the simulated system after a sequential evaluation must be the same as the states reached if concurrent evaluation had taken place.

It is interesting to observe the similarity of the LALD modeling philosophy with that of the specification methodologies described earlier in Chapter 2, particularly the directed-graph and RTM techniques, for example, the separation into control and data structures and the use of "hand-shake" procedures to initiate and control the operations in the data structure. A similar hierarchical approach, utilizing a modular highway-connected structure has been adopted in the HILO system (14). Whilst not providing for the simulation of concurrent processes, HILO does allow fault simulation to take place at both gate and systems level.

One important characteristic of both these languages is the ability to simulate at the systems level. However, there is generally a "loss of definition" in the simulation at this level, owing to the need to use a functional specification of the subsystem modules or units, and it is necessary to drop down to a lower level for detailed structural analysis. For example, Boolean equations, state tables, register-transfer statements, etc., describe the overall logical behavior of a unit but are independent of the actual hardware used in the implementation. However, in order to simulate the fault mode of a circuit it is necessary to model the actual implemented circuit (to determine, for instance, the effect of a particular terminal s-a-1). Thus, fault modeling at the systems level can only be accomplished on a general basis, and specific faults introduced by a particular method of implementation could be undetected. One method of overcoming this, but still leading to some fuzziness in interpretation, is to perform a gate-level simulation for each subsystem module and then compile a restricted fault dictionary which is referenced during a high-level simulation.

### 3.4.1. General-Purpose Simulation Languages

Theoretically, general-purpose simulation languages (33, 34) are intended for use with any system which can be assumed to change in a discrete manner. Thus, though not specifically developed for digital systems, unlike the languages described in § 3.1, they can nevertheless be used for the modeling of computer systems (35). The internal structure of general-purpose simulators follow usual practice, and may be either event-driven, employing a list-structured data base, or interpretive systems using compiled code. Using a general-purpose simulation language it is possible to express the structure of a network, its behavior, and the required simulation conditions; moreover, timing controls, output formats, and diagnostics are generally built into the software. In general, general-purpose simulators are used to model the overall performance of computer systems; the major objectives of these simulation studies can be categorized into five different areas (36); these are as follows.

(a) The feasibility of performing a given workload on a certain class of computer.

(b) Comparison of computer systems (and the evaluation of software systems) against a specific "benchmark" to assist in procurement decisions.

(c) Determination of processing capability for various system configurations and operating conditions.

(d) Investigation of the effect of changes in the system structure etc. during the design process.

(e) Improvement of system performance by identifying and modifying the critical hardware/software component of a system—a process known as "tuning".

Note that the system is normally simulated at the behavioral user level rather than at the lower structural or functional levels. (It is possible, however, to simulate logic-gate networks using general-purpose simulators but the process is very time consuming and suffers an inherent loss of definition.) For example, it might be required to investigate the effects of changing hardware modules, software, or scheduling routines in a computer system. Typical of these investigations would be whether increasing the size of store buffers results in increasing message throughput, or the determination of the optimum size of a cache store. Note that in these cases only that part of the system under investigation needs to be accurately simulated; the remainder of the system, such as processor operation, disk storage, file layout, etc. can be less accurately defined. Care must be taken, however, to ensure that the manner of interaction with the other parts of the system are well defined. Note that general-purpose simulators provide a statistical model, their main purpose being to supplement, rather than replace, gate-level simulators by allowing the examination of *large* blocks of logic within the system.

The two most commonly used languages are SIMSCRIPT (4), which requires a good basic knowledge of FORTRAN and is an event-driven simulator, and GPSS (3), which is an interpretive language allowing the simulated model to be set up using a block-structured approach. The GPSS language defines as its basic components the following entities.

(a) *Transactions* which progress through the system model generating prescribed actions.

(b) *Facilities* which are operated upon by the transactions one at a time, and *storages* which can be operated upon simultaneously.

(c) *Blocks* which specify the rules for operating on the transitions.

(b) *Queues* for controlling progress through the system.

In use, a direct analogy must be made between these entities and the system to be modeled. The development of a GPSS model is performed from the point of view of a transaction (also known as a job) and its execution and progress through the system. Block types are used to specify the operations performed by the transactions, the job flow being implicit in the way the blocks are connected. Typical blocks are SEIZE and RELEASE facilities, and ENTER and LEAVE storage space; QUEUE and DEPART blocks are used to enter and remove transactions from queues. Control blocks are also available, such as GENERATE, ADVANCE, TERMINATE, TEST, LOOP, and TRANS-FER, which are used to establish and control the flow of transactions. The simulation model is described as a block diagram using the special block types to specify the required system transactions. The GPSS language also provides for the output of simulation statistics as a built-in facility, including the utilization of facilities, storage, and queues.

The SIMSCRIPT language resembles FORTRAN in format and general computation facilities. It deals with *entities* described by parameters called *attributes*, with *sets* of related entities, and with *events*. Entities may be permanent, existing for the duration of the simulation, or temporary, arriving and leaving during the course of the simulation run. In general, permanent entities would be system resources, such as CPU, storage, etc., while transactions or jobs would be temporary entities. Queues in the system are defined as sets, with the elements of a set ordered on a stack basis. A simulation program written in SIMSCRIPT would take the form of a set of event routines, analogous to a subroutine, beginning with an EVENT statement and terminated by an END statement; subsequent statements are concerned with the scheduling of events. The usual FORTRAN statements such as READ, WRITE, IF, DO, etc., all have their equivalent SIMSCRIPT forms.

A similar, but sometimes simpler, approach is to construct a set of special simulation routines which can be embedded in the FORTRAN language to provide a simulation language; one such language is GASP (37), which gives high computation speeds but is relatively unsophisticated.

There are many problems associated with the use of general-purpose simulators. From the users point of view it is necessary to learn the syntax and semantics of the language (particularly SIMSCRIPT) as well as under-standing the concept of the simulation procedures. Since the model is algorithmically based, without necessarily any exact correspondence to the actual system, the software processes must always be interpreted in terms of system behavior. Because of this the fidelity of the simulation cannot always be assumed correct (the results must be validated in some other way), since the simulation could be invalidated by inconsistencies or ambiguities in the simulation language or its interpretation. These arguments apply of course to any simulator, but the problems are far more apparent with a general-purpose simulator since a general process is being modeled.

Another problem area is concerned with exercising the model, which is not necessarily a straightforward process. The running of *ad hoc* experiments to test out particular functions of the system can be an unreliable and time-consuming process, and a systematic approach must be developed. Equally important is the consideration of boundary conditions, that is the interface between the detailed subsystem under study and the rest of the system, and the detail and accuracy required by the simulation.

At a more simple, but vital, level is the amount of resources required by the simulation. This must be considered both in terms of manpower (to produce the simulation model) and the CPU time required to execute the simulation study. It is important to establish the problem areas to be studied and then "tailor" the simulation accordingly; a too ambitious simulation can easily lead to over-investment of resources.

## 3.5. SUMMARY

The designer who wishes to use a simulator package is faced with a difficult choice of alternative languages. At the systems level there are several important factors to be considered. Among these are the ease of learning the language and describing the system model, the host computer, compilation and execution times, whether conversational or batch-processing mode, output facilities, storage requirements, general computing requirements, and tracing and debug facilities.

At the logic-gate level the situation is similar, and in this case the following additional factors must be taken into account.

(a)  Compiled-code or table-driven (event) simulator.
(b)  Time-shared terminal system or batch processing.
(c)  Synchronous or asynchronous mode of logic operation.
(d)  Whether all gates or only active paths are simulated.
(e)  Fault simulation, including parallel or deductive simulation of several faulty machines.
(f)  Two- or three-valued logic signals, including hazard detection.
(g)  Delay facilities.
(h)  Maximum number of gates that can be simulated.

(i) Hierarchical, block structured.

(j) Number of machine cycles that can be simulated in one second on the host computer.

A major consideration is that a digital logic simulator must be both accurate and cost effective in order to justify its adoption as a design tool.

The relative importance of all these factors depends ultimately on the problem to be solved and the size of simulation required, and a choice can only be made after careful consideration of all the parameters involved. For example, on average a parallel fault simulator uses less storage but more CPU time than a deductive simulator (38). Thus, if storage requirements are an overriding factor and CPU time is unimportant the parallel fault simulation approach is more efficient. However, when sufficient storage is available it is more effective to use the deductive technique.

Simulation has become an essential computer aid for the design and testing of digital systems, both at the gate and system level. However, there are still many problems to be solved. A particular difficulty exists with complex LSI circuits (postulated to have logic-gate densities of some 3000 gates per chip) where even now the available logic simulators are woefully inadequate (39). In this case it is essential to have powerful multi-level and logic-level simulators (including timing analysis) and for fault-test generation to be integrated into the design process. Moreover, a "top-down" approach to LSI design must be adopted (40) using a high-level behavioral simulator, which enables the system to be partitioned along the physical boundaries of the real system as well as a lower gate-level analysis.

Many of these problems are associated with the lack of formal specification and design methods. The simulation results can only be as good as the model itself, and it seems inevitable that some constraints (or approximations) must be made in establishing a viable model of the system. This fact, coupled with the inevitable and inherent loss of definition at the higher levels (which may well be a fundamental computational constraint, analogous to the "combinational explosion" encountered in artificial intelligence) has lead to a natural suspicion of simulation results. Nevertheless, if allowances are made for the limitations of the simulated model, and the results carefully validated against the real environment, the technique can provide an extremely powerful design tool.

## REFERENCES AND BIBLIOGRAPHY

1. MacDougall, H. H. Computer system simulation: an introduction. *Computer Surv.* **2**, 191–210, 1970.
2. Lake, D. W. Logic simulation in digital systems. *Computer Des.* **9**, 77–83, 1970.

3. Efron, R., and Gordon, G. General purpose digital simulation and examples of its applications. *IBM Systems J.* 3, 22–34, 1964.

4. Markowitz, H. M., Hausner, B., and Kerr, H. N. *Simscript–A Simulation Programming Language.* Prentice Hall, Englewood Cliffs, N. J., 1963.

5. Hays, G. G. Computer aided design–Simulation of digital design logic. *IEEE Trans. Computers* C18, 1–10, 1969.

6. Kahn, H. J., and May, J. W. R. Logic simulation in the design of a large computer system. *Radio Electron. Eng.* 43, 497–503, 1973.

7. Reynolds, J. S. A conversational logic simulator for use with a time sharing computer. *IEE Conference on CAD*, pp. 608–615. IEE Publ. No. 51, 1969.

8. Pai, D., and Lewin, D. Analysis of sequential logic circuits. *Computer J.* 17, 64–68, 1974.

9. McClure, R. M. A programming language for simulating digital systems. *J. ACM* 12, 14–22, 1965.

10. Shalla, L. Automatic analysis of electronic digital circuits using list processing. *Comm. ACM* 9, 372–380, 1966.

11. Arden, B. W., Geller, B. A., and Graham, R. M. An algorithm for translating Boolean expressions. *J. ACM* 9, 222–240, 1962.

12. Boyce, A. H. Marconi Company Ltd., Research Division, Great Baddow, Essex. Private communication.

13. Kirkpatrick, T. I., and Clark, N. R. PERT as an aid to logic design. *IBM J. Res. Dev.* 10, 135–141, 1966.

14. Flake, P. L., Musgrave, G., and White, I. J. A digital system simulator– HILO. *Digital Processes* 1, 39–53, 1975.

15. *Digital Systems Simulation–LOGICS.* GE Information System Users Guide, March 1970.

16. Breuer, M. A. Technique for the simulation of computer logic. *Comm. ACM* 7, 443–446, 1964.

17. Ulrich, E. G. Time sequenced logical simulation based on circuit delay of active network paths. *Proceedings of ACM 20th National Conference 1965*, pp. 437–448.

18. Kaposi, A. A. Logic testing by simulation. *IEE Conference on CAD*, pp. 31–40. IEE Publ. No. 51, 1969.

19. Duke, K. A., Schnurman, H. D., and Wilson, T. I. System validation by three level modelling synthesis. *IBM J. Res. Dev.* 15, 166–174, 1971.

20. Yoell, M., and Rinon, S. Application of ternary algebra to the study of state hazards. *J. ACM* 11, 84–97, 1964.

21. Eichelberger, B. Hazard detection in combinational and sequential switching circuits. *IBM J. Res. Dev.* 9, 90–99, 1965.

22. Jephson, J. S., McQuarrie, R. P., and Vogelsberg, R. E. Three-value computer design verification system. *IBM Systems J.* 8, 178–188, 1969.

23. Breuer, M. A. Functional partitioning and simulation of digital circuits *IEEE Trans. Computers* C19, 1038–1046, 1970.

24. Szygenda, S. A., and Thompson, E. W. Fault injection techniques and models for logical simulation. *AFIPS FJCC* 41, 875–884, 1972.

25. Seshu, S., and Freeman, D. N. The diagnosis of asynchronous sequential switching systems. *IRE Trans. Electron. Computers* **EC11**, 459–465, 1962.
26. Hardie, F. H., and Suhocki, R. J. Design and use of fault simulators for Saturn computer design. *IEEE Trans. Computers* **EC16**, 412–429, 1967.
27. Armstrong, B. A deductive method for simulating faults in logic circuits. *IEEE Trans. Computers* **C21**, 464–471, 1972.
28. Ulrich, E. G., and Baker, R. Concurrent simulation of nearly identical digital networks. *IEEE Computer* **7**, 39–44, 1974.
29. Roth, J. P., Bouricius, W. G., and Schneider, P. R. Programmed algorithms to compute tests to detect and distinguish between failures in logic circuits. *IEEE Trans. Computers* **EC16**, 567–580, 1967.
30. Baray, M. B., and Su, S. Y. H. A digital system modelling philosophy and design language. *Proceedings of 8th Annual Design Automation Workshop, Atlantic City, N. J., June 1971*, pp. 1–22.
31. Baray, M. B., Su, S. Y. H., and Carberry, R. L. The structure and operation of a design language compatible simulator. *Proceedings of 8th Annual Design Automation Workshop, Atlantic City, N. J., June 1971*, pp. 22–34.
32. Su, S. Y. H., Baray, M. B., and Carberry, R. L. A system modelling language translator. *Proceedings of 8th Annual Design Automation Workshop, Atlantic City, N. J., June 1971*, pp. 35–49.
33. Gordan, G. *System Simulation*. Prentice Hall, Englewood Cliffs, N. J., 1969.
34. Naylor, T. H., Balinty, J. L., Burdick, D. S., and Chu, K. *Computer Simulation Techniques*. John Wiley, New York, 1966.
35. Huesman, R. L., and Goldberg, R. P. Evaluating computer systems through simulation. *Computer J.* **10**, 150–156, 1967.
36. Bell, T. E. Objectives and problems in simulating computers. *AFIPS FJCC* **41**, 287–297, 1972.
37. Kiviat, P. J. *GASP–A General Activity Simulation Program*. Project No. 90.17-019(2), Appl. Res. Labs. U.S. Steel, Monroeville, Pa., 1963.
38. Chang, H. Y. P., Chappell, S. G., Elmendorf, C. H., and Schmidt, L. D. Comparison of parallel and deductive fault simulation methods *IEEE Trans. Computers* **C23**, 1132–1138, 1974.
39. Teets, J. J. The role of simulation in LSI design. *AFIPS SJCC* **40**, 1065–1070, 1972.
40. Caplener, H. D., and Janku, J. A. Top down approach to LSI system design. *Computer Des.* **13**(8), 143–148, 1974.
41. Szygenda, S. A., and Thompson, E. W. Digital logic simulation in a time-based, table driven environment. Part 1. Design verification. *IEEE Computer* **8**(3), 24–36, 1975.
42. Thompson, E. W., and Szygenda, S. A. Logic simulation in a time-based, table driven environment. Part 2. Parallel fault simulation. *IEEE Computer* **8**(3), 38–49, 1975.

# Logic-Network Synthesis

## 4.1. INTRODUCTION

In this chapter the techniques and algorithms developed for the computer-aided synthesis of logic circuits will be discussed. The main objective of this work is the hardware realization of logic networks specified either formally using Boolean equations or tabular methods (such as truth and state tables) or as register-transfer language statements.

Much of the earlier work relied heavily on classical switching theory and was concerned primarily with the minimization of combinational circuits based on Quine-McClusky (1) or decomposition methods (2, 3). Unfortunately, though the literature contains many examples of algorithms for the synthesis of logic circuits, few of them are really suitable for the design of large systems (in the order of 20 primary switching variables) owing to the vast amounts of computation involved. The fundamental difficulty is the rapid build-up of derived data (and hence computational requirements) as the number of input variables is increased. Moreover, in many cases the number of intermediate products that are generated, for example multiple-output prime-implicant terms, is often excessively large. It is also essential to effect some form of data reduction on the input variables (for example, in the simplest case, the use of non-canonical terms to describe a switching function), since it is generally impracticable to store all possible input combinations for a very large problem.

As a consequence of these problems heuristic procedures must generally be employed to obtain a vaible solution in terms of time and cost. The use of these techniques inherently implies a non-optimal solution and in some cases the sacrifice of certain design criteria, such as the optimal sharing of output functions in a multi-output circuit [called "satisficing" the requirements (4)]. In many cases, however, the circuits generated using heuristic techniques are equal to, if not better than, those obtained by an experienced logic designer.

There are numerous advantages to be gained from using computer-assisted logic design. As well as the general advantages outlined in § 1.1 there are also a number of more specific benefits, of which the following are examples.

(a) The use of automated synthesis reduces the need for simulation in test generation. In fact the only way to solve the testing problem may well be to design circuits that can be tested, that is by imposing design constraints on the engineer.

(b) Engineers with little or no experience of logic design can produce viable circuits in a minimum of time; this is particularly useful for engineers in other disciplines who are not professional logic designers.

(c) The creative ability of the designer increases as he continually learns through man–machine interaction. (The computer-design algorithm eliminates the computational effort, not the creative ability.)

(d) Research on switching theory and logic design can be accelerated, since new ideas and methods may be quickly and reliably evaluated on an empirical basis.

However, to take full advantage of such a scheme a methodology must be developed to specify complex digital subsystems, which, as we have seen in Chapter 2, still remains a difficult problem. In fact, though a great deal of research has been carried out in the synthesis field, very few, if any, design systems are currently in use. There are many CAD schemes in existence for printed-circuit-board layout, placement, interconnections, fault simulation, etc., but in the main the logic-design process is still performed manually. It is essential to automate this aspect of digital systems design if the objectives of an overall design-automation scheme are to be achieved.

Another difficulty that exists is the lack of a suitable design theory at the subsystems level. At the present time technology has advanced to such an extent that the value of minimization and implementation in terms of basic NOR/NAND gates is rather dubious (5). With modern LSI, MOS, and IC technologies the cost of a single gate, transistor, or diode is insignificant. Moreover, with the increasing use of complex modules such as ROM's, programmable logic arrays (PLA), arithmetic and logic units, shift registers, etc., logic design with basic gates is becoming rather academic. Unfortunately, theory has not kept pace with practice, and we have now reached a stage where the lack of a suitable formal design theory at the subsystems level is becoming a severe handicap.

Nevertheless in some cases a minimal solution is still relevant. For example, in LSI manufacture circuit area and the interconnection between gates and modules are important parameters. The number of interconnections determines to a large extent the final size of the module (most chips are pin limited), while decreasing circuit area enhances the production yield (by reducing the number of processing steps). In both cases minimization of the logic circuits can result in worthwhile savings. Similarly, the programmable logic array, and some versions of the ROM, will utilize multiple-output, minimal sums of products expressions directly to effect a realization which economizes on the number of words required in the memory.

Notwithstanding these criticisms there is still a considerable advantage to be gained in studying the existing techniques of logic-circuit design, and in particular their computer realizations. Switching theory as we know it must inevitably form the basis of any new technique for the interconnection of subsystem components, and consequently a knowledge of these techniques must be an essential prerequisite to future theory. In fact it is conceivable that many of the established concepts are fundamental and the ideas will apply at all system levels. For example, the basic covering problem (the selection of a irredundant set of terms which cover or contain a specified function) appears in many different areas of switching theory such as logic minimization, fault-test generation, state reduction, etc. Again, the concept of functional decomposition may well apply to the implementation of logic using ROM's (6). Moreover, there is still a definite requirement for the established techniques, especially in areas other than computer engineering. For instance, the ASM design approach, mentioned in § 2.7, relies on conventional switching theory to translate the control flow charts into a hardware implementation.

In the following sections of this chapter we shall briefly outline the basic theoretical concepts of the subject and then carry on to describe in detail some of the techniques which have emerged for the design and implementation of combinational and sequential circuits.

## 4.2. SYNTHESIS OF COMBINATIONAL LOGIC

Most algorithmic methods employ the normal forms (that is, sum of products or product of sums) to represent Boolean switching functions; however, in many cases a topological representation due to Roth (7) is to be preferred. The *cubic notation* is based on the methods used to specify error-correcting codes in which points in *n*-dimensional space are used to represent the possible binary codes, or *n-tuples*, and the *distance* between them. The K-map can be considered as an attempt to project this *n*-dimensional space onto a two-dimensional map, which is usually only effective for up to five or six variables. An *n*-tuple is an ordered sequence of *n* binary digits; for example, the binary sequence 0111 can be thought of as a 4-tuple. The distance between *n*-tuples is the number of variables that must change value in going from one *n*-tuple to another, that is the *Hamming distance.*

Using the cubic notation a Boolean function in three variables $(a, b, c)$, for instance, may be represented as a three-dimensional unit cube, as shown in Fig. 4.1*a*. Note that each canonical product term (minterm) of the function is associated with a unique point (or *vertex*) of the 3-cube. Moreover, since each vertex is distance-one apart (that is, they are adjacent and differ in one variable only), it is possible to represent non-canonical product terms by *planes* and *edges* of the cube, as shown in Figs. 4.1*b, c, d,* and *e*. Thus the 3-cube may be considered as comprising eight vertices (0-cubes) six planes (2-cubes), and twelve edges (1-cubes). The expression *n*-cube is used to describe the number of literals in a product term; for example, a product term of $n-1$ literals, where *n* is the number of variables, is represented by an edge or line segment, that is a one-dimensional cube or 1-cube. Thus, in this case for example, we have the 1-cubes $10X$, $1X0$, $X00$ and the 2-cubes $0XX$, $X1X$, $1XX$; the order of the cube is determined by the number of $X$'s, i.e. missing literals.

Consider the Boolean function

$$Z = ab\bar{c} + \bar{a}bc + abc + \bar{a}b\bar{c} \tag{4.1}$$

which may be represented in the cubic notation as shown in Fig. 4.1*f*. Note that only the vertices corresponding to the product terms are indicated (by dots) in the diagram. The set of 3-tuples is referred to as the *ON array*, that is the set of product terms which gives $Z = 1$. The set of vertices not picked out correspond to $Z = 0$ and is called the *OFF array*. Together the ON and OFF arrays give the same information as a truth table, "don't-care" terms (the *DC array*) being obtained by default. Thus, we may formally specify the function in equation (4.1) as

$$\text{ON-array} \quad \overset{abc}{\left\{ \begin{matrix} 000 \\ 011 \\ 110 \\ 111 \end{matrix} \right\}} \qquad \text{OFF-array} \quad \overset{abc}{\left\{ \begin{matrix} 001 \\ 010 \\ 100 \\ 101 \end{matrix} \right\}}.$$

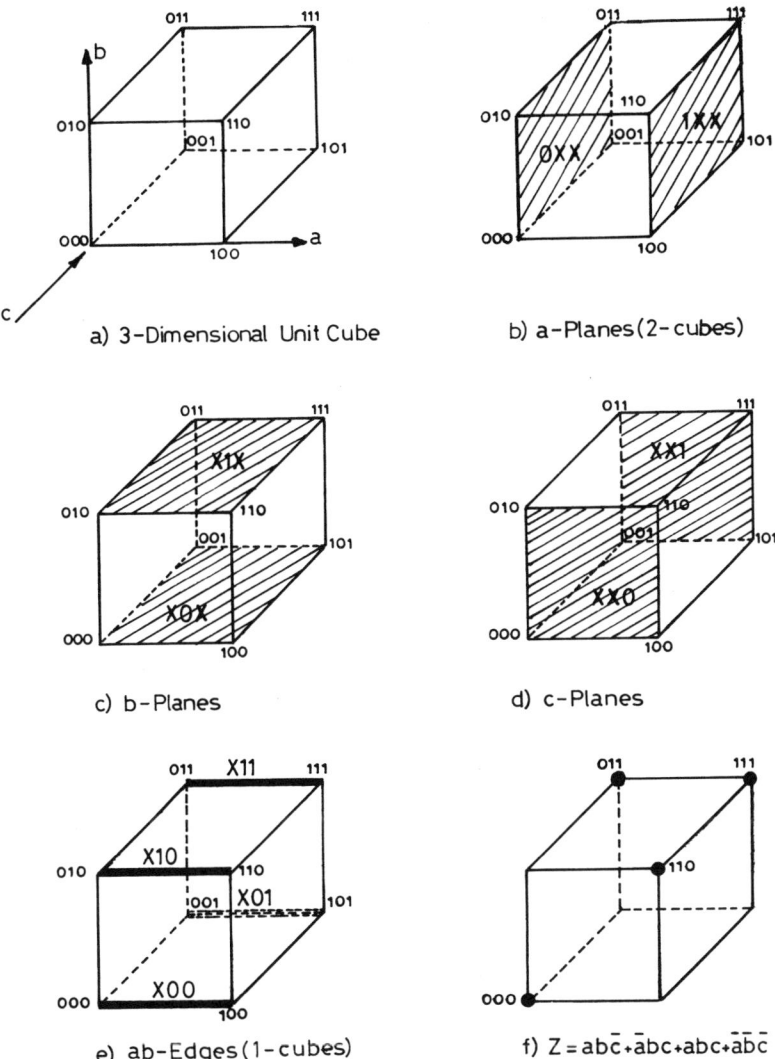

**Figure 4.1.** Cubic notation for Boolean functions

Using the cubic notation it is possible to specify and manipulate switching functions expressed as arrays of $n$-tuples and a complete algebra may be established (8) with defined operations on arrays of cubes.

### 4.2.1. Generation of Prime Implicants

Standard minimization algorithms, such as the Quine–McClusky procedure, can be restated and processed using the cubic notation. This technique, however, suffers from the drawback that the minterm (0-cube) form of the Boolean function must be used as the initial starting point, iteratively generating the 1-cubes, 2-cubes, etc. (to extract the prime implicants) until no further reduction is possible. For large switching circuits this can be a severe disadvantage, since on average some $2^{n-1}$ minterms are required for an $n$-variable system.

Alternative minimization techniques have been described which do not require the use of minterm equations. These algorithms are based on array operations such as the *sharp* and *star* (concensus) functions. The sharp product (denoted by #) is a cubical method of extracting the prime implicants of a function; it is based on De Morgan's theory and can be thought of as a subtraction process. For example, let us consider the function

$$Z = \bar{a}b + bc. \tag{4.2}$$

Complementing and expanding we obtain

$$\bar{Z} = \overline{\bar{a}b + bc} = (a + \bar{b})(\bar{b} + \bar{c}).$$

Therefore

$$\bar{Z} = a\bar{c} + \bar{b}.$$

Note that each expression is a prime implicant of $\bar{Z}$ and there are no others; this is shown in Table 4.1$a$ using K-maps. In effect we have "subtracted" the function $Z$ from the unit cube and obtained the prime implicants of the residual function.

The sharp product $a \# b$, where $a$ and $b$ are two sets, is defined as containing all elements of $a$ not in $b$. The sharp product between two arrays of cubes $A$ and $B$ is the set of cubes such that $P(A \# B)$ is the set of all prime implicants of the function defined by $P(A)\overline{P(B)}$. Thus, $A \# B$ is the set of the largest cubes containing those 0-cubes (minterms) in $A$ but not in $B$.

It is also possible to define the sharp product algebraically by means of a co-ordinate table, as shown in Table 4.2, and the following rules:

$$a \# b = a \quad \text{if} \quad a_i \# b_i = \phi \quad \text{for any } i$$

$$a \# b = \psi \quad \text{if} \quad a_i \# b_i = Z \quad \text{for all } i$$

$$a \# b = U_i(a_1, a_2, \ldots, \alpha_i, \ldots, a_n) \quad \text{for all } i \text{ for which}$$

$$\qquad a_i \# b_i = \alpha_i \in \{0,1\}.$$

## Table 4.1. Sharp Product on $K$-Maps

(a) $\bar{Z} = a\bar{c} + \bar{b}$

(b) $(01X) \# (X11) = (010)$

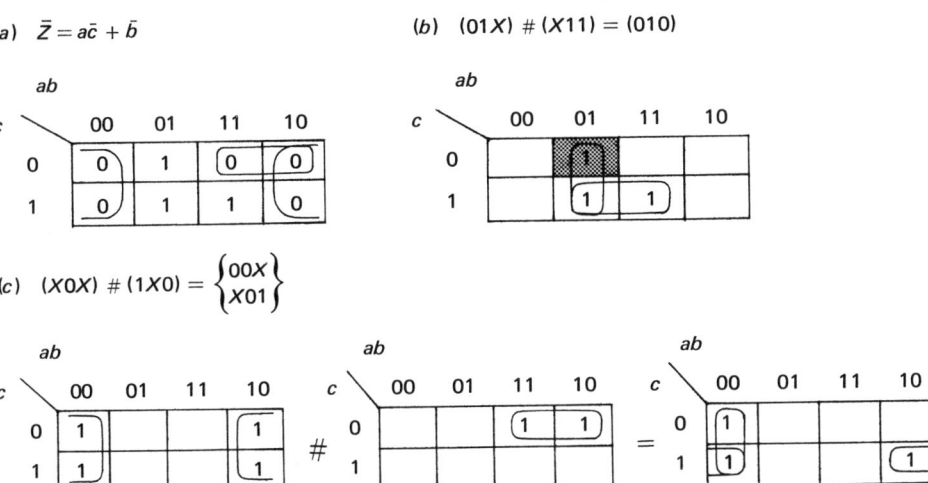

(c) $(X0X) \# (1X0) = \begin{Bmatrix} 00X \\ X01 \end{Bmatrix}$

(Note that $\psi$ is the null cube and $\phi$ the empty set; the entire $n$-dimensional unit cube being denoted by $U_n = xxx \ldots x$.) For example, to compute the sharp product of the cubes $01X$ and $X11$ the cubes are combined according to the co-ordinate table; thus

$$123$$

$$a \quad 01X$$

$$\#b \quad \underline{X11} \qquad (01X) \# (X11) = 010.$$

$$\underline{ZZ0}$$

Note that no cubes can be formed for the $Z$ terms and the only cube obtainable is $a_1 a_2 0 = 010$; this is shown on the K-map in Table 4.1$b$ where it is clear that the cube 010 is the only element in $a$ which is not

## Table 4.2. Coordinate Sharp Product

|  |  | $b_i$ |  |  |
|---|---|---|---|---|
| $a_i \# b_i$ |  | 0 | 1 | $X$ |
| | 0 | $Z$ | $\phi$ | $Z$ |
| $a_i$ | 1 | $\phi$ | $Z$ | $Z$ |
| | $X$ | 1 | 0 | $Z$ |

contained in $b$. Again, consider the sharp product of the cubes $X0X$ and $1X0$; we have

$$\begin{array}{c} X0X \\ \# \underline{1X0} \\ 0Z1 \end{array} \qquad (X0X) \, \# \, (1X0) = \left\{ \begin{array}{c} 00X \\ X01 \end{array} \right\}$$

which is given by $0a_2 a_3 = 00X$ and $a_1 a_2 1 = X01$ as shown in Table 4.1$c$.

When sharping a cubical array $A$ by a cube $b$, that is $A \, \# \, b$, the product is given by

$$A \, \# \, b = [(a_1 \, \# \, b) \sqcup (a_2 \, \# \, b) \sqcup \ldots]$$

where the operator $\sqcup$ is called the *cube-union* and is the *cover* of the union of the individual cubes. A cube $b$ is said to cover another cube $a$ if it has a 0 (or 1) in all co-ordinate positions in which $a$ has a 0 (or 1); those positions of $b$ corresponding to positions in which $a_i = X$ may be filled with either value. In this way the absorption theory of Boolean algebra is employed to remove redundant cubes of smaller dimension. The sharp product of $a \, \# \, B$ is given by

$$a \, \# \, B = [(a \, \# \, b_1) \, \# \, b_2] \, \# \, b_3 \ldots$$

When the sharp product of two arrays is required either procedure may be used. We have seen that Boolean functions may be alternatively specified in terms of ON, OFF, and DC arrays of input $n$-tuples for which the function $Z = 1$, 0, and $X$ (don't-care) respectively. Only two of these three arrays, however, are required, since the third one can always be computed using the sharp function. Now since

$$U_n = \text{ON} \sqcup \text{OFF} \sqcup \text{DC}$$

it follows that

$$\text{ON} = U_n \, \# \, (\text{OFF} \sqcup \text{DC})$$
$$\text{OFF} = U_n \, \# \, (\text{ON} \sqcup \text{DC})$$

and

$$\text{DC} = U_n \, \# \, (\text{ON} \sqcup \text{OFF}).$$

Thus, given any two of the three arrays it is always possible to compute the third array.

Let us illustrate these ideas by considering the function $Z = \bar{a}b + bc$; the ON array is given by

$$ON = \begin{Bmatrix} 01X \\ X11 \end{Bmatrix}$$

and there are no don't-care conditions. Now the OFF array may be obtained by performing the sharp function between $U_n$, the $n$-dimensional unit cube, that is $XXX$, and the ON array; thus

$$OFF = U_n \,\#\, ON = XXX \,\#\, \begin{Bmatrix} 01X \\ X11 \end{Bmatrix}$$

$$= (XXX \,\#\, 01X) \,\#\, X11 = \begin{Bmatrix} 1XX \\ X0X \end{Bmatrix} \,\#\, X11$$

$$= (1XX \,\#\, X11) \sqcup (X0X \,\#\, X11)$$

$$= \begin{Bmatrix} 10X \\ 1X0 \end{Bmatrix} \,\#\, X0X = \begin{Bmatrix} X0X \\ 1X0 \end{Bmatrix}$$

which is the OFF array as established earlier (see Table 4.1$a$) and is equivalent to $\bar{Z} = a\bar{c} + \bar{b}$; note that these terms are the prime implicants of the function $\bar{Z}$. It can be shown (3) that the set of all prime implicants of a function $Z$ are given by

$$PI(Z) = U_n \,\#\, (U_n \,\#\, ON)$$

or when don't-cares are present

$$PI(Z) = U_n \,\#\, (U_n \,\#\, (ON \sqcup DC)).$$

Note that canonical terms are not required. In practice the function would be described in terms of its OFF array and DC array, and the prime implicants computed using the expression

$$PI(Z) = U_n \,\#\, OFF.$$

The sharp product generates the complete set of prime implicants, but does not in general give a minimum cover of the function. Continuing with our example the prime implicants of $Z = \bar{a}b + bc$ would be computed as follows:

$$PI(Z) = U_n \, \# \, \text{OFF} = XXX \, \# \, \begin{Bmatrix} X0X \\ 1X0 \end{Bmatrix}$$

$$= (XXX \, \# \, X0X) \, \# \, 1X0$$

$$= (X1X \, \# \, 1X0) = \begin{Bmatrix} 01X \\ X11 \end{Bmatrix}$$

which is equivalent to $Z = \bar{a}b + bc$, the prime implicants of the original function.

Another procedure which forms the basis for finding prime implicants is the *concensus* method first described by Quine (1). The concensus operation may be stated as follows: the concensus of two product terms $A$ and $B$ is the largest product $P$ such that $P$ does not imply either $A$ or $B$, but $P$ implies $A + B$. Thus, implicant $a$ is the concensus of implicants $ab$ and $a\bar{b}$, and, more generally, $ac$ is the concensus of $ab$ and $\bar{b}c$; this is shown in Table 4.3a.

For cubes the equivalent operation is the *star (*) product* [first described by Roth (7)] defined by the co-ordinate table shown in Table 4.4 and the following rules:

$$a * b = \phi \quad \text{if} \quad a_i * b_i = \phi \quad \text{for more than one } i$$

$$a * b = c \quad \text{where} \quad c_i = a_i * b_i \neq \phi \quad \text{and} \quad c_i = X$$

$$\text{when} \quad a_i * b_i = \phi.$$

For example, the concensus of $XX01$ and $011X$ is given by

$$\begin{array}{ll} a & XX01 \\ * \, b & \underline{011X} \\ & 01\phi1 \end{array} \quad XX01 * 011X = 01X1$$

**Table 4.3. The Concensus Operation**

(a) Concensus of $ab$ and $a\bar{b}$

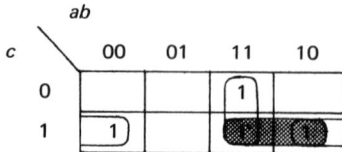

(b) Concensus of $\bar{c}d$ and $\bar{a}bc$

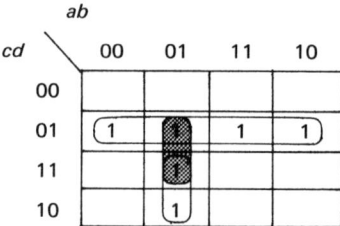

**Table 4.4. The Star Product**

| $a_i * b_i$ | | $b_i$ | |
|---|---|---|---|
| | 0 | 1 | $X$ |
| $a_i$    0 | 0 | $\phi$ | 0 |
| $a_i$    1 | $\phi$ | 1 | 1 |
| $a_i$    $X$ | 0 | 1 | $X$ |

which is equivalent to $\bar{a}bd$ as shown in Table 4.3$b$. The star product does not generate prime implicants by itself, but by combining the product with the absorption operation an algorithm can be developed which gives all prime implicants. This procedure is called *iterative concensus* and consists of the successive addition of derived concensus terms to a sum-of-products expression (which may or may not be canonical) and the removal of terms which are included in other terms, using the relationship $x + xy = x$; the iteration of this procedure will result in the set of all prime implicants. The algorithm may be stated as follows.

Form the star product of all cubes $c_i$ and $c_j$ of the given cover $C$ (expressed as ON and DC arrays); if $c_i * c_j \neq \phi$ replace $C$ with $C \sqcup (c_i * c_j)$ and repeat. Continue until no more concensus terms can be formed or they are found redundant when the absorbed union is formed. For example, consider the function

$$Z = ab + bc + \bar{a}b\bar{c}.$$

The ON array is given by

$$ON = \begin{Bmatrix} 11X \\ X11 \\ 010 \end{Bmatrix}.$$

then comparing $11X$ with all other cubes we obtain

$$11X * X11 = 111 \subseteq 11X$$

$$11X * 010 = \phi10 = X10 \supseteq 010 \text{ delete } 010 \text{ add } X10.$$

The list is now modified to

$$ON = \begin{Bmatrix} 11X \\ X11 \\ X10 \end{Bmatrix}$$

Continuing we have

$$X11 * X10 = X1\phi = X1X \supseteq 11X$$
$$\supseteq X11$$
$$\supseteq X10$$

therefore

$$PI = X1X = b.$$

Though the method is more efficient than the Quine–McClusky algorithm it still requires an excessive amount of computation, since cubes must be examined for non-trivial star products and the products then compared to find those which can be subsumed; in many cases this will involve comparing each cube with every other cube.

The concept of concensus has been generalized by Tilson (8), who has evolved an efficient algorithm for generating prime implicants based on the close relationship between the operations of star and intersection. The *Intersection* ($\cap$) operation between two $n$-tuples is defined by the same co-ordinate table as that given for the star operation, but the results are interpreted using slightly different rules; these are

$$a \cap b = \phi \quad \text{if } any \quad a_i \cap b_i = \phi$$

otherwise

$$a \cap b = c \quad \text{where} \quad c_i = a_i \cap b_i.$$

Now consider the two cubes

$$a = a_1 a_2 \ldots a_n$$
$$b = b_1 b_2 \ldots b_n.$$

If $a_1 = 1$ and $b_1 = 0$, or vice versa, then it can be shown that the star product is given by

$$a * b = X \square [(a_2 \ldots a_n) \cap (b_2 \ldots b_n)]$$

where $\square$ is the *concatenation* operator. For example

$$a_i = 0101 \quad b_i = 11XX \quad \text{and} \quad 101 \cap 1XX = 101$$

then

$$a_i * b_i = X \,\square\, 101 = X101.$$

Note that

$$0 * 1 \quad \text{or} \quad 1 * 0 = \phi.$$

The operation can be generalized to handle concensus between two arrays by partitioning the original cover array into three subarrays obtained by collecting together all those cubes which contain a 1, 0, or $X$ in the first column; thus

$$C = \begin{Bmatrix} 000 \\ 011 \\ 110 \\ 111 \\ X01 \\ X11 \end{Bmatrix} \quad C_0 = \begin{Bmatrix} 000 \\ 011 \end{Bmatrix} \quad C_1 = \begin{Bmatrix} 110 \\ 111 \end{Bmatrix} \quad C_X = \begin{Bmatrix} X01 \\ X11 \end{Bmatrix}.$$

Two new arrays, $D_0$ and $D_1$, may be formed from $C_0$ and $C_1$ by deleting column 1 giving

$$D_0 = \begin{Bmatrix} 00 \\ 11 \end{Bmatrix}, \quad D_1 = \begin{Bmatrix} 10 \\ 11 \end{Bmatrix}.$$

Now

$$\begin{Bmatrix} 00 \\ 11 \end{Bmatrix} \cap \begin{Bmatrix} 10 \\ 11 \end{Bmatrix} = \left[ \begin{Bmatrix} 00 \\ 11 \end{Bmatrix} \cap 10 \right] \cup \left[ \begin{Bmatrix} 00 \\ 11 \end{Bmatrix} \cap 11 \right]$$

$$= [(00 \cap 10) \cup (11 \cap 10)] \cup [(00 \cap 11) \cup (11 \cap 11)]$$

$$= 11.$$

Therefore $G_1 = X11$ is the generalized concensus with respect to column 1; in a similar manner $G_2, G_3, \ldots, G_n$ may be obtained for the other columns. The generalized concensus for the cover array is then given by $G_c = G_1 \cup G_2 \cup G_3 \ldots \cup G_n$. The prime implicant array is obtained by adding $G_c$ to $C$ and deleting redundant terms, that is $\text{PI} = C \cup G_c$.

Thus the algorithm calls for the computation of the generalized concensus with respect to each column in turn and the formation of the subsumed union of each generalized concensus with the original array. Though the method is very similar to iterative concensus, the column-by-column operations eliminate a large number of repetitious cube comparisons.

### 4.2.2. The Covering Problem

The final step in the minimization of Boolean functions is to find a minimal *cover* of the original switching terms; note that there can be many different covers for the same function. The concept of a cover is derived from set theory; thus if $A_1, A_2, \ldots, A_n, S$ are subsets of the same universe, and

$$S \subseteq \bigcup_{i=1}^{n} A_i$$

then,

$$A = \{A_1, A_2, \ldots, A_n\}$$

is said to cover the set $S$, and is expressed as

$$S \sqsubseteq A.$$

Any cube $a$ can be decomposed to a sum of minterms (set of 0-cubes) called its *base* $K^0(a)$; cube $a$ then covers the individual members of its base. Thus, an $n$-cube is said to cover $2^n$ 0-cubes, that is all those 0-cubes which can be obtained by replacing $X$'s by 0's and 1's in the original $n$-cube. For example, the 2-cube $0XX$ covers the set of cubes $\{000,001,010,011\}$. The cover relationship may be alternatively stated as follows: cube $a$ covers cube $b$ if the position of all 0's and 1's in the two $n$-tuples correspond; where $X$'s appear in the $a$ $n$-tuple any entry may occur in the $b$ $n$-tuple. Conversely, cube $b$ is said to *subsume* (or include) cube $a$ if, and only if, all the other 0-cubes covered by $b$ are also covered by $a$. Thus, cube $0X1$ subsumes $XX1$ since the 0-cubes $\{001,011\}$ are contained in the set $\{001,011,101,111\}$. Note that cube $a$ covers cube $b$.

   When minimizing combinational circuits it is necessary to have a criterion for minimality. In general the criteria used are based on some form of cost function related to such parameters as the number of inputs (pin connections), interconnections, gates, etc. The simplest procedure is to assign a cost factor to each PI cube; thus the problem is to find a minimal cost cover, comprising a set of prime implicants, for a given switching function. A cover $C$ of a switching function $Z$ is said to be *minimal* or *irredundant* if each cube in $C$ is a prime implicant of $Z$ and no cube subsumes the logical sum of two or more cubes. Moreover, it is necessary to include in any minimal cover all the essential prime implicants (*extremals*) of the function $Z$. A prime implicant is an essential prime implicant of $Z$ if it contains at least one 0-cube of the ON-array which cannot be covered by any other prime implicants.

The usual method of determining essential prime implicants is by constructing a prime-implicant chart, using the PI terms and 0-cubes as co-ordinates, and then extracting the PI terms corresponding to rows containing a single entry. However, it would be pointless to expand the ON-array into its $K^0(Z)$ base when the essence of the methods used to extract PI($Z$) has been the use of non-canonical terms. An alternative method, which operates directly on the PI array, is as follows: let

$$PI = \{P_1, P_2, P_3, \ldots, P_n\}$$

be the set of cubes of PI's and also let $(PI - p_i)$ denote the PI array less cube $p_i$. Now define $A = p_i \# (PI - p_i)$ for $DC = 0$, where cube $p_i$ covers some members of $K^0(Z)$ and $(PI - p_i)$ the rest. Now if $A = \phi$ then all the 0-cubes covered by $p_i$ are also covered by other prime implicants and $p_i$ is not an essential prime implicant; if $A \neq \phi$ then $p_i$ is an essential PI. If the original function contained don't-cares then the 0-cubes covered by $p_i$ may be don't-care terms; this possibility may be eliminated by computing the expression

$$A = (p_i \# (PI - p_i)) \# DC.$$

As an example, consider the PI array:

$$PI = \begin{Bmatrix} XX11 \\ X11X \\ X1X1 \\ 1XX1 \end{Bmatrix}$$

then

$$XX11 \ \# \begin{Bmatrix} X11X \\ X1X1 \\ 1XX1 \end{Bmatrix} = 0011$$

thus $XX11$ is an essential PI. Again,

$$X11X \ \# \begin{Bmatrix} XX11 \\ X1X1 \\ 1XX1 \end{Bmatrix} = \phi$$

therefore $X11X$ is not essential. Thus, by testing each member of the PI array in turn it is a simple matter to find all the essential prime implicants.

In order to generate a minimal cover, however, it is necessary to incorporate the extraction procedure into a computer algorithm. A simple and rapid algorithm for generating a near-minimal irredundant cover may be obtained by simply disregarding the non-essential prime implicants as follows.

(1) Compute the prime-implicant terms, using the generalized concensus method, and form a PI array.

(2) For each $p_i$, $i = 1, 2, \ldots, n$, in the PI array

    (a)  replace PI by $(\text{PI} - p_i)$
    (b)  compute $A = p_i \,\#\, \text{PI}$
    (c)  if $A = \phi$ disregard $p_i$ and increment $i$
            if $A \neq \phi$ compute $B = A \,\#\, \text{DC}$
            if $B = \phi$ disregard $p_i$ and increment $i$
            if $B \neq \phi$ replace $M_c$ by $M_c \cup p_i$, replace DC by $\text{DC} \cup p_i$ and increment $i$.

Note that in order to facilitate the computation an array $M_c$ is allocated in which the members of a minimal cover are assembled. Note also that if the test for essential prime implicants gives $A \neq \phi$ (or $B \neq \phi$ in the case of don't-care terms), indicating that $p_i$ is an extremal, $p_i$ is placed in the $M_c$ array. Furthermore, since an essential prime implicant covers some members of the ON array it no longer needs to be considered in the computation, and hence these PI cubes can be treated as don't-care terms and included in the DC array. If $p_i$ is not an essential prime implicant $(A = \phi)$ it is returned to the PI array. An important point to note is that the order of cubes in the PI array affects the results. The procedure will give the minimal cover if the PI's are in the correct order; unfortunately this order cannot be predicted.

There are two general procedures for generating a minimal cost cover: one is an *extraction technique* (9, 10) and the other is a *matrix technique* (11). Both methods use the concepts of essential prime implicants and row and column dominance; linear-programming (12) or branch-and-bound (13) methods are employed to generate the optimal solution. *Dominance* is usually defined in terms of a prime-implicant chart (or table) in the following manner.

A row $R_1$ of a prime-implicant table is said to dominate another row $R_2$ of the same table (written $R_1 \supset R_2$) if row $R_1$ has entries in all the columns in which $R_2$ has entries and if, in addition, row $R_1$ has at least one entry in a column in which row $R_2$ does not have an entry. If row $R_1$ dominates row $R_2$, $R_2$ may be removed from the table. Column dominance may also be defined in a similar manner, and the concept can be extended to include cube arrays.

The extraction procedure consists essentially of computing the PI array and then extracting the essential PI's. The array of essential PI's is then reduced using dominance, taking into account the cost factors associated with the PI cubes and the upper bounds on circuit cost. If no essential PI's are found and there is no column or row dominance the array is said to be *cyclic*. In this case it is necessary to employ branch-and-bound techniques which involve (sometimes arbitrarily) selecting a particular path (equivalent to assuming that a particular cube is essential to a minimal cover) and evolving a minimal cover in terms of the remaining cubes using dominance techniques. The process may be terminated when an upper bound on cost has been exceeded, and the computation must then back-track to the last branch point and start again with an alternative path. The major disadvantage of the extraction technique is the large (often excessive) amounts of storage and computation time required for large circuits, particularly when many branch points are involved. The matrix method consists of solving what is essentially a cost-weighted prime-implicant table using either linear-programming or branch-and-bound techniques in conjunction with row and column dominance.

### 4.2.3. Multiple-Output Circuits

So far we have only dealt with single-output switching functions, whereas in practice the majority of circuits are multiple output. The main computational distinction between single- and multiple-output circuits is that the definition of prime implicant must be broadened to embrace multiple-output prime implicants (MOPI) which can cover 0-cubes in more than one output function. Thus the advantage of MOPI's is that once generated they can be shared and combined to implement different output functions. McCluskey and Schorr (14) have shown that the circuit cost of an $m$-output circuit may be significantly reduced (over a separate minimization) by considering the irredundant cover to be comprised of MOPI's. For example, in Table 4.5 if the cover of $Z_2$ is chosen as

$$Z_2 = \begin{Bmatrix} 01X \\ X01 \\ 1X0 \end{Bmatrix}$$

the cube $01X$ appears in both $Z_1$ and $Z_2$, as indicated in the K-map for $Z_1 Z_2$, and can be shared between the outputs.

The most convenient way of representing and handling multiple-output circuits is to use a *tag method* (15) to identify the outputs associated with each 0-cube; this is called the function array $Z$. Thus, the multiple-output circuit in Table 4.5 would be represented as

$$abc \qquad Z_1 Z_2 Z_3$$

$$
Z = \begin{cases}
000 & 101 \\
001 & 011 \\
010 & 111 \\
011 & 110 \\
100 & 110 \\
101 & 011 \\
110 & 010
\end{cases}.
$$

A multiple-output prime implicant can also be expressed as a cube with an associated function tag. The function tag identifies the output function for which the cube is a MOPI; thus the cubes $01X$, $X01$ and $0X0$ shown in Table 4.5 would be represented as

$$01X \,\square\, 110$$
$$X01 \,\square\, 011$$
$$0X0 \,\square\, 101$$

It has been shown (16) that concensus techniques can be used to form MOPI's if the encoding of the output variable is altered by replacing each 1 in the tag by an $X$. The major problem that is encountered when deriving MOPI's, even when generalized concensus is used, is the formation of trivial intermediate products (for example, cubes with all zero tags) which must be generated and temporarily stored.

**Table 4.5. Multiple-Output Function**

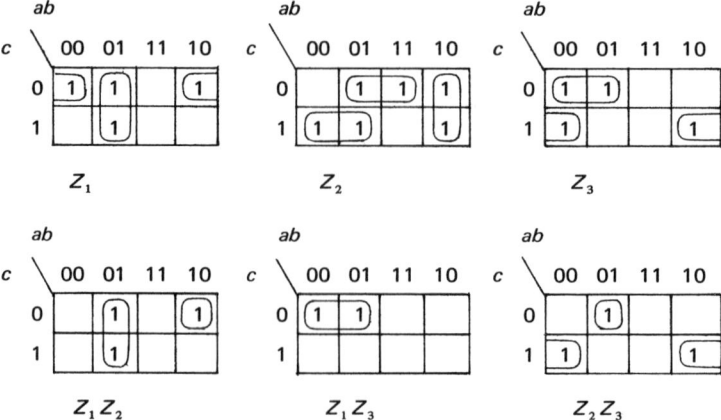

The process of finding a cover for a Boolean function can be summarized as a three-part problem, namely (1) the generation of a set of prime implicants PI, (2) the selection of a minimal cost cover which is a subset of PI, and (3) the construction of an irredundant cover, also a subset of PI. Note that in all the cases described above the complete set of prime implicants is found and then a minimal subset is selected according to some cost criteria. In general this procedure requires an excessive amount of computation and storage, and consequently other methods must be sought, for instance techniques which do not require all prime implicants to be found prior to finding a minimal cover.

### 4.2.4. Decomposition Techniques

The concept of functional decomposition was first described by Ashenhurst (2), and is based on the idea of breaking a switching function down into smaller subparts each of which can be realized more easily than the original function. Thus the synthesis procedure proceeds from the input terminals through to the output terminals and leads to a multi-level cascade of gates. In addition, the technique can take into account physical constraints such as fan-in factors and types of available module. Let $X$ be the set of input variables $X = \{x_1, x_2, \ldots, x_n\}$ of a single-output function $Z(x)$; also let $\lambda$ and $\mu$ be subsets of $X$ such that $X = \lambda \cup \mu$. Then function $Z(x)$ is said to have a *simple decomposition* if, and only if, there exist functions $g$ and $h$ such that

$$Z(x_1, x_2, \ldots, x_n) = g[h(x_i, \ldots, x_{i_p}), x_{i_{p+1}}, \ldots, x_{i_n}]$$

where $(x_i, \ldots, x_{i_p}) = \lambda$ and $(x_{i_{p+1}}, \ldots, x_{i_n}) = \mu$ and $i_1, \ldots, i_n$ is some ordering of the integers 1 to $n$. The equivalent network is shown in Fig. 4.2. When $\lambda$ and $\mu$ are disjoint subsets of $Z$, that is $\lambda \cap \mu = \phi$, the decomposition is referred to as *disjoint*; otherwise it is termed *non-disjoint*. Thus the function

$$Z = \Sigma\,(4,5,6,7,8,10,13,15) \qquad\qquad (4.3)$$

shown in Table 4.6$a$ has the disjoint decomposition

$$Z = \bar{x}_2\bar{x}_4 h + x_2\bar{x}_4\bar{h}$$

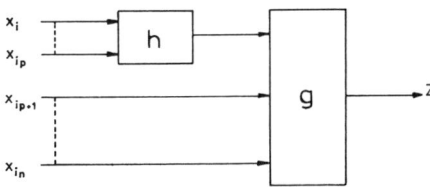

**Figure 4.2.** Functional decomposition.

where

$$h = x_1 x_3 + x_1 \bar{x}_3.$$

The existence of a disjoint decomposition is best determined using the *partition matrix*. Let us consider, for example, the partition $(x_1 x_3)(x_2 x_4)$ on the function $Z(x_1, x_2, x_3, x_4)$. Now a partition matrix may be drawn, similar to a K-map, in which the variables in $(x_1 x_3)$ define the columns, with the rows being defined in a similar manner by $(x_2 x_4)$. Thus, the combination of a row heading with a column heading specifies an input combination. Partition maps may be drawn for all partitions of the original function. Table 4.6 illustrates a number of cases for the function given in Eq. (4.3). Two important properties of the partition matrix are the number of distinct rows, called *row multiplicity* $\delta$, and the *column multiplicity* $\nu$ which is the number of distinct columns. Now a switching function $Z(x_1, x_2, \ldots, x_n)$ has a

**Table 4.6. Partition Matrices**

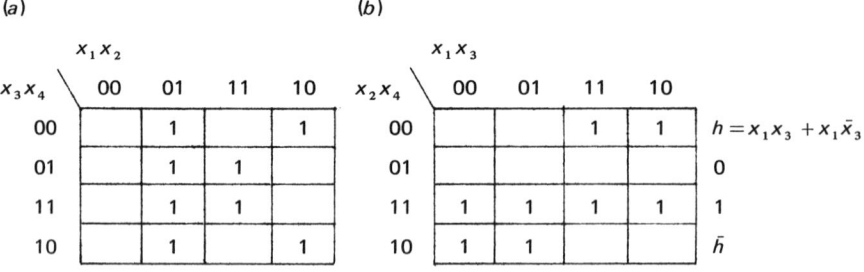

(a)

$x_1 x_2$

| $x_3 x_4$ | 00 | 01 | 11 | 10 |
|---|---|---|---|---|
| 00 |  | 1 |  | 1 |
| 01 |  | 1 | 1 |  |
| 11 |  | 1 | 1 |  |
| 10 |  | 1 |  | 1 |

(b)

$x_1 x_3$

| $x_2 x_4$ | 00 | 01 | 11 | 10 | |
|---|---|---|---|---|---|
| 00 |  |  | 1 | 1 | $h = x_1 x_3 + x_1 \bar{x}_3$ |
| 01 |  |  |  |  | 0 |
| 11 | 1 | 1 | 1 | 1 | 1 |
| 10 | 1 | 1 |  |  | $\bar{h}$ |

(c)

$x_1 x_4$

| $x_2 x_3$ | 00 | 01 | 11 | 10 | |
|---|---|---|---|---|---|
| 00 |  |  |  | 1 | $h = x_1 \bar{x}_4 \bar{x}_2 \bar{x}_3$ |
| 01 |  |  |  | 1 | |
| 11 | 1 | 1 | 1 |  | $\bar{h}$ |
| 10 | 1 | 1 | 1 |  | |

(d)

$x_2 x_3 x_4$

| $x_1$ | 000 | 001 | 010 | 011 | 100 | 101 | 110 | 111 |
|---|---|---|---|---|---|---|---|---|
| 0 |  |  |  |  |  | 1 | 1 | 1 |
| 1 | 1 |  | 1 | 1 |  | 1 |  | 1 |

disjoint decomposition if, and only if, there exists a partition matrix for $Z$ which contains at most four distinct kinds of row; these are (1) all zeros (2) all ones, (3) any pattern of ones and zeros, and (4) the inverse of the pattern in (3). This condition is equivalent to the requirement that the partition matrix has at most two distinct columns. Thus, we may say that a switching function has a simple disjoint decomposition if, and only if, the column multiplicity $v \leqslant 2$. For example in Table 4.6$b$ there are only two distinct columns, and for the first row, where $x_2 = 0$ and $x_4 = 0$, we have

$$h = 0 . \bar{x}_1 \bar{x}_3 + 0 . \bar{x}_1 x_3 + 1 . x_1 x_3 + 1 . x_1 \bar{x}_3 = x_1 x_3 + x_1 \bar{x}_3 ;$$

similarly for the fourth row, where $x_2 = 1$ and $x_4 = 0$, we have

$$\bar{h} = \bar{x}_1 \bar{x}_3 + \bar{x}_1 x_3 .$$

Note that an alternative decomposition is obtained for the partition $(x_1 x_4)(x_2 x_3)$, but $(x_1 x_2)(x_3 x_4)$ and $(x_2 x_3 x_4)(x_1)$ do not give decompositions since $v > 2$.

In order to establish the existence of a disjoint decomposition for a given function, partition maps must be constructed for all possible partitions of the function and exhaustively tested for the condition $v \leqslant 2$. Since a function of $n$ variables requires $2^n - n - 2$ non-trivial partition maps to be investigated, the amount of computation involved soon becomes excessive. One approach (17) which has been used to reduce the search time is to constrain $h$ in the function $Z(x) = g[h(\lambda), \mu]$ to be a *vertex function*. A vertex function $h(x_1, x_2, \ldots, x_n)$ of $n$ variables assumes one of its two possible values for *one* particular combination of the $n$ variables and the inverse value for all other combinations. Now, if $h(x)$ is a vertex function, then it can always be decomposed into $\beta[\alpha(t), u]$, where $t$ and $u$ are partitions of the literals of $x$, and $\beta$ and $\alpha$ are vertex functions. It may be shown that, if a disjoint vertex decomposition of a function of $n$ variables into sets $\{n_1, n_2\}$ of free and bounded variables exists, then all disjoint vertex decompositions into sets $\{n'_1, n'_2\}$ also exist, where $n'_2$ is a subset of $n_2$. Conversely, if no disjoint vertex decomposition exists for the function with $n_2$ containing $K$ variables, then no disjoint decomposition can exist for larger values of $K$. Using this fact an upper bound can be established on the amount of computation required, since if no disjoint vertex decompositions are found for $n_2 = K$ then decompositions with larger values of $K$ can be disregarded.

### 4.2.5. Computer Algorithms

In general the computer generation of prime implicants using a classical approach has been evolved to a comparatively simple process due mainly to the efforts of Roth (18), and Morreale (19), and Slagle *et al.* (20).

Morreale's *partitioned-list algorithm* is basically a modification of the Quine–McCluskey method. In this technique prime implicants are first generated from vertices differing in the least significant variable, followed by the prime implicants arising from vertices differing in the next most significant co-ordinate, and so on until the most-significant co-ordinate has been examined. The resultant set of prime implicants is then treated in the same way until no further reduction is possible. This procedure will generate the complete set of prime implicants and has the advantage over the Quine–McCluskey method in that the number of comparisons between cubes is considerably reduced. In practice the technique employs a reduction operator $R$, which is similar to the concensus operation, but in this case only individual bit positions are inspected. The operator is applied in a specific order obtained by partitioning the 0-cubes in the ON array into a tree structure; this is shown in Fig. 4.3 for four variables. Note that $R_1$ refers to the operation of comparing vertices which differ in the least significant position and generating the resultant PI terms; $R_2$ refers to a comparison of the next-most-significant digits, etc. For example, consider the 0-cube cover shown below:

$$C_{15} = \begin{Bmatrix} 0000 \\ 0100 \\ 0101 \\ 0110 \\ 1001 \\ 1101 \\ 1110 \\ 1111 \end{Bmatrix}$$

$$C_{14} = \begin{Bmatrix} 010X \\ 111X \end{Bmatrix} \qquad C_{13} = \begin{Bmatrix} 01X0 \\ 11X1 \end{Bmatrix}$$

$$C_{11} = \begin{Bmatrix} 0X00 \\ 1X01 \end{Bmatrix} \qquad C_7 = \begin{Bmatrix} X101 \\ X110 \end{Bmatrix}$$

$$C_{12} = \phi, \qquad C_{10} = \phi, \qquad C_6 = \phi$$

which gives the complete set of prime implicants for the cover $C_{15}$.

The main attribute of the method is that at most $n$ (where $n$ is the number of variables) arrays or lists must be stored at any one time; the original 0-cube array, however, must stay in the store throughout the calculation. The method can be used to determine multiple-output prime implicants but suffers from the disadvantage of requiring canonical forms. Though the method has been redefined recursively (21), to make it more

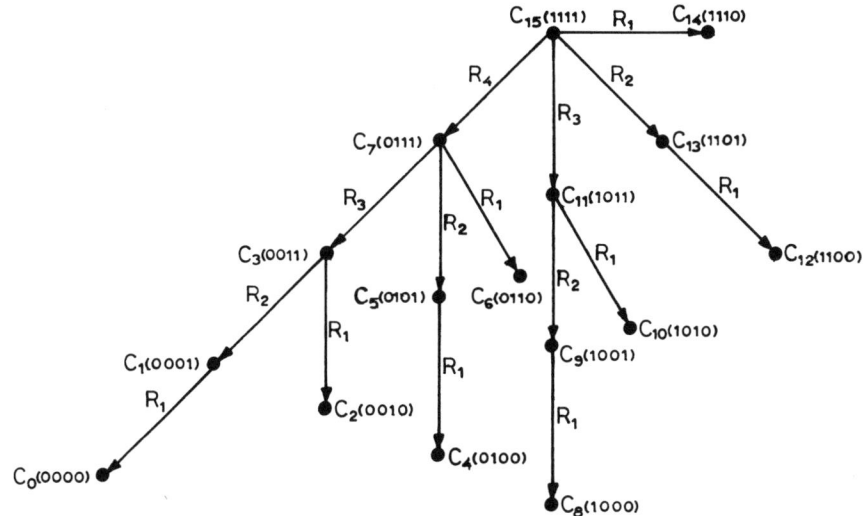

**Figure 4.3.** Order for applying operator $R$.

efficient the computational overheads created by organizational programming tend to absorb the savings achieved by the reduced number of comparisons.

For many switching functions the number of prime implicants evolved can be prohibitively large; for instance, Miller (22) has shown that for one class of $n$-variable functions the number of PI's is proportional to $3^n/n$. Heuristic methods have been described, however, which reduce the computational requirements of extracting and selecting PI's by not generating the entire set of prime implicants. These techniques determine directly the irredundant normal form (INF) of a Boolean function to produce a solution which is near minimal. One such algorithm has been described by Necula (23), who uses a modified form of ON and OFF arrays, called the $\langle 0,1 \rangle$ representation, to specify the Boolean function. This is shown in Table 4.7$b$ where the original truth table has been turned on its side, the don't-care terms omitted, and the remaining 0-cubes partitioned into ON and OFF sets. The Boolean function is completely specified by

$$\langle x_4 \rangle_0 = 010110, \quad \langle x_4 \rangle_1 = 0110101$$

$$\langle x_3 \rangle_0 = 000110, \quad \langle x_3 \rangle_1 = 1100011 \text{ etc.}$$

Note that there will be a total of $2n$ cubes where $n$ is the number of variables. Also, each 1 (0) bit in the code represents a true (false) minterm in the $n$-variable canonic form, the respective minterms being determined by the

### Table 4.7. $\langle 0,1 \rangle$ Representation of Boolean Function

(a)  Truth table

| $x_1$ | $x_2$ | $x_3$ | $x_4$ | $Z$ |
|-------|-------|-------|-------|-----|
| 0 | 0 | 0 | 0 | 0 |
| 0 | 0 | 0 | 1 | 0 |
| 0 | 0 | 1 | 0 | 1 |
| 0 | 0 | 1 | 1 | 1 |
| 0 | 1 | 0 | 0 | 0 |
| 0 | 1 | 0 | 1 | 1 |
| 0 | 1 | 1 | 0 | $X$ |
| 0 | 1 | 1 | 1 | 0 |
| 1 | 0 | 0 | 0 | 1 |
| 1 | 0 | 0 | 1 | 1 |
| 1 | 0 | 1 | 0 | $X$ |
| 1 | 0 | 1 | 1 | 0 |
| 1 | 1 | 0 | 0 | 0 |
| 1 | 1 | 0 | 1 | $X$ |
| 1 | 1 | 1 | 0 | 1 |
| 1 | 1 | 1 | 1 | 1 |

(b)  Rearranged and reduced truth table

| $Z'$ | 0 0 0 0 0 0 1 1 1 1 1 1 1 |
|------|---------------------------|
| $x'_4$ | 0 1 0 1 1 0 0 1 1 0 1 0 1 |
| $x'_3$ | 0 0 0 1 1 0 1 1 0 0 0 1 1 |
| $x'_2$ | 0 0 1 1 0 1 0 0 1 0 0 1 1 |
| $x'_1$ | 0 0 0 0 1 1 0 0 0 1 1 1 1 |

column that contains the bit under consideration. For example, the first 1 in code $\langle x_3 \rangle_1$ in Table 4.7b represents the minterm $0100 = \bar{x}_4 x_3 \bar{x}_2 \bar{x}_1$ which is contained in the canonic sum-of-products expression for $Z$. The $\langle 0,1 \rangle$ representation has (among others) the following important properties.

(a)  If a reduced term $t$ is an implicant of $Z$ then $\langle t \rangle_0 = 0$ and $\langle t \rangle_1 \neq 0$ and conversely. Thus, for the function $Z$ in Table 4.7 we obtain

$$\langle x_1 \bar{x}_2 \bar{x}_3 \rangle_0 = (000011)(\overline{001101})(\overline{000110}) = 000000$$

and

$$\langle x_1 \bar{x}_2 \bar{x}_3 \rangle_1 = (0001111)(\overline{0010011})(\overline{1100011}) = 0001100$$

and hence $x_1 \bar{x}_2 \bar{x}_3$ is an implicant of $Z$.

(b)  If the implicant $t$ of $Z$ is an implicant of the implicant $t_1$ of $Z$, then $\langle t \rangle_1 \cdot \langle t \rangle_0 = 0$ and conversely.

Using these properties an algorithm can be developed for generating prime implicants from a $\langle 0,1 \rangle$ representation. This is achieved by testing for the inclusion of all possible $3^n - 1$ terms (both reduced and canonical) within $Z$, starting with the largest terms first. Each generated implicant term must be checked to ensure that the 0-cubes covered are not already included in a previously generated prime implicant.

The basic method has been extended to allow the direct extraction and selection of PI's to give an irredundant Boolean function for both canonical and partially reduced truth tables. The algorithm is well suited for computer implementation and considerably reduces the computation requirement; successful results are claimed for strongly minimizable Boolean functions when starting from the canonical form.

Another method which is similar in principle is the *relaxation algorithm* due to Waters (24) and used in the CALD suite of synthesis programs (25). As before the objective of the method is to reduce the number of intermediate derived products and hence the amount of computation. In this case the algorithm, which is based on the cubical notation, commences by looking for the largest prime implicants (that is those which cover the maximum number of 0-cubes) and then progressively searches for smaller prime implicants until a complete cover is obtained.

Using the relaxation approach the function to be minimized is specified in terms of ON and OFF arrays; the don't-care terms, if they exist, are generated automatically (using the sharp product) and included in the ON array. In order to illustrate the method let us take the function

$$Z = \Sigma (2,3,5,7,8,9,10,11,13,15)$$

the ON and OFF arrays for which are shown in Table 4.8. Now let the first literals of the first vertex of the ON array $(X)$ form an $n - 1$ cube (where $n$ is

**Table 4.8. Relaxation Method of Minimization**

| a | b | c | d | | a | b | c | d | | Prime implicants |
|---|---|---|---|---|---|---|---|---|---|---|
| 0 | 0 | 1 | 0 | ✓ | 0 | 0 | 0 | 0 | | $X$ 0 1 $X$ |
| 0 | 0 | 1 | 1 | ✓ | 0 | 0 | 0 | 1 | | $X$ 1 $X$ 1 |
| 0 | 1 | 0 | 1 | | 0 | 1 | 0 | 0 | | 1 0 $X$ $X$ |
| 0 | 1 | 1 | 1 | | 0 | 1 | 1 | 0 | | |
| 1 | 0 | 0 | 0 | | 1 | 1 | 0 | 0 | | |
| 1 | 0 | 0 | 1 | | 1 | 1 | 1 | 0 | | |
| 1 | 0 | 1 | 0 | ✓ | | | | | | |
| 1 | 0 | 1 | 1 | ✓ | | | | | | |
| 1 | 1 | 0 | 1 | | | | | | | |
| 1 | 1 | 1 | 1 | | | | | | | |

ON array $(X)$      OFF array $(Y)$

| First vertex | 0010, $n - 1$ cubes | $0XXX, X0XX, XX1X, XXX0$ |
|---|---|---|
| | $n - 2$ cubes | $00XX, \underline{X01X}, XX10, 0XX0$ |
| | | $X0X0, 0X1X$ |
| | $n - 3$ cubes | $X010, 0X10, 00X0, 001X$ |

the number of variables) that is $0XXX$ which is equivalent to the prime implicant $\bar{A}$. Next, determine if any vertex of the OFF array ($Y$) is included in this $n-1$ cube by forming the logical intersection. The test for logical intersection may be simply performed by determining whether or not any vertex of $Y$ has the same value in the co-ordinate corresponding to the bound component of $X$. If the vertex is not included it must be, by definition, a prime implicant, since there can be no higher cube that could include it. If the cube does contain a vertex of $Y$ the current search can be immediately concluded and the next $n$-cube in sequence tested. This procedure is then repeated for $n-2$, $n-3$ cubes, etc., the process terminating with the 0-cubes. Once a prime implicant has been found all the vertices of $X$ included in the cube may be marked as covered and need not be considered further. Continuing with the example shown in Table 4.8, the first vertex of $X$ is 0010 and all the 3-cubes include a vertex of $Y$. The 2-cube $X01X$ does not include a vertex of $Y$ and is hence a prime implicant; this cube covers 0-cubes 0010, 0011, 1010, and 1011 which can be checked off in the $X$ list. Vertex 0101 is considered next; the 1-cube $X1X1$ covers terms 0101, 0111, 1101, and 1111. The process is continued to yield the PI's $X01X$, $X1X1$, and $10XX$. Note that the method is ideally suited for list structures (a list-processing language was used to effect a realization) and as there are no derived terms the computation is considerably reduced. The method is, however, dependent on the initial ordering of the 0-cubes in the ON and OFF arrays. As with other techniques the algorithm cannot guarantee the generation of the complete set of prime implicants and consequently the irredundant cover obtained is not necessarily minimal.

The method can easily be extended to multiple-output circuits by using a tagging technique to identify the output functions. In this case the starting point is an *L-array* which consists of all those 0-cubes generating a 1 in an output function together with tag bits (duplicated) which denote the functions concerned. Thus, in Table 4.9b, the row 0010 110 110 in the $L$-array indicates that outputs $Z_1$ and $Z_2$ go to 1 for the 0-cube 0010. The OFF arrays called *M-arrays* are formed separately for each output function and consist of the 0-cubes which cause the function to go to zero; these are shown in Table 4.9c.

The multiple output relaxation algorithm consists of the following steps.

(1) Form (*a*) the OFF set $M$ for each output function, (*b*) the ON set $L$ omitting don't-care terms, and (*c*) an empty set $C$ to store the multiple-output PI's.

(2) Set a counter $N = 1$; this is used to generate the $n-N$ cubes, where $n$ is the number of variables. Now commencing with the first row of the $L$-array (see Table 4.9b) we have 0010 110 110, which generates the 3-cubes $0XXX$, $X0XX$, $XX1X$, and $XXX0$. These are compared with the entries in the

# Table 4.9. Multiple-Output Relaxation Algorithm

(a) Truth table

| $x_1$ | $x_2$ | $x_3$ | $x_4$ | $Z_1 Z_2 Z_3$ |
|---|---|---|---|---|
| 0 | 0 | 0 | 0 | 0 0 0 |
| 0 | 0 | 0 | 1 | 0 0 0 |
| 0 | 0 | 1 | 0 | 1 1 0 |
| 0 | 0 | 1 | 1 | 1 1 0 |
| 0 | 1 | 0 | 0 | 0 0 0 |
| 0 | 1 | 0 | 1 | 1 1 0 |
| 0 | 1 | 1 | 0 | 0 1 1 |
| 0 | 1 | 1 | 1 | 1 1 0 |
| 1 | 0 | 0 | 0 | 1 0 1 |
| 1 | 0 | 0 | 1 | 1 0 1 |
| 1 | 0 | 1 | 0 | 1 1 0 |
| 1 | 0 | 1 | 1 | 1 1 0 |
| 1 | 1 | 0 | 0 | 0 0 0 |
| 1 | 1 | 0 | 1 | 1 0 1 |
| 1 | 1 | 1 | 0 | 0 0 1 |
| 1 | 1 | 1 | 1 | 1 1 1 |

(b) ON array

$$L = \begin{Bmatrix}
0010 & 110 & 110 \\
0011 & 110 & 110 \\
0101 & 110 & 110 \\
0110 & 011 & 011 \\
0111 & 110 & 110 \\
1000 & 101 & 101 \\
1001 & 101 & 101 \\
1010 & 110 & 110 \\
1011 & 110 & 110 \\
1101 & 101 & 101 \\
1110 & 001 & 001 \\
1111 & 111 & 111
\end{Bmatrix}$$

(c) OFF arrays

$$M_1 = \begin{Bmatrix} 0000 \\ 0001 \\ 0100 \\ 0110 \\ 1100 \\ 1110 \end{Bmatrix}$$

$$M_2 = \begin{Bmatrix} 0000 \\ 0001 \\ 0100 \\ 1000 \\ 1001 \\ 1100 \\ 1101 \\ 1110 \end{Bmatrix}$$

$$M_3 = \begin{Bmatrix} 0000 \\ 0001 \\ 0010 \\ 0011 \\ 0100 \\ 0101 \\ 0111 \\ 1010 \\ 1011 \\ 1100 \end{Bmatrix}$$

(d)

$$L = \begin{Bmatrix}
0101 & 110 & 110 \\
0110 & 011 & 011 \\
0111 & 110 & 110 \\
1000 & 101 & 101 \\
1001 & 101 & 101 \\
1101 & 101 & 101 \\
1110 & 001 & 001 \\
1111 & 111 & 111
\end{Bmatrix}$$

$$C = \{X01X \quad 110\}$$

**Table 4.9.** (*continued*)  **Multiple-Output Relaxation Algorithm**

(e)

$$L = \begin{cases} 0101 & 010 & 110 \\ 0110 & 011 & 011 \\ 0111 & 010 & 110 \\ 1000 & 101 & 101 \\ 1001 & 101 & 101 \\ 1101 & 001 & 101 \\ 1110 & 001 & 001 \\ 1111 & 011 & 111 \end{cases} \quad C = \begin{cases} X01X & 110 \\ X1X1 & 100 \end{cases}$$

(f)

$$L = \{\phi\} \quad C = \begin{cases} X01X & 110 \\ X1X1 & 100 \\ 01X1 & 110 \\ 0X1X & 010 \\ X110 & 001 \\ 10XX & 100 \\ 100X & 101 \\ 11X1 & 101 \\ XX11 & 101 \end{cases}$$

OFF sets $M_1$ and $M_2$ (as indicated in the function tag bits), when it is found that all the 3-cubes include vertices of $M_1$ and $M_2$ and hence cannot be prime-implicant terms.

(3) The counter is now increased to $N = 2$ and the 2-cubes formed. After inspection it is found that the cubes $00XX$, $0X1X$ and $0XX0$ all include vertices of $M_1$ and $M_2$, but the cube $X01X$ does not. Thus $X01X$ is a multiple-output PI of $M_1$ and $M_2$, and the term $X01X$ 110 is added to the set $C$. The vertices 0010, 0011, 1010, and 1011 which are covered by $X01X$ are removed from the $L$-array; the resultant arrays are shown in Table 4.9$d$.

(4) Starting again with the first row of the reduced $L$-array the first cube formed from 0101 that does not include vertices of both $M_1$ and $M_2$ is the 2-cube $X1X1$. This cube includes vertices of $M_2$ but not $M_1$; hence the MOPI term $X1X1$ 100 is added to set $C$. The vertices 0101, 0111, 1101, and 1111 are included by the MOPI, and hence function 1 is removed from the tag bits; note that none of the vertex rows can be removed as their output terms are not completely covered.

(5) Continuing the procedure the first cube of 0101 that does not include a vertex of $M_2$ (the remaining function that needs to be covered) is the 1-cube $01X1$. At this stage it is necessary to back-track to check if the cube $01X1$ includes any vertices of $M_1$; if it does not then it is a MOPI of both $M_1$ and $M_2$. In this case it dos not; therefore the term $01X1$ 110 can be added to set $C$, and the vertices 0101 and 0111 removed from the $L$-array

This procedure is repeated until the $L$-array is empty, that is when all the terms in $L$ are covered by the cubes of the set $C$; the continued application of the algorithm produces a subset of all possible MOPI's. For the example problem, the total set of MOPI's contains fourteen terms; the algorithm has generated nine of these as shown in Table 4.9$f$.

The relaxation algorithm was programmed for an ICL 1907 series computer using a list-processor language, the ON–OFF arrays being treated as list structures. The maximum size problem that can be handled is a 20-variable expression with 10 output functions. The main advantage of the relaxation algorithm is that prime implicants are generated only if they are likely to contribute to a reduced solution. The number of prime implicants generated is considerably reduced, with the majority being essential PI's, thus simplifying the selection of the final cover. Unfortunately the method requires the use of canonical terms for the initial circuit specification.

Waters (24) also describes a simple, yet effective, heuristic procedure for the solution of cyclic prime-implicant tables. This is called the *cover-most* procedure and is based on the premise that the PI which covers the greatest number of input vertices of a cyclic PI table is most likely to form part of a solution, which, if not minimal, is a close approximation. The algorithm may be described as follows.

**(1)** For each PI calculate the number of 0-cubes covered by the PI; let this be $N$.

**(2)** Select the PI with the greatest $N$. If more than one PI has the same value of $N$ select the PI with the lowest cost criteria. If the cost factors are equal, arbitrarily select a PI term.

**(3)** Add the PI selected in step (2) to the set $C$ of PI terms. Remove all vertices covered by the selected PI and any other PI terms which, as a result of selecting the initial PI, now covers an empty set of vertices.

**(4)** Return to step (1) if the set of vertices is non-empty.

The algorithm is claimed to be easier to compute and more economical than normal algebraic methods.

The process is illustrated in Table 4.10. The prime implicant $E$ covers four vertices and has the highest value of $N$; therefore it is selected first. This results after reduction in the PI table shown in Table 4.10$b$. In this table PI's $G$ and $I$ both have the same value of $N$, but $G$ has the lowest cost and is therefore selected next. The final table shown in Table 4.10$c$ indicates that PI's $B$ and $C$, which have the lowest cost, should be chosen; this must be determined by successive iteration. Thus the final solution is given by $EGBC$, which in this case also happens to be the minimal. However, the algorithm cannot be guaranteed to find the minimal solution, particularly for large-variable problems.

Another reduction technique, again with the objective of producing a low, but not necessarily minimum, cost multiple-output circuit, is that due to Su and Dietmeyer (26). The starting point for the method is basically an $n$-input $m$-output truth table, called the function array $C$, which specifies *both* the ON and DC vertices for a combinational circuit. The function array is considered to be the union of $2^m - 1$ subarrays, each of which is the subset of all cubes of $C$ with the *same* output $m$-tuple, that is

$$C = \sum_{j=1}^{2^m - 1} C^{\lambda_j}$$

where $\lambda$ is the set of output-column designators and each $C^\lambda$ consists of all cubes of $C$ which have 1's in all the output columns specified by $\lambda$ and in no others; some sets of $C^\lambda$ may of course be empty. The union of the single-output cover of the vertices of each $C^\lambda$ forms a cover for the complete set $C$ and represents a reduced circuit. Thus a minimum cover of the input

## Table 4.10. Cover-Most Algorithms

(a) Prime-implicant table

| PI | $V_1$ | $V_2$ | $V_3$ | $V_4$ | $V_5$ | $V_6$ | $V_7$ | $V_8$ | Cost factor | $N$ |
|---|---|---|---|---|---|---|---|---|---|---|
| A | X | X | | | | | | | 2 | 2 |
| B | | X | | X | | | | | 2 | 2 |
| C | | | X | | | | | | 2 | 1 |
| D | | | | | | | X | X | 3 | 2 |
| * E | X | X | | | | X | | X | 3 | 4 |
| F | X | | | | | X | | | 3 | 2 |
| G | | | | | X | | X | | 3 | 2 |
| H | | X | | X | | | | X | 4 | 3 |
| I | | | X | | X | | | | 4 | 2 |

Vertices (column group header over $V_1$–$V_8$)

(b) Reduced PI table

| PI | $V_3$ | $V_4$ | $V_5$ | $V_7$ | Cost factor | $N$ |
|---|---|---|---|---|---|---|
| B | | X | | | 2 | 1 |
| C | X | | | | 2 | 1 |
| D | | | | X | 3 | 1 |
| * G | | | X | X | 3 | 2 |
| H | | X | | | 4 | 1 |
| I | X | | X | | 4 | 2 |

Vertices (column group header over $V_3$–$V_7$)

(c) Final PI table

| PI | $V_3$ | $V_4$ | Cost factor | $N$ |
|---|---|---|---|---|
| B | | X | 2 | 1 |
| C | X | | 2 | 1 |
| H | | X | 4 | 1 |
| I | X | | 4 | 1 |

Vertices (column group header over $V_3$–$V_4$)

$n$-tuples of each subarray may replace those input $n$-tuples to obtain a compressed array which suggests a more economical circuit. In this way the reduction of an $n \times m$ multiple-output problem is converted into $2^m - 1$ $n$-input, single-output problems. The paper describes methods of reducing the function array to obtain a near-minimal covering.

It is assumed in the algorithm that the cost of the circuit is given by the number of diodes required in a two-level AND–OR (NAND) network, which may be related to the number of circuit connections which must be made. However, since the prime implicants are selected to cover the maximum number of output functions, rather than vertices, the number of interconnections required could be greater than that obtained by the usual classical methods.

A more recent and highly original heuristic minimization procedure which can handle large practical problems with up to 20–30 input variables is the MINI system due to Hong *et al.* (27). In this approach the cost function is simplified by assigning equal weights to each prime implicant, and the final solution is obtained by iteratively improving on an initial solution, rather than by generating and covering prime implicants. The process is basically one of modifying the implicant terms in order to reduce the number and increase the size of the prime implicants; the procedure is similar in concept to the manual operations normally performed on a K-map.

There are primarily three modification procedures that are performed on the implicant terms; these are as follows.

(a) Implicants are expanded to their maximum size and any other implicants that are covered removed.

(b) Each implicant term is reduced to its smallest possible size while still maintaining the necessary cover of the original minterms (note in this context smallest size means containing the minimal number of literals).

(c) Implicants are examined in pairs to see if they can be transformed into another pair (by reducing one and enlarging the other) which can be more easily merged with other terms during the expansion process; this process is called *reshaping*.

Processes (a) and (b) both have the effect of reducing the number of implicants in the final solution, while (c) facilitates the expansion and reduction processes. The general approach used in MINI is to iterate through the three main procedures until no further reduction can be obtained; note that the order in which the procedures are applied is crucial and can radically effect the resulting solutions.

The MINI procedure uses a modified cubical notation, termed a *positional* cube, which is more convenient for machine representation. In this notation the variables 0, 1, and $X$ are recoded as binary pairs, that is representing 0 as

10, 1 as 01, and $X$ as 11, the code 00 representing no value or a null cube. The notation was first described by Su and Cheung (28) to represent multiple-value logic; Table 4.11 shows a typical example of positional encoding. Multiple-output functions are represented in the usual way by a tag field catenated to the input cube to denote a multiple-output implicant. For generality, the input variables are grouped into a set of multiple-value variables such that the new variable $X_i$, comprising $n_i$ of Boolean input variables, has $2^{n_i}$ values; the coding for a multiple-output function using this notation is shown in Table 4.12. Note that $X_1$ and $X_2$ can take on values 00, 01, 10, and 11, and must be encoded using a 4-tuple to allow for the don't-care terms.

An important point is that for conciseness the designer can specify the problem in a reduced manner (see Table 4.12$a$), but this can give rise to *conflicts* between a specified 1 output and a don't-care term (shown as an encircled entry in Table 4.12$c$). In the MINI system conflicts of this type are automatically resolved by forcing the don't-care terms to 1. (There is, however, another form of conflict which can arise with a reduced specification this is between a specified 0 and 1 output which can only be resolved by designer intervention).

Boolean specifications are encoded into the positional cube format as shown in Table 4.12$b$. The first four cubes in the ON cover are the cubes shown in Table 4.12$a$ with the output don't-cares replaced with 0's. The DC cover is obtained by encoding only those cubes containing don't-care terms in their output and replacing $X$'s in the output tag with 1's and all other values with 0's. The minimization procedure starts from the initial ON and DC covers, and has the objective of minimizing the number of cubes in the ON cover by iterative merging. This corresponds to minimizing the number of NAND gates in a two-level AND–OR circuit without regard to the number of input terms (modifications are described in the paper, however, which do incorporate cost criteria).

The initial stage in the MINI process is to expand the cubes in the ON cover into a *disjoint cover*, which has the advantage of modifying the initial specification into a more suitable form for effecting successful mergers. A process called *disjoint sharp*, represented by the symbol $\oplus$, is used to obtain the disjoint cover of the ON array. This operator is derived from the normal

**Table 4.11. Positional Encoding**

| Cubes | Encoded cubes | | | |
|-------|------|------|------|------|
| 0101  | 10 | 01 | 10 | 01 |
| 1$X$11  | 01 | 11 | 01 | 01 |
| $XXXX$  | 11 | 11 | 11 | 11 |
| 00$XX$  | 10 | 10 | 11 | 11 |

## Table 4.12.  Specification of Multiple-Output Functions

(a)  Partial truth table

| $ABCD$ | $Z_1 Z_2 Z_3$ |
|---|---|
| 00X0 | 0  0  1 |
| 10X0 | 1  1  0 |
| 11XX | 1  X  0 |
| X010 | 1  0  X |

(b)  Encoded format

| $X_1 = \{A,B\}$ | $X_2 = \{C,D\}$ | Output | |
|---|---|---|---|
| 0001 | 1010 | 001 | |
| 0010 | 1010 | 110 | ON |
| 1000 | 1111 | 100 | |
| 1010 | 0010 | 100 | |
| 1000 | 1111 | 010 | DC |
| 1010 | 0010 | 001 | |

(c)  K-maps

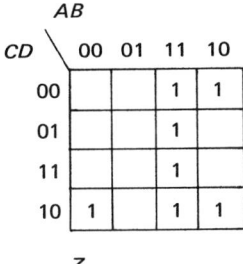
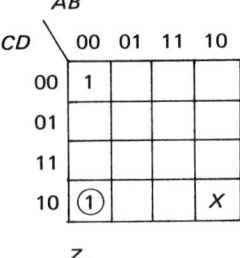

$Z_1$                                $Z_2$                                $Z_3$

sharp function, $A \# B$, which, as we have seen in § 4.2.1, can be defined as $A \cap \bar{B}$ and used to generate the prime implicants of $A\bar{B}$. The disjoint sharp function is defined as having the same cover as $A\bar{B}$ but with the resultant cubes of $A \oplus B$ being mutually disjoint. Note that the disjoint cover so obtained is also the complement of the original cube. The function can also be defined procedurally in the following manner. Consider two cubes, $A = a_1 a_2 a_3 \ldots a_n$ and $B = b_1 b_2 b_3 \ldots b_n$, then let

$$A \oplus B = C = \prod_{i=1}^{n} C_i$$

where $C_i$ is given by

$$C_1 = (a_1 \bar{b}_1) a_2 a_3 a_4 \ldots a_n$$
$$C_2 = (a_1 b_1)(a_2 \bar{b}_2) a_3 a_4 \ldots a_n$$
$$C_3 = (a_1 b_1)(a_2 b_2)(a_3 \bar{b}_3) a_4 \ldots a_n$$
$$C_n = (a_1 b_1)(a_2 b_2)(a_3 b_3) \ldots (a_n \bar{b}_n)$$

where the AND and NOT functions are performed on a bit-by-bit basis. When $C_i$ becomes a null cube, that is $a_i \bar{b_i} = \phi$, $C_i$ is deleted from the $A \oplus B$ list.

As an example, consider the disjoint sharp function between $A = XXXX$, the entire four-dimensional unit cube, and $B = X1X1$. Applying the basic rules above we have

$$C_1 = (X\bar{X})\, X\, X\, X \ldots \qquad\qquad \text{null cube}$$

$$C_2 = (XX)(X0)\, X\, X \ldots \qquad\qquad X\,0\,X\,X$$

$$C_3 = (XX)(X1)(X\bar{X})\, X \ldots \qquad \text{null cube}$$

$$C_4 = (XX)(X1)(XX)(X0) \ldots \qquad X\,1\,X\,0.$$

Thus the disjoint cubes are $X0XX$ and $X1X0$; this is shown in Table 4.13. The disjoint sharp function applies equally to cubes encoded in the positional notation, as do all other cubical-array operators.

The principal procedure in the MINI system is the *cube-expansion* process. This procedure examines each individual cube in a predetermined order and attempts to generate a prime cube which covers the original cube and other cubes in the solution. The covered cubes are replaced by the prime cubes before the next cube in sequence is expanded. The ordering of the cubes important, and MINI puts the cubes which are difficult to merge (corresponding in the main to essential primes) on the top of the list to be examined. Cube expansion is done one part at a time, where a part may be one literal or a group of digits in the positional notation. Before we can specify the cube-expansion procedure, however, it is necessary to define the following terms.

(a) Two disjoint cubes $A$ and $B$ are called *K-conjugates* if, and only if, $A$ and $B$ have *one* part $K$ where the intersection of the corresponding parts is

**Table 4.13. Disjoint Sharp Function**

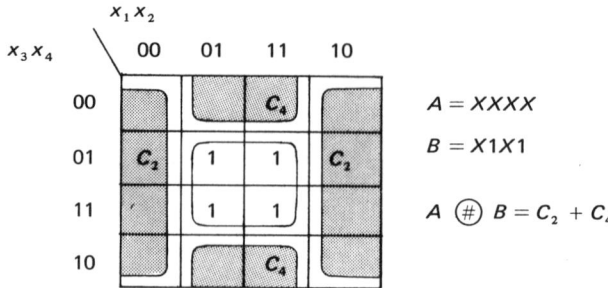

$$A = XXXX$$

$$B = X1X1$$

$$A \oplus B = C_2 + C_4$$

null. For example, cubes $A = 0X1X$ and $B = 10X1$ are 1-conjugate since they differ only in the first digit; note that don't-care terms can assume any value.

**(b)** The set of all cubes in $\bar{F}$, the OFF array, that are $K$-conjugates of a given cube $f$ in $S$, the solution in progress, is defined as $H(f:K)$. Further, $S$ is defined as the set of cubes which covers all the vertices in $F$, the ON array (and possibly some in the DC array), but none in $\bar{F}$. Also,

$$H = \{g_i \mid f \text{ and } g_i \text{ are } K\text{-conjugates}\}$$

where $g_i$ are the disjoint cubes comprising $\bar{F}$ (obtained as a by-product in the disjoint $F$ computation).

**(c)** The bit-by-bit OR of the part $K$ of all cubes in $H(f:K)$ is denoted by $Z(f:K)$.

Now, using these definitions we may procedurally define the single-part expansion of a cube $f$ along a part $K$ as

$$SPE(f:K) = a_1 a_2 a_3 \ldots a_{K-1} \overline{Z(f:K)} \, a_{K+1} \ldots a_n.$$

The SPE procedure can be considered as a generalized implementation of Roth's coface operation (18) on variable $K$.

The expansion process is more easily explained using an example. Consider the K-map shown in Table 4.14a which shows the $f$ and $g_i$ terms. The

**Table 4.14. Cube Expansion**

(a)  K-map

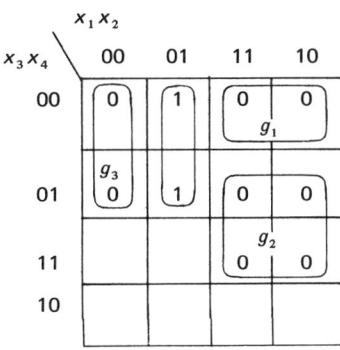

$f = 010X$

$$\bar{f} = \begin{cases} 1X00 = g_1 \\ 1XX1 = g_2 \\ 001X = g_3 \end{cases}$$

(b)  Single-part expansion

| $K$ | $H(f:K)$ | $\overline{Z(f:k)}$ | $SPE(f:K)$ |
|---|---|---|---|
| 1 | $g_3$ | 1 | $1X01$ |
| 2 | null | $X$ | $0\bar{X}01$ |
| 3 | $g_1$ | 1 | $0\bar{X}11$ |
| 4 | $g_2$ | 0 | $0\bar{X}0\bar{0}$ |

evaluation of the SPE function is shown in Table 4.14$b$; note that the $g_i$ terms are compared with the $f$ terms to obtain $H(f:K)$; thus

$$f = 0X01 \qquad\qquad 0X01 \qquad\qquad 0X01$$

$$g_1 = 0X\underline{1}X \quad g_2 = 0X0\underline{0} \quad g_3 = \underline{1}1XX$$

Prime implicants may be extracted using this process according to the theorem: A cube is a prime if, and only if, every part of the cube is a prime part. A cube can be expanded in every part by repeatedly applying the SPE as follows:

$$\text{expand } (f) = \text{SPE } ( \ldots \text{SPE(SPE(SPE}(f:1):2):3) \ldots n).$$

Furthermore, it is also possible to extend this technique to obtain the essential primes.

   The expansion process leaves the cubes in the current solution in a near-prime form, and the next step is to attempt to reduce the size of the cubes in $S$ without affecting the cover. The smaller the size of the cubes the more likely it will be covered by another expanded cube in a later step. The *cube-reduction* process goes through the list of cubes in the solution list $S$ in a predetermined manner and reduces each of them. The reduction of one cube $A$ against another cube $B$ assumes that $B$ does not cover $A$ and that the two cubes differ in at least two parts. Cube $A$ can be reduced if, and only if, all parts of $B$ cover $A$ except in one part; let that be part $j$. Now given

$$A = a_1 a_2 a_3 \ldots a_j \ldots a_n$$

and

$$B = b_1 b_2 b_3 \ldots b_j \ldots b_n$$

the reduced version of $A$ (called the *trimmed $A$*) is

$$A'_. = a_1 a_2 \ldots (a_j \bar{b}_j) \ldots a_n.$$

   After the expansion and reduction steps are performed the current solution contains minimal vertex-sharing cubes. The next step is to reorganize the size of the cubes into a more convenient form, the reshaping process, without changing their coverage or number. Thus, reshaping transforms a pair of cubes into another disjoint pair such that the vertex coverage is not affected. Assume that in $S$, the current solution list of cubes, no cube covers another and the distance between any two cubes is greater than or equal to two. Then if $A = a_1 a_2 \ldots a_n$ and $B = b_1 b_2 \ldots b_n$ are two cubes in $S$, the necessary and sufficient conditions for reshaping are as follows.

(a) The distance between $A$ and $B$ is exactly two.
(b) One part of $A$ covers the corresponding part of $B$.

Let $i$ and $j$ be the two parts in which $A$ and $B$ differ and let $j$ be the part in which $A$ covers $B$, that is $a_j$ covers $b_j$. The two cubes

$$A' = a_1 a_2 \ldots a_i \ldots (a_i \wedge \bar{b}_i) \ldots a_n$$

and

$$B' = a_1 a_2 \ldots (a_i \vee b_i) \ldots b_j \ldots a_n$$

are called the reshaped cubes of $A$ and $B$. The process is called Reshape $(A;B)$. This process is illustrated in Table 4.15; the reshaping process can also be considered as a special case of the concensus operation.

The procedures described above are incorporated into a heuristic algorithm which iteratively applies the processes of expansion, reduction, and reshaping until there is no further decrease in solution size. The main steps in the algorithm are shown below.

S1—Accept the Boolean specification.
S2—Accept the partition description, defining part sizes etc.

**Table 4.15. Reshaping Process**

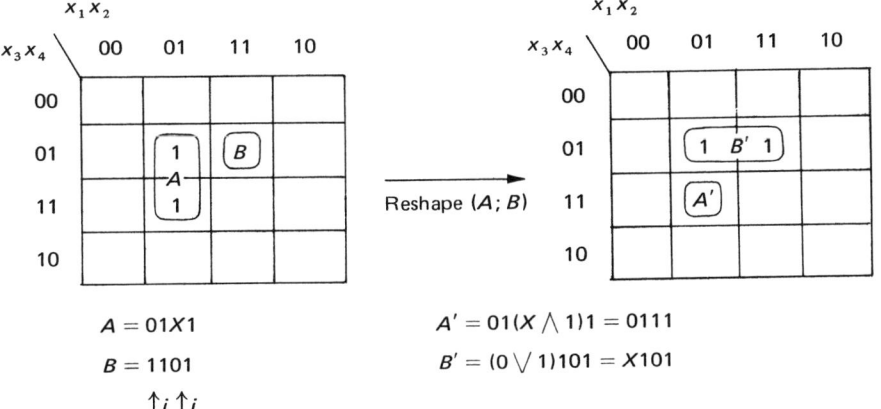

$A = 01X1$

$B = 1101$

$\uparrow_i \uparrow_j$

$A' = 01(X \wedge 1)1 = 0111$

$B' = (0 \vee 1)101 = X101$

S3—Extract the ON terms and decode into positional cube format according to the partition description; assign these cubes to the ON array $F$.
S4—Generate don't-care specification due to any inputs which appear in more than one part.
S5—Extract the don't-care terms from the original specification and add to the list generated in S4.
S6—Decode the list of DC terms into cubes and assign to DC array
S7—Generate partition description in the format required by subsequent programs.
S8—Compute the disjoint OFF cover $\bar{F} = U_n \oplus F$.
S9—Expand $\bar{F}$ against $F$ to generate new $\bar{F}$.
S10—Generate the disjoint ON cover $F = U_n \oplus (\bar{F} \cup \mathrm{DC})$.
S11—Expand $F$ against $\bar{F}$ and compute solution size.
S12—Reduce each cube of $F$ against the other cubes in $F \cup \mathrm{DC}$.
S13—Reshape $F$.
S14—Expand $F$ against $\bar{F}$ and compute solution size.
S15—If the size of the new solution is smaller than the previous one (obtained in S11) go to S12, otherwise $F$ is the solution.

Note that steps S1–S6 are only required for functions specified in the Boolean form; if the original specification is in the cube notation the algorithm may be entered at step S7. The steps S12–S15 form the main iterative loop which produces decreasing size solutions; the solutions contain all of the $F$ vertices and possibly some of the DC vertices. Each step of the algorithm is described in detail in the original paper.

The MINI process does not generate all prime implicants nor perform the classical covering procedure, but it does efficiently compute a near-minimal solution. Moreover, the procedures used in the MINI process are novel and could prove to be new and effective tools for minimization.

The MINI algorithms have been programmed for an IBM 360/75 using APL with a 65-kbyte work space. Claims are made that almost all problems with 20–30 effective input variables can be handled; a nine-variable symmetric function was minimized to a two-level circuit containing 85 cubes in about 20 min 360/75 (APL) CPU time (the minimal solution contains 84 cubes).

As with all CAD procedures of this type the results obtained are extremely problem dependent and hence difficult to evaluate. The two main criteria used to evaluate heuristic minimization programs are the minimality of the solution and the associated computation time. The degree of minimality can only be determined by minimizing examples for which a minimal solution is already known. As the number of input variables is increased (and most algorithms are concerned with large-variable problems), it becomes increasingly difficult to find examples with a known minimum The usual procedure is to obtain a minimal solution by using an alternate algorithmic procedure often based on classical methods. For example, Waters used a standard Quine-McCluskey algorithm, in conjunction with a random truth-table generator, to establish the effectiveness of the relaxation algorithm. An alternative approach is to generate a specific class of many variable Boolean functions with known (or easily computed) minimal prime-implicant covers. Ostapko and Hong (29) have described a method of computing many-variable test-case problems based on the relationship between the covering problem and the classic map-coloring problem.

### 4.2.6. Logic Implementation

Though the minimization process can lead to an economical two-level circuit, this is not necessarily the best realization of a network (except perhaps in the specific case of a PLA). For instance, in many practical cases it is necessary to consider the fan-in–fan-out factors of the modules, circuit hazards (related to the number of logic levels), and of course the type of module itself. Thus the process of circuit implementation involves not only Boolean minimization but also the consideration of engineering and circuit constraints. Thus, the output of an implementation program should be a logic diagram or wiring schedule, showing the interconnection of specific logic modules to effect an economical solution with due regard to engineering constraints.

One method of handling this problem is to employ *factorization*, which enables a given network specification to be converted to a logically equivalent implementation which satisfies fan-in and fan-out restrictions. The principle of factorization is a simple one and can be illustrated by the algebraic factoring of a Boolean sum-of-products expression. For example, the expression

$$Z_1 = a\bar{b}c\bar{e} + a\bar{b}\bar{d}\bar{e} + a\bar{c}d\bar{e} \tag{4.4}$$

requires two-level AND–OR logic for its implementation and utilizes 15 inputs and 4 gates. Now, if this expression is factored to

$$Z_1 = a\bar{e}\,(\bar{b}c + b\bar{d} + \bar{c}d)$$

the function may be implemented as a three-level circuit using 13 inputs and 6 gates; $a\bar{e}$ is called a *factor*. Note that the factorization has led to extra gates and logic levels, but an overall reduction in the fan-in factor has been achieved. In general, implementing a factored expression leads to (*a*) an increase in logic levels and hence circuit delays, (*b*) a decrease in both fan-in and fan-out factors, and (*c*) a change in circuit costs which may be greater or less than the original unfactored implementation.

Algorithmic methods for the implementation of combinational circuits using factored expressions have been described by Dietmeyer and Su (30). The objective of the work was to implement a single-output Boolean expression, defined as a cubic array, using only NAND gates with a specified maximum fan-in of $I$ inputs. Earlier, Dietmeyer and Schneider (31) proposed a formal method of extracting factors using array algebra, where a factor ($\gamma$) is defined as a product of variables common to more than one cube in the original array. For example, the factorization of the function $Z_1$ given in Eq. (4.4) may be represented in the array notation as follows:

$$C = \begin{Bmatrix} 101X0 \\ 10X00 \\ 1X010 \end{Bmatrix} \qquad \gamma = 1XXX0 \qquad D = \begin{Bmatrix} X01XX \\ X0X0X \\ XX01X \end{Bmatrix}$$

where for $C = \{c^1, c^2, \ldots, c^q\}$ the factor $\gamma$, common to vertices $c^i$ and $c^j$ of the array $C$, may be determined using the *factor product* $c^i F c^j$ defined by Table 4.16 and the following rule:

$$\gamma = (\gamma_1, \gamma_2, \ldots, \gamma_n)$$

where $\gamma_k = c_k{}^i F c_k{}^j$ with the proviso that if $\gamma = U_n$ no factors exist. Thus, given an array of cubes $C$, the common factor is given by

$$\gamma = (\ldots (c^1 F c^2) F c^3) \ldots F c^q)$$

that is

$$\gamma = (101X0 \, F \, 10X00) \, F \, (1X010) = (10XX0 \, F \, 1X010)$$
$$= 1XXX0$$

which corresponds to the factor $a\bar{c}$ obtained earlier by Boolean algebra.

The choice between alternative factors is decided using an heuristic figure of merit for each factor, which consists of the number of variables in the

**Table 4.16. Factor Product**

|  | | $c_k{}^j$ | | |
|---|---|---|---|---|
| $F$ | | 0 | 1 | X |
|---|---|---|---|---|
| $c_k{}^i$ | 0 | 0 | X | X |
|  | 1 | X | 1 | X |
|  | X | X | X | X |

factor (the *width* $\omega$) multiplied by the number of cubes in which the factor appears (the *height* $q$). Thus, the figure of merit ($M$) of factor $\gamma$ of array $C$ is given by

$$M(C, \gamma) = \omega q.$$

Dietmeyer and Su present an algorithm which generates the factor with the highest figure of merit for a given array. When an array contains more than one factor the factorization proceeds by stages, removing in turn those factors with the highest figure of merit. That is, after extracting each factor, the factor-finding algorithm is then applied to the reduced array of cubes ($D$) to obtain the next factor having the highest figure of merit.

The figure of merit described above does not necessarily give an adequate measure of the true cost savings which can be achieved by factorization, since it is based on an implementation using NAND gates with $I$ inputs. Consequently, using this criteria to select alternative factors does not guarantee a minimal-cost circuit.

An alternative measure of the cost of a term is simply the number of its inputs, the cost increasing when the number of inputs rises above the predetermined value of $I$. (In the Dietmeyer method this term-cost is used to restrict the number of factors considered.) Since in a practical situation a number of different types of gate would be used to achieve a realization, each with differing values of $I$, a more general figure of merit which takes these practical considerations into account is required.

The basic Dietmeyer and Su algorithms have been programmed for the IBM 1620 computer (using FORTRAN), but a disclaimer is made that they are not suitable for a design automation scheme without considerable modification both to the algorithm and the software implementation. Nevertheless typical 10-variable problems were solved in under 10 s of CPU time.

A more recent factorization technique which attempts to implement combinational circuits within the constraints imposed by a practical environment is the IMPS system due to Bumstead (32). The algorithm accepts a near-minimal sum-of-products expression as its input and then implements the SOP terms using a set of NAND–NOR gates with specified cost and fan-in constraints (which may be selected by the designer). The constraints imposed by fan-out, propagation delays (i.e., number of logic levels), and logic hazards are also considered. The method makes use of a look-up table giving the costs of implementing all possible product terms, and employs a modified branch-and-bound technique (33) to generate the product factors.

The method is based on the premise that the cost of implementing each product term of a sum-of-products expression depends only on its input.

Therefore a minimum-cost implementation can be effected by *independently* realizing each SOP term at minimum cost. In some instances, however, the cost factors for individual product terms can interact; these cases are as follows.

(a) When the outputs from the previous level implementation determines whether or not the inputs to the unit under consideration need to be complemented. This can arise in a mixed-logic-gate realization where the choice of an AND or NAND gate at one level determines the logic polarity of the output to subsequent levels.

(b) If complex gates such as AND–OR–INVERT are used it is possible to implement a group of product terms with a single unit; this raises the problem of selecting the best group of SOP terms.

(c) When realizing a circuit with a specified number of logic levels in order to reduce the overall propagation delay or prevent hazards In this case the implementation of a term can affect the number of levels passed through by the output signal.

When NAND gates only are used a minimum-cost circuit is obtained by implementing each product term as a NAND subcircuit. For other gate modules, and when constrained by circuit delays, special algorithms, described in Bumstead's thesis, have to be employed.

The method used to tabulate the minimal-cost subcircuit implementation of a product term relies on the characterization of SOP terms by the number of uncomplemented $(n_1)$ and complemented $(n_2)$ inputs; the parameter $(n_1, n_2)$ is also used as the key to access the cost table. Note that an optimal implementation depends only on the number and polarity of the inputs. For instance, the term $ab\bar{c}d\bar{e}$ with $n_1 = 3$ and $n_2 = 2$ yields the same optimal circuit as $\bar{a}bcde$, which can easily be shown by simply relabeling the inputs. As an example, consider the implementation of the seven-variable function

$$Z = abZ' + c\bar{d}eZ' + f\bar{g}$$

**Table 4.17. Gate Cost Specification**

| Gate type | Fan-in | Cost |
|-----------|--------|------|
| NAND      | 1      | 10   |
|           | 2      | 15   |
|           | 3      | 20   |
|           | 4      | 30   |
|           | 8      | 60   |
| NOR       | 1      | 10   |
|           | 2      | 15   |

**Table 4.18. Minimal-Cost Implementations of SOP Terms**

| Term | $n_1/n_2$ | Circuit | Cost |
|---|---|---|---|
| $Z' = \bar{f}g$ | 1/1 | g, f → (inverter) → (NOR gate) | 25 |
| $\bar{t}_1 = abZ'$ | 3/0 | a, b, Z' → (NAND gate) | 20 |
| $\bar{t}_2 = c\bar{d}eZ'$ | 3/1 | d → (inverter); c, e, Z' → (NAND gate) | 40 |
| $\bar{t}_3 = f\bar{g}$ | 1/1 | g → (inverter); f → (NAND gate) | 25 |
| $Z_1 = t_1 + t_2 + t_3$ $= \overline{\bar{t}_1\,\bar{t}_2\,\bar{t}_3}$ | | $t_1$, $t_2$, $t_3$ → (NAND gate) | 20 |

where $Z' = \bar{f}g$ is a factor. The cost factors for the gates required to be used for the implementation are given in Table 4.17, with the minimal subcircuits for the individual SOP terms in Table 4.18; in the IMPS system these circuits would be obtained by accessing the cost table with the appropriate $(n_1, n_2)$ keys. The final circuit, which is the minimal configuration, is shown in Fig. 4.4.

The cost table is derived by considering a SOP term to be represented by a cascaded circuit consisting of NAND and NOR gates with limited

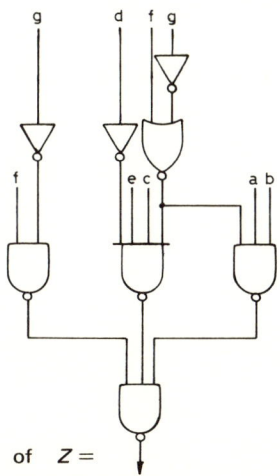

**Figure 4.4.** Implementation of $Z = abZ' + c\bar{d}eZ' + f\bar{g}$.

fan-in; this is shown in Fig. 4.5. The technique used is to reduce successively the original $(n_1, n_2)$ input signal paths until the output level is reached, when there will be only one signal path $(0,1)$ carrying the output. In the general case shown in Fig. 4.5 the NAND–NOR blocks can comprise a subcircuit consisting of a number of gates, with the state of the signal reductions at any stage $i$ being defined by $(n_1^i, n_2^i)$. A modified form of dynamic programming (34) is used to generate the cost table. The required incremental change of state is related to an alteration of the number of uncomplemented and complemented signals from $(n_1^1, n_2^1)$ to $(n_1^2, n_2^2)$, etc., subject to a given cost criteria.

The cost program may be set up prior to an implementation pass for any specified set of modules with a given cost and fan-in factor. A typical run time for the COST program is quoted as requiring 17 s of CPU time on an ICL 1906A machine to generate a cost table for 20 inputs $(n_1 + n_2)$ and four-logic levels.

In the IMPS system the factorized form of the switching function is obtained by extracting factors from a minimal sum-of-products expression

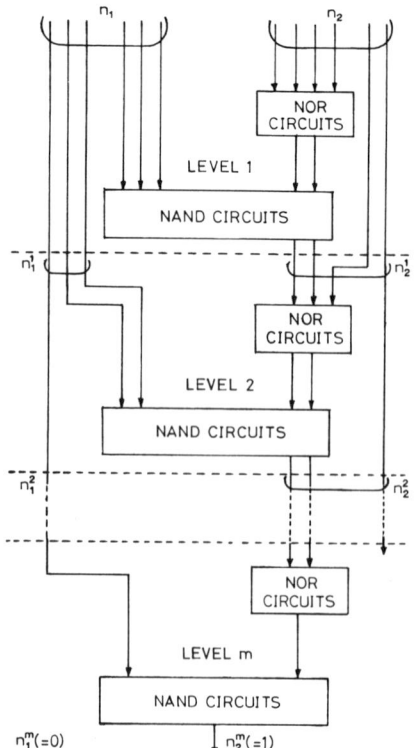

**Figure 4.5.** Cascaded NAND-NOR model.

which is generated using the relaxation method of minimization described earlier. The factors are restricted to particular types with special properties which are more likely to lead to an economical implementation; for example, factors with redundant terms are not considered.

The special factors used in the IMPS system are defined as follows.

(a) *A product-term factor (PF)* of an SOP expression consists of a set of literals which are included in more than one term of the expression; it follows from the definition that a single literal can be a PF. Thus if

$$Z = ab\bar{c}d + ab\bar{c}f + abde \qquad\qquad (4.5)$$

than $(ab\bar{c})$, $(ab)$, $(b\bar{c})$, $(ad)$, $(a\bar{c})$, and $(bd)$ are product-term factors. Removing PF's from an expression reduces the fan-in factors of the modules but increases their number. Note that for the product-term factor $PF = \{x_1, x_2, \ldots, x_n\}$ of a function $Z$, where $n$ is the number of variables, all product terms consisting of a subset of the variables of PF are also factors of the function. For instance, $ab$ and $a\bar{c}$ are also PF's of function $Z$ in Eq. (4.5).

(b) *A maximal product-term factor (MPF)* is such that for

$$PF = \{x_1, x_2, \ldots, x_n\}$$

there exists no other product term

$$PF' = PF\, x_k$$

where $k \neq 1, \ldots, n$ such that $PF'$ is a factor of all terms in the SOP expression of which PF is a factor. For example, the MPF's of Eq. (4.5) are

$ab\bar{c}$ in terms 1, 2

$bd$ in terms 1, 3

$ab$ in terms 1, 2, and 3.

(c) *A sum-of-product factor (SF)* is a factor in $n$ variables $(x_1, x_2, \ldots, x_n)$ which represents a multi-term switching function which cannot be covered by a single prime implicant and is therefore irreducible a distinction is made between single sum-of-product factors (SSF) which occur once in an expression and common sum-of-product factors (CSF) which occur more than once. For example, in the expression

$$ab\bar{e}\,(cd + \bar{c}\bar{d}) + \bar{a}\bar{b} \qquad\qquad (4.6)$$

$(cd + \bar{c}\bar{d})$ is a SSF since the switching function cannot be reduced; however, in the expression

$$\bar{a}b\,(\bar{c}df + \bar{c}d\bar{f}) + a\bar{b}$$

the factor $(\bar{c}df + \bar{c}d\bar{f})$ is not a SF since it can be reduced to $\bar{c}d$ which is a prime implicant of the expression. A SSF is always associated with a product-term factor; for instance in the expression above, Eq. (4.6), the SSF $(cd + \bar{c}\bar{d})$ is called the *cofactor* of the PF $(ab\bar{e})$. The set of all possible SSF's of a given sum-of-products expression can be generated by forming the set of PF's and then deriving their cofactors; it can be shown that only MPF s need be considered in this process.

The input to the IMPS system consists of a set of sum-of-products expressions which are then factorized to generate the factors described above. Since it is not possible to select an optimal set of factors to give a minimal cost cover by evaluating each factor independently using the cost table (owing to interaction between factors), it is necessary to search all alternative choices of factors in order to determine a minimal-cost implementation. If a sum-of-products expression has $n$ maximal product-term factors then there are $3^n$ ways of selecting factors to form alternative expressions: each MPF may be selected, or the cofactor of each MPF, or neither of these. Since the number of MPF's for an expression can be quite large, it is obviously impracticable to use exhaustive search methods, and a means of limiting the number of alternative expressions which are examined must be found.

One method of solving this problem of minimizing a function $f$ in a discrete set $X$ is to use the branch-and-bound method already successfully employed in other implementation schemes (17, 36). In the present case the set $X$ consists of $3^n$ elements, each of which is an alternative factorized expression derived from the original SOP expression $Z$ by removing a subset of the $K$ MPF's of $Z$ and their cofactors. Let the function $f(x)$, where $x \in X$, be the cost of a factorized expression of $x$ evolved using the cost-table technique. Then the requirement to find a minimum-cost factorized expression may be stated as determining an element $x'$ of $X$ such that $f(x') \leqslant f(x)$ for all $x \in X$. In order to apply the branch-and-bound method a means of evaluating a lower bound function $g(A)$, where $A \subseteq X$, on the value of $f(x)$ for any $x \in A$ must be defined; this creates the major difficulty in applying the technique to minimal-cost searches. The IMPS algorithm proceeds by partitioning the set $X$, stage by stage, into progressively smaller subsets until a subset $x'$ is reached which is the minimal-cost solution. At each stage only one subset $A$ of $X$, for which $g(A)$ is minimum, is partitioned.

The actual method is best illustrated by way of an example: consider the expression

$$Z = a\bar{c}\bar{d} + \bar{c}\bar{d}e + \bar{c}\bar{d}f + a\bar{d}e$$

**Table 4.19. Factor Sets**

| No. | MPF | Cofactor (SSF) | Cost |
|-----|-----|----------------|------|
| 1 | $\bar{d}e$ | $\bar{c} + a$ | 25 |
| 2 | $\bar{d}$ | $a\bar{c} + \bar{c}e + \bar{c}f + ae$ | 120 |
| 3 | $\bar{c}\bar{d}$ | $a + e + f$ | 40 |

which has the MPF and SSF factors shown in Table 4.19. The table also shows the cost of implementing each factor (derived from the cost table) with the set of gates shown in Table 4.17. The partitions on this expression performed by the branch-and-bound algorithm are shown in Fig. 4.6 in the form of a tree graph, where each node in the graph represents a stage in the partitioning process. Thus, node $X_0$ represents the complete unpartitioned set of all possible expressions, and nodes $X_1$ and $X_2$ the two disjoint subsets formed by partitioning $X_0$ into the set of expressions for which the SSF $(\bar{c} + a)$ has been removed (indicated in the graph by the notation $1XX$ since there are three SSF's) and the set for which $(\bar{c} + a)$ has not been removed (denoted by $0XX$). Note that each factor is taken in a prescribed sequence, the order of which can affect the final result.

Associated with each stage of the partitioning process is the calculation of the value of $g(A)$. For nodes representing subsets containing more than one expression, such as $X_7$, $g(A)$ is obtained by summing the individual cost of

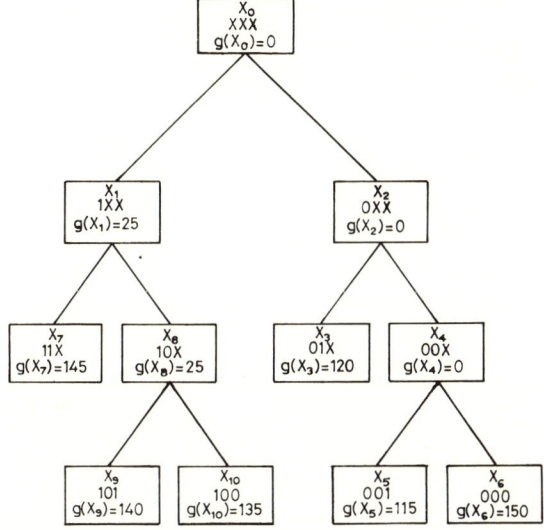

**Figure 4.6.** Branch-and-bound search.

the removed SSF's; thus for node $X_7$, $g(X_7) = 25 + 120 = 145$. When a node represents subsets of $X_0$ containing a single expression, such as $X_9$, $g(A)$ is obtained by evaluating the expression using the cost table. For instance in node $X_9$ the 3-tuple 101 indicates that SSF's 1 and 3 are removed; therefore the expression

$$Z = \bar{d}eZ_1' + \bar{c}\bar{d}Z_2'$$

where

$$Z_1' = \bar{c} + a \quad \text{and} \quad Z_2' = a + e + f$$

is evaluated to obtain a value for $g(X_9)$.

One of the novel features of the IMPS system is that the implementation routine preserves the hazard conditions of the original circuit and will realize a network within a specified overall propagation delay. Providing the original switching equations are free of logical hazards, for example if all the prime implicants are present and represented in a sum-of-products form (37), the IMPS factorization routines will not introduce additional hazards. This is achieved by using only the hazard-preserving transformations described by Ungar (38); based on this work factoring operations are restricted to the following Boolean laws and transformations: (a) the generalized De Morgan theorem; (b) the associative law; (c) factoring, but not multiplying out; (d) the relations $a + ab = a$ and $a + \bar{a}b = a + b$.

Following this procedure results in a multi-level implementation which contains only those hazards which were inherent in the original two-level sum-of-products expression. The effect of propagation delays through the network can also be compensated; these delays can give rise to hazardous conditions in a circuit when signals have different path lengths. In some cases it is also important to obtain a minimum delay between input and output signals to conform to timing constraints. Propagation delays are specified in the IMPS system by the user, who must assign an allowed signal delay called the *delay set number*, to each variable in the expression to be implemented. When an AND term is implemented as a cascade of NAND–NOR circuits the algorithm ensures that each variable belonging to the same delay set traverses the same number of gates. Owing to the signal inversions produced by the NAND–NOR gates the unit of delay is taken to be the propagation delay of two gates. The relative delay between variables is brought about by specifying that variables belonging to delay set $d$ should pass through one more unit of delay than variables belonging to delay set $(d - 1)$. The technique is realized by modifying the dynamic-programming algorithm to generate a cost table of minimal-cost implementations in which all the variables in the term pass through the same number of gates.

The IMPS system has been successfully programmed for the ICL 1900 series computer and tested using randomly generated problems and standard design examples. The output of the system is a tabulated wiring schedule describing gate types and their interconnections, but this could easily be modified to produce a graphical output. Comparisons were also made against circuit examples quoted in the literature by other authors and circuits produced by manual (that it intuitive) logic design techniques; the results of these comparisons are shown in Table 4.20. It will be seen that the IMPS algorithms compare very favorably with earlier published results and in all cases produce a comparable cost solution. The results obtained with manually designed circuits indicate in general a small improvement in cost, but of course the reduction in design time is drastic, showing clearly the advantages of CAD.

### 4.2.7. Design Automation Schemes

The minimization and implementation procedures discussed in the preceding sections would normally be included as part of an overall logic design automation (DA) system; for instance, the relaxation and IMPS algorithms are both part of the CALD system (39). The characteristics of the design automation scheme must of necessity effect the design of individual packages and the overall performance required from the software; thus it is not viable to develop synthesis packages in isolation. The CALD system, for instance, requires a tabular input in terms of ON and OFF arrays [generated by the

**Table 4.20.  IMPS Test Results**

| Circuit | Number of | | IMPS data | | | Control data | | |
|---|---|---|---|---|---|---|---|---|
| | Variables | Outputs | Run-time (s) | Store (K words) | Cost | Run-time (s) | Cost | Computer |
| Ref. 30 | 10 | 1 | 4 | 3 | 160 | 27 | 160 | IBM 1620 |
| Ref. 31 | 8 | 1 | 2 | 2 | 105 | 13.5 | 130 | IBM 1620 |
| Ref. 36 | 10 | 6 | 11 | 4 | 580 | 2.4 | 710 | CDC 6400 |
| Ref. 17 | 8 | 1 | 4 | 3 | 26 | 45.6 | 23 | IBM 704 |
| Control logic | 15 | 1 | 2 | 2 | 370 | – | 455 | – |
| Control logic | 14 | 4 | 19 | 4 | 815 | – | 710 | – |
| Register transfer | 10 | 10 | 4 | 2 | 350 | – | 335 | – |
| Register transfer | 7 | 4 | 4 | 2 | 195 | – | 170 | – |
| Decoding | 9 | 5 | 8 | 3 | 385 | – | 425 | – |
| Decoding | 4 | 7 | 8 | 3 | 340 | – | 275 | – |

designer using a problem-oriented language or a flow-table description (40)] which constrains the design of subsequent synthesis packages. Other DA schemes described in the literature are the IBM ALERT system (41) and the Singer Corporation System (42). In the ALERT system, discussed earlier in § 2.7.4, the IBM logic automation system is used to implement the Boolean equations derived from the initial Iverson description. The implementation routine simply checks for redundant expressions (no factorization is performed) and realizes the equations directly as NAND or AND- OR- INVERT gates using IBM solid-state technology. The system is very inefficient due mainly to the inherent redundancy in generating the Boolean equations from the Iverson language descriptions. It is doubtful whether the use of a more sophisticated implementation program would be cost effective. The Singer system uses a low-level register-transfer language called LOGICSPEC to describe the Boolean equations effecting the transfer and processing operations between registers. Again, a very simple implementation procedure is adopted which performs a direct realization without undue attention to minimal cost criteria, the onus being on the designer to manipulate the original equations into an economical form.

It is perhaps unfair to contrast the implementation routines in these DA schemes, since the main emphasis in the work was placed on system specification and documentation. However, the fact remains that there is no DA scheme as yet which adequately satisfies the criteria for the automated design of combinational (and sequential, as we shall see in the next section) logic systems. The CALD system satisfies many of the requirements for the design of subsystems, but the major problem of implementing design equations in terms of complex LSI modules (such as ROM's, PLA's, $\mu$-processors, etc.) still remains to be solved.

## 4.3. SYNTHESIS OF SEQUENTIAL CIRCUITS

The design of sequential systems conventionally falls into four distinct phases (43).

(a) The representation of the required machine function in terms of a state or flow table.
(b) Reduction and merging of the state table or flow table to obtain a minimum number of internal states and hence bistables in the final implementation.
(c) The assignment of a binary code to the internal states of the machine; this may be done primarily for economic reasons in the case of synchronous machines or to eliminate critical races in asynchronous machines.
(d) Extraction and minimization of the next-state and output combinational logic functions which are defined by the assigned state table.

It will be seen from (d) above that an essential component of any automated system for sequential-circuit design is the minimization and implementation routines discussed earlier. In fact it is more realistic to consider combinational-circuit design as a special case of the more general problem of sequential-circuit design.

Though a large number of research papers have appeared on all the above aspects of sequential-circuit design, very few of the theoretical ideas described have found direct application in design automation schemes. The reasons for this are numerous, not the least of which is the reluctance of the logic designer to use sequential-machine concepts. As we have seen, state tables are not easy to derive for complex circuits, even when partitioned into control–data structures, and a method of specifying the system which renders the theory "invisible" to the user must be developed. Another important disadvantage is that, though the theoretical work is formally consistent and leads to an optimum solution, the mathematics can seldom be programmed efficiently for a digital computer. Moreover, in many cases undue emphasis is placed on particular aspects of economical design. For instance, state reduction has been performed on the basis of decreasing the number of internal states, and hence bistables, on the assumption that this will produce the most economical circuit. In many cases, however, this is not the case, since reducing the number of bistables can often lead to increased complexity in the associated combinational logic. This becomes quite pertinent when using LSI modules, since storage devices, being regular in structure and easier to fabricate, are cheap and readily available, whereas random logic arrays must be custom designed. This leads quite naturally to the concept of implementing sequential machines using ROM's or RAM's with the minimum of external logic; note that in this case reducing the number of states in the machine will reduce the number of words required in the ROM. A similar situation exists with state-assignment algorithms where the objective is to reduce the input logic to the bistable circuits; in many cases this is done without consideration of the effect that the assignment may have on the output circuits. In the case of ROM implementation, however, the output values would normally be stored in the ROM words so the question does not arise; moreover, the input logic need not be reduced to a minimum since in effect it becomes part of the address-decoding network of the ROM.

An overall criticism is that much of the work has been done in isolation without too much regard for the constraints imposed by the necessity to effect a computer implementation. For example, the theory of synchronous and asynchronous machines has in the main been treated separately owing to its historical evolution. However, it is important in a DA scheme to have common synthesis procedures which can handle both types of machine in order to reduce the software overheads. Similarly, very little attempt has been made to apply heuristic methods to allow an efficient computational algorithm to be obtained.

It will be apparent that, as in the case of combinational switching theory, there still exists a considerable amount of basic research to be performed. However, though very few software systems exist for the automated design of sequential circuits there is nevertheless sufficient theory to establish a good foundation for DA schemes and in the following sections we shall discuss some of these techniques.

### 4.3.1. State-Table Reduction

We shall restrict out discussion to incompletely specified state tables, that is, those in which some internal and output states either cannot occur or their condition is immaterial, since most practical machines fall into this category; the fully specified table can of course be treated as a special case. The objective of state-table reduction is to seek a machine with the smallest number of states which is equivalent to at least one of the machines represented by the incompletely specified state table.

The main advantage of state-table reduction is that the number of bistables required for an implementation can be reduced; for example, an $n$-state machine (or rows in the case of an asynchronous circuit) requires $\log_2 n$ storage devices (to the nearest integer). However, reduction can only be achieved when $n$ crosses a $2^s$ threshold, where $s$ is the number of state variables, and $(n, s)$ obviously become further apart as $n$ increases. This means that for very large machines state-reduction techniques seldom yield savings in storage elements. Nevertheless, state minimization is a worthwhile procedure, since the inevitable increase in don't-care values allows more economical state assignments and consequently bistable input logic to be obtained. The advantages are more apparent, however, when ROM implementations are employed (44), since in this case the number of rows, and hence words in the ROM, is the determining factor. A further advantage is obtained in the generation of diagnostic test sequences, since the length of the sequence is directly proportional to the number of states.

Another important point which is not generally realized is that a reduced state table masks the structure of a machine. This is particularly important when decomposition techniques are employed (45), since many regular structures are inherently redundant (for example, shift-register configurations) and an irredundant machine is often impossible to decompose into a regular structure. One approach to the problem is to start with a fully reduced machine and then progressively add redundancy (by state splitting) until a decomposition is possible.

The original work on state reduction was performed by Ginsberg (46) and Paull and Ungar (47) and is well reported in the standard textbooks (43). The basic method involves deriving an *implication chart* from the state table for a given machine which delineates all possible equivalences between pairs of states. Two states are said to be equivalent (or *compatible*) if (*a*) they have the same output state, and (*b*) for all possible input changes their next-state transitions result in the same (or equivalent) states. Note that the unspecified conditions can be allotted in such a way as to effect these requirements and that states with different output states can never be equivalent.

In order to generate the complete set of *maximal compatibles* the implication chart must be exhaustively searched for all compatible state pairs which are then combined into compatible sets (or *c-classes*) in which *all* elements of the set are pair-wise compatible. A maximal compatible is a set of compatible pairs that is not contained in any other compatible set. For example, from the state table shown in Table 4.21 we obtain the following set of pair-wise compatibles:

$(2,3)(2,6)(2,7)(3,4)(3,6)(3,7)(4,5)(4,7)(4,8)(5,8)(6,7)$

which can be combined to give the maximal compatibles

$(2,3,6,7),(3,4,7)$, and $(4,5,8)$.

Note that, since all states in a compatible set are equivalent, all but one state may be removed from the state table, thereby giving a reduction in its size.

In order to obtain a minimal machine it is necessary to select a set of compatibles which fulfils the following conditions.

(**a**) Every internal state of the machine is contained in at least one compatible term in the set—called the *covering* condition.

**Table 4.21. Incompletely Specified State Table**

| Present state | Input X | |
|---|---|---|
| | Next state | Output Z |
| | 0   1 | 0   1 |
| 1 | 2   8 | 1   1 |
| 2 | 1   7 | 0   0 |
| 3 | X   6 | 0   X |
| 4 | 4   X | 0   1 |
| 5 | 3   4 | 0   X |
| 6 | 1   3 | X   0 |
| 7 | X   2 | X   X |
| 8 | 7   5 | 0   X |

**(b)** The next states of every state pair in a compatible for all input conditions must be included in at least one other compatible of the set—known as the *closure* condition.

**(c)** The number of elements in the set of compatibles must be a minimum whilst still satisfying the covering and closure conditions—called the *minimality* condition.

Thus the reduction of a state table consists of generating all possible maximal compatibles and then selecting a minimal cover of the machine which satisfies the closure condition. This is analogous to the combinational minimization problem and presents similar computational difficulties. The Paull and Ungar method for extracting maximal compatibles has been successfully programmed for small-variable problems, and alternative algebraic methods, but difficult to program, have been described by Marcus (48) and Bouchet (49). However, the problem of selecting a minimal cover remains a difficult one; satisfying the covering condition is comparatively simple but meeting the closure conditions for large state tables can become very involved. The problem has been considered by Graselli and Luccio (50) using the concept of *prime compatibles* (PC's) which reduces the number of sets of compatibles which have to be considered for a minimal solution.

As an example of the closure problem consider the machine shown in Tables 4.21 and 4.22. Now $C_3 = (4,5,8)$ is a compatible, but what other compatibles must be included to constitute a closed set? From the table we can establish that the implied sets are

$$(4,3)(4,7)(3,7) \text{ and } (4,5)$$

and it is necessary that the sets $(4,3)(4,7)$ and $(3,7)$ be contained in the other compatibles which are selected for the minimal cover. If we denote the closure requirement by $P_k$ then we can say that $P_3 = \{(4,3)(4,7)(3,7)\}$. Consider, however, the compatible $C_1 = (2,3,6,7)$ for the same machine; in this case the implied sets are

$$(7,6)(7,3)(7,2)(6,3)(6,2) \text{ and } (3,2)$$

and we see that $C_1$ satisfies all its own closure requirements and we can set $P_1 = \{\phi\}$, where $\phi$ is the empty set. Since $C_1 = (2,3,6,7)$ is a compatible any subset of $C_1$ is also a compatible; consequently, for

$$C_1' = (3,6,7)$$

we have

$$P_1' = \{(3,6)(6,2)(3,2)\}.$$

Note that $C_1 \supset C_1'$ and $P_1 \subseteq P_1'$; when this condition is met we say that compatible $C_1'$ is *excluded* by compatible $C_1$. It will be obvious that in selecting a minimal closed cover of compatibles that $C_1$ would be a far better choice than $C_1'$.

A *prime compatible* is defined as one that is not excluded by any other compatible (notice the close analogy with prime implicants). Note also that, though maximal compatibles must obviously be prime compatibles, a prime compatible is not necessarily a maximal compatible. Prime compatibles are important in state-table reduction, since it can be shown that there always exists at least one set of PC's which satisfies the covering, closure, and minimality requirements for a given machine.

The complete set of PC's for a machine can be generated from the set of maximal compatibles using an enumerative procedure. For example, in Table 4.22 starting with the maximal compatible with the largest number of states $(n)$ we delete one state at a time to form the set of $n-3$ compatibles

**Table 4.22. Generation of Prime Compatibles**

|  |  | $C_k$ |  | $P_k$ |
|---|---|---|---|---|
| $n = 4$ | $C_1$ | (2,3,6,7) |  | $\{\phi\}$ |
| $n = 3$ |  | (2,3,6) | ✓ | $\{(7,6)(7,3)(6,3)\}$ |
|  |  | (2,3,7) | ✓ | $\{(7,6)(2,7)(6,2)\}$ |
|  |  | (2,6,7) | ✓ | $\{(7,3)(7,2)(3,2)\}$ |
|  |  | (3,6,7) | ✓ | $\{(6,3)(6,2)(3,2)\}$ |
|  | $C_2$ | (3,4,7) |  | $\{6,2\}$ |
|  | $C_3$ | (4,5,8) |  | $\{(4,3)(4,7)(7,3)(4,5)\}$ |
| $n = 2$ | $C_4$ | (3,4) |  | $\{\phi\}$ |
|  |  | (3,7) | ✓ | $\{6,2\}$ |
|  | $C_5$ | (4,7) |  | $\{\phi\}$ |
|  | $C_6$ | (4,5) |  | $\{4,3\}$ |
|  | $C_7$ | (4,8) |  | $\{4,7\}$ |
|  | $C_8$ | (5,8) |  | $\{(7,3)(4,5)\}$ |
|  | $C_9$ | (1) |  | $\{\phi\}$ |
|  |  | (2) | ✓ | $\{\phi\}$ |
|  |  | (3) | ✓ | $\{\phi\}$ |
|  |  | (4) | ✓ | $\{\phi\}$ |
|  | $C_{10}$ | (5) |  | $\{\phi\}$ |
|  |  | (6) | ✓ | $\{\phi\}$ |
|  |  | (7) | ✓ | $\{\phi\}$ |
|  | $C_{11}$ | (8) |  | $\{\phi\}$ |

(including the original maximal compatibles containing $n-3$ states). The implied state sets are then derived (from the state table of Table 4.21) and each compatible tested for primality using the relationships $C_i \supseteq C_k$ and $P_i \subseteq P_k$; the compatibles which are excluded are checked off and ignored in later processing. The $n-2$ set of compatibles is formed next, and the procedure continued until no further decomposition is possible; the complete set of PC's is shown in Table 4.22.

Once all the prime compatibles for a machine are available, the next step is to choose a minimal set satisfying the cover and closure conditions. Though in CAD systems this would be performed using an algorithmic procedure, we shall illustrate the principles involved using a tabular method based on a covering and closure table called a *CC-table*, shown in Table 4.23. The covering section of the table is similar to the prime-implicant chart and is comprised of entries indicating the states covered by each prime compatible; for instance, CI covers states 2, 3, 6, and 7 and $X$'s are placed at the appropriate intersections of the table.

The closure section displays the corresponding closure requirements for each prime compatible. For example, suppose C2 was selected as a possible candidate for a minimal set, then the compatible C1 must be included in the set to satisfy the implied state conditions. This is indicated in the closure section of the chart by placing a circle at row C2, column 1, and a cross at row C1, column 1. (Note that since the choice of C1 does not include any closure requirements there is no need to insert a circle in the C1 row.) Similarly, if we selected compatible C8 it is necessary to include C3 and either C1 or C2, that is (C3)(C1 + C2); this is shown in columns 5 and 6.

Using the CC table a set of PC's $(S_p)$ which satisfy the covering and closure conditions for a machine can immediately be determined. For example, from Table 4.23 we obtain

**Table 4.23. CC-Table**

| | Covering section | | | | | | | | Closure section | | | | | |
|---|---|---|---|---|---|---|---|---|---|---|---|---|---|---|
| | S1 | S2 | S3 | S4 | S5 | S6 | S7 | S8 | 1 | 2 | 3 | 4 | 5 | 6 |
| C1 | | X | X | | | X | X | | X | | | | X | |
| C2 | | | X | X | | | X | | 0 | X | X | X | X | |
| C3 | | | | X | X | | | X | | 0 | | | | X |
| C4 | | X | X | | | | | | | | | | | |
| C5 | | | | X | | | X | | | | | | | |
| C6 | | | | X | X | | | | | | 0 | | | |
| C7 | | | | X | | | | X | | | | 0 | | |
| C8 | | | | | X | | | X | | | | | 0 | 0 |
| C9 | X | | | | | | | | | | | | | |
| C10 | | | | | X | | | | | | | | | |
| C11 | | | | | | | | X | | | | | | |

$$S_{p_1} = (C9)(C1)(C3)(C2)$$
$$S_{p_2} = (C9)(C1)(C6)(C2)(C7)$$
$$S_{p_3} = (C9)(C1)(C2)(C8)(C3) \quad \text{etc.}$$

Note that $S_{p_1}$ represents the minimal machine since only four states are required.

The CC-table can be reduced using the same methods as those employed for prime-implicant charts, that is, algorithms based on row and column dominance. Similarly it is possible to identify *essential prime compatibles* (for example, C1 and C9 in the example above) and *cyclic tables*, thus once again indicating the close similarity of the two approaches and the fundamental nature of the covering problem.

Numerous extensions to the original work of Grasselli and Luccio have been reported in the literature. Luccio (51) has redefined prime compatible classes to allow the number of compatibles considered for a minimal cover to be reduced. Bennetts (52) has described a method for deriving prime C-classes which does not require the generation of maximal compatibles, since the C-classes are constructed from a list of pair-wise compatibles obtained directly from the state table together with the implied class sets. Algebraic procedures for determining irredundant prime closed sets have been described by de Sarkar *et al.* (53, 54) while Yang (55) has presented a partition method of minimization.

The use of state-table decomposition techniques for the determination of maximal compatibles has been proposed by Sinha Roy and Sheng (56), and Kella (57) has reported a method of obtaining a minimal cover for a machine by recursively adding new states rather than starting with the complete set of MC's. Note that the algorithms of both Bennetts and Kella dispense with the necessity of generating the complete set of MC's as a preliminary step. A somewhat different approach, based on heuristic principles, is the reduction of state tables using a randomized search as described by Stentiford and Lewin (58). A more recent paper by Biswas (59) describes a systematic procedure based on a compatiblity-graph representation of the implication chart for generating a minimal cover for a machine.

Unfortunately practically all of the methods mentioned above would be extremely inefficient if implemented on a computer. This is particularly true of the graphical and decomposition methods, but applies generally to all techniques—as shown by the lack of any reported computer implementations. One exception to this is the work by Bennetts *et al.* (60) who describe a heuristic procedure for generating minimal covers based on the determination of a closure function for each maximal or prime compatible set. The algorithm commences by generating all the maximal compatibles for the machine together with their associated closure functions; from the set of maximal compatibles the essential MC's can then be identified. The next step is to compute, in turn, for each essential MC a tree structure showing the chain of implied MC's until termination (indicating closure) is obtained. The algorithm includes heuristic criteria which ensure an early termination obtained by ignoring the exploration of minor alternative branches. The subset of MC's obtained in this way is tested for machine cover, and if covering is not achieved another essential MC is selected and the process repeated. The algorithm does not normally result in a minimal machine, but in general a near-minimal solution is obtained which is comparable to a good engineering design obtained by manual methods.

The algorithm was programmed for an ICL 1900 series machine, using a list-processing language embedded in FORTRAN, and forms part of the CALD suite. Results are difficult to quote since they are obviously problem dependent, but a 22-state machine was minimized to 12 states in 251 s using 12 K of core for program and 14 K for working space.

One of the major computing problems associated with state reduction is the amount of core required to generate and select the maximal and prime compatible classes. This is particularly so with PC's, since there are in general many more PC's than MC's for a given machine (rather like multiple-output prime implicants). For instance, in the result quoted above the number of prime compatible sets is 261 requiring more than 32 K of core for generation. Thus in a practical case, unless a theoretical minimum machine is required, it would appear better practice to calculate MC's only.

Most of the work on state-table reduction has been described in relation to synchronous machines. However, the same techniques can be used for asynchronous machines but certain restrictions have to be applied (61). The principle modification is that it is necessary to allocate the output values of the unstable states in the primitive flow table prior to commencing the reduction routine in order to avoid spurious signals on the output lines. Transient output pulses can occur if the unstable output states are left unallocated and treated as don't-cares in the reduction process. For example, if a transition occurs from a stable state with output value 0 to another stable state with output value 0, the intermediate unstable-state output must also be 0. If the unstable-state output is left as a don't-care value, it could be allocated to a 1 in the reduction process and thus give rise to a spike on the output. Note that the reduction process not only eliminates redundant stable states in the flow table but also simultaneously merges the rows. In general a Mealy machine results, in which the output values are different for stable states in the same row of the flow table, and consequently it is not possible to realize the output as a sole function of the state variables. If a Moore machine is required it is necessary first to eliminate the redundant stable states and then perform the row merging independently.

### 4.3.2. State Assignment

Once a minimal state table for a machine has been produced the next step in the synthesis process is to effect a hardware realization. In order to achieve this the rows of the state table (corresponding to the internal states of the machine) must be coded using a unique binary code for each row. For an $r$-row machine the minimum number of storage devices required is specified by the relationship

$$2^{s-1} < r \geqslant 2^{s}$$

where $s$ is the number of state variables; for a logically correct assignment each state must be allocated to one of the $2^{s}$ possible combinations. Note that there are

$$\frac{2^{s}\,!}{(2^{s} - r)!}$$

ways of allocating the $2^{s}$ combinations to an $r$-row state table. However, it has been shown (62) that, under certain conditions when alternative assignments differ only in a re-ordering or complementing of their columns, they may be considered equivalent. In this case the number of state assignments reduces to

$$A_{(r)} = \frac{(2^{s} - 1)!}{(2^{s} - r)!\,s!}\ .$$

In all practical cases (say circuits with more than five states) to attempt to determine an optimal assignment by enumerative methods is obviously impossible and algorithmic techniques must be used. Thus the major problem in state assignment resides in determining an algorithm for coding the internal states of a machine so that an economical and, in the case of asynchronous circuits, race-free realization is obtained. There is a fundamental difference between assigning synchronous and asynchronous machines. In the case of the former, any set of state codes, providing each member is uniquely assigned to a particular state, can be used to generate a correctly functioning circuit, and the main design criterion is circuit economy. Asynchronous machines, on the other hand, because of their unclocked, logic-level mode of operation, require to be assigned in such a way as to eliminate critical races which can occur if more than one secondary variable changes at a time—circuit economy, therefore, is not a primary design consideration.

Another important consideration is that the type of bistable used for the implementation can often determine the optimal assignment (63, 64). This rather obvious factor is often neglected in work on state assignment. The effect of bistable type is perhaps more relevant to synchronous machines where there is a greater choice of storage devices, for example D-type (delay elements) set–reset and J–K devices, but it also applies to asynchronous circuits where either feedback (direct implementation of the excitation equations corresponds to using delay elements) or DC set–reset bistable circuits are used. Owing to the swing in logic systems design from implementation using discrete gates and bistables to complex MSI components such as ROM's, PLA's, etc., the economical state assignment of synchronous machines has become of less importance (except for the realization of LSI chips). Asynchronous machines, on the other hand, irrespective of how they are implemented, require to be assigned in a race-free manner (races can occur in a ROM realization owing to switching delays in the indigenous storage elements).

A considerable literature has arisen on the subject of state assignment for both synchronous and asynchronous systems; unfortunately very little of the formal theory can be fully utilized in CAD systems and it has been necessary to draw heavily on heuristic methods. In the remainder of this section we shall review, from the point of view of CAD, the more relevant work that has emerged in the theory of synchronous- and asynchronous-machine assignments.

### 4.3.3. Synchronous-Machine Assignment

One of the first programmable algorithms for state assignment described in the literature was due to Armstrong (65), and was based on the fact that a given state assignment will lead to a "good" realization if in the excitation and output K-maps the entries are clustered into separate large groups of 0's and 1's. This may be achieved by examining the rows and columns of the state table for state pairs which can be given adjacent codes and so directly yield simplified Boolean equations for the next-state variables in terms of the present state and input variables; a procedure for obtaining a state assignment of this type was first described by Humphrey (66).

Armstrong defined two adjacency conditions based on the relationships between states.

(a) *Type-I adjacency.* This occurs when two present states have identical next states for the same given input state. The adjacencies are determined by examining all of the state-table columns for the condition

$$N(q_i, I_m) = N(q_j, I_m)$$

where $N$ signifies the next-state function and $q$ and $I$ are the internal and input states respectively; $q_i$ and $q_j$ would be assigned adjacent codings to effect a good assignment.

(b) *Type-II adjacency.* This is present when two next states have the same present state in the state table and the input codes for the respective columns are adjacent. Thus each row of the state table is evaluated for the condition

$$N(q_i, I_m) = q_j \quad \text{and} \quad N(q_i, I_p) = q_k$$

where $I_m$ and $I_p$ are adjacent input states; in this case $q_j$ and $q_k$ would be given adjacent codings.

Table 4.24 shows the type-I and type-II adjacencies for the given state table; note that it is possible for the adjacency condition to occur more than once for each state pair.

In order to understand the logic behind the choice of type-I and type-II adjacency conditions it is necessary to consider the switching terms which form the ON and OFF sets of the next state function. The minterms obtained from a pair of states with a type-I adjacency will give rise to a 1 (0) in the ON (OFF) sets of the next state function depending on the coding of the next state. Since the next state is the same for both states in a type-I adjacency the function will be simplified if the state pairs are given an adjacent coding. Consider the assigned table shown in Table 4.24c, then the next-state function is given by

$$Y_1 = (1)(\bar{x}_1 \bar{x}_2) + (3)(\bar{x}_1 \bar{x}_2) + (4)(\bar{x}_1 \bar{x}_2) + (1)(\bar{x}_1 x_2) + (2)(\bar{x}_1 x_2) \quad \text{etc.}$$

Substituting the state code we have

$$Y_1 = \bar{y}_1 \bar{y}_2 \bar{x}_1 \bar{x}_2 + y_1 y_2 \bar{x}_1 \bar{x}_2 + \bar{y}_1 y_2 \bar{x}_1 \bar{x}_2 + \bar{y}_1 \bar{y}_2 \bar{x}_1 x_2 + y_1 \bar{y}_2 \bar{x}_1 x_2.$$

If we consider the simplification of this function we find that

$$(\bar{y}_1 \bar{y}_2 \bar{x}_1 \bar{x}_2) + (\bar{y}_1 y_2 \bar{x}_1 \bar{x}_2) = \bar{y}_1 \bar{x}_1 \bar{x}_2$$

corresponding to total states $(1)(\bar{x}_1 \bar{x}_2) + (4)(\bar{x}_1 \bar{x}_2)$ which both have the same next states.

Similarly the minterms in the next-state function resulting from a pair of states with a type-II adjacency will occur in the ON (OFF) sets if the code for both states has a 1 (0) for that function. If the two states are assigned adjacent codes the next-state expression will be simplified.

## Table 4.24. State Assignment using Adjacency Conditions

(a) State table

| Present state | Input $x_1 x_2$ | | | | | | | |
|---|---|---|---|---|---|---|---|---|
| | Next state | | | | Output $Z$ | | | |
| | 00 | 01 | 11 | 10 | 00 | 01 | 11 | 10 |
| 1 | 3 | 3 | 4 | 1 | 1 | 1 | 0 | 1 |
| 2 | 1 | 2 | 4 | 4 | 1 | 1 | 0 | 1 |
| 3 | 3 | 4 | 4 | 2 | 0 | 1 | 1 | 1 |
| 4 | 3 | 3 | 4 | 1 | 0 | 1 | 1 | 1 |

(b) Adjacencies

| State pairs | Number of occurrences | | | |
|---|---|---|---|---|
| | Type I | Type II | Type III | Type IV |
| 1,2 | 1 | 1 | 4 | 0 |
| 1,3 | 2 | 2 | 2 | 0 |
| 1,4 | 4 | 3 | 2 | 0 |
| 2,3 | 1 | 1 | 2 | 0 |
| 2,4 | 1 | 2 | 2 | 0 |
| 3,4 | 2 | 3 | 4 | 1 |

(c) Assigned table

| Present state | $Y_1 Y_2$ | Input $x_1 x_2$ | | | | | | | |
|---|---|---|---|---|---|---|---|---|---|
| | | Next state | | | | Output $Z$ | | | |
| | | 00 | 01 | 11 | 10 | 00 | 01 | 11 | 10 |
| 1 | 0 0 | 11 | 11 | 01 | 00 | 1 | 1 | 0 | 1 |
| 2 | 1 0 | 00 | 10 | 01 | 01 | 1 | 1 | 0 | 1 |
| 3 | 1 1 | 11 | 01 | 01 | 10 | 0 | 1 | 1 | 1 |
| 4 | 0 1 | 11 | 11 | 01 | 00 | 0 | 1 | 1 | 1 |

Ideally, when state assignments are determined using adjacency conditions, each internal state pair with an adjacency relationship should be assigned adjacent codes. It will be obvious that in the majority of cases it will be impossible simultaneously to satisfy all the adjacency conditions, and it becomes necessary to determine those adjacent state pairs which make the greatest contribution to a simplified set of circuit equations. In this context it appears that the type-II adjacency is less important than type I.

Armstrong used the concept of an *adjacency graph* to depict the type-I and type-II relationships; a type-I adjacency graph for the state table of Table 4.24 is shown in Fig. 4.7. The nodes in the graph represent the states, and the branches joining a pair of nodes indicate the adjacency condition; each branch is labeled with the number of occurrences in the state table of the adjacency conditions, called the *branch weight*. The problem of finding optimal adjacent codings for the set of state pairs which satisfy the adjacency condition resolves into assigning the nodes of the adjacency graph to the vertices of an $n$-cube, for some $n$, in such a way that as many branches of the graph as possible coincide with edges of the cube. At the same time the branches which do not coincide with edges should be those with small branch weights.

Armstrong describes various heuristic methods for performing this "embedding" function based on minimizing the function

$$W = \sum_{ij} w_{ij}d_{ij}$$

where $w_{ij}$ is the branch weight (for both type-I and type-II adjacencies) for nodes $i$ and $j$ in the adjacency graph and $d_{ij}$ is the distance between these nodes. The $w_{ij}$ are given quantities and $d_{ij}$ are unknowns dependent upon the particular assignment.

The method did not, however, give minimal results, owing in part to the difficulty of minimizing $W$ and the adjacency conditions employed. The algorithm was programmed for an IBM 7090 in assembly language and could handle state tables with up to 100 states and 30 inputs (that is 3000 cells or total states). Execution times varied from a few seconds for machines with less than 16 states to 2 min for a 3000-cell problem.

New, higher-order adjacencies were described in a second paper by Armstrong (67), where the state table was considered as a mapping of present states to next states under control of the inputs. Subsets of these mappings, called *pr mappings*, are allocated a numerical scoring function which is a measure of the desirability of including each mapping in a basic assignment set; the type-I and type-II adjacencies are the simplest types of pr mappings. Armstrong describes algorithms which are claimed to give nearly minimal results, but which unfortunately would be very inefficient if programmed for a computer.

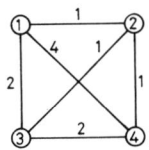

**Figure 4.7.** Type-I adjacency graph.

The concept of scoring adjacent state pairs is basic to the direct method of assignment and is employed by a number of workers in the field. Friedman and Menon (68) have described an assignment method based on scoring, and introduce two new adjacency conditions in addition to the type-I and type-II conditions considered earlier; these are as follows.

*Type-III adjacency.* The next output state values are examined, and if the values are the same for two states under the same input conditions they are made adjacent; thus each output column is examined for the condition

$$Z_k(q_i, I_m) = Z_k(q_j, I_m).$$

*Type-IV adjacency.* If two present states occur as their own next states, or as the next states of each other, under the same input conditions, they are made adjacent. Thus the following conditions must be fulfilled for each column:

$$N(q_i, I_m) = q_i \quad \text{and} \quad N(q_j, I_m) = q_j$$

or

$$N(q_i, I_m) = q_j \quad \text{and} \quad N(q_j, I_m) = q_i.$$

The adjacency conditions are scored by attributing a weight $w(q_i, q_j)$ to each state pair; initially $w(q_i, q_j)$ is set equal to 0. The conditions are scored according to the following order of merit:

Type I—add $S_0 = \lceil \log_2 n \rceil$ where $n$ = number of states to $w(q_i, q_j)$
Type II—add 1 to $w(q_i, q_j)$
Type III—add 1 to $w(q_i, q_j)$
Type IV—add $S_0 - 1$ to $w(q_i, q_j)$.

The effectiveness of a particular state assignment may be assessed by summing all those weights associated with the state pairs which were given adjacent codings. State assignment with a high total weight will tend to yield an economical realization. A state assignment with a relatively high weighting may be obtained by allocating adjacent codings to as many as possible state pairs with large weights. The method has not been programmed but would form the basis of a good computer algorithm. A similar method was employed by Waters (24), who used type-I and type-II conditions in conjunction with a new adjacency condition (type V) which considered states which occur as present and next states in the same row of the table, that is $N(q_i I_m) = q_j$. This type of adjacency condition ensures that the bistable input equations will contain don't-care conditions, since only one next-state variable is required to change.

Minimal assignments are obtained by maximizing the expression

$$W = \sum_{ij} (a\, X_{ij} + b\, Y_{ij} + c\, Z_{ij})$$

where $a$, $b$, and $c$ are factors denoting the relative contribution of the adjacency conditions types I, II, and V (represented by $X$, $Y$, and $Z$ in the equation for $W$). Note also that $a > b > c$, since the adjacency conditions do not contribute equally to an economic assignment.

The scoring procedure takes into account the number of state-pair adjacencies in which each individual state is involved as well as the number of adjacencies between each state pair. Moreover, the score allocated to type-I adjacencies depends on whether or not there are two or more occurrences of the same next state. A lower score is given for occurrences greater than two in order to reduce the problem of choosing an assignment, since it is known *a priori* that it is not feasible to realize all possible adjacencies. From an examination of the state table score arrays are derived for the state and state-pair scores. In order to accomplish the assignment of adjacent codes to those state pairs with the highest scores, the state with the highest state score (called the *selecting state*) is used as the starting point and given an all-zero code. Next the scores of the state pairs which contain the selecting state are examined and the pair with the highest state-pair score determined; the other member of this state pair is then assigned a code which is adjacent to the selecting state. This step is followed by an examination of the scores of those state pairs which have one of the assigned states as a member of the pair with the highest state-pair score. An attempt is then made to code the unassigned state with an adjacent code which also satisfies the other adjacency conditions. At each step the codes must be selected so as to satisfy as many adjacency requirements as possible. Waters describes a computer algorithm to determine a good assignment heuristically, though of course it does not necessarily produce an optimal assignment. The assignment algorithm was programmed using a list structure for the ICL 1900 series machine and assigned 30 cell machines in some 8 s of CPU time using 11 K of core.

Attempting to produce an optimal assignment for a state table by enumerative methods soon leads to an insuperable amount of computation. Dolotta and McCluskey (69), however, have proposed a method, based on the concept of *codable columns*, whereby a good encoding may be chosen without the necessity of trying all possible codes. The number of distinct codable columns (that is, with no complementary pairs of columns) for an $r$-row state table is given by

$$C_{(r)} = \frac{1}{2} \sum_{i=r-2^{s-1}}^{2^{s-1}} \binom{r}{i}$$

which gives rise to a considerably smaller number of columns than distinct state assignments $A_{(r)}$, as shown in Table 4.25a. For example, the four-row table shown in Table 4.25b has only three possible distinct assignments (00,01,10,11), (00,01,11,10), and (00,11,01,10), and all others may be derived by relabeling or complementing the variables (70). Dolotta and McCluskey assumed a delay-element realization (obtained by extracting application equations for a D-type bistable); other forms of realization would necessitate a different approach, particularly with regard to the consideration of complemented codes (71).

The state codings are represented in terms of codable columns $C_1$, $C_2$, and $C_3$ which may be combined to give the actual assignments $(C_1 C_2)$, $(C_1 C_3)$, and $(C_2 C_3)$; thus all possible codings for a state table can be obtained by choosing subsets of the complete set of codable columns. A codable column for an $r$-row state table is any column of 0's and 1's which have the following properties: (a) is of length $r$, (b) has a leading (uppermost) 0, (c) has not greater than $2^{s-1}$ 0's, and (d) has not greater than $2^{s-1}$ 1's where $s$ is the number of state variables. Table 4.25c shows the derivation of the codable columns for a four-row table. It is obviously more economic to manipulate the codable columns, with the objective of choosing an appropriate column subset, than investigate all possible assignments. The codable columns for a state table may be represented as an $r \times C_{(r)}$ base matrix, where each row of the matrix may be identified with an internal state of the machine and $C_{(r)}$ is the number of codable columns. The next state for each input combination may be represented in the same way; the matrices for the state table of Table 4.25b are shown in Table 4.25d. Note that the codable columns are represented using octal notation with the least significant digit at the bottom. Columns which have 1's uppermost are complemented and represented as a negative octal number.

It is interesting to observe the similarity with the adjacency method of assignment, since the matrices represent the mapping of codable columns into the next-state columns. By examining each column mapping in turn and evaluating the result in terms of some suitable minimization criteria the best coding can be determined.

Dolotta and McCluskey describe a "scoring" procedure for performing this function which requires the comparison of each base entry column with the next-state entries on a column-by-column basis and allocating a score according to the following criteria.

## Table 4.25. Codable Columns

(a)

| No. of rows $r$ | No. of state variables $s$ | No. of distinct state assignment columns $C_{(r)}$ | No. of distinct state assignments $A_{(r)}$ |
|---|---|---|---|
| 1 | 0 | — | — |
| 2 | 1 | 1 | 1 |
| 3 | 2 | 3 | 3 |
| 4 | 2 | 3 | 3 |
| 5 | 3 | 15 | 140 |
| 6 | 3 | 25 | 420 |
| 7 | 3 | 35 | 840 |
| 8 | 3 | 35 | 840 |
| 9 | 4 | 255 | 10,810,800 |
| 10 | 4 | 501 | 21,621,600 |

(b)

| Present state | Input $x$ 0 | Input $x$ 1 | Assignment codings | | | Codable columns $C_1$ | $C_2$ | $C_3$ |
|---|---|---|---|---|---|---|---|---|
| 1 | 2 | 3 | 00 | 00 | 00 | 0 | 0 | 0 |
| 2 | 1 | 2 | 01 | 01 | 11 | 0 | 1 | 1 |
| 3 | 4 | 3 | 10 | 11 | 01 | 1 | 0 | 1 |
| 4 | 4 | 2 | 11 | 10 | 10 | 1 | 1 | 0 |

(c)

|  |  |
|---|---|
| Length $r = 4, n = 2$ | 0 0 0 0 0 0 0 0 1 1 1 1 1 1 1 1 |
|  | 0 0 0 0 1 1 1 1 0 0 0 0 1 1 1 1 |
| $C_{(r)} = 3$ | 0 0 1 1 0 0 1 1 0 0 1 1 0 0 1 1 |
|  | 0 1 0 1 0 1 0 1 0 1 0 1 0 1 0 1 |

(d)

| Present state | Base matrix | | | | $x = 0$ Matrix | | | $x = 1$ Matrix | |
|---|---|---|---|---|---|---|---|---|---|
| 1 | 0 | 0 | 0 | 0 | 1 | 1 | 1 | 0 | 1 |
| 2 | 0 | 1 | 1 | 0 | 0 | 0 | 0 | 1 | 1 |
| 3 | 1 | 0 | 1 | 1 | 1 | 0 | 1 | 0 | 1 |
| 4 | 1 | 1 | 0 | 1 | 1 | 0 | 0 | 1 | 1 |
| Octal coding | 03 | 05 | 06 | 03 | —04 | —07 | —05 | 05 | —00 |

(a)   An all 0 entry in the row scores 20 marks.

(b)   An all 1 entry (complement of all 0's) in the row scores 10 marks.

(c)   Identical entries in adjacent columns (change of one variable) score 20 marks.

(d)   Identical entry to base entry scores 4 marks.

(e)   Identical entry to complement of base entry scores 4 marks.

All scores are expressed in octal notation to facilitate computer manipulation. As a result of this comparison the base vector with the highest score is chosen as the first codable column. The scoring procedure is modified in the search for the second and subsequent codable columns to the following.

(a)   The occurrence of an entry corresponding to a chosen column scores 4 marks.

(b)   The occurrence of similar entries to those in the chosen column (this is a condition for output sharing in multi-terminal circuits) scores 20 marks.

These scores are added to any existing scores to form a cumulative total. Having chosen two codable columns it is necessary to test if they will form a valid code, that is will generate a code with $2^s$ distinct rows. It does not necessarily follow that any set of codable columns will form a valid code. For a code to be valid it must satisfy the following conditions.

(a)   For each pair of codable columns, $C_1$ and $C_2$, of a set $\{C_1, C_2, \ldots, C_n\}$ the number of 1's obtained by performing the AND operation between all possible combinations of the column $(\bar{C}_1 \bar{C}_2, \bar{C}_1 C_2, C_1 \bar{C}_2, C_1 C_2)$ must be less than, or equal to, $2^{s-2}$ in each case.

(b)   In the general case for a complete code to be valid the same operation must be performed on all columns in all possible combinations. That is, for three columns we have $\bar{C}_1 \bar{C}_2 \bar{C}_3, \bar{C}_1 \bar{C}_2 C_3, \ldots, C_1 C_2 C_3$ and the sum of the 1's in each case must be less than, or equal to, $2^{s-k}$ where $s$ is the number of state variables and $k$ the number of columns.

The algorithm has been programmed for an IBM 7090 computer and tested for machines with up to eight internal states. The paper also describes extensions to the basic algorithm for large state tables, for dealing with incompletely specified machines, and for minimizing output logic.

A general and more rigorous approach to the problem of state assignment based on partition algebra has been described by Stearns and Hartmanis (72, 73). In this method the state assignment is made in such a way that each binary variable describing the next state depends on as few variables of the present state as is possible. The complexity of an assignment realization can be determined from its associated logic equations

$$Y_i = f_i (y_1, \ldots, y_r, x_1, \ldots, x_s) \ i = 1, \ldots, r$$

where $y$ and $x$ are the present state and input variables and $Y$ is the next-state variable. Normally one would expect that $Y_i$ would depend on all of the $y$ variables being present in an expression. However, if the next-state variable $Y_i$ depends only on a small subset of the present-state variables $y_i$ (ignoring the input conditions) it can be shown that the resulting *reduced dependency* assignments are more economical. The state variables which are absent from the next-state functions are termed *vacuous* variables, while those which do appear are *non-vacuous.*

The *degree of dependency* for a next-state function $Y_i$ is defined as the number $(d_i)$ of its non-vacuous-state variables. Since the realization of a secondary assignment takes the form of a set of $N$ next-state functions, the goodness factor of an assignment may be expressed as a cost measure given by the arithmetical sum of the individual $d_i$ values.

Procedures for determining assignments that lead to a low number of non-vacuous variables are based on partitions of the set of internal states. A partition of a set $S$ of internal states is a collection of disjoint subsets, called the *blocks* of the partition. For example, consider the assignment of the state table shown in Table 4.26. The assignment can be considered as the combination of three *elementary* assignments for the state variables $y_1$, $y_2$, and $y_3$. Thus, for $y_1$ states 1, 5, and 7 are assigned the bit value 0 and states 2, 3, 4, and 6 the value 1, giving the blocks $b_0 = \{1,5,7\}$ and $b_1 = \{2,3,4,6\}$ and the partition

$$\pi_{(y_1)} = \{\overline{1,5,7}; \overline{2,3,4,6}\}$$

on the set of states $S = \{1,2,3,4,5,6,7\}$. Similarly

$$\pi_{(y_2)} = \{\overline{1,2,3}; \overline{4,5,6,7}\}$$

and

$$\pi_{(y_3)} = \{\overline{1,3,6,7}; \overline{2,4,5}\}.$$

Note also from Table 4.26 that the state of $y_1$ alone will enable the state of the machine to be identified as belonging to one or other of the blocks of $\pi_{(y_1)}$, while a knowledge of the state of $y_2$ will narrow the search still further to a block of $\pi_{(y_2)}$. For instance, if $y_1 = 1$ then the machine is in one of the states 1, 5, or 7; if $y_2$ also equals 1 then the machine must be in either state 5 or 7; finally, if $y_3 = 1$ the state of the machine (5) is completely resolved.

## Table 4.26. Partition Assignment

(a) State table

| | Input $x_1 x_2$ | | | | | | | | | | |
|---|---|---|---|---|---|---|---|---|---|---|---|
| | Next state | | | | Output $Z$ | | | | Assignment | | |
| Present state | 00 | 01 | 11 | 10 | 00 | 01 | 11 | 10 | $y_1$ | $y_2$ | $y_3$ |
| 1 | 2 | 3 | 2 | 3 | 0 | 0 | 0 | 0 | 1 | 0 | 1 |
| 2 | 6 | 4 | 6 | 4 | 0 | 0 | 0 | 0 | 0 | 0 | 0 |
| 3 | 4 | 4 | 4 | 4 | 0 | 0 | 0 | 0 | 0 | 0 | 1 |
| 4 | 5 | 5 | 5 | 5 | 0 | 0 | 0 | 0 | 0 | 1 | 0 |
| 5 | 1 | 1 | 1 | 1 | 0 | 0 | 0 | 0 | 1 | 1 | 0 |
| 6 | 7 | 5 | 7 | 5 | 0 | 0 | 0 | 0 | 0 | 1 | 1 |
| 7 | 1 | 1 | 1 | 1 | 1 | 0 | 1 | 0 | 1 | 1 | 1 |

(b) Next-state equations

$$Y_1 = y_2$$

$$Y_2 = \bar{y}_1$$

$$Y_3 = y_1 y_2 + y_1 y_3 x_1 \bar{x}_2 + y_2 y_3 \bar{x}_1 \bar{x}_2 + \bar{y}_1 \bar{y}_2 \bar{y}_3 \bar{x}_1 \bar{x}_2 + y_2 y_3 x_1 x_2 + y_1 y_3 \bar{x}_1 x_2$$
$$+ \bar{y}_1 \bar{y}_2 \bar{y}_3 x_1 x_2$$

(c) Table for computation of $M(\pi)$

| | Inputs | | | |
|---|---|---|---|---|
| States | 00 | 01 | 11 | 10 |
| 1 | b | a | b | a |
| 2 | a | b | a | b |
| 3 | b | b | b | b |
| 4 | b | b | b | b |
| 5 | a | a | a | a |
| 6 | a | b | a | b |
| 7 | a | a | a | a |

Partitions can be combined algebraically; for the partitions $\pi_1$ and $\pi_2$ of the same set we have the following relationships.

(a) $\pi_1$ is said to be greater than, or equal to, $\pi_2 (\pi_1 \geqslant \pi_2)$ if each block of $\pi_2$ is contained in a block of $\pi_1$.

(b) The sum of two partitions, $\pi_1 + \pi_2$ (also called *least upper bound*), is the partition whose blocks are the union of overlapping (i.e. containing common members) blocks of $\pi_1$ and $\pi_2$.

(c) The product of two partitions, $\pi_1 . \pi_2$ (also called *greatest lower bound*), is the partition whose blocks are the intersections of blocks of $\pi_1$ with blocks of $\pi_2$.

The partition with one block (that is the complete state set) is called the *unit partition* (1), while the partition which contains each member of the set in a separate block is called the *zero partition* (0). A set of partitions which contains the unit and zero partitions, and every sum and product of its members, is called a *lattice*.

In order to effect an assignment with reduced dependency it is necessary to consider a class of partitions which have a characteristic called the *substitution* property (also known as *preserved* partitions). The substitution condition is satisfied if any two internal states in any block of the partition, under the same and any input conditions, go to next states that are all contained in a *single* block of the same partition (this is equivalent to a *closed* partition). Partitions with the substitution property may be computed from the state table by considering in turn each pair of internal states and ascertaining their next states for all possible input conditions. The process is continued by finding the pairs of next states for these pairs, and so on, until a list of state pairs is ohtained. The final list is then examined and appropriate pairs combined, using the transitive property, to form the smallest SP partition; these are then combined using the summation relationship to give the complete lattice.

A better approach to reduced dependency assignments is to compute the *partition pairs* for a machine. An ordered pair of partitions $(\pi, \pi')$ on the set of states $S$ of a sequential machine is a partition pair if, and only if, any two internal states in the same block of $\pi$, under any input conditions, go to next states in the same block of $\pi'$. Thus we have the substitution property between partitions, and an SP partition may be said to form a partition pair with itself. Furthermore, given two partition pairs $(\pi_1, \pi_1')$ and $(\pi_2, \pi_2')$ on the states of a completely defined machine $S$, we may say that

(a) $(\pi_1 . \pi_2, \pi_1' . \pi_2')$ is a partition pair

and

(b) $(\pi_1 + \pi_2, \pi_1' + \pi_2')$ is a partition pair.

It can be shown (74) that for any partition $\pi$ on a set of states of machine $S$ there is a smallest partition $\pi'$ such that $(\pi, \pi')$ is a partition pair; partition $\pi'$ is called $m(\pi)$. The computation of $m(\pi)$ is easily carried out by deriving from the state table all those sets of next states generated by the blocks of $\pi$ under all input conditions, and then constructing the minimal partition which contains these sets. For instance, if

$$\pi = \{\overline{1,5,7};\ \overline{2,3,4,6}\}$$

for the machine in Table 4.26$a$, then the state sets generated under all input conditions are

$$\overline{1,5,7} = (2,1)(3,1)$$

and

$$\overline{2,3,4,6} = (4,5,6,7)(4,5).$$

Combining these we have

$$m(\pi) = \{\overline{1,2,3};\ \overline{4,5,6,7}\}.$$

Again, for any partition $\pi$ on a set of states of machine $S$ there is a largest partition $\pi'$ such that $(\pi', \pi)$ is a partition pair. This partition, called $M(\pi)$, can also be obtained from the state table by identifying those (present) states which all go into the same block of $\pi$ under each input condition; that is, we must look up in the state table the states in each block of $\pi$, for the same input conditions, and note the present states. The computation of $M(\pi)$ may be facilitated by constructing a next-state partition table shown in Table 4.26$c$. In this table each next-state entry is replaced by a symbol indicating the block of $\pi$ which contains the state. Identical next-state rows are then identified to obtain $M(\pi)$. Thus if we have the partition

$$\pi = \{\overline{1,3,6,7} : \overline{2,4,5}\}$$

and let $a$ denote the first block and $b$ the second, we obtain from Table 4.26$c$ the partition

$$M(\pi) = \{\overline{1};\ \overline{2,6};\ \overline{3,4};\ \overline{5,7}\}.$$

As well as defining partition pairs based on the substitution property [called a state–state (S–S) pair], other partition pairs are also possible based on input–state (I–S), state–output (S–O), and input–output (I–O) conditions (74). The S–S or S–O partition pairs imply state-variable reduced dependencies, while I–S or I–O pairs reduce input dependencies.

The importance of partition pairs is that a complete algebra, *pair algebra*, may be established for them which can be used to detect reduced dependencies in the equations corresponding to any given assignment. Moreover, the mathematical techniques are perfectly general and enable an insight into the structure and information flow of sequential machines; consequently the ideas of partition theory are being applied in many areas of switching theory (75).

Though in general partition pairs can contain any number of blocks, a maximal reduction in the dependency of the state variables can be achieved if two-block partitions are used. In such a case each state variable would be independent of the remaining state variables. Thus we can define a reduced-dependency state assignment as follows:

A set of partitions $\{\pi_1, \pi_2, \pi_3, \ldots, \pi_r\}$ of a set of machine states $S$ is called an assignment (or *r-assignment*) of $S$ if, and only if, (*a*) each of the partitions contain two blocks, and (*b*) $\pi_1 . \pi_2 \ldots \pi_r = 0$, the zero partition.

Note that there are $2^{n-1} - 1$ distinct two-block partitions for an $n$-state machine. It will be seen that the three partitions $\pi_{(y_1)}$, $\pi_{(y_2)}$, and $\pi_{(y_3)}$ constitute an assignment for the machine of Table 4.26.

In order to obtain a reduced-dependency assignment using two-block partitions it is necessary to compute all possible partitions and then select a set of partitions such that

$$D = d_1 + d_2 + \ldots + d_n$$

is minimized, where $d_i$ is the number of non-vacuous variables for each state variable. Curtis (76) was the first to suggest an algorithmic method for performing this operation, while Karp (77) described a systematic procedure for selecting two-block partitions using the idea of an *admissibility test*. In this test a set of partitions $\{\psi_1, \psi_2, \ldots, \psi_p\}$ is said to be *r-admissible* if, and only if, there exists an $r$-assignment $\{\theta_1, \theta_2, \ldots, \theta_r\}$ such that each of the given $\psi$ partitions can be expressed as a product of the $\theta$ partitions, and there does not exist any $(r-1)$-assignment with this property. For example, if we let $p = 1$ and $\psi_1 = \{\overline{1,5,7}; \overline{2,3,4,6}\}$ and suppose that the following set of three $\theta$'s are proposed for the machine in Table 4.26, then

$$
\begin{array}{llllllll}
 & 1 & 2 & 3 & 4 & 5 & 6 & 7 \\
\theta_1 & 1 & 0 & 0 & 0 & 1 & 0 & 1 \\
\theta_2 & 1 & 1 & 1 & 0 & 0 & 0 & 0 \\
\theta_3 & 1 & 0 & 1 & 0 & 0 & 1 & 1 \\
\end{array}
$$

The set of $\theta$'s constitutes an assignment since each state has a distinct code; furthermore $\psi_1$ is the product of some $\theta$'s since $\psi_1 = \theta_1$. Note also that it is impossible for a set of two $\theta$'s to meet these requirements.

Checking to see if there exists an $r$-assignment that employs all partition pairs of an arbitrary collection can be accomplished by testing the set of partitions occurring in the partition pairs to see if it is $r$-admissible. A non-enumerative technique was devised by Karp, but the method is restrictive (to machines with a total number of states greater than $2^{r-1}$) and involves lengthy computations. A more general approach to evaluating the admissibility of a set of two-block partitions to produce an assignment $\theta$ has been described by Weiner and Smith (78) using the following two theorems.

(i) Let $\{\psi_1, \psi_2, \ldots, \psi_s\}$ denote a set of distinct two-block partitions and let $\psi = \psi_1 \cdot \psi_2 \ldots \psi_s$. This set is $r$-admissible where $r = s + e(\psi);$ $e(\psi) = \lceil \log_2 \epsilon (\psi) \rceil$ and $\epsilon (\psi)$ denotes the number of elements in the largest block of $\psi$. Note that any appropriate assignment $\{\theta_1, \theta_2, \ldots, \theta_r\}$ must contain (within a re-ordering) $\theta_1 = \psi_1$, $\theta_2 = \psi_2, \ldots, \theta_s = \psi_s$.

(ii) Let $\{\psi_1, \psi_2, \ldots, \psi_p\}$ denote a set of partitions such that $\psi_1$, $\psi_2, \ldots, \psi_{p-1}$ are distinct two-block partitions and the number of blocks of $\psi_p$, $\beta(\psi_p)$, is greater than 2. Now assume without loss of generality that

$$\psi_p \leqslant \psi_i \quad \text{for} \quad i = 1, 2, \ldots, q \quad \text{where} \quad 0 \leqslant q < p.$$

Let $\alpha = \psi_1 \cdot \psi_2 \ldots \psi_q$ and also let

$$\psi = \psi_1 \cdot \psi_2 \ldots \psi_p = \psi_{q+1} \cdot \psi_{q+2} \ldots \psi_p.$$

Then the set is $r$-admissible where

$$r = (p - 1) + e(\alpha \mid \psi_p) + e(\psi).$$

In this case

$$e(\alpha \mid \psi_p) = \lceil \log_2 \epsilon (\alpha \mid \psi_p) \rceil$$

where $\alpha \mid \psi_p$ denotes the quotient partition of $\alpha$ whose elements are the blocks of $\psi_p$; $\epsilon (\alpha \mid \psi_p)$ denotes the largest number of blocks of $\psi_p$ in a block of $\alpha$.

The $r$-admissibility test is a constructive procedure in that once the set of partitions is specified the value of $r$ may be calculated. Note also that the two-block partitions

$$(\psi_1 = \theta_1), (\psi_2 = \theta_2) \ldots , (\psi_{p-1} = \theta_{p-1})$$

come from a partial assignment and that if $e(\alpha \mid \psi_p) \neq 0$ the test indicates that the $\psi_p$ partition requires certain $\theta$ to be added to the assignment. The process of obtaining an admissible assignment may be iterated by using the quotient partition $\alpha \mid \psi_p$ to generate an appropriate $\theta$ and then calculating a new quotient partition $\alpha \mid (\psi_p \cdot \theta)$.

As an example of theorem (i) consider the two-block partitions

$$\psi_1 = \{\overline{1,5,7}; \overline{2,3,4,6}\}, \qquad \psi_2 = \{\overline{1,2,3}; \overline{4,5,6,7}\}$$

and

$$\psi_3 = \{\overline{1,3,6,7}; \overline{2,4,5}\}.$$

Now

$$\psi = \psi_1 \cdot \psi_2 \cdot \psi_3 = \{\overline{1}; \overline{2}; \overline{3}; \overline{4}; \overline{5}; \overline{6}; \overline{7}\} = 0$$

and $e(\psi) = \log_2 1 = 0$. Therefore for $s = 3$ the partition set is 3-admissible and three partitions are required to effect an assignment; these are $\theta_1 = \psi_1$, $\theta_2 = \psi_2$ and $\theta_3 = \psi_3$.

Let us now consider an example employing theorem (ii). Let

$$\psi_1 = \{\overline{1,2}; \overline{3,4,5,6}\}, \qquad \psi_2 = \{\overline{1,5,6}; \overline{2,3,4}\},$$

and

$$\psi_3 = \{\overline{1}; \overline{2}; \overline{3,5}; \overline{4,6}\}.$$

Then $q = 1$ and $\alpha = \psi_1$, since $\psi_1 \geqslant \psi_3$ and $\psi = \psi_2 \cdot \psi_3 = 0$. The set of partitions $\{\psi_1, \psi_2, \psi_3\}$ is 3-admissible where $p - 1 = 2$,

$$e(\alpha \mid \psi_p) = \lceil \log_2 2 \rceil = 1 \quad \text{and} \quad e(\psi) = \lceil \log_2 1 \rceil = 0.$$

(Note that if there are no $\geqslant$ relationships in the partition set $q = 0$ and $\alpha = I$, the identity partition.) Now $\theta_1 = \psi_1$ and $\theta_2 = \psi_2$, but, since $e(\alpha \mid \psi_3) = 1$,

$\psi_3$ requires another $\theta$ to complete the assignment. From the definition of $\alpha \mid \psi_p$ we can represent it as

$$\alpha \mid \psi_p = \{\overline{A, B}; \overline{C, D}\}$$

where $A$, $B$, $C$, $D$ denote the respective blocks of $\psi_3$. The additional $\theta$ corresponds to a two-block partition $\theta'$ of the set of blocks of $\psi_p$ such that

$$e(\alpha \mid \psi_p . \theta') = 0;$$

there are two such $\theta'$ that satisfy this condition, $\{\overline{A, C}; \overline{B, D}\}$ and $\{\overline{A, D}; \overline{B, C}\}$, and thus the additional $\theta$ may be chosen to be either $\{\overline{1,3,5}; \overline{2,4,6}\}$ or $\{\overline{1,4,6}:\overline{2,3,5}\}$. If the number of additional $\theta$'s required is greater than 1 it becomes necessary to iterate the procedure. Suppose that

$$e(\alpha \mid \psi_2) = 2$$

for

$$\psi_1 = \{\overline{1,2}; \overline{3,4,5,6}\}$$

and

$$\psi_2 = \{\overline{1,3}; \overline{2,4}; \overline{5}; \overline{6}\} \quad \text{and} \quad \alpha = I.$$

Then

$$\alpha \mid \psi_p = \overline{ABCD}$$

and the *first* additional $\theta$ to be added corresponds to a two-block partition $\theta'$ such that

$$e(\alpha \mid \psi_p . \theta') = 1;$$

there are three such $\theta'$, which are $\{\overline{A, B}; \overline{C, D}\}$, $\{\overline{A, C}; \overline{B, D}\}$, and $\{\overline{A, D}; \overline{B, C}\}$. Once one of the partitions has been chosen for $\theta'$ the process can be repeated to obtain the other.

Weiner and Smith describe an assignment algorithm based on the use of admissibility tests and the generation of a *dependency profile* to select an optimal set of two-block partitions. The dependency profile takes into account those quantities which affect the expected cost of the implemented circuit and must be defined by the user. The user must provide a subroutine which calculates an appropriate figure of merit (the expected cost) from the set of $d_i^s$ and $d_j^0$ values for the logic equation. Thus the dependency profile is defined as

$$D = \{d_1{}^s, \ldots, d_r{}^s; d_1{}^0, \ldots, d_t{}^0\}$$

where $d_i^s$ and $d_j^0$ are the number of non-vacuous variables occurring in the next-state and output equations for $Y_i$ and $Z_j$.

The algorithm obtains the best assignment from a set of partition pairs that contains a two-block partition as the right-hand member; $M$-partitions are utilized in their derivation. To assist in the computation of the $M$-partitions for each two-block partition, an arithmetical procedure is used based on row numbers (RN) and column numbers (CN). Partitions are represented using a *partition number* (PN). For example, the two-block partition $\{\overline{1,2}; \overline{3,4,5,6}\}$ is represented in octal by expressing the partition as a binary column and then reading from top to bottom to obtain octal 17. For certain partitions the PN value may be used as a generating function (for the *representation set*) by expressing the octal number in the binary radix notation and then converting each term to a two-block partition. Thus, the PN octal 17 can be expressed as $1 \times 2^0 + 1 \times 2^1 + 1 \times 2^2 + 1 \times 2^3$ to yield the partition numbers $07 + 10$ (adding together the terms less than $2^3$) and the partitions $\{\overline{1,2,3}; \overline{4,5,6}\}$ and $\{\overline{1,2,4,5,6}; \overline{3}\}$.

A partially encoded state table (using an elementary assignment two-block partition) may be represented by octal row and column numbers. Now, each row number (column number) associated with a given two-block partition is equal to the sum of the corresponding row number (column number) associated with the generating partitions in the representation set. Thus using the state table to establish the initial row and column numbers for a given two-block partition the full set of RN's and CN's may be obtained by using the initial numbers as generating functions. Note that the technique is very similar to Dolotta and McCluskey's method of representation, but the connection between column numbers and $M$-partitions was not established.

The algorithm was programmed for an IBM 7094 computer using the low-level linked-list language developed by Bell Telephones, and solved eight variable problems (both input and state variables) in under 1 s of machine time. In common with most methods of state assignment based on partition-pair algebra, the method is difficult to program efficiently for large variable problems owing to the considerable amount of algebraic manipulation required.

Curtis (64, 79) has generalized the methods of Dolotta and McCluskey and Weiner and Smith to apply to machines employing T, SR, and JK bistables or combinations of these types. Torng (80) has proposed a method of evaluating the cost of an assignment based on the examination of elementary assignments (two-block partitions). The method consists of searching for a set of next-state functions that satisfy certain criteria, rather than an exhaustive determination of the actual implemented circuit corresponding to a particular assignment.

If an elementary assignment (EA) is made for one state variable $y_i$, the corresponding next-state function is given by

$$Y_i = \sum_j (XS)_j$$

where $X$ and $S$ are the input and internal states and $j$ covers all the total states with $0 \rightarrow 1$ transitions (note this is assuming delay-type implementation). Consider the machine in Table 4.26$a$; the variable $y_1$ is given by the EA $\{\overline{1,5,7};\ \overline{2,3,4,6}\}$. Now

$$Y_1 = \bar{x}_1 \bar{x}_2 (S_4 + S_5 + S_6 + S_7) + \bar{x}_1 x_2 (S_4 + S_5 + S_6 + S_7)$$
$$+ x_1 \bar{x}_2 (S_4 + S_5 + S_6 + S_7) + x_1 x_2 (S_4 + S_5 + S_6 + S_7).$$

Therefore

$$Y_1 = S_4 + S_5 + S_6 + S_7.$$

Note that the expression can be resolved into a number of reduced product terms; these generally take the form of

$$I_\alpha (S_m + S_n + \ldots)$$

where $I_\alpha$ is called the *I-factor* and $(S_m + S_n + \ldots)$ the *S-factor*. The number of products in the realization of $Y_i$ is defined as the cost of the corresponding EA. Each product term is given a cost value of 1, the sum of the product values being called the cost factor for an EA.

An optimum solution can be obtained by enumerating all allowable EA's (which effect an assignment) and evaluating their respective costs. This procedure can present considerable computational problems, and Torng has suggested an algorithm which reduces the choice of EA's based on the idea of product factors. The algorithm does not produce an optimal solution but does lead to a good implementation.

Story *et al.* (81) have described an algorithm for deriving optimum (minimal-cost) assignments for JK bistables (though the method can be extended to other types) based on the lower-bound approach first described by Davis (82) and extending the costing philosophy proposed by Torng. In the Story method a set of columns, each of which is composed of a binary element for each row of a partially assigned state table, is derived; from this matrix it is possible to generate all possible distinct state assignments for the machine. General input equations for JK bistables are derived from the machine matrix based on one-column partial-state assignments (PSA's), and then a minimum number (MN), which represents a lower bound on cost, is selected for each column. The optimum state assignment is then found by comparing the sets of MN's with corresponding actual cost numbers for complete state-assignment schemes consisting of a set of PSA's. (Note that the partial state assignments correspond to the codable columns defined by Dolotta and McCluskey.)

As we have already seen, in a given $r$-row state table there are $C_{(r)}$ distinct columns from which groups of $s$ columns may be assembled to form an assignment. In the algorithm a cost number is associated with each of the $C_{(r)}$ columns which is independent of the other columns. This is accomplished by calculating a cost number $M_{(x)}$ for each column $C_{(x)}$ under consideration. The value of $M_{(x)}$ represents a lower bound on the cost of implementing that part of the combinational circuit corresponding to the selected column in a particular state assignment. A lower bound, such as $M_{(x)}$, for a distinct column is called a minimum number (MN). The minimum number is calculated for a particular column by applying the column to the given state table as if the column were a complete state assignment and then deriving the input equations for a JK bistable in the usual way; in general the resulting combinational equations must be minimized. For JK bistables a generalized expression may be written for the J input; thus

$$J_d = \sum_i XS + 0.5 \sum_j XS$$

where $\Sigma_i$ covers all total states with present to next state transitions of $0 \rightarrow 1$, $\Sigma_j$ covers all don't-care total states with transitions $1 \rightarrow 0$, $1 \rightarrow 1$, $1 \rightarrow DC$, or $0 \rightarrow DC$, and $X$ and $S$ are the input and internal states respectively; a similar expression can be written for $K_d$.

The cost number for a given column $C_d$ may be calculated using the expression

$$MN_d = AOI_{j_d} + AOI_{k_d}$$

where AOI is the number of AND-OR inputs required for the J and K combinational input logic. A *lower bound* for a complete assignment scheme is taken to be equal to the sum of the MN's associated with the $s$ distinct columns of the assignment. The actual cost number (AN) for an assignment scheme is defined to be the sum of the number of *actual* (not lower-bound)

AND–OR inputs for each bistable input equation minimized separately. In the algorithm the values of MN and AN are compared for each PSA combination to determine the optimum state-assignment scheme.

The algorithm has been programmed for a digital computer but no programming details or run times are given. Comparison of the technique with earlier methods suggests that it is very effective in producing an optimum design. However, only small machines have been designed as of yet with up to eight rows and some 50 cells. Since the amount of computation, and hence execution time, increases rapidly with the number of distinct columns associated with a given state table (it is necessary to evaluate MN for each column), it is doubtful if the method could ever be economic for large machines. The advantage of the algorithm lies in its ability to produce an optimal assignment without the necessity for a complete enumeration.

Though considerable work has been published on the subject of synchronous-machine assignment, an efficient (in the computational sense) algorithm which generates good, rather than optimal, realizations for large machines has yet to be developed. Moreover, much of the reported work concentrates on the minimization of the bistable input equations (ignoring in the main the output logic) when implemented in terms of two-level NAND–NOR logic. What is really required is a general assignment algorithm which takes into account MSI modules such as shift registers, ROM's, etc., and the efficient realization of machines using these devices (83). Searching for an optimal solution in terms of basic elements is only worthwhile for custom-designed LSI chips; even then work is required to relate the design more closely to the actual technology, for example, in terms of MOS gates.

### 4.3.4. Asynchronous Machine Assignment

The absence of any synchronizing (clock) pulses in an asynchronous sequential machine introduces a major design problem, that of ensuring that the circuit will function correctly irrespective of any variations in transmission delays through the circuit. Note that the asynchronous machine is essentially a combinational network with feedback, and that active elements (NAND–NOR gates) must be included in the loop. Hazards can be generated when two or more variables are required to change state at the same time. Owing to unequal delaying paths through the network it is improbable that the variables will change state simultaneously and hence unpredictable circuit conditions can arise. The main types of hazard encountered in asynchronous machines are as follows.

(a) Static, dynamic, and function hazards in the combinational (excitation) network (43).

**(b)** Races between secondary variables which will be *critical* if the correct behavior of the circuit depends on the outcome of the race, and *non-critical* if the circuit functions correctly independently of the outcome of the race.

**(c)** Essential hazards (37), which are multiple-order hazards involving a critical race between an input and a secondary variable. Essential hazards are characteristic to asynchronous systems and cannot be corrected by logical methods. Ungar has defined the essential hazard in terms of a flow table and has also proved that if a flow table contains an essential hazard the resulting network must contain at least one explicit delay (to ensure the input signal always wins the race) to function correctly.

Static, dynamic, and function hazards may be eliminated by employing the following design technique

**(i)** Operating the circuit in the *fundamental mode* whereby the machine is assumed to have reached a stable state before the next input change occurs.

**(ii)** Ensuring that the input variables can only change one at a time.

**(iii)** Adding extra logic gates to the network to eliminate static hazards, or realizing the circuit using set–reset bistables (84).

Essential hazards may be overcome by reconfiguring the circuit to incorporate extra delaying paths in the network using standard gating elements (85). Critical races between secondary state variables in a fundamental-mode machine can be avoided by suitably encoding the states of the machine. This then is the significant difference between state assignment for a synchronous and asynchronous machine—in the case of a synchronous machine any state assignment will suffice, whereas asynchronous machines must be coded to prevent critical races.

Flow tables can be assigned non-critically by investigating all possible state (row) transitions and then allocating a code such that only one secondary variable changes during any allowable row transition. The absolute minimum number of state variables ($s$) that can be used to realize an $r$-row flow table in this way is given by

$$s_{min} = \lceil \log_2 r \rceil.$$

In many cases, however, it is not possible to code a table using $s_{min}$ variables and also abide by the change of one variable constraint. A *normal flow table* is one in which all unstable states lead *directly* to a stable state, and in this case the maximum speed of the circuit is obtained, since there are no intermediate states and thus only one pass through the excitation network is required to effect the transition. Table 4.27a shows a normal flow table which has been assigned using the minimum number of state variables.

## Table 4.27. Asynchronous State Assignment

(a)

|   | Inputs ab 00 | 01 | 11 | 10 | State variables $y_1$ | $y_2$ |
|---|---|---|---|---|---|---|
| 1 | ① | 2 | 4 | ① | 0 | 0 |
| 2 | ② | ② | 3 | 1 | 0 | 1 |
| 3 | 2 | ③ | ③ | 4 | 1 | 1 |
| 4 | 1 | 3 | ④ | ④ | 1 | 0 |

(b)

|   | Inputs $x_1 x_2$ 00 | 01 | 11 | 10 |
|---|---|---|---|---|
| a | ① | ② | 8 | 4 |
| b | 5 | ③ | 8 | ④ |
| c | ⑤ | 7 | 9 | ⑥ |
| d | 1 | ⑦ | ⑧ | 6 |
| e | 5 | 3 | ⑨ | ⑩ |

(c)

| $y_3$ \ $y_1 y_2$ | 00 | 01 | 11 | 10 |
|---|---|---|---|---|
| 00 | a | d | d' | b |
| 1 | e | c | $b'_2$ | $b'_1$ |

|   | $y_1$ | $y_2$ | $y_3$ | Inputs $x_1 x_2$ 00 | 01 | 11 | 10 |
|---|---|---|---|---|---|---|---|
| a | 0 | 0 | 0 | 000 | 000 | 010 | 100 |
| e | 0 | 0 | 1 | 011 | 101 | 001 | 001 |
| d | 0 | 1 | 0 | 000 | 010 | 010 | 011 |
| c | 0 | 1 | 1 | 011 | 010 | 001 | 011 |
| b | 1 | 0 | 0 | 101 | 100 | 110 | 100 |
|   | 1 | 0 | 1 | 111 | 100 | — | — |
|   | 1 | 1 | 0 | — | — | 010 | — |
|   | 1 | 1 | 1 | 011 | — | — | — |

**Table 4.27.** (*continued*)   **Asynchronous State Assignment**

(*d*)

|         | $y_1 y_2$ |     |     |     |
|---------|-----------|-----|-----|-----|
| $y_3$   | 00        | 01  | 11  | 10  |
| 0       | a         | d   |     |     |
| 1       | b         |     | c   | e   |

|     | $y_1$ | $y_2$ | $y_3$ | Inputs $x_1 x_2$ | | | |
|-----|-------|-------|-------|------|------|------|------|
|     |       |       |       | **00** | **01** | **11** | **10** |
| a   | 0     | 0     | 0     | 000  | 000  | 010  | 001  |
| b   | 0     | 0     | 1     | 111  | 001  | 010  | 001  |
| c   | 1     | 1     | 1     | 111  | 010  | 101  | 111  |
| d   | 0     | 1     | 0     | 000  | 010  | 010  | 111  |
| e   | 1     | 0     | 1     | 111  | 001  | 101  | 101  |

(*e*)

| $r_1$ | $r_2$ | $r_3$ | Input |
|-------|-------|-------|-------|
| $y_1$ | $y_2$ | $y_3$ | **01** |
| 0     | 0     | 0     | ②     |
| 0     | 0     | 1     | ③     |
| 1     | 1     | 1     | 7     |
| 0     | 1     | 0     | ⑦     |
| 1     | 0     | 1     | 3     |

If we now consider the flow table shown in Table 4.27b we find that it is not possible to assign this as a normal flow table with direct transitions and the table must be made *abnormal* to effect an assignment. This is done by using directed cycles to produce the required race-free transitions. For example, the transition from row *b* state ③ to row *c* state ⑤ is directed via the internal states $100 \to 101 \to 111 \to 011$, thus necessitating three passes through the network. In general if we define a time unit as the time required for one state variable to change, this time being assumed constant, then a directed transition will take $T$ units of time when $T$ state variables are required to change. The assignment of secondary variables to an *r*-row flow table may be considered as a mapping of the *s*-state variables into the vertices of an *s*-dimensional unit cube. A set of vertices from an *n*-cube is said to be *equidistant* if the distance between every pair of vertices in this set is the same. If the states are encoded to satisfy the Hamming-distance relationship of the cube, critical races can be avoided; this is shown in Fig. 4.8 for the flow table of Table 4.27*b*.

So far we have considered the case where one state variable only is changed at a time for any inter-row transition. However, it has been shown by Liu (86) that it is possible to have an assignment where multiple changes of state variable can occur, the ensuing races being non-critical. Moreover, the transition times obtained with this type of circuit may be the same as that obtained with adjacent row assignments, since the non-critical races set up a free-running condition. Thus, a *direct* transition between internal states $S_i$ to $S_j$ written $S_i, S_j$ may be defined as a transition whereby all internal state variables that are to undergo a change of state are simultaneously excited. A direct transition $[S_i, S_j]$ races critically with another direct transition $[S_m, S_n]$ if the possibility exists that unequal transmission delays may cause these two transitions to share a common internal state (either stable or unstable). It also follows that when direct transitions occur a minimum transition-time assignment is obtained. This form of assignment, which approximates in response time to that obtained with a normal flow table, is called a *single-transition-time* (STT) assignment (also known as a unicode single transition time, USTT). The SST assignment is illustrated in Table 4.27*d*—note that the transition from row $b$ to row $d$ simultaneously excites the variables $y_2$ and $y_3$ and could involve the state changes

$$001 \rightarrow 011 \rightarrow 010$$

$$001 \rightarrow 010 \rightarrow 010$$

$$001 \rightarrow 000 \rightarrow 010.$$

Since there are no stable states which have codings corresponding to the transition-state values, and the set of unstable transition states for transitions occurring in the same column is disjoint, the assignment is free of critical races.

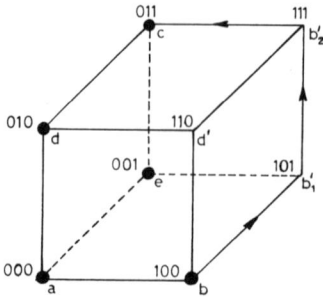

**Figure 4.8.** Assignment using *n*-cubes.

Liu has also shown that a state-variable assignment in which the row assignments correspond to an equidistant error-correcting code will be free of critical races. Note that an equidistant error-correcting code of $2^m$ message words requires $2^m - 1$ bits; hence the number of state variables required for a flow table with $2^m$ rows will be $2^m - 1$. Note also that a Hamming distance of 3 is the minimum requirement for an error-correcting code.

Most of the methods described above would be either difficult to program or give rise to a large and hence uneconomical number of state variables. The first algorithmic approach for generating STT assignments was described by Tracey (87) and was based on an extension of Liu's work. In Tracey's method partitions on the set of internal states are used to determine the assignments. For example, in Table 4.27d variable $y_1$ induces the two-block partition

$$r_1 = \{\overline{a, b, d}; \overline{c, e}\}$$

$y_2$ induces

$$r_2 = \{\overline{a, b, e}; \overline{c, d}\}$$

and $y_3$ induces

$$r_3 = \{\overline{a, d}; \overline{b, c, e}\}.$$

The assignment is said to consist of the collection of partitions (*r*-partitions) $r_1, r_2$, and $r_3$ induced by the variables $y_1, y_2$, and $y_3$.

A row assignment allocating one *y*-state per row can be used for STT realization of normal flow tables without critical races if, and only if, for every transition $[S_i, S_j]$ the following conditions are satisfied.

(a) If $[S_m, S_n]$ is another transition in the same column, then at least one *y* variable partitions the pair $[S_i, S_j]$ and pair $[S_m, S_n]$ into separate blocks.

(b) If $S_k$ is a stable state in the same column, then at least one *y* variable partitions the pair $[S_i, S_j]$ and the state $S_k$ into separate blocks.

(c) For $i \neq j$, $S_i$, and $S_j$ are in separate blocks of at least one *y* variable.

It will be seen from Table 4.27e, if we examine the transitions $3 \to ③$ and $7 \to ⑦$, that the above conditions are fulfilled. For example, $\{3, ③\}$ and $\{7, ⑦\}$ are partitioned into separate blocks by $y_2$; moreover $\{3, ③\}$ are in separate blocks of $\pi_1$. The pair $\{3, ③\}$ and ② are partitioned into separate blocks by $y_3$.

The separation of like stable and unstable states into separate blocks ensures that transitions between rows involve row assignments that contain a non-changing part that is different from the corresponding part (same digit positions) in any other row assignment in the flow table. Moreover, every transition within a column has a different non-changing part in the row assignments involved. It therefore follows that the set of intermediate unstable states in each column transition must be disjoint. As an example, consider the transitions ③→⑤ and ⑦→① in Table 4.27$b$; then we have

|        | $y_1$ | $y_2$ | $y_3$ |
|--------|-------|-------|-------|
| $S_i$  | 0     | 0     | 1     |
| $S_j$  | 1     | 1     | 1     |
| $S_m$  | 0     | 1     | 0     |
| $S_n$  | 0     | 0     | 0     |

Now unequal transmission delays could cause the direct transition $[S_i, S_j]$ momentarily to assume any of the internal states $(- - 1)$ where dashes represent all combinations of 0 and 1. Similarly the transition $[S_m, S_n]$ could assume the values $(0 - 0)$. The existence of the the the 0 and 1 values for $y_3$ ensures that a critical race cannot occur. If $[S_i, S_j]$ and $[S_m, S_n]$ are transitions in the same column of a flow table and if $S_k$ is a stable state also in the same column, then the collection of all two-block partitions $\{\overline{S_i, S_j};$ $\overline{S_m, S_n}\}$ and $\{\overline{S_i, S_j}; \overline{S_k}\}$ of a flow table comprise the *partition list* of the flow-table. The partition list for the machine of Table 4.27$b$ is given below:

$$\pi_1 = \{\overline{a, d}; \overline{b, c}\}$$
$$\pi_2 = \{\overline{a, d}; \overline{c, e}\}$$
$$\pi_3 = \{\overline{a}; \overline{b, e}\}$$
$$\pi_4 = \{\overline{a}; \overline{c, d}\}$$
$$\pi_5 = \{\overline{a, d}; \overline{c, e}\}$$
$$\pi_6 = \{\overline{b, d}; \overline{c, e}\}$$
$$\pi_7 = \{\overline{a, b}; \overline{c, d}\}$$
$$\pi_8 = \{\overline{a, b}; \overline{e}\}$$
$$\pi_9 = \{\overline{c, d}; \overline{e}\}$$
$$\pi_{10} = \{\overline{b, e}; \overline{c, d}\}$$

In order to obtain a minimum transition-time assignment free of critical races it is necessary that each partition of the partition list is $\leqslant r_i$, where $r_i$ is a member of the set of two-block partitions induced by the internal state variables $y_i$ to give the assignment. Since optimum assignments are those which contain the least number of $y$ variables it is necessary to derive the minimum number of $r$-partitions for the flow table. For the example quoted the set of $r$-partitions are

$$r_1 = \{\overline{a, b, d}; \overline{c, e}\}$$
$$r_2 = \{\overline{a, b, e}; \overline{c, d}\}$$
$$r_3 = \{\overline{a, d}; \overline{b, c, e}\}.$$

Note that partitions

$$\pi_2, \pi_5, \pi_6, \text{ and } \pi_8 \text{ are } \leqslant r_1$$
$$\pi_4, \pi_7, \pi_9, \text{ and } \pi_{10} \text{ are } \leqslant r_2$$
$$\pi_1, \pi_2, \pi_3, \text{ and } \pi_5 \text{ are } \leqslant r_3.$$

The $r$-partitions are generated from the partition list by expressing the list as a Boolean matrix, with the $\pi$ partitions as rows and the partition elements as columns, and then performing a Boolean reduction process; note that the order is arbitrary. For example, we can express the partition $\pi_1 = \{\overline{a, d}; \overline{b, c}\}$ as 0110 –, where the elements of block $(\overline{a, d}) = 0$, $(\overline{b, c}) = 1$, and the missing elements are dashed; continuing in this way we obtain the Boolean matrix shown in Table 4.28a.

There are various ways of solving this matrix. One technique is to compute the maximal intersectables (analogous to Paull and Ungar's method for maximal incompatibles); this method is due to Tracey and is called *Matrix Reduction Algorithm #1*. First, a list of intersectables is obtained; for example, from Table 4.28a

1   0 1 1 0 –
2   0 – 1 0 1

intersect since all the declared terms are the same, dashed terms taking any value. The complete list of pair-wise intersectables is shown below:

(12)(13)(15)
(23)(25)(26)(28)
(34)(35)(39)(3$\overline{10}$)
(47)(48)(4 10)(49)
(56)(58)
(68)
(7, 10)(7$\overline{9}$)
(89)
(9 $\overline{10}$)

## Table 4.28.  Matrix Reduction Algorithm # 1

(a)

|     | a  | b  | c  | d  | e  |
|-----|----|----|----|----|----|
| 1   | 0  | 1  | 1  | 0  | –  |
| 2   | 0  | –  | 1  | 0  | 1  |
| 3   | 0  | 1  | –  | –  | 1  |
| 4   | 0  | –  | 1  | 1  | –  |
| 5   | 0  | –  | 1  | 0  | 1  |
| 6   | –  | 0  | 1  | 0  | 1  |
| 7   | 0  | 0  | 1  | 1  | –  |
| 8   | 0  | 0  | –  | –  | 1  |
| 9   | –  | –  | 0  | 0  | 1  |
| 10  | –  | 0  | 1  | 1  | 0  |

(b)

|      | 1 | 2 | 3 | 4 | 5 | 6 | 7 | 8 | 9 | 10 |
|------|---|---|---|---|---|---|---|---|---|----|
| *A   | x | x | x |   | x |   |   |   |   |    |
| *B   |   | x |   |   | x | x |   | x |   |    |
| *C   |   |   |   | x |   |   | x |   | x | x  |
| D    |   | x |   | x |   |   |   |   |   |    |
| E    |   | x |   |   |   |   |   |   | x |    |
| F    |   | x |   |   |   |   |   | x | x |    |

Note that 4 intersects with the inverse of 9; this is allowable since the original designation of terms was arbitrary. We now compute the maximal intersectables by combining terms together; this gives

$$A\ (1\ 2\ 3\ 5),\ B\ (2\ 5\ 6\ 8),\ C\ (4\ 7\ \bar{9}\ 10)$$

$$D\ (\ 3\ 4),\ E\ (3\ 9),\ F\ (8\ 9).$$

The final step is to select a covering of MI's over the partition-list matrix. Note that the problem is analogous to the McCluskey selection of prime implicants and may be solved in the usual way using a chart technique (see Table 4.28$b$). In this case $A$, $B$, and $C$ cover all rows; that is

$$A(1\ 2\ 3\ 5) = 01101 = r_3 = \{\overline{a, d}; b, c, e\}$$

$$B(2\ 5\ 6\ 8) = 00101 = r_1 = \{\overline{a, b, d}; c, e\}$$

$$C(4\ 7\ \bar{9}\ 10) = 00110 = r_2 = \{\overline{a, b, e}; c, d\}.$$

The table may also be evaluated algebraically; for example

$$MI = (A)(A + B)(A + D + E)(C + D)(A + B)(B)(C)(B + F)(C + D + F)(C)$$

$$= ABC.$$

In this case we obtain a unique answer; in general this method gives all the solutions including the optimum, and the product with the fewest literals is the required term. The main disadvantage of this method is that for large-variable problems the amount of computation becomes excessive, and it is necessary to employ more efficient algorithms which give a "good", if not optimum, solution.

Such an algorithm (called Matrix Reduction Algorithm #2 by Tracey) will now be discussed. This is based on the assumption that for many Boolean matrices an optimum or near-optimum reduction may be obtained by constructing an intersectable that covers a large number of rows, removing the covered rows from the matrix, and then constructing another intersectable that covers a large number of the remaining rows, etc., until all rows of the original matrix are covered. The algorithm is as follows.

(1) Select a column of the matrix with the largest number of specified entries and identify it with the letter $A$. If several columns have the same largest number of specified entries, arbitrarily select one of them.

(2) Complement appropriate rows of the matrix so that all specified entries in the column selected in step 1 agree.

(3) Identify those rows that are not specified under the column selected in step 1 with the letter $B$.

(4) Examine each column not identified with an $A$ and determine the difference between the number of 1's and 0's in each of these columns. Ignore for this count those rows identified with a $B$ or $C$.

(5) Select the column from step 4 that has the largest difference magnitude. Set that column to a 1 or 0, whichever was larger, and identify the column with an $A$. If several columns have the same largest difference, arbitrarily select one of them.

(6) Examine those rows not identified with a $B$ or $C$. If a row does not agree with the setting of the column in step 5, identify that row with a $C$.

(7) Consider those rows identified with a $B$ and specified under the column selected in step 5. Remove the $B$ identification from these rows and complement them, if necessary, so that they agree with the selected column setting in step 5.

(8) Go back to step 4 unless all columns are identified with an $A$. If all columns are identified with an $A$, go to step 9.

(9) All rows not identified with a $C$ have an intersection. This intersection represents one of the partitions to be used in the assignment.

Determine the intersection and remove the covered rows from the matrix. Remove all identifiers from the remaining matrix and go back to step 1. The algorithm is ended when there are no rows remaining in the matrix.

In order to illustrate this procedure consider again the matrix shown in Table 4.28*a*. This is reproduced, together with the resulting matrices produced during the algorithmic procedure in Tables 4.29 and 4.30. The following notes will assist the reader in understanding the procedure.

### Table 4.29. Matrix Reduction Algorithm # 2

(*a*)

|  | | $A = 0$ | | $A$ | | |
|---|---|---|---|---|---|---|
|  |  | a | b | c | d | e |
|  | 1 | 0 | 1 | 1 | 0 | – |
|  | 2 | 0 | – | 1 | 0 | 1 |
| B | 3 | 0 | 1 | – | – | 1 |
|  | 4 | 0 | – | 1 | 1 | – |
|  | 5 | 0 | – | 1 | 0 | – |
|  | 6 | – | 0 | 1 | 0 | 1 |
|  | 7 | 0 | 0 | 1 | 1 | – |
| B | 8 | 0 | 0 | – | – | 1 |
|  | 9 | – | – | $\phi1$ | $\phi1$ | $\cancel{1}0$ |
|  | 10 | – | 0 | 1 | 1 | 0 |
| Difference |  | 5 | 2 |  | 0 | 0 |

Pass 1

(*b*)

|  | | $A = 0$ | | $A$ | | $A = 1$ |
|---|---|---|---|---|---|---|
|  |  | a | b | c | d | e |
|  | 1 | 0 | 1 | 1 | 0 | – |
|  | 2 | 0 | – | 1 | 0 | 1 |
|  | 3 | 0 | 1 | – | – | 1 |
|  | 4 | 0 | – | 1 | 1 | – |
|  | 5 | 0 | – | 1 | 0 | – |
|  | 6 | – | 0 | 1 | 0 | 1 |
|  | 7 | 0 | 0 | 1 | 1 | – |
|  | 8 | 0 | 0 | – | – | 1 |
| C | 9 | – | – | 1 | 1 | 0 |
| C | 10 | – | 0 | 1 | 1 | 0 |
| Difference |  |  | 2 |  |  | 2 |

Pass 2

**Table 4.29.** (continued)  **Matrix Reduction Algorithm #2**

(c)

|  |  | $A = 0$ |  | $A$ | $A = 0$ | $A = 1$ |
|---|---|---|---|---|---|---|
|  |  | a | b | c | d | e |
|  | 1 | 0 | 1 | 1 | 0 | – |
|  | 2 | 0 | – | 1 | 0 | 1 |
|  | 3 | 0 | 1 | – | – | 1 |
| C | 4 | 0 | – | 1 | 1 | – |
|  | 5 | 0 | – | 1 | 0 | – |
|  | 6 | – | 0 | 1 | 0 | 1 |
| C | 7 | 0 | 0 | 1 | 1 | – |
|  | 8 | 0 | 0 | – | – | 1 |
| C | 9 | – | – | 1 | 1 | 0 |
| C | 10 | – | 0 | 1 | 1 | 0 |
| Difference |  | 0 |  |  | 2 |  |

Pass 3
$$r_1 = \{\overline{a,d}; \overline{b,c,e}\}$$

(d)

|  |  | $A = 0$ | $A = 1$ | $A$ | $A = 0$ | $A = 1$ |
|---|---|---|---|---|---|---|
|  |  | a | b | c | d | e |
|  | 1 | 0 | 1 | 1 | 0 | – |
|  | 2 | 0 | – | 1 | 0 | 1 |
|  | 3 | 0 | 1 | – | – | 1 |
| C | 4 | 0 | – | 1 | 1 | – |
|  | 5 | 0 | – | 1 | 0 | – |
| C | 6 | – | 0 | 1 | 0 | 1 |
| C | 7 | 0 | 0 | 1 | 1 | – |
| C | 8 | 0 | 0 | – | – | 1 |
| C | 9 | – | – | 1 | 1 | 0 |
| C | 10 | – | 0 | 1 | 1 | 0 |

Pass 4

(1)  Columns $c$ and $d$ have eight specified entries each; column $c$ is selected and identified with an $A$.

(2)  Row 9 needs to be complemented.

(3)  Identify rows 3 and 8 with $B$.

(4)  Count 1's and 0's in columns $a$ $b$ $d$ $e$.

(5)  Column $a$ has largest difference, i.e. five zeros. Set column $a$ to 0 and identify it with an $A$.

(6)  Not necessary as all rows contain zeros.

(7)  Remove $B$ identifier; no complementation necessary.

(8)  Return to step 4.

(4)  Count 1's and 0's in columns $b$ $d$ $e$.

**Table 4.30. Matrix Reduction Continued.**

(a)

|          |    | *a* | *b* | *A* *c* | *A* = 1 *d* | *e* |
|----------|----|-----|-----|---------|-------------|-----|
|          | 4  | 0   | –   | 1       | 1           | –   |
| *C*      | 6  | –   | 0   | 1       | 0           | 1   |
|          | 7  | 0   | 0   | 1       | 1           | –   |
| *B*      | 8  | 0   | 0   | –       | –           | 1   |
|          | 9  | –   | –   | 1       | 1           | 0   |
|          | 10 | –   | 0   | 1       | 1           | 0   |
| Difference |  | 2   | 3   |         | 3           | 2   |

(b)

|          |    | *A* = 0 *a* | *A* = 0 *b* | *A* *c* | *A* = 1 *d* | *A* = 0 *e* |
|----------|----|-------------|-------------|---------|-------------|-------------|
|          | 4  | 0           | –           | 1       | 1           | –           |
| *C*      | 6  | –           | 0           | 1       | 0           | 1           |
|          | 7  | 0           | 0           | 1       | 1           | –           |
| *C*      | 8  | 0           | 0           | –       | –           | 1           |
|          | 9  | –           | –           | 1       | 1           | 0           |
|          | 10 | –           | 0           | 1       | 1           | 0           |
| Difference |  | 3           | 3           |         |             | 1           |

$$r_2 = \{\overline{a,b,e}\,;\overline{c,d}\}$$

(c)

|   | *a* | *b* | *c* | *d* | *e* |
|---|-----|-----|-----|-----|-----|
| 6 | –   | 0   | 1   | 0   | 1   |
| 8 | 0   | 0   | –   | –   | 1   |

$$r_3 = \{\overline{a,b,d}\,;\overline{c,e}\}$$

(5) Columns *b* and *e* have same difference; select *e* and put column to 1.
(6) Identify rows 9 and 10 with *C.*
(7) No rows identified with *B.*
(8) Return to step 4.
(4) Count 1's and 0's in column *a b.*
(5) Column *d* has largest difference; set to 0.
(6) Identify rows 4 and 7 with *C.*
(7) No rows with *B.*
(8) Return to step 4.
(4) 5. Set *b* to 1.
(6) Identify rows 6 and 8 with *C.*
(7) No rows with *B.*
(8) Finish; go to 9.
(9) Rows 1 2 3 5 have an intersection.

The procedure must now be repeated on the remaining rows in the matrix, that is rows 4, 6, 7, 8, 9, and 10; this is shown in Table 4.30. The reader may easily verify that the resulting partitions are those previously found.

The limitations of the algorithm are as follows.

(1) The algorithm does not always produce an intersection covering a maximum number of rows in a matrix.

(2) There exist matrices where none of the members of the minimum set of covering partitions cover a maximum number of rows in the matrix.

Important advantages of this method are that it is easily programmed for a computer and is capable of handling large matrices.

To summarize, the STT assignment procedure discussed above (called *assignment method #1* by Tracey) consists of the following steps.

(a) Convert the merged flow table to a partition list.

(b) Convert the partition list to a Boolean matrix.

(c) Reduce the Boolean matrix.

(d) Let the reduced matrix define the state assignment.

Unfortunately assignment method #1 can become very laborious for flow tables with more than 40 cells, and to overcome this Tracey described two other algorithms which, though less efficient in terms of the number of $y$ variables, involves considerably less computation.

*Assignment method #2* is based on the concept of *k-sets*. A *k*-set exists in a single column of a flow table and consists of all $k - 1$ unstable entries leading to the same stable state, together with that stable state. A direct transition in *k*-set $k_q$ does not race critically with a direct transition in *k*-set $k_r$ if an assignment has been made such that at least one $y$ variable partitions the elements of $k_q$ and the elements of $k_r$ into separate blocks. The first step in the assignment procedure is to construct a partition list from the *k*-sets of a flow table instead of from the transition pairs. From Table 4.27*b* we obtain

$$\pi_1 = \{\overline{a, d}; \overline{b, c, e}\}$$

$$\pi_2 = \{\overline{a}; \overline{b, e}\}$$

$$\pi_3 = \{\overline{a}; \overline{c, d}\}$$

$$\pi_4 = \{\overline{b, e}; \overline{c, d}\}$$

$$\pi_5 = \{\overline{a, b, d}; \overline{c, e}\}$$

$$\pi_6 = \{\overline{a, b}; \overline{c, d}\}$$

$$\pi_7 = \{\overline{c, d}; \overline{e}\}$$

$$\pi_8 = \{\overline{a, b}; \overline{e}\}.$$

Clearly $\pi_7 \leqslant \pi_4$; $\pi_4$, $\pi_2 \leqslant \pi_1$; $\pi_3 \leqslant \pi_6$; $\pi_8 \leqslant \pi_5$. Therefore partitions $\pi_2$, $\pi_3$, $\pi_4$, $\pi_7$, and $\pi_8$ may be removed from the list. If the remaining four $\pi$-partitions are converted to Boolean matrix form, it is clear that no further reduction is possible; the resulting assignment for the machine is shown in Table 4.31. Note that the assignment is incompletely specified, but is nevertheless free of critical races regardless of how the unspecified entries are allocated. The assignment requires more state variables than assignment method #1, but it is quote possible that the final circuit equations could be just as economical. Note that if the $k$-sets contain no more than two states, method #2 degenerates to method #1.

*Assignment method #3* described by Tracey is very similar to the Liu method. In this case the state assignment is constructed from the column partition of a flow table and results in an even greater saving in computation. A column partition is a partition constructed from a single column of a flow table with each $k$-set of the column appearing as a separate block. It can be either completely or incompletely specified. A state assignment constructed from the set of column partitions of a flow table contains no critical races, even if all transitions are direct. Before the column partitions are coded to give the assignment, those partitions equal to or less than some other partition of the set should be discarded. From Table 4.27$b$ the column partitions are

$$\pi_1 = \{\overline{a, d}; \overline{c, b, e}\}$$
$$\pi_2 = \{\overline{a}; \overline{b, e}; \overline{c, d}\}$$
$$\pi_3 = \{\overline{a, b, d}; \overline{c, e}\}$$
$$\pi_4 = \{\overline{a, b}; \overline{c, d}; \overline{e}\}.$$

By inspection there are no partitions that can be discarded, and the partitions $\pi_1$, $\pi_2$, $\pi_3$, and $\pi_4$ must be used for the assignment. Note that six $y$ variables are required for the assignment: one to distinguish between the blocks of $\pi_1$, two for $\pi_2$, one for $\pi_3$, and two for $\pi_4$. The final assignment is shown in Table 4.32.

**Table 4.31. Assignment Method #2**

|   | $y_1 = \pi_1$ | $y_2 = \pi_6$ | $y_3 = \pi_5$ | $y_4 = \pi_4$ |
|---|---|---|---|---|
| $a$ | 0 | 0 | 0 | – |
| $b$ | 1 | 0 | 0 | 0 |
| $c$ | 1 | 1 | 1 | 1 |
| $d$ | 0 | 1 | 0 | 1 |
| $e$ | 1 | – | 1 | 0 |

**Table 4.32.  Assignment Method # 3**

| | $\pi_1$ | $\pi_2$ | $\pi_3$ | $\pi_4$ |
|---|---|---|---|---|
| | $y_1$ | $y_2 y_3$ | $y_4$ | $y_5 y_6$ |
| a | 0 | 0  0 | 0 | 0  0 |
| b | 1 | 0  1 | 0 | 0  0 |
| c | 1 | 1  1 | 1 | 0  1 |
| d | 0 | 1  1 | 0 | 0  1 |
| e | 1 | 0  1 | 1 | 1  1 |

Method # 3 can be considered to yield an upper bound on the number of variables for methods # 1 and # 2; method # 2 is an upper bound on method # 1. All the assignment methods work equally well for completely or incompletely specified machines, and either of the Boolean reduction techniques described earlier may be used to effect a minimal assignment.

Smith *et al.* (88) have described an implementation of the Tracey algorithms (# 1 and # 2) programmed for the IBM 360/50 using PL/1. Matrix reduction was performed using Tracey's reduction algorithm # 2 which generates a near-minimal assignment. Computation times were from 1.5 to 8 min for machines with up to 32 cells and 15 min for a 72-cell table; in all cases the computation times were found to be extremely problem dependent.

In a later paper Smith (89) described a critical comparison of the Tracey assignment algorithms, and reported that for large tables of more than 75 cells the minimal reduction of $k$-set matrices becomes computationally impracticable. It is also suggested that the use of $k$-set, rather than transition, partitions introduces less than 20% additional state variables. Using $k$-sets (assignment method # 2) and the non-minimal reduction routine the computation times become excessive (over 100 s of CDC 1604 machine time) for tables with greater than 200 cells. It would appear that the major computational effort is involved in the reduction of the Boolean matrix, increasing proportionally to the square of the matrix size.

An efficient computational algorithm is also described by Smith which is claimed to be suitable for machines with up to 400 cells. The method has the distinct advantage that the computational requirements increase linearly with the size of the flow table. The algorithm consists of generating the $k$-set partitions and the corresponding rows of a Boolean matrix in a piecemeal fashion, with the matrix being partially reduced each time it reaches a predetermined size. For example, the $k$-set partitions would be obtained from the flow table column by column and converted into Boolean matrix form. When the size of the Boolean matrix reaches a predetermined limit (say 20–30 rows) it is partially reduced until a lower limit (2–8 rows) is reached or the reduction can proceed no further. The process is continued until all the $k$-set partitions have been extracted and reduced; a $k$-set partition is not added to the Boolean matrix if it can be covered by an existing row. When all the $k$-set partitions have been found, the state variable and partition list must be checked to ensure that each flow-table row is partitioned by some variable from every other flow-table row. This requirement must be satisfied (by adding extra $k$-set partitions) to ensure the absence of critical races. Note that the method also can be adopted to overcome the problem of storing large flow tables in main core. Since the examination of the flow table is performed column by column, it is possible to store large tables on backing store (say a disk-file) and to read a column at a time into main store.

The algorithm has been programmed in FORTRAN for the CDC 1604 machine. A wide variety of flow tables have been assigned using the segmented-reduction (SR) method with typical computation times varying from 4 s for flow tables with up to 60 cells to 179 s for a 400-cell machine. In all cases the times obtained were considerably less than those obtained for corresponding machines using an implementation of the Tracey algorithm.

An alternative approach for dealing with large flow tables has been reported by Elsey (90). The method does not generate STT assignments or an optimum solution, but it does enable large tables to be handled using a backing-store technique. The method examines the flow table row by row (hence necessitating the minimum storage space in main core) and performs a simultaneous merging and assignment procedure based on the standard method of adjacent coding and shared-row states (91).

The principle of the method may be illustrated by considering an example based on the primitive flow table shown in Table 4.33. The initial step is to write the first row of the table into the result store (RS) (see Table 4.34a)

## Table 4.33. Primitive Flow Table[†]

|  | Inputs $x_1 x_2$ | | | |
|---|---|---|---|---|
|  | 00 | 01 | 11 | 10 |
| 1 | ①/0 | 2 | – | 5 |
| 2 | 1 | ②/0 | 3 | – |
| 3 | – | 6 | ③/1 | 4 |
| 4 | 1 | – | 3 | ④/1 |
| 5 | 1 | – | 7 | ⑤/0 |
| 6 | 8 | ⑥/1 | 3 | – |
| 7 | – | 9 | ⑦/0 | 5 |
| 8 | ⑧/1 | 6 | – | 10 |
| 9 | 1 | ⑨/0 | 7 | – |
| 10 | 8 | – | 3 | ⑩/1 |

[†]Suffixes relate to output states.

## Table 4.34. Elsey Algorithm[†]

| | | | | | |
|---|---|---|---|---|---|
| (a) | 00 | ①/00 | 2 | – | 5 |
| (b) | 00 | ①/00 | ②/00 | 3 | 5 |
| (c) | 00 | ①/00 | ②/00 | 3/01 | 5 |
| | 01 | – | 6 | ③/01 | 4 |
| (d) | 00 | ①/00 | ②/00 | 3/01 | 5/10 |
| | 01 | – | 6 | ③/01 | 4 |
| | 10 | 1 | – | 7 | ⑤/10 |
| (e) | 00 | ①/00 | ②/00 | 3/01 | 5/10 |
| | 01 | 1/00 | 6 | ③/01 | ④/01 |
| | 10 | 1 | – | 7 | ⑤/10 |
| (f) | 00 | ①/00 | ②/00 | 3/01 | 5/10 |
| | 01 | 1/00 | 6/11 | ③/01 | ④/01 |
| | 10 | 1 | – | 7 | ⑤/10 |
| | 11 | 8 | ⑥ | 3 | – |
| (g) | 00 | ①/00 | ②/00 | 3/01 | 5/10 |
| | 01 | 1/00 | 6/11 | ③/01 | ④/01 |
| | 10 | 1/00 | ⑨/10 | ⑦/10 | ⑤/10 |
| | 11 | 8 | ⑥ | 3 | – |
| (h) | 00 | ①/00 | ②/00 | 3/01 | 5/10 |
| | 01 | 1/00 | 6/11 | ③/01 | ④/01 |
| | 10 | 1/00 | ⑨/10 | ⑦/10 | ⑤/10 |
| | 11 | ⑧/11 | ⑥/11 | 3/01 | ⑩/11 |

[†]Suffixes relate to secondary assignment

which will be expanded as the algorithm proceeds. The first entry in the result store, taken in sequence across the row (called the *E-entry*), is stable-state ① which is assigned 00. After inspecting the flow table the RS row is merged with rows 1 and 2 of the flow table (see Table 4.34b). As the E-entry is stable the next entry ② is considered and again an attempt is made to merge rows; in this case no rows merge. The next E-entry is unstable 3; in this case the following procedure is followed.

**(1)** If the corresponding stable entry (S) has already been processed, i.e. in an earlier row of RS, assign a proper code path from E to S.

**(2)** If the stable entry has not yet been processed then:

   *(a)* Try to merge the S row with any unprocessed row of the RS which is adjacent to the row containing E. Assign a code path from E to S.

   *(b)* Try to merge the S row with any other unprocessed row of RS and assign a proper code path from E to S.

   *(c)* Write the S row into RS with a code adjacent to the processed row; if such a code is available within the number of secondary variables used. Otherwise an attempt it made to use any unused assignment which

can give a cycle between already used states. If this fails a code adjacent to the processed row is selected using an extra secondary variable.

In our example the stable row (that is the row containing ③) has yet to be processed, i.e. it is still in data store. Consequently the stable row is written into RS and the state assigned a code adjacent to the processed row (see Table 4.34c). Continuing, entry 5 is now examined. This is unstable and no rows merge and furthermore the stable row has yet to be processed; thus the stable row is written into RS with a code adjacent to the processed row (see Table 4.34d). The next row of RS (taken in sequence) is now examined and the first E-entry is found to be a don't-care. The flow-table is then inspected and it is apparent that row 4 will merge with the processed row. After merging, the E-entry is unstable and the S row already processed, so a code path is assigned to the stable row (Table 4.34e). Proceeding to the next E-entry, which is unstable 6, we find no rows merge and the S row will not merge with any row of RS; hence it is written into RS and assigned a code adjacent to the processed row, i.e. 11 (see Table 4.34f). The next E-entry is ③', no rows merge, and the E-entry is stable. Passing to the next E-entry ④' the same situation exists and the procedure carries on to the next RS row. Here the first E-entry is unstable 1 and rows 9 and 7 will merge (see Table 4.34g); the unstable 1 is assigned the code 00. For E-entries ⑨, ⑦, and ⑤ no rows merge and all entries are stable, and row 4 of RS is considered next. The first E-entry is unstable 8, and this row will merge with rows 8 and 10; the resulting E-entry is stable (see Table 4.34h). The next E-entry is ⑥ and no rows merge; the following E-entry is unstable 3 and the stable row is already processed, so a code-path $11 \to 01$ is allocated. The final E-entry is ⑩ which is stable and there are no more data rows left. The final assigned flow table is shown in Table 4.34h.

An interesting variant on the state-assignment problem is the work done by Burton and Noakes (92) and Tan (93) in which STT assignments are derived in such a way as to evolve minimal excitation equations directly. Using this technique the usual extraction and Boolean minimization procedures can be avoided. The method consists of examining in turn each input column of a flow table and forming sets of those rows in the table whose states go to the same next state (called *destination* sets by Tan). For instance, the flow table shown in Table 4.36 has the following destination sets:

Input $I_1$, $D_{11} = (\underline{a})$, $D_{12} = (b, \underline{c}, d)$

Input $I_2$, $D_{21} = (a, \underline{b}, c)$, $D_{22} = (\underline{d})$

Input $I_3$, $D_{31} = (\underline{a}, c)$, $D_{32} = (\underline{b}, d)$

Input $I_4$, $D_{41} = (\underline{a})$, $D_{42} = (b, \underline{d})$, $D_{43} = (\underline{c})$

where $D_{ij}$ denotes the destination sets, $i$ the input column from which the set is derived, and $j$ the reference number of that set; stable states are indicated by underlining. Now, in order to derive an assignment a secondary variable $y_n$ is allocated to each destination set and the value of $y_n$ made equal to 1 when the elements in the corresponding set contain the row element, otherwise $y_n$ is made equal to 0; the full assignment is shown in Table 4.35.

The next-state equations may be extracted directly from the assignment in the form of simple product terms (containing only one state variable) which cover the unique destination set containing those states involved in a $0 \rightarrow 1$ or $1 \rightarrow 1$ transition in the assigned flow table. For example, consider the set $D_{11}(y_1)$, with input $I_1$; the stable states are $a$ and $c$. Now, since $a$ is an element of $D_{11}$, and also $D_{31}$ under $I_3$, we can add the single product terms $I_1 y_1 + I_3 y_5$ to the next-state equations for $y_1$; the remaining stable state $c$ is covered by $D_{43}$ with input $I_4$. Thus we can write

$$Y_1 = I_1 y_1 + I_3 y_5 + I_4 y_9$$

similarly

$$Y_2 = I_1 y_2 + I_2 y_3 + I_2 y_4 + I_3 y_6 + I_4 y_6 + I_4 y_9$$
$$Y_3 = I_1 y_1 + I_1 y_2 + I_2 y_3 + I_3 y_5 + I_3 y_6 + I_4 y_7 + I_4 y_9$$
$$Y_4 = I_2 y_4 + I_4 y_8$$
$$Y_5 = I_1 y_1 + I_1 y_2 + I_3 y_5 + I_4 y_7 + I_4 y_9$$
$$Y_6 = I_2 y_3 + I_2 y_4 + I_3 y_6 + I_4 y_8$$
$$Y_7 = I_1 y_1 + I_3 y_5 + I_4 y_7$$
$$Y_8 = I_2 y_3 + I_2 y_4 + I_3 y_6 + I_4 y_8$$
$$Y_9 = I_1 y_2 + I_4 y_9.$$

Note that all the $y$ terms are in the uncomplemented form and that the assignment obtained is equivalent to a Liu assignment. Note also that, since

**Table 4.35. State Assignments Using Destination Sets**

| $I_1$ | $I_2$ | $I_3$ | $I_4$ | $y_1 (D_{11})$ | $y_2 (D_{12})$ | $y_3 (D_{21})$ | $y_4 (D_{22})$ | $y_5 (D_{31})$ | $y_6 (D_{32})$ | $y_7 (D_{41})$ | $y_8 (D_{42})$ | $y_9 (D_{43})$ |
|---|---|---|---|---|---|---|---|---|---|---|---|---|
| $a$ ① 2 ① ① | | | | 1 | 0 | 1 | 0 | 1 | 0 | 1 | 0 | 0 |
| $b$ 3 ② ② 4 | | | | 0 | 1 | 1 | 0 | 0 | 1 | 0 | 1 | 0 |
| $c$ ③ 2 1 ③ | | | | 0 | 1 | 1 | 0 | 1 | 0 | 0 | 0 | 1 |
| $d$ 3 ④ 2 ④ | | | | 0 | 1 | 0 | 1 | 0 | 1 | 0 | 1 | 0 |

the flow table is used in its standard form, any two states corresponding to the same $y$ state can be merged into a single state. Using this fact redundancy in the equations can be reduced by simple algebraic manipulation using the union operation. Thus $D_{11} \cup D_{12}$ is the set $(a, b, c, d)$ which is the set of all states, and consequently the term $I_1(y_1 + y_2)$ in the equation for $Y_3$ and $Y_5$ may be replaced by 1; similarly $D_{42} \cup D_{43} = (b, c, d) = D_{12}$ which allows $I_4 y_2$ to be substituted for $I_4(y_8 + y_9)$ in the equation for $Y_2$.

Tan has described a heuristic algorithm based on this technique (and also defined an upper bound on gate inputs), while Burton (94) has extended the method to extract the input equations for set–reset bistables. Unfortunately, though the method gives reasonable realizations for small machines, it is unlikely to prove an efficient computational algorithm owing to the amount (and type) of computation involved. The method also tends to generate a larger number of state variables than other STT assignment procedures and furthermore it does not take into account the output logic.

Other work in state assignment which is worth noting is the use of graph-theoretic methods proposed by Saucier (95), which gives rise to difficult computational problems, and the generation of shared-row assignments using parity-coding techniques (96, 97). The use of minimum-distance codes to effect race-free (but not necessarily STT) assignments would appear to hold considerable promise for CAD application, particularly when coupled with table look-up techniques (98).

To date the Tracey STT assignment technique, or some version of the method, has been the one most successfully applied in computer-assisted methods. The major problems come about, as with all this work, in the handling of very large flow tables.

### 4.3.5. State-Assignment Selection Tests

In establishing an assignment for an asynchronous machine it is often possible to develop several legitimate assignments with the same number of state variables. Maki and Tracey (99) have described a method whereby it is possible to predict which of the generated state assignments will yield a relatively simple set of next-state equations. The method considers the determination of the next-state expressions for a given machine on a column-by-column basis. The next-state equations can be assumed to be of the following form:

$$Y_1 = f_{11}(y_1, y_2, \ldots, y_n)I_1 + f_{12}(y_1, y_2, \ldots, y_n)I_2 + f_{1m}(y_1, y_2, \ldots, y_n)I_m$$

$$Y_2 = f_{21}(y_1, y_2, \ldots, y_n)I_1 + f_{22}(y_1, y_2, \ldots, y_n)I_2 + f_{2m}(y_1, y_2, \ldots, y_n)I_m$$

$$\vdots$$

$$Y_n = f_{n1}(y_1, y_2, \ldots, y_n)I_1 + f_{n2}(y_1, y_2, \ldots, y_n)I_2 + f_{nm}(y_1, y_2, \ldots, y_n)I_m$$

where $y_1, y_2, \ldots, y_n$ are the present state variables, $Y_1, Y_2, \ldots, Y_n$ are the next-state variables, $I_1, I_2, \ldots, I_m$ are the input states and $f_{11}, f_{12}, \ldots, f_{nm}$ are functions of the internal-state variables.

The objective of the selection method is to obtain an assignment that will tend to minimize the function $f_{11}, f_{12}, \ldots, f_{nm}$ so as to yield simplified sum-of-products expressions. For NAND-gate implementation (excitation or delay equations) the selection process requires finding those coefficients $f_{ij}$ which correspond to the conditions

(a)  $f_{ij} = 1$ or $0$

and

(b)  $f_{ij} = y_i$ or $\bar{y}_i$.

Consider the flow table shown in Table 4.36; the $r$-partitions for assignments (1) and (2) are given by

$$\text{assignment (1)} \quad r_1 = \{\overline{a, d, e}; \overline{b, c}\}$$

$$r_2 = \{\overline{a, d}; \overline{b, c, e}\}$$

$$r_3 = \{\overline{a, c, e}; \overline{b, d}\}$$

$$\text{assignment (2)} \quad r_1' = \{\overline{a, d}; \overline{b, c, e}\}$$

$$r_2' = \{\overline{a, e}; \overline{b, c, d}\}$$

$$r_3' = \{\overline{a, c, e}; \overline{b, d}\}$$

Now a column partition $a_j$ is defined as a collection of $k$-sets of the column of the flow table with input state $I_j$ where each $k$-set constitutes a single block; thus we have

$$a_1 = \{\overline{\underline{a}, d, e}; \overline{b, c}\}$$
$$a_2 = \{\overline{a, b, \underline{d}}; \overline{\underline{c}}; \overline{\underline{e}}\}$$
$$a_3 = \{\overline{a, c, \underline{d}}; \overline{\underline{b}, e}\}$$

where the stable states are underlined for convenience.

It can be shown that if all the stable states of a column partition $a_j$ are in the *same* block of an $r$-partition $r_i$, then the next-state coefficient $f_{ij}$ will be either 0 or 1. Constant coefficients can be easily determined by identifying the stable state of each column partition in the blocks of the set of $r$-partitions. For example, considering $a$, above, the stable states are $a$ and $c$;

by inspection of the $r$-partitions we see that all the stable states are included in the same block of $r_3$ but not in $r_1$ or $r_2$, and therefore coefficient $f_{31}$ will be constant. If the first block of $r_1$ is coded with 0, then the partial next-state equation will be given by $Y_1 = 0.I_1$. Thus by ensuring that all the stable states in a column have a value of either 0 or 1 the next-state variable is dependent only on the input value.

In order to obtain a simple set of next-state equations it is clearly necessary to have as many constant coefficients as possible. The total number of such constant coefficients $(A_t)$ for a given assignment can be used as a measure of the complexity of the resulting next-state expressions. The second desirable characteristic of an assignment is that it should produce a number of $f_{ij}$'s equal to $y_i$; this ensures that the next-state $Y_i$ will be dependent only on the input and the present state of $y_i$. It has been shown by Maki and Tracey that a coefficient $f_{ij}$ will equal $y_i$ if $a_i \leqslant r_i$. For instance, comparing the $a$-partitions with the $r$-partitions for our example, we find that only $a_1 \leqslant r_1$ satisfies this relationship. This means that for all the transitions occurring in column $I_1$ the internal state variable $y_1$ will not change state. The total number of terms of the form $f_{ij} = y_i(B_1)$ in a given assignment can also be used as a measure of a good internal-state assignment.

In order to compare two (or more) state assignments the values of $A_t$ and $B_t$ are obtained and a weight (figure of merit) calculated for each assignment of the form

$$W_t = pA_t + B_t$$

where $p$ is a variable that allows for adjustment of the relative weights of $A_t$ and $B_t$ (it is assumed that constant coefficients yield more economical results than literal coefficients). The value of $p$ would normally be chosen by the designer, based on the cost of implementing constant-coefficient terms as opposed to literal coefficients; in general $p$ will vary with each type of implementation.

As an example of the use of the figure of merit $W_t$ consider the two alternative assignments for the machine shown in Table 4.36. Now for assignment (1) we find for the condition $f_{ij} = 0$ or 1 that stable states $a$ and $c$ in partition $a_1$ are included in partition $r_3$, and stable states $d$ and $b$ in partition $a_3$ are included in $r_3$. Thus, $Y_3 = 0.I_1$ and $Y_3 = 1.I_3$ to yield the score $A_t = 2$. Similarly, for assignment (2) stable states $a$ and $c$ in $a_1$ are included in $r'_3$, and stable states $d$ and $b$ in $a_3$ are included in $r'_2$ and $r'_3$. This gives $Y_3 = 0.I_1$, $Y_2 = 1.I_3$ and $Y_3 = 1.I_3$ to yield $A'_t = 3$. Applying the test for $f_{ij} = y_i$ we find that for assignment (1) $a_1 = r_1$ giving $B_t = 1$; there are no such conditions for assignment (2), therefore $B'_t = 0$. Now if we assume a value of $p = 2$ we obtain

$$W_t = 2A_t + B_t$$

then

$$W_t = 5 \text{ for assignment (1)}$$

and

$$W'_t = 6 \text{ for assignment (2).}$$

Therefore it is possible to predict that assignment (2) will be the most economical.

The test can be applied in CAD synthesis systems to determine the efficiency of particular assignments or, in the case of converging algorithms (where repeated computation yields progressively better assignments), to determine the termination point. The Maki-Tracey test has been programmed in PL/1 and forms part of a large synthesis program for asynchronous circuits (88). Improved state-assignment tests (based on the same principles) have been proposed by Maki *et al.* (100) which take into account the sharing of gates in a NAND implementation and realizations using set-reset bistables (SR-FF). Moreoever, the improved technique allows the comparison of assignments with a differing number of state variables, and also takes into consideration the complexity of the output equations. A general method for the selection of state assignments has also been proposed by Saucier (101) using the partition algebra of Hartmanis; the Maki-Tracey algorithm is shown to be a special case of the general theorem.

### 4.3.6. Derivation of Next-State Equations

Once the assigned state table has been generated, either for a synchronous or asynchronous machine, the next and final step is to realize the table in terms of logic elements. This is a fairly straightforward process in the case of synchronous circuits, since it is only necessary to examine the present and next-state transitions on the assigned table, applying the rules dictated by the

**Table 4.36. State-Assignment Selection**

|   | $I_1$ | $I_2$ | $I_3$ | (1) $y_1$ | $y_2$ | $y_3$ | (2) $y_1$ | $y_2$ | $y_3$ |
|---|---|---|---|---|---|---|---|---|---|
| a | ① | 4 | 4 | 0 | 0 | 0 | 0 | 0 | 0 |
| b | 3 | 4 | ② | 1 | 1 | 1 | 1 | 1 | 1 |
| c | ③ | ③ | 4 | 1 | 1 | 0 | 1 | 1 | 0 |
| d | 1 | ④ | ④ | 0 | 0 | 1 | 0 | 1 | 1 |
| e | 1 | ⑤ | 2 | 0 | 1 | 0 | 1 | 0 | 0 |

characteristic equations or transition table of the specified bistable, to generate the required input equations. The equations must then be simplified, using normal Boolean minimization techniques, and implemented in terms of standard logic modules. As we have seen, the type of bistable used for the implementation can radically effect the complexity (and hence economy) of the input equations; consequently many CAD systems allow alternative bistable types to be specified by the designer.

Owing to the absence of a clock pulse, asynchronous circuits present slightly more difficult problems, since the possible presence of circuit hazards in the excitation or next-state equations must be taken into account during the implementation stages; similar hazards can also exist of course in the output logic. The usual practice is to arrange that single-variable static hazards which arise due to a violation in practice of the Boolean expressions $A + \bar{A} = 1$ and $A\bar{A} = 0$, are compensated by the inclusion of redundant terms in the equations which maintain the correct output during the input changes. This technique is not usually applied directly to CAD systems owing to the difficulty involved in translating the graphical or algebraic procedures to an algorithmic form. A much better approach is to implement the flow table using a direct-coupled set–reset bistable (84, 102, 103). Not only does this technique overcome the static-hazard problem but also enables the same algorithms for equation extraction to be used for both synchronous and asynchronous machines (note that excitation equations correspond to the input equations for D-type bistable implementation for a synchronous machine). This procedure unfortunately does not compensate for all possible circuit hazards; the essential hazard, which is peculiar to asynchronous circuits, must be treated separately. This hazard is basically a critical race between an input signal change and a secondary variable change, and can be overcome by logical means provided the stray line delays never exceed the gate delays; this assumption is valid for most practical implementations. The most useful method of correction, due to Armstrong *et al.* (102), assumes an STT assignment and single-rail inputs (that is in the uncomplemented form).

In general, the logical equations of a sequential circuit require uncomplemented as well as complemented input variables. However, if the inputs are supplied as double rail or if invertors are used on the inputs, then a change in an $x$ input would not result in a change in $\bar{x}$ until after some delay time $D$ associated with the bistable or invertor. Therefore single-rail inputs must be assumed and an alternative method of generating $\bar{x}$ is employed in order to ensure that the $x$-variable change is seen before the subsequent $y$-variable change. This can be done by replacing first-level AND gates in the sum of products form of the logical equations by NOR–AND pairs where necessary. For example, suppose a sum-of-products equation contained the term $x_1\bar{x}_2y_2\bar{y}_3$, this would be replaced by

$$\overline{x_1(\bar{x}_2 y_2 \bar{y}_3)} = x_1 \overline{(x_2 + \bar{y}_2 + y_3)}$$

which can be realized as a NOR–AND pair (see Fig. 4.9a). What is effectively happening is that those $x$ variables which must be complemented and the $y$ variables with which the former are racing are passed through the same NOR gate. This resolves the race so that the first-level gates see the $x$ change before any $y$ change. If this technique is combined with the use of d.c. SR bistables for the circuit realization, a hazard-free circuit results.

Consider the assigned flow table shown in Table 4.37; extracting the $Y_1 Y_2$ set and reset conditions and minimizing in the usual way results in the equations

$$Y_1 \text{ set } = \bar{x}_1 \bar{x}_2 y_2 + x_1 x_2 y_2 + x_1 \bar{x}_2 \bar{y}_2$$

$$Y_1 \text{ reset} = x_1 x_2 \bar{y}_2 + x_1 \bar{x}_2 \bar{y}_2$$

$$Y_2 \text{ set } = \bar{x}_1 x_2 \bar{y}_1$$

$$Y_2 \text{ reset} = \bar{x}_1 x_2 y_1$$

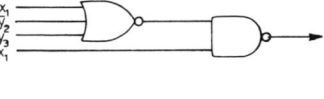

a) NOR–NAND pair

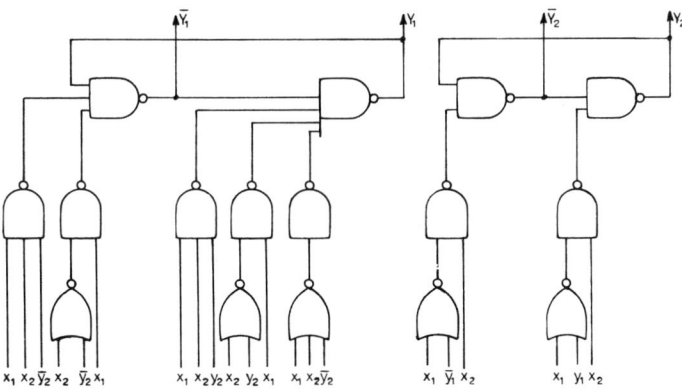

b) Delay-free Realization

**Figure 4.9.** Essential hazard correction.

**Table 4.37. SR Bistable Realization**

| $y_1 y_2$ | $x_1 x_2$ 00 | 01 | 11 | 10 | $y_1 y_2$ | $x_1 x_2$ 00 | 01 | 11 | 10 |
|-----------|------|-----|-----|-----|-----------|------|-----|-----|-----|
| 00 | ① | 2 | ① | 4 | 00 | 00 | 01 | 00 | 10 |
| 01 | 3 | ② | 3 | ② | 01 | 11 | 01 | 11 | 01 |
| 11 | ③ | 4 | ③ | 2 | 11 | 11 | 10 | 11 | 01 |
| 10 | ④ | ④ | 1 | ④ | 10 | 10 | 10 | 00 | 10 |

Applying the NOR–AND technique we have

$$Y_1 \text{ set } = \overline{(x_1 + x_2 + \bar{y}_2)} + x_1 x_2 y_2 + x_1 \overline{(x_2 + y_2)}$$
$$Y_1 \text{ reset} = x_1 x_2 \bar{y}_2 + x_1 \overline{(x_2 + \bar{y}_2)}$$
$$Y_2 \text{ set } = x_2 \overline{(x_1 + y_1)}$$
$$Y_2 \text{ reset} = x_2 \overline{(x_1 + \bar{y}_1)}.$$

The circuit is shown implemented in Fig. 4.9b; note the use of the NOR-NAND elements to obtain the inversion required with NAND bistables.

An alternative method has been described by Hlavicka (104) using a correction element, which is an additional sequential circuit inserted in the network to generate a correction variable. Though the method leads to circuits with fewer logic levels the total number of elements tends to be greater than that required by the Armstrong method.

As might be suspected, ROM's are also ideal devices for the realization of synchronous and asynchronous sequential circuits (44, 105). Using ROM's the initial conceptual design procedure remains unchanged, and the starting point for implementation is the assigned flow table. Table 4.38 shows a typical assigned flow table for a divide-by-two asynchronous counter stage; the transition table shows the required transitions from present to next states of the counter when the external input $x$ is applied. The circuit is shown in Fig. 4.10. Note that the $y_1 y_2$ outputs are fed directly back to the address input of the ROM to give the required sequential, that is feedback, action. Note also that the circuit represents a Moore machine; the more general Mealy machine can easily be accommodated by allocating appropriate bits in the ROM words to generate the output functions directly.

An implementation of this form is possible because the integrated-circuit ROM is constructed from active devices, which give the necessary gain round the feedback loop. The equivalent in the ROM to an asynchronous stable-state condition is when the output word is used to address its own location—a form

**Table 4.38.  ROM Implementation of Binary Counter Stage**

(a)  Assigned flow table

| State variables | Input $x$ | | Output |
|---|---|---|---|
| $y_1 y_2$ | 0 | 1 | $z$ |
| 00 | 00 | 01 | 0 |
| 01 | 11 | 01 | 0 |
| 11 | 11 | 10 | 1 |
| 10 | 00 | 10 | 1 |

(b)  Transition table

| Address | Output word |
|---|---|
| $xy_1 y_2$ | $y_1 y_2 z$ |
| 000 | 000 |
| 100 | 010 |
| 001 | 110 |
| 101 | 010 |
| 011 | 111 |
| 111 | 101 |
| 010 | 001 |
| 110 | 101 |

of dynamic loop. Thus the ROM circuit is directly analogous to the conventional NAND–NOR implementation of the excitation equations. However, in this case there is an added advantage in that there is no longer any need to examine and correct for static hazards. The occurrence of static hazards arises during the minimization procedures and since when using ROM's all the basic switching terms are effectively used, hazards of this type are eliminated. However, owing to the differing switching times of the memory devices in the ROM it is still necessary to have a race-free state assignment. For a minimum-dependence address-calculation network (straight-through connection of the ROM address word) an $s$-variable STT state assignment for an $n$-input column flow table requires $\lceil \log_2 n \rceil + s$ address variables. When ROM addresses are calculated externally to the ROM in a separate network (a procedure used to reduce the amount of ROM storage), care must be taken to ensure that any hazardous conditions in the address network are eliminated.

Synchronous machines can be implemented using ROM's in a similar manner, though in this case secondary races can be ignored; there is, however, a timing problem to be considered. In some cases the ROM is provided with an enable or strobe line which can be used like a system clock; for instance, the outputs can be disabled until the transients on the input lines have died

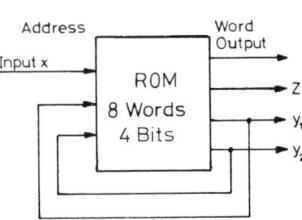

**Figure 4.10.**  Divide-by-two counter.

away. However, the required delay round the loop may be obtained by using external bistable devices (for example MSI D-type bistable latch units) to register (that is, delay) the outputs prior to returning them to the address inputs.

Maki *et al.* (106) have described a means whereby the next-state and output equations for a machine can be obtained directly from the flow table and state assignment, thereby eliminating the need to construct a transition table and excitation matrix. The technique can be applied to any valid assignment, including STT and shared-row assignments. The method assumes that the input states are uncoded, thus permitting the determination of the next-state equations on a partial column-by-column basis. The general form of the next-state equations for a machine with $n$ internal states and $m$ input states is given by

$$Y_n = f_{n1}(y_1, y_2, \ldots, y_n)I_1 + f_{n2}(y_1, y_2, \ldots, y_n)I_2$$
$$+ f_{nm}(y_1, y_2, \ldots, y_n)I_m$$

where $y_n$ is the present-state variable, $Y_n$ the next-state variable, and $I_m$ the input state; $f_{nm}$ is a function of the internal-state variables only. Similarly the output equations can be represented by;

$$Z_k = g_{k1}(y_1, y_2, \ldots, y_n)I_1 + g_{k2}(y_1, y_2, \ldots, y_n)I_2$$
$$+ g_{km}(y_1, y_2, \ldots, y_n)I_m$$

where $Z_k$ is the output and $g_{km}$ is a function of the internal-state variables. Once the next-state and output equations are generated in this form the input states can be coded and the set of Boolean equations minimized in the usual way. However, in order to obtain a minimal set of next-state equations it is necessary to determine the 1's (or 0's) and the "don't-care" terms for each next-state variable [as we have seen the "don't-care" terms can be obtained by complementing the list of specified ON (or OFF) conditions]. The extraction of the ON conditions for the next-state variables is performed by determining the $k$-sets for each column of the assigned flow table and then investigating the row transitions for each state pair. Consider the flow table shown in Table 4.39. In column $I_1$ there are two $k$-sets $(a, d, e)$ and $(b, c)$; thus there are three transition pairs $bc$, $ad$, $ae$. Since states $ade$ belong to the same $k$-set they will have the same next-state entry of 000, which is the code for stable state ① (row a), and similarly for states $bc$ which have the next-state entry of 110. Now during a transition between states $b$ and $c$ any of the internal states 11– could momentarily be assumed; thus to ensure that the circuit reaches its proper terminal state all the states represented by 11– must have a next-state

## Table 4.39. Generation of Next-State Equations

(a) Flow table

| | Inputs | | | Outputs | | |
|---|---|---|---|---|---|---|
| | $I_1$ | $I_2$ | $I_3$ | $I_1$ | $I_2$ | $I_3$ |
| a | ① | – | 4 | 10 | – | – |
| b | 3 | 4 | ② | – | – | 01 |
| c | ③ | ③ | – | 01 | 00 | – |
| d | 1 | ④ | ④ | – | 11 | 00 |
| e | 1 | ⑤ | 2 | – | 10 | – |

(b) Assigned flow table

| $y_1 y_2 y_3$ | $I_1$ | $I_2$ | $I_3$ |
|---|---|---|---|
| 0 0 0 | 000 | – | 001 |
| 1 1 1 | 110 | 001 | 111 |
| 1 1 0 | 110 | 110 | – |
| 0 0 1 | 000 | 001 | 001 |
| 0 1 0 | 000 | 010 | 111 |

entry of 110 (note that in the case of an STT assignment, however, these transitory states are normally assumed to be zero). The internal states that can be entered by the circuit during a state transition can be represented as a $p$-subcube of an $n$-cube. Thus, in the transition between rows $b$ and $c$ in columns $I_1$ we have the resultant $p$-subcube $y_1 y_2$ (11–), and for rows $d$ and $e$ to row $a$ we have the $p$-subcubes $\bar{y}_1 \bar{y}_2$ (00–) and $\bar{y}_1 \bar{y}_3$ (0–0). Since it is possible to represent the $p$-subcubes as a function of the internal-state variables we may write a Boolean sum-of-products expression which denotes those states requiring specified entries (in this case 1's) under input $I_1$; thus

$$P_{I_1} = y_1 y_2 + \bar{y}_1 \bar{y}_2 + \bar{y}_1 \bar{y}_3.$$

Partial next-state equations may now be obtained by noting that if $y_1$ is 1 in the stable-state row code, then the next-state variable $Y_1 = 1$ for *all* states in the $p$-subcube associated with that stable state. In other words all $p$-subcubes associated with transitions to a stable state will appear in the next-state equations for $Y_i$ if digit $i$ of the stable-row code is 1. Thus we can obtain for columns $I_1$ the following partial next-state equations:

$$Y_1 = y_1 y_2 I_1; \quad Y_2 = y_1 y_2 I_1; \quad Y_3 = 0 . I_1.$$

This process would of course be followed through column by column to obtain the complete set of equations.

Maki *et al.* describe algorithms for the derivation of all the $p$-subcubes and the generation of 1-sets, that is those subcubes which have next-state variables equal to 1 (0-sets could of course have been derived as an alternative). The resulting Boolean equations represent those terms which cause the next-state variables to go to 1, that is the excitation equations.

In order to obtain a minimal set of next-state equations it is also necessary to determine the "don't-care" conditions for each column of the flow table and include these in the equations. Since the unspecified $p$-subcubes will be common for all the design equations the logical complement of the $P_{I_i}$ equations will provide the required "don't-care" terms. Complementation is performed using the algebraic processes of inversion, multiplication, and simplification employing the standard forms $A(A + B) = A$ and $A(\bar{A} + B) = AB$. The "don't-care" terms obtained in this manner are added to the 1-sets for each state variable and the equations minimized in the normal way.

The same procedure can be extended to generate the output equations; it is interesting to note that it is necessary to make the stable and unstable output states identical. Furthermore, it is claimed that static hazards can be determined and eliminated using these techniques. The algorithms have been programmed for an IBM 360/50 using PL/1 (88) with satisfactory results but rather long computation times.

## REFERENCES AND BIBLIOGRAPHY

1. Quine, W. V. A way to simplify truth functions. *Am. Math. Mon.* **62**, 627–31, 1955.
2. Ashenhurst, R. L. The decomposition of switching functions *Ann. Harvard Computational Lab.* **29**, 74–116, 1959.
3. Roth, J. P., and Karp, R. M. Minimisation over Boolean graphs. *IBM J. Res. Dev.* **6**, 227–38, 1962.
4. Simon, H. A. *The Sciences of the Artificial*, pp. 64–5. MIT Press, Cambridge, Mass., 1969.
5. Lewin, D. Outstanding problems in logic design. *Radio Electron. Eng.* **44**, 9–17, 1974.
6. Kramme, F. Standard read-only memories simplify complex logic design. *Electronics* **43**, 88–95, Jan. 1970.
7. Roth, J. P. Algebraic topological methods for the synthesis of switching systems. I. *Trans. Am. Math. Soc.* **88**, 301–26, 1958.
8. Tilson, P. Generalization of concensus theory and application to the minimisation of Boolean functions. *IEEE Trans.–Computers* **EC16**, 446–56, 1967.
9. Ewing, A. C., Roth, J. P., and Wagner, E. G. Algorithms for logical design. *AIEE Trans. Comm. Electron.* pp. 450–8, Sept. 1961.
10. Su, Y. H. Automated logic design via a new local extraction algorithm. *Proc. NEC* pp. 651–6, Dec. 1969.
11. Cobham, A., Fridshal, R., and North, J. H. An application of linear programming to the minimisation of Boolean function. *Proceedings of AIEE Symposium on Switching Circuit Theory*, pp. 3–9, 1961; see also IBM Res. Rep. No. RC-472, June 1961.
12. Vajda, S. *Mathematical Programming.* Addison Wesley, Reading, Mass., 1961.

13. Little, J. D. C., Murty, K. G., Sweeney, D. W., and Karel, G. An algorithm for the travelling salesman problem. *Operations Res.* **11**, 972–89, 1963.
14. McCluskey, E. J., and Schorr, H. Essential multiple-output prime implicants *Mathematical Theory of Automata* Vol. 12, pp. 437–57. Polytechnic Press, 1962.
15. Bartee, T. C. Computer design of multiple-output networks. *IRE Trans. Electron. Computers* **EC10**, 21–30, 1961.
16. Bartee, T. C., Lebow, I. L., and Read, I. S. *Theory and Design of Digital Machines*. McGraw-Hill, New York, 1962.
17. Karp, R. M., McFarlin, F. E., Roth, J. P., and Wilts, J. R. A computer program for the synthesis of combinational switching circuits. *Proceedings of AIEE 2nd Annual Symposium on Switching Circuit Theory*, pp. 182–94, 1961.
18. Roth, J. P. *A Calculus and an Algorithm for the Multiple-Output 2-level Minimisation Problem*. Res. Rep. No. RC 2007, IBM T. J. Watson Research Center, Feb. 1968.
19. Morreale, E. Partitioned list algorithm for prime implicant determination from canonical forms. *IEEE Trans. Electron. Computers* **EC16**, 611–20, 1967.
20. Slagle, J. R., Chang, C. L., and Lee, R. C. T. A new algorithm for generating prime implicants. *IEEE Trans. Computers* **C19**, 304–10, 1970.
21. Morreale, E. Recursive operators for prime implicant and irredundant normal form determination. *IEEE Trans. Computers* **C19**, 504–9, 1970.
22. Miller, R. E. *Switching Theory, Vol. I, Combinational Circuits*. John Wiley, New York, 1965.
23. Necula, N. N. An algorithm for the automatic approximate minimization of Boolean functions. *IEEE Trans. Computers* **C17**, 770–82, 1968.
24. Waters, M. C. *Computer Aids to Logic System Design*. PhD Thesis, Dept. of Electronics, University of Southampton, 1972.
25. Lewin, D. W., and Waters, M. C. Computer aids to logic system design. *Computer Bull.* **13**, 382–8, 1969.
26. Su, Y. H., and Dietmeyer, D. L. Computer reduction of two-level, multiple output switching circuits. *IEEE Trans. Computers* **C18**, 58–63, 1969.
27. Hong, S. J., Cain, R. G., and Ostapko, D. L. MINI—A heuristic approach for logic minimisation. *IBM J. Res. Dev.* **18**, 443–58, 1974.
28. Su, S. Y. H., and Cheung, P. T. Computer minimisation of multi-valued switching functions. *IEEE Trans. Computers* **C21**, 995–1003, 1972.
29. Ostapko, D. L., and Hong, S. J. Generating test examples for heuristic Boolean minimisation. *IBM J. Res. Dev.* **18**, 459–64, 1974.
30. Dietmeyer, D. L., and Su, Y. H. Logic design automation of fan-in limited NAND circuits. *IEEE Trans. Computers* **C18**, 11–22, 1969.
31. Dietmeyer, D. L., and Schneider, P. R. A computer-orientated factoring algorithm for NOR logic design. *IEEE Trans. Electron. Computers* **EC14**, 868–74, 1965.

32. Bumstead, D. *Computer Aided Implementation of Switching Functions.* PhD Thesis, Dept. of Electronics, University of Southampton, 1974.
33. Lawler, E. L., and Wood, D. E. Branch and bound methods—A survey. *Operations Res.* 14, 699–719, 1966.
34. Larson, R. E. *State Increment Dynamic Programming.* Elsevier, New York, 1968.
35. Davidson, E. S. An algorithm for NAND decomposition under network constraints. *IEEE Trans. Computers* C18, 1098–109, 1969.
36. Su, S. Y. H., and Nam, C. W. Computer aided synthesis of multiple output multilevel NAND networks with fan-in and fan-out constraints. *IEEE Trans. Computers* C20, 1445–55, 1971.
37. Ungar, S. H., Hazards and delays in asynchronous sequential switching circuits. *IRE Trans. Circuit Theory* CT6, 12–25, 1959.
38. Ungar, S. H. *Asynchronous Sequential Switching Circuits.* John Wiley Interscience, New York, 1969.
39. Lewin, D. W., Purslow, E., and Bennetts, R. G. Computer assisted logic design—the CALD system. *IEEE Conference on CAD*, pp. 343–51. IEE Publ. No. 86, 1972.
40. Kaletzky, A., and Lewin, D. W. Problem orientated language for logic design. *Computer J.* (Paper not yet published: due Autumn, 1976.)
41. Friedman, T. D., and Yang, S. C. Methods used in an automatic logic design generator (ALERT). *IEEE Trans. Computers* C18, 593–614, 1969.
42. Orr, W. K. Computer aided design for custom integrated circuits. *AFIPS Proc. FJCC* 35, 599–611, 1969.
43. Lewin, D. W. *Logical Design of Switching Circuits* (2nd edn.), Chaps. 5 *et seq.* Nelson, London, 1974.
44. Sholl, H. A. Direct transition memory and its application in computer design. *IEEE Trans. Computers* C23, 1048–61, 1974.
45. Hennie, F. C. *Finite-State Models for Logical Machines*, Chap. 4. John Wiley, New York, 1968.
46. Ginsberg, S. A synthesis technique for minimal state sequential machines. *IRE Trans. Electron. Computers* EC8, 13–24, 1959.
47. Paull, M. C., and Ungar, S. H. Minimising the number of states in incompletely specified sequential switching functions. *IRE Trans. Electron. Computers* EC8, 356–66, 1959.
48. Marcus, M. P. Deriviation of maximal compatibles using Boolean algebra. *IBM J. Res. Dev.* 8, 537–8, 1964.
49. Bouchet, A. An algebraic method for minimising the number of states in an incomplete sequential machine. *IEEE Trans. Computers* C17, 795–8, 1968.
50. Grasselli, A., and Luccio, F. A method for minimising the number of internal states in incompletely specified sequential networks. *IEEE Trans. Computers* EC14, 350–9, 1965.
51. Lucio, F. Extending the definition of prime compatible classes of states in incomplete sequential machine reduction. *IEE Trans. Computers* C18, 537–40, 1969.

52. Bennetts, R. G. An improved method of prime C-class derivation in the state reduction of sequential networks. *IEEE Trans. Computers* **C20**, 229–31, 1971.

53. de Sarkar, S. C., Basu, A. K., and Choudhury, A. K. Simplification of incompletely specified flow tables with the help of prime closed sets. *IEEE Trans. Computers* **C18**, 953–5, 1969.

54. de Sarkar, S. C., Basu, A. K., and Choudhury, A. K. On the determination of irredundant prime closed sets. *IEEE Trans. Computers* **C20**, 933–8, 1971.

55. Yang, C. Closure partition method for minimising incomplete sequential machines. *IEEE Trans. Computers* **C22**, 1109–22, 1973.

56. Sinha Roy, P. K., and Sheng, C. L. A decomposition method of determining maximum compatibles. *IEEE Trans. Computers* **C21**, 309–12, 1972.

57. Kella, J. State minimisation of incompletely specified sequential machines. *IEEE Trans. Computers* **C19**, 342–8, 1970.

58. Stentiford, F. W. H., and Lewin, D. W. Heuristic procedure for the reduction of finite-state machines. *IEE Electron. Lett.* **7**, 700–2, 1971.

59. Biswas, N. State minimisation of incompletely specified sequential machines. *IEEE Trans. Computers* **C23**, 80–4, 1974.

60. Bennetts, R. G., Washington, J. L., and Lewin, D. W. A computer algorithm for state-table reduction. *Radio Electron. Eng.* **42**, 513–20, 1972.

61. Paull, M. C., and Waldbaum, G. A note on state minimisation of asynchronous sequential functions. *IEEE Trans. Electron. Computers* **EC16**, 94–7, 1967.

62. McCluskey, E. J., and Ungar, S. H. A note on the number of internal variable assignments for sequential switching circuits. *IRE Trans. Electron. Computers* **EC8**, 439–40, 1959.

63. Harlow, C., and Coates, C. L. On the structure of realisations using flip–flop memory elements. *Inf. Control* **10**, 159–74, 1967.

64. Curtis, H. A. Systematic procedures for realising synchronous machines using flip–flop memory, Part 1. *IEEE Trans. Computers* **C18**, 1121–7, 1969.

65. Armstrong, D. B. A programmed algorithm for assigning internal codes to sequential machines. *IRE Trans. Electron. Computers* **EC11**, 466–72, 1962.

66. Humphrey, W. S. *Switching Circuits with Computer Applications*, Chap. 10. McGraw-Hill, New York, 1958.

67. Armstrong, D. B. On the efficient assignment of internal codes to sequential machines. *IRE Trans. Electron. Computers* **EC11**, 611–22, 1962.

68. Friedman, A. D., and Menon, P. R. *Theory and Design of Switching Circuits*. Computer Science Press, Woodland Hills, Calif., 1975.

69. Dolotta, T. A., and McCluskey, E. J. The coding of internal states of sequential circuits. *IEEE Trans. Electron. Computers* **EC13**, 549–62, 1964.

70. McCluskey, E. J., and Ungar, S. H. A note on the number of internal variable assignments for sequential switching circuits. *IRE Trans. Electron. Computers* **EC8**, 439–40, 1959.

71. Weiner, P., and Smith, E. J. On the number of distinct state assignments for synchronous sequential machines. *IEE Trans. Electron. Computers* **EC16**, 220–1, 1967.

72. Hartmanis, J. On the state-assignment problem for sequential machines I. *IRE Trans. Electron. Computers* **EC10**, 157–65, 1961.

73. Stearns, R. E., and Hartmanis, J. On the state-assignment problem for sequential machines II. *IRE Trans. Electron. Computers* **EC10**, 593–603, 1961.

74. Hartmanis, J., and Stearns, R. E. *Algebraic Structure Theory of Sequential Machines.* Prentice Hall, Englewood Cliffs, N. J., 1966.

75. Kohavi, Z. *Switching and Finite Automata Theory.* McGraw Hill, New York, 1970.

76. Curtis, H. A. Multiple reduction of variable dependency of sequential machines. *J. ACM* **9**, 322–44, 1962.

77. Karp, R. M. Some techniques of state assignment for synchronous sequential machines. *IEEE Trans. Electron. Computers* **EC13**, 507–18, 1964.

78. Weiner, P., and Smith, E. J. Optimisation of reduced dependencies for synchronous sequential machines. *IEEE Trans. Electron. Computers* **EC16**, 835–47, 1967.

79. Curtis, H. A. Systematic procedures for realising synchronous sequential machines using flip–flop memory, Part II. *IEEE Trans. Computers* **C19**, 66–73, 1970.

80. Torng, H. C. An algorithm for finding secondary assignments of synchronous sequential circuits. *IEEE Trans. Computers* **C17**, 461–9, 1968.

81. Story, J. R., Harrison, H. J., and Reinhard, E. A. Optimum state-assignment for synchronous sequential circuits. *IEEE Trans. Computers* **C21**, 1365–73, 1972.

82. Davis, W. A. An approach to the assignment of input codes. *IEEE Trans. Electron. Computers* **EC16**, 435–42, 1967.

83. Davis, W. A. Single shift-register realisations for sequential machines. *IEEE Trans. Computers* **C17**, 421–31, 1968.

84. Lewin, D. W. A new approach to the design of asynchronous logic. *Radio Electron. Eng.* **36**, 327–34, 1968.

85. Armstrong, D. B., Friedman, A. D., and Menon, P. R. Realisation of asynchronous sequential circuits without inserted delay elements. *IEEE Trans. Computers* **C17**, 129–34, 1968.

86. Liu, C. N. A state variable assignment method for asynchronous sequential switching circuits. *J. ACM* **10**, 209–16, 1963.

87. Tracey, J. H. Internal state assignments for asynchronous sequential machines. *IEEE Trans. Computers* **EC15**, 551–60, 1966.

88. Smith, R. J., II, Tracey, J. H., Schoeffel, W. L., and Maki, G. K. Automation in the design of asynchronous sequential circuits. *IFIPS SJCC* **32**, 55–60, 1968.

89. Smith, R. J., II. Generation of internal state assignments for large asynchronous sequential machines. *IEEE Trans. Computers* **C23**, 924–32, 1974.

90. Elsey, J. *An Algorithm for the Synthesis of Large Sequential Switching Circuits.* Rep. No. R-169, Coordinated Science Labs., University of Illinois, 1963.

91. Ungar, S. H. *Asynchronous Sequential Switching Circuits*, Chap. 3. John Wiley Interscience, New York, 1969.

92. Burton, D. P., and Noakes, D. R. Maximum speed STT state-assignment for sequential machines. *IEEE Electron. Lett.* **4**, 464–5, 1968.

93. Tan, C. State assignment for asynchronous sequential machines. *IEEE Trans. Computers* **C20**, 382–91, 1971.

94. Burton, D. P. *Flip–Flop Realisation of Asynchronous Sequential Machines with STT State Assignments.* Res. Memo., Dept. of Electronics and Electrical Engineering, University of Birmingham, 1969.

95. Saucier, G. State assignment of asynchronous sequential machines using graph techniques. *IEEE Trans. Computers* **C21**, 282–8, 1972.

96. Maki, G., and Tracey, J. H. A state assignment procedure for asynchronous sequential circuits. *IEEE Trans. Computers* **C20**, 666–8, 1971.

97. Kashef, R. S., and McGhee, R. B. Augmented parity check codes for encoding of asynchronous sequential machines. *IEEE Trans. Computers* **C22**, 891–6, 1973.

98. Barry, R., and Lewin, D. W. Table-look up method for the state assignment of asynchronous machines. *IEE Electron. Lett.* **9**, 574–6, 1973.

99. Maki, G. K., and Tracey, J. H. State assignment selection in asynchronous sequential circuits. *IEEE Trans. Computers* **C19**, 641–4, 1970.

100. Maki, G. K., Sawin, D. H., III, and Jeng, B. A. Improved state assignment selection tests. *IEEE Trans. Computers* **C21**, 1443–9, 1972.

101. Saucier, G. Next-state equations of asynchronous sequential machines. *IEEE Trans. Computers* **C21**, 397–9, 1972.

102. Armstrong, D. B., Friedman, A. D., and Menon, P. R. Realisation of asynchronous sequential circuits without inserted delay elements. *IEEE Trans. Computers* **C17**, 129–34, 1968.

103. Langdon, O. G. Delay-free asynchronous circuits with constrained line delays. *IEEE Trans. Computers* **C19**, 175–81, 1969.

104. Hlavicka, J. Essential hazard correction without the use of delay elements. *IEEE Trans. Computers* **C19**, 232–8, 1970.

105. Sholl, H. A., and Yang, S. C. Design of asynchronous sequential networks using read-only memory. *IEEE Trans. Computers* **C24**, 195–206, 1975.

**106.** Maki, G. K., Tracey, J. H., and Smith, R. J., II. Generation of design equations in asynchronous sequential circuits. *IEEE Trans. Computers* **C18**, 467–72, 1969.

**107.** Shiva, S. G., and Nagel, H. T. Bypass multivariable Karnaugh maps. *Electron. Des.* **22**(21), 86–91, 1974.

**108.** Shiva, S. G., and Nagel, H. T. Reduce state tables by computer. *Electron. Des.* **22**(22), 122–7, 1974.

**109.** Shiva, S. G., and Nagel, H. T. Let a computer design memory circuits. *Electron. Des.* **22**(23), 122–7, 1974.

# Logic-Circuit Testing

## 5.1. INTRODUCTION

The design of reliable digital systems is rapidly becoming a problem of paramount importance. One of the fundamental requirements of the design process is to be able to test the final system in order to verify and maintain its specified performance. The testing procedure is essentially one of applying specified input signals to the network under test and then measuring the output response compared to some standard reference.

Though various techniques have emerged for the testing of digital systems (1, 2) these are still far from satisfactory, particularly when sequential networks are involved. The problem of designing reliable software is even more acute; no trustworthy methods exist at present for the testing and evaluation of software systems, though work is in progress in the general area of software engineering (3, 4). The proper solution to the problem lies in designing systems which are both testable and failure tolerant, including self-diagnosis, rather than in attempting, as we do at the moment, to devise tests for existing (and often intuitively designed) systems. It is in this area that CAD techniques will play an essential role, since the design of reliable systems will only become feasible if a formal design and evaluation methodology based on computer assistance is developed.

Hardware testing may be performed at two basic levels, the systems level which requires diagnosis down to a faulty subsystem module, and the logic gate or LSI package level which must detect a fault in a particular module.

Once a system fault has been traced to a particular logic subsystem, the unit may either be repaired off-line or, ideally, simply thrown away—the "disposable" LSI or MSI circuit. However, we have not, as yet, truly reached the expendable-element stage, and most logic boards are repaired and put back into operation. Thus, the logic designer has the further responsibility of devising suitable test schedules to detect and diagnose faults in the logic subsystems. Moreover, there is a very pressing need to test the manufactured boards prior to final assembly in the machines; this requirement will still persist (perhaps with greater emphasis) when LSI circuits are fully utilized. For LSI the prime requirement is for an input–output check only and subsequent fault location is not generally required.

With complex circuits containing many variables, the exhaustive test approach, that of applying all possible input conditions and observing the outputs, becomes prohibitive in terms of time and cost. Consequently, it is necessary to determine in some way a minimal set of inputs which, when applied to the logic circuit, will produce a defined output indicating whether or not the circuit is operating correctly and according to specification. Currently, the problem of testing large logic assemblies is partially overcome by using randomized input sequences, a technique which has found favor, in the absence of any formal methods, with the manufacturers of automatic test equipment (ATE).

The basic problem is illustrated in Fig. 5.1, which shows a typical combinational logic circuit with primary inputs A, B, C, D, E. The objective is to detect a logical fault on any of the interconnection lines by examining the output Z; for example, if input A was permanently stuck at logical values of 1 or 0 it would be necessary to *sensitize* a path from A to Z to enable the fault on A to be detected. For instance, by setting B = 0, C = 1, D = 0, and E = 0 the input line A may be tested for being stuck at 1 by testing with A = 0, since Z = 0 under correct conditions and Z = 1 under fault conditions; similarly A stuck at 0 can be detected by using A = 1.

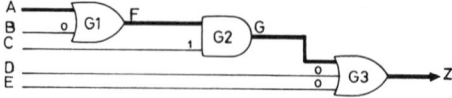

**Figure 5.1.** Path Sensitization.

The philosophy of requiring the design engineer to devise test sequences on an intuitive basis is not a good one, since there is a strong possibility, particularly with large circuits, that errors or omissions could result. The advantages of a formal algorithmic approach to test sequence generation over intuitive methods are as follows.

(a) With large arrays up to 1000–3000 gates the intuitive approach becomes impossible to handle.

(b) All possible fault conditions can be identified and tested, thereby ensuring full fault cover.

(c) Diagnostic information may be readily obtained.

(d) Ideally, testing could be performed without introducing additional monitor points.

(e) Test-sequence generation becomes an integral part of a CAD system.

(f) The design engineer is not constrained in any way.

The major disadvantage of automatically generated tests is that the initial derivation can be costly in computer time. However, this is normally a once-off calculation and the subsequent repeated use of minimal test sequences considerably reduces the overall cost of testing.

Logic circuits (or systems) are normally tested in two ways; these are as follows.

(a) *Single-flow*, in which the complete set of test inputs is applied in sequence to the actual circuit under test; when a faulty output is detected, the testing is terminated and the unit pronounced faulty. If the complete set of tests is run through (irrespective of any faulty outputs that may occur) it is possible to obtain diagnostic information from the fault-covering properties of the individual tests. In the literature this method of testing is often called a *combinational* procedure; unfortunately the term is confusing, since the technique can be applied to both combinational and sequential circuits (that is those containing feedback loops).

(b) *Multi-flow* testing requires each test input to be applied separately to the circuit, with the result of an individual test being used to determine the next test input to be applied. This form of test procedure is sometimes called *sequential* testing, which is also misleadingly named since, as in the case above, it can be used for both types of switching circuit.

Of the two methods, the multi-flow procedure is more generally employed since it tends to be more efficient in operation; it is also particularly well suited for diagnostic routines. Seshu and Freeman (5) have described the relative merits of the two methods in their paper on asynchronous logic testing.

Almost exclusively, the work on test-sequence generation and related topics has assumed a fairly simple *fault model*, which nevertheless appears to be adequate for the vast majority of faults. The model assumes that only single logical faults, resulting in an input or output line being *permanently* stuck at logic levels 0 or 1, can occur in the circuit. Thus no account is taken of multiple or intermittent fault conditions, or those arising from physical defects in the circuit. The argument for adopting this model is that it is highly improbable that faults will develop simultaneously, and that testing will be done frequently enough to detect and repair a single fault before another can occur. It is also assumed that manufacturing and device faults, such as shorts on printed-circuit-board tracks, open-circuit package connections, etc., will normally materialize as single logical faults. In the main these assumptions have been warranted in practice, but it will be apparent that a small percentage of fault must inevitably lead to intermittent and multiple fault conditions which could defy detection tests based on the simple model.

Before attempting to devise test sequences for a logic circuit it is obviously necessary to have a relevant model or description of the circuit itself. The description may be formulated in two ways: (*a*) as an actual topological description of the *implemented* circuit in terms of gates, packages, etc., and their interconnections, or (*b*) as a formal mathematical model employing Boolean equations, state tables, etc. In order to determine the true fault characteristics of the unit it is essential to utilize a model which relates to the physical circuit, that is describing the actual packages and interconnections used in the implementation. Using a formal description, such as a state table, the circuit can be evaluated for logical correctness under all necessary and sufficient input conditions, but in general this will lead to unnecessarily large test sets, in the worst case of course involving all possible input sequences. Moreover it is also possible that the actual implementation will produce circuit configurations (such as the inclusion of redundant elements) which will give rise to indistinguishable faults etc., thus preventing full fault-diagnostic operation to be achieved. However, in order to apply algorithmic methods of test-sequence generation, in contrast to the use of simulation methods as discussed in Chapter 3, it is essential to have a formal description of the circuit, but if possible one that is related to the actual circuit configuration. This in general means that the Boolean equations for a circuit must be construed in terms of the actual devices, and their connecting paths, used for its realization. For circuits which have been intuitively designed this involves an analytical procedure prior to the application of any test-generation algorithm. The problem is more difficult with sequential machines, and in general the approach adopted is to partition the circuit into combinational and sequential (memory) components and generate individual tests. Alternatively the circuit may be converted into an iterative combinational circuit by detecting and breaking feedback loops, and tests generated using a modified form of the combinational-circuit techniques. In both cases

Boolean equations can be used to describe the combinational part of the circuit; however, when state-table analysis (6) is employed it is far better to use the assigned table, which has a closer relationship to the actual circuit in its implemented form.

It will be apparent that it is far more convenient to generate test sequences at the initial design stages than attempt to analyze existing intuitively designed logic circuits. In the latter case a time-consuming analysis procedure is required and, more important, it may not be feasible, because of the defined configuration, to establish a satisfactory fault cover. It is becoming evident that constraints must eventually be placed on the logic designer, and the use of computer-assisted methods employing design algorithms is one way of introducing such a constraint, to enable logic designs which are easily testable to be produced.

Considerable work has been reported on the subject of designing testable logic circuits (7), both from the viewpoint of the logic design itself and the more practical aspects of circuit implementation. Reddy (8) has defined the properties of an easily testable circuit as follows.

(a) Requires a small test set.
(b) The test set must be easily established, either during the design stage or after implementation.
(c) The test set must be easy to apply and interpret.
(d) Faults should be locatable to any required degree.
(e) Ideally circuits should be irredundant.

From the viewpoint of circuit realization the following guidelines have been suggested (9, 10).

(a) Access should be made available to specified internal nodes of the circuit; it has been suggested that this should particularly apply to bistable circuits. This requirement will inevitably increase the overall cost of the board or package.
(b) Where possible redundant elements or connections should be avoided.
(c) Faults should be as easy to locate as possible; for instance (i) independent subsystems on a board should be physically separated, (ii) uniform layout and numbering system for printed-circuit boards should be employed, (iii) analog and digital subsystems should be separated, (iv) MSI and LSI chips should be mounted in sockets, etc.
(d) Synchronous (clocked) circuitry should be used as far as possible, but clock lines must be isolated from logic lines to allow different clock rates to be applied during testing. In general it is recommended that asynchronous circuits should be avoided, since differences in speed of response between the automatic test equipment and the circuit under test could result in output changes going undetected.

(e) Provision must be made to initialize sequential circuits (that is, to set the starting conditions) prior to testing using a synchronizing sequence, or, preferably, a master reset pulse should be provided.

(f) The operational characteristics of the ATE to be used must be taken into account in devising the test sequences.

All these guidelines, and it is possible to think of many more, must be taken into account during the design stages and considered on a cost-effective basis.

One of the important characteristics of a testable logic circuit is that it should contain few or no redundant components. The reason for this is that a fault occurring in the redundant logic may not be observable at an output terminal, unless of course special monitor points are provided. Moreover, it is also possible for the fault to mask other faults occurring in the non-redundant part of the network. Consider the circuit shown in Fig. 5.2; the input term $\bar{y}_1 y_2$ has been included to overcome the effect of a static hazard in the circuit which forms part of the excitation network for an asynchronous machine. If we investigate the effect of a stuck-at-0 (s-a-0) fault on the output of G3 it will be obvious that this will cause the output $Y_2$ to be permanently set to 1 and consequently will mask any stuck-at-1 (s-a-1) faults on the other gates G1 and G2. Note also that it is impossible to diagnose the fault, since in order to do this it would be necessary to choose an input combination which would set G1, G2, and G3 all to 1, thus making it impossible to distinguish between s-a-0 faults on any of the gates.

This example illustrates to some extent the relevance of using CAD techniques for the synthesis of testable logic. Boolean minimization techniques can obviously be very helpful in this context, and the actual circuit itself would be better synthesized in terms of set–reset bistables in order to eliminate the necessity for the bridging term $\bar{y}_1 y_2$.

Another area where the use of CAD techniques becomes imperative is that of designing *failure-tolerant systems* (11, 12, 13). This is a philosophy of designing logic systems such that the system has the ability to execute

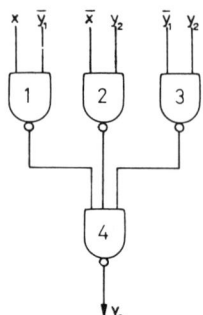

**Figure 5.2.** Logic redundancy.

specified algorithms correctly, regardless of any hardware or software failures. We shall concentrate our attention on hardware systems in which fault tolerance is considered to be an integral factor in the initial design phases. Fault tolerance is normally achieved by the means of *protective redundancy*, for instance the inclusion of extra logic circuits or error-detecting coding techniques (note that this is at variance with the concept of testable logic circuits). In hardware systems there are two main methods of employing redundancy.

(a) The *masking* or *static* approach which uses replication of circuit modules or components. The most favored method is that of *triple modular redundancy* (TMR) with triplicated units being arranged in a voting configuration (14).

(b) The *recovery* or *dynamic* approach requires two consecutive actions, the detection of the fault followed by a recovery action which either eliminates the fault or corrects the error. This process normally entails the use of error-detecting and error-correcting codes, monitoring circuitry, etc. (15); in general the recovery method requires less redundancy than the masking technique.

Another approach which has received some attention is the idea of *fail-safe* logic circuits (16), which has as its objective the design of circuits which resort to a safe condition (as defined by the system characteristics) when a fault occurs.

The only efficient way to apply testable logic and failure-tolerant techniques, especially to complex systems involving LSI components, is to use computer-assisted methods. To date no work has been reported on the CAD of failure-tolerant circuits, but since the techniques are basically those of logic design there is no reason to suppose that they would not be readily amenable to implementation in a CAD system.

The remainder of this chapter is concerned with reviewing the basic concepts of fault diagnosis and failure-tolerant techniques in order to establish the fundamental ideas and their relevance to computer-assisted design systems.

## 5.2. FAULT-DIAGNOSIS TECHNIQUES FOR COMBINATIONAL CIRCUITS

There are four basic methods of detecting fault conditions in a combinational logic circuit: these are the *fault-matrix, path-sensitization, Boolean-difference,* and *partitioning* techniques. All these methods use the single-fault model of logical s-a-0 and s-a-1 faults with the techniques applying to single static faults only. The path-sensitizing method has also been successfully employed to detect faults in sequential circuits. In order to illustrate the ideas involved in these techniques we shall consider each of them in some detail.

### 5.2.1. The Fault-Matrix Method

The fault matrix (also called a fault table) was originally proposed by Chang (17), who used the concept of a Boolean matrix (called a D-matrix) to describe the fault characteristics of a network. In the D-matrix the $d_{ij}$ entry (where $i$ and $j$ represent the rows and columns respectively) is set to 1 if a fault $f_i$ is detected by a test $t_j$, otherwise the entry is set to 0. The technique was extended later by Kautz (18), who proposed a similar method of representation, called an F-matrix, in which the entries correspond to the expected output under test and fault conditions.

The fault matrix of Kautz relates the set of all possible input tests, for a given circuit, to their associated faults. The entries within the F-matrix are the output values resulting from applying a given test input under specified fault conditions. For example, consider the simple exclusive-OR circuit shown in Fig. 5.3a and its associated fault matrix detailed in Table 5.1a. There are two inputs and hence four different input tests, termed $t_0 - t_3$. Since the circuit contains seven connections $(C_1 - C_7)$, there are 14 possible fault conditions, $f_1 - f_{14}$, referred to as C1/0, C1/1, etc., where C1/0 denotes connection C1

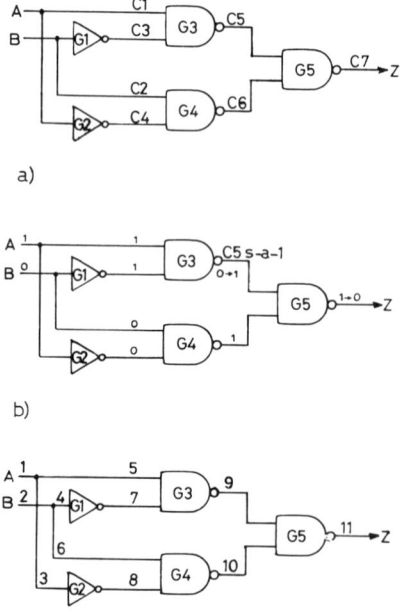

a)

b)

c)

**Figure 5.3.** Exclusive-OR circuits.

# Table 5.1. Fault-Matrix Method of Fault Detection

(a) F-matrix

| AB | Test | $f_0$ | $f_1$ C1/0 | $f_2$ C1/1 | $f_3$ C2/0 | $f_4$ C2/1 | $f_5$ C3/0 | $f_6$ C3/1 | $f_7$ C4/0 | $f_8$ C4/1 | $f_9$ C5/0 | $f_{10}$ C5/1 | $f_{11}$ C6/0 | $f_{12}$ C6/1 | $f_{13}$ C7/0 | $f_{14}$ C7/1 |
|----|----|----|----|----|----|----|----|----|----|----|----|----|----|----|----|----|
| 00 | $t_0$ | 0 | 0 | 1 | 0 | 1 | 0 | 0 | 0 | 0 | 1 | 0 | 1 | 0 | 0 | 1 |
| 01 | $t_1$ | 1 | 1 | 0 | 0 | 1 | 1 | 1 | 0 | 1 | 1 | 1 | 1 | 0 | 0 | 1 |
| 10 | $t_2$ | 1 | 0 | 1 | 1 | 0 | 0 | 1 | 1 | 1 | 1 | 0 | 1 | 1 | 0 | 1 |
| 11 | $t_3$ | 0 | 1 | 0 | 1 | 0 | 0 | 1 | 0 | 1 | 1 | 0 | 1 | 0 | 0 | 1 |

(b) $G_D$-matrix

| | $f_0 f_1$ | $f_0 f_2$ | $f_0 f_3$ | $f_0 f_4$ | $f_0 f_5$ | $f_0 f_6$ | $f_0 f_7$ | $f_0 f_8$ | $f_0 f_9$ | $f_0 f_{10}$ | $f_0 f_{11}$ | $f_0 f_{12}$ | $f_0 f_{13}$ | $f_0 f_{14}$ |
|----|----|----|----|----|----|----|----|----|----|----|----|----|----|----|
| $t_0$ | | 1 | | 1 | | | | | 1 | | 1 | | | 1 |
| $t_1$ | | 1 | 1 | | | | 1 | | | | | 1 | 1 | |
| $t_2$ | 1 | | | 1 | 1 | | | | | 1 | | | 1 | |
| $t_3$ | 1 | | 1 | | | 1 | | 1 | 1 | | 1 | | | 1 |

s-a-0 etc. The entries within the table may be calculated by hand computation (i.e., the circuit is considered with test input 00, and the output function for each fault condition C1/0, C1/1, etc., is derived; the process is then repeated for all test inputs). Alternatively a computer fault-simulation model may be used.

The F-matrix is usually transformed into a $G_D$-matrix for ease of manipulation; this is done by performing an exclusive-OR operation between the correct (no-fault) output column $f_0$ and all the other fault columns. We are now in a position to select a minimal set of input tests that will cover all possible fault conditions. This is analogous to the basic prime-implicant covering problem, and may be solved using the same techniques, such as row and column dominance. For example, the first step is to determine the *essential tests*, that is those tests which detect one particular fault only (analogous to essential PI's); in practice this amounts to scanning the $G_D$-matrix for fault columns with a single entry.

In this case from Table 5.1b we have:

$t_1$—only test for $f_0 f_7$ and $f_0 f_{12}$, i.e. C4/0 and C6/1

$t_2$—only test for $f_0 f_5$ and $f_0 f_{10}$, i.e. C3/0 and C5/1

$t_3$—only test for $f_0 f_6$ and $f_0 f_8$, i.e. C3/1 and C4/1.

The essential tests are therefore $t_1$, $t_2$, and $t_3$, and in fact these three tests also cover all other faults. If this was not so, it would be necessary to add other tests until a complete fault cover was obtained. The full test set, expressed in terms of input–output vectors, is thus

01/1,    10/1,    11/0.

If these tests are applied sequentially to the input terminals of the circuit, any deviation from the defined output sequence would indicate the existence of an error.

Though the fault matrix provides a useful tool for the determination of fault-detection tests it is impractical to use for large variable circuits since the computational requirements increase rapidly with the number of connections $N$ and input variables $n$ (the size of the matrix is given by $N \times 2^{n+1}$). It is also possible to extend the fault-matrix technique to allow the actual location of a fault to be diagnosed; unfortunately the method generates a prohibitive amount of computation.

### 5.2.2. Path Sensitization

The basic one-dimensional path sensitization technique (19, 20) relies on three processes.

**(a)** The postulation of a specific fault within the circuit structure, e.g., C5 s-a-1.

**(b)** The propagation of the logical effect of this fault, from its original location to the output terminals, along a *sensitive path*; this is called the *forward trace*.

**(c)** A *backward-trace* phase, in which the necessary gate conditions required to propagate the fault along the sensitive path are established.

In this technique the inputs to each circuit element on the sensitive path are grouped into a *control* input, which is part of the sensitized path and must be allowed to vary in order to detect a fault, and the *static* inputs, which are held at a constant value to maintain the sensitized path.

An example will best serve to clarify these points. Consider the fault C5 stuck at 1 in the circuit shown in Fig. 5.3*a*. The first step is to determine those gates through which the fault will be propagated before it reaches the output Z; in our example this is trivial since only gate G5 needs to be considered. However, in order to detect the presence of C5 s-a-1, on the output of G5, the other input to the gate, C6, must be held at 1. Under these conditions, with G5 specified at 0 and C6 held constant at 1, the output C7 would be 1; consequently if C5 was s-a-1 (i.e., the fault condition) the output of G5 would go to 0, indicating a fault.

We must now establish the necessary primary input conditions to ensure that C6 is held at 1 and C5 at 0 for the correctly functioning circuit, i.e., the backward trace. The static inputs for the output C6 to be held at 1 is given by $\overline{C2} + \overline{C4}$, i.e. $\overline{C2} + C1$; for C5 to be 0 it is necessary for the inputs to be $C1 + C3$, i.e. $C1 + \overline{C2}$. Thus, the input combination 10 (i.e. test $t_2$) is the only test that will detect C5/1, as we ascertained earlier using the fault-matrix approach. The sensitive path is thus through gates G3 and G5, as shown in Fig. 5.3*b*, with gate G4 being used to maintain the path.

Once an input test has been established all other faults detected by that test are derived. The process is then repeated, using the same procedure with an as yet undetected fault condition until all faults are covered. In practice the forward- and backward-trace phases would be combined, and a computer fault simulation used to establish the input test conditions.

Though one-dimensional path-sensitization procedures have been successfully programmed and employed to locate faults in the IBM System 360 processors (21), the technique nevertheless contains a major defect in that some possible fault tests may not be detected by the method. This is due to the existence of fan-out paths from the point of failure in the circuit. Should these paths reconverge later, and the number of signal inversions that occur along the paths be unequal, then the effect of a fault could be masked. The answer to this problem is to *simultaneously sensitize all possible paths* from the point of failure to the circuit outputs. This approach, known as *n-dimensional path sensitization* was first described by Roth (22, 23). The basic procedure is as follows.

(a) For each pass through the circuit all possible paths from a chosen fault site to all circuit outputs are generated simultaneously, canceling any reconvergent fan-out paths that may occur. This operation is called the *D-drive* and is a generalization of the forward-trace technique.

(b) Using a backward-trace process, the primary input conditions which are required to generate the static input conditions on the gates for the D-drive are derived. This is called the *consistency* operation and enables the sensitive paths in the network to be realized.

The procedures described above are based on the *calculus of D-cubes* which allows a formal mathematical model of the network, under fault conditions, to be set up. No attempt will be made to explain the D-calculus method in detail; nevertheless the theory is of sufficient importance to warrant establishing some of the fundamental definitions and premises of the theory.

The starting point for the D-calculus is the idea of a *singular cover* which may be used to represent the logic signal changes in a gate or network. Let us consider a two-input AND gate with inputs I1 and I2 and output Z; the singular cover for this circuit is shown in Table 5.2a. Note that the table

## Table 5.2. Singular Covers

(a) AND gate

|    | I1 | I2 | Z |
|----|----|----|---|
| C1 | 1  | 1  | 1 |
| C2 | 0  | X  | 0 |
| C3 | X  | 0  | 0 |

(b) OR gate

|    | I1 | I2 | Z |
|----|----|----|---|
| C1 | 1  | X  | 1 |
| C2 | X  | 1  | 1 |
| C3 | 0  | 0  | 0 |

(c) Combinational network

|    |     | I1 | I2 | I3 | I4 | I5 | Z |
|----|-----|----|----|----|----|----|---|
| G1 | {   | 1  | 1  | X  | 1  |    |   |
|    |     | 0  | X  | X  | 0  |    |   |
|    |     | X  | 0  | X  | 0  |    |   |
| G2 | {   |    | 1  | 1  | X  | 1  |   |
|    |     |    | 0  | X  | X  | 0  |   |
|    |     |    | X  | 0  | X  | 0  |   |
| G3 | {   |    |    |    | 1  | X  | 1 |
|    |     |    |    |    | X  | 1  | 1 |
|    |     |    |    |    | 0  | 0  | 0 |

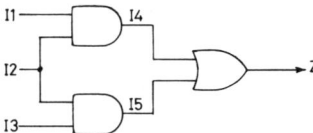

**Figure 5.4.** Singular cover for network.

(similar to a truth table) describes the logical functions of the AND gate, but also illustrates that there are two don't-care input conditions, that is when either input is at logic 0. The singular cover for the AND-gate function is given by the set of cubes, which may be expanded in the usual way to yield the vertices. In a similar way the singular cover for a network can be built up from the singular covers of the individual constituent gates, as shown in Fig. 5.4 and Table 5.2*c*. Note that each gate in the table is treated separately, according to its covering table, and that the inputs (both primary and secondary) which do not effect the gate output are assigned don't-cares. For example, G1 has the inputs I1 and I2 and output I4, which correspond to the covering table, and input I3 is a don't-care.

In the D-calculus theory singular covers are extended to embrace the concept of *propagation D-cubes*, which are used to signify those gate inputs which have sole responsibility for determining the output. A new variable $D$ is introduced which may assume either of the Boolean values 0 and 1, but is constrained to take the *same* value in a particular cube (the D-cube could thus be considered as a constrained don't-care term). The D-cube can be derived from the singular cover of a function by algorithmic methods or by inspection. For instance, the D-cubes $D1D$ and $1DD$ represent the controlling inputs of the AND gate; the cube $D1D$ can be interpreted as stating that, for correct operation, the output Z is controlled by input I1 when I2 has the static value 1. Note that the D-cubes may be expanded to give the vertices; thus $D1D \equiv 010$, 111 and $1DD \equiv 100$, 111. In addition the D-cubes can also indicate fault-test conditions; for example, the input vector 111 constitutes a test for I1 s-a-0 and I4 s-a-0, and similarly 010 is a test for both lines s-a-1.

Roth has described an algorithm, based on a binary operation of intersection, which may be used to derive the D-cubes from a singular cover. For cubes with *different* output values the new input values are obtained by intersection using the following algebraic rules:

$$0 \cap 0 = 0 \cap X = X \cap 0 = 0$$
$$1 \cap 1 = 1 \cap X = X \cap 1 = 1$$
$$X \cap X = X$$
$$1 \cap 0 = D, 0 \cap 1 = \bar{D}.$$

Thus, from the singular cover for the two-input AND gate shown in Table 5.2*a* we have, applying the rules,

$C1 \cap C2 = D1D$

$C1 \cap C3 = 1DD.$

The *primitive D-cube of failure* is conceptually very different in nature to the propagation D-cube though identical in formalism; this can cause considerable confusion! The primitive D-cube of failure is used to express fault tests in terms of the input–output vertices of the faulty gate. Suppose, for instance, that our two-input AND-gate example had an s-a-0 fault on the output Z; then the corresponding D-cube of failure would be $11D$, which indicates that with I1 and I2 forced to 1 the output would be 0 if the fault is present and 1 if absent. Similarly for a two-input NAND gate the primitive D-cube of failure would be $11\bar{D}$, which states that the correct output is 0 and the faulty output 1 with $I1 = I2 = 1$.

Algorithmic rules have been described by Roth for the derivation of primitive D-cubes of failure from the singular covers which are very similar to those for the propagation D-cubes. In this case, however, the intersection operation is applied between the cubes of the covers for the good and faulty circuits, and includes the following rule for complementation:

$$C_{\text{fault}} \cap C_{\text{good}} = 1 \cap 0 = \bar{D}$$

$$\text{and} \quad 0 \cap 1 = D.$$

One final definition is required in order to appreciate the full D-algorithm procedure, and that is the concept of *D-intersection* which provides a basic tool for building sensitized paths. Consider once again the circuit shown in Fig. 5.1 and suppose we require to sensitize a path from input A through to output Z. Then the relevant propagation D-cubes for the three gates are, respectively,

$$
\begin{array}{ccccccccc}
 & A & B & C & D & E & F & G & Z \\
G1 = & D & 0 & X & X & X & D & X & X \\
G2 = & X & X & 1 & X & X & D & D & x \\
G3 = & X & X & X & 0 & 0 & X & D & D
\end{array}
$$

By inspection a propagation D-cube that represents the path from $A \to Z$ would be

$$Z = D\ 0\ 1\ 0\ 0\ D\ D\ D.$$

The same result can be obtained by applying a further binary intersection operation, called by Roth the D-intersection, between propagation D-cubes; the operation is fully defined by Table 5.3 and the following rules.

(a) The symbols $\phi$ and $\psi$ mean that the D-intersection is empty and undefined respectively.

(b) If no $\phi$ or $\psi$ co-ordinates exist and if *both* $\lambda$ and $\mu$ occur, the D-intersection coordinate is undefined.

(c) If only $\lambda$ (but not $\mu$) occurs in the D-intersection, then in the second factor change all those coordinates which are $D$ to $\bar{D}$ and those which are $\bar{D}$ to $D$.

(d) If only $\mu$ (but not $\lambda$) occurs in the D-intersection, then for these coordinates let $D \cap D = D$ and $\bar{D} \cap \bar{D} = \bar{D}$.

It is easy to see that the result obtained earlier for Z in Fig. 5.1 can be derived by applying the D-intersection operator, for instance

$$G1 \cap G2 = 001XXDDX = G12$$

$$G12 \cap G3 = D0100DDD = Z.$$

The D-algorithm, which is excellently described by Friedman and Menon (24), consists initially of deriving the propagation D-cubes for each element in the network and then a D-cube of failure for each postulated fault in the circuit (this would be done step by step). The next stage necessitates performing a D-drive which drives the effect of the failure through to the primary outputs of the circuit; this is done using the D-intersection technique and evaluating all possible paths. Finally, the consistency operation is performed which establishes the primary input conditions required for the sensitive paths. This is achieved by using a reverse D-intersection technique whereby Boolean values are assigned to the don't-care terms in the sensitive paths; during this final stage any inconsistencies in the gate input–output conditions will automatically emerge from the algorithm.

Though the D-algorithm is a powerful method of establishing fault-detection tests, practical implementations are still very rare, particularly

**Table 5.3. D-Intersection Operator**

|        | 0 | 1 | $X$ | $D$ | $\bar{D}$ |
|--------|---|---|-----|-----|-----------|
| 0      | 0 | $\phi$ | 0 | $\psi$ | $\psi$ |
| 1      | $\phi$ | 1 | 1 | $\psi$ | $\psi$ |
| $X$    | 0 | 1 | $X$ | $D$ | $\bar{D}$ |
| $D$    | $\psi$ | $\psi$ | $D$ | $\mu$ | $\lambda$ |
| $\bar{D}$ | $\psi$ | $\psi$ | $\bar{D}$ | $\lambda$ | $\mu$ |

for large-variable systems. The algorithm has been programmed in **APL** (23), but no conclusive results were obtained owing to the inefficient execution of the interpretive **APL** code. Warburton (25) has also reported that the algorithm has been successfully programmed to produce fault-test sequences for combinational and sequential LSI circuits.

### 5.2.2. Boolean-Difference Technique

The use of Boolean differences for deriving test sequences for combinational networks has been reported by Sellers *et al.* (26), Amar and Condulmari (27), and Bennetts (28). Boolean difference is a mathematical technique which enables the action of a logic circuit to be analyzed for the effect of an error occurring in the primary inputs. The method is based on the exclusive-OR operation between two Boolean functions, one representing a good machine and the other a faulty model of the machine. If the Boolean difference is equal to 1 then an error is indicated, and the error function can be used as the basis of a fault test sequence.

Consider a Boolean function $Z$ given by

$$Z = f(x_1, x_2, \ldots, x_i, \ldots, x_n)$$

where $x$ are primary inputs to a circuit. If the input $x_i$ is in error then a new function $Zx_i$ may be defined as

$$Zx_i = g(x_1, x_2, \ldots, \bar{x}_i, \ldots, x_n)$$

which is formed from $Z$ by replacing $x_i$ by $\bar{x}_i$ and *vice versa.* The Boolean difference, $dZ/d_{x_i}$ is defined by

$$\frac{dZ}{d_{x_i}} = Z \oplus Z_{x_i} = h(x_1, x_2, \ldots, x_n)$$

where $\oplus$ is the exclusive-OR operation. As an example consider the exclusive-OR circuit shown in Fig. 5.3 where the output is given by

$$Z = \bar{C}1\,C2 + C1\overline{C2}$$

Suppose CI is in error; then

$$Z_{C1} = C1C2 + \overline{C1}\ \overline{C2}$$

and

$$\frac{dZ}{d_{C1}} = (\overline{C}1C1 + C1\overline{C2}) \oplus (C1C2 + \overline{C1C2})$$

$$= \overline{C1}\,\overline{C2} + \overline{C1}C2 + C1\overline{C2} + C1C2 \qquad (5.1)$$

The exclusive-OR operations may be performed mathematically (15) but for a small number of variables it is convenient to use K-maps.

The technique is to map the functions $Z$ and $Z_{x_i}$ onto separate K-maps and then derive a K-map representing $dZ/d_{x_i}$. This is performed by comparing corresponding cells on the $Z$ and $Z_{x_i}$ maps, and inserting a 1 in the derived $dZ/d_{x_i}$ map if there is a difference in the two values, otherwise a zero; the technique is illustrated in Table 5.4.

Returning to the example above, $Z_{C1}$ defines the function that is realized by the faulty network when there is a fault in the value of C1. Under fault conditions the output will differ from the true output for those terms that make $dZ/d_{C1} = 1$. Thus $dZ/d_{C1}$ defines the full set of input tests that will cause an observable output if there is a logical fault in the value of C1. These tests include all logical faults of both the s-a-0 and s-a-1 type, and $dZ/d_{C1}$ must therefore be partitioned into separate lists. This is achieved by splitting the list of all tests into those containing $x_i$ and those containing $\bar{x}_i$; the former will demand a 1 on $x_i$ and therefore test for $x_i$ s-a-0, and the latter conversely will test for $x_i$ s-a-1. Thus, from Eq. (5.1) we have

$$(\overline{C}_1\overline{C}_2, \overline{C}1C2)_{C1 \text{ s-a-1}} \quad \text{and} \quad (C1\overline{C}2, C1C2)_{C1 \text{ s-a-1}}$$

which corresponds to the tests $(t_0, t_1)$ and $(t_2, t_3)$ respectively, as shown in the $G_D$-matrix in Table 5.1$b$.

The technique may also be extended to determine tests for faults on non-primary input lines (28), for example C5 in Fig. 5.3. From Fig. 5.3 we have

**Table 5.4. Boolean Difference**

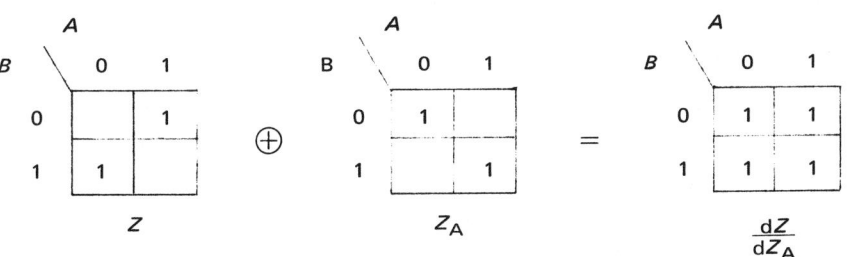

$$Z = C1\overline{C2} + \overline{C1}C2 \quad \text{and} \quad C5 = C1\overline{C2}$$

therefore

$$Z = C5 + \overline{C1}C2$$

and

$$Z_{C5} = \overline{C5} + \overline{C1}C2$$

giving

$$\frac{dZ}{dZ_{C5}} = \overline{C5}\,\overline{C1}\,\overline{C2} + \overline{C5}\,C1C2 + \overline{C5}\,C1\,\overline{C2} + C5\,\overline{C1}\,\overline{C2} + C5\,C1C2 + C5\,C1\overline{C2}.$$

Now since $C5 = C1\overline{C2}$ the only time it will be 0 will be when $C1 = 1$ and $C2 = 0$. Thus in order to detect for C5 s-a-1 the input must contain the term C1C2; the other combinations will test for C5 s-a-0. Thus we have $t_2$ for C5/1, and $t_0$, $t_3$ for C5/0 as confirmed by the $G_D$-matrix in Table 5.1$b$.

The Boolean-difference method is rather limited to small-variable circuits but can be effectively programmed for a digital computer. The major difficulty is caused by the amount of algebraic manipulation required to generate and simplify the error functions (the problem can in some cases by handled by standard minimization techniques); this particularly applies to faults on non-primary input lines. Its main advantage is in spotting essential tests, and once these are known the path-sensitizing method can be used to determine all other faults detected by these tests.

### 5.2.4. Partitioning Method of Fault Diagnosis

The partitioning method has been extensively used in practice, notably by Seshu (5, 29) who has described a sequential analyzer based on this technique. The sequential analyzer is basically a digital fault simulator which can automatically derive test sequences, or if presented with a set of test inputs deduce a fault-detection or diagnostic procedure; the analyzer can be applied to both combinational and sequential systems. Though the partitioning method can be employed with both single- and multi-flow test strategies it is best suited to the multi-flow procedure. From the viewpoint of CAD the technique is not so interesting since it is usually applied to existing designs rather than being integrated into the initial design phases.

In the partitioning method the circuit is usually simulated (using fault-simulation techniques as described in § 3.3.3) to generate the detection test sets. The simulated model is successively changed from the good no-fault version $f_0$ to each of the defined faulty versions, in our running example $f_1$ through $f_{14}$. A test is applied to all versions of the circuit and this will effect a partition (or decision tree) based on the logic values at the primary outputs. Since the members of each fault equivalence class generate the same output, further tests are required to increase the degree of resolution until either $f_0$ is identified alone (fault detection) or all faulty versions are isolated separately (fault location). The value of this method lies in its ability to try different test sets and ascertain which one is best for the current application. This implies the use of certain criteria to choose the tests, and one such method is the *check-out criterion.*

For our example circuit shown in Fig. 5.1, the initial equivalence class is $f_0$–$f_{14}$ inclusive; suppose it is required to isolate $f_0$ as quickly as possible. This amounts to determining which tests separate the largest number of faulty circuits from the good circuit—this is the check-out criterion. If we look at the detection matrix $G_D$ of Table 5.1b, it is possible to list the number of detectable faults for each test—this is shown in column $N_1$ of Table 5.5. From the table $t_3$ is the first choice and this test will generate the two equivalent classes $E_1{}^1$ and $E_1{}^0$, where

$$E_1{}^1 = \{f_1, f_3, f_6, f_8, f_9, f_{11}, f_{14}\}$$

and

$$E_1{}^0 = \{f_0, f_2, f_4, f_5, f_7, f_{10}, f_{12}, f_{13}\}.$$

The procedure is now repeated on the equivalence class containing $f_0$, and the corresponding test weightings are shown in column $N_2$ of Table 5.5. Note that there are two possible tests $t_1$ and $t_2$, and we shall arbitrarily choose $t_1$ giving the partitions

$$E_2{}^1 = \{f_0, f_4, f_5, f_{10}\}$$
$$E_2{}^0 = \{f_2, f_7, f_{12}, f_{13}\}.$$

**Table 5.5.  Check-Out Weighting**

| Test | No. of faulty circuits detected | | |
|------|------|------|------|
| | $N_1$ | $N_2$ | $N_3$ |
| $t_0$ | 5 | 2 | 1 |
| $t_1$ | 5 | ④ | — |
| $t_2$ | 5 | 4 | 3 |
| $t_3$ | ⑦ | — | — |

The procedure is repeated until eventually $f_0$ is isolated and the full detection set is defined; the partition sequence is shown diagrammatically in Fig. 5.5.

### 5.2.5. SPOOF Representation of Networks

The major drawback associated with the test-generation methods described in the preceding sections is that multiple faults are difficult, if not impossible, to handle. Moreover, while the Boolean-difference method is algebraically elegant, it requires a Boolean function specification rather than the more relevant topological description of the actual circuit. The D-algorithm, on the other hand, provides considerable insight into the structure of a circuit but requires fault-simulation techniques in order to exploit the method.

A method for describing both the network structure and its output function in a single algebraic expression has been proposed by Clegg (30) using the concept of SPOOF's (structure and parity observing output function). The technique provides an easy means of determining the effect of "stuck-at" single or multiple faults on the functional characteristics of a combinational logic circuit. The elements of a SPOOF are *terms*, which are analogous to the use of literals in a conventional Boolean expression. A term is a literal expressed together with a path list which denotes the path through the network from the literal to a specified output. In other words topological information can be carried in a Boolean expression by subscripting the variables according to the leads on which they appear. For example, if we consider the circuit shown in Fig. 5.3c we can express the input to gate G5 on lead 9 as

$$S_9 = \overline{A}_{\overline{1},\overline{5},9} B_{2,4,\overline{7},9}.$$

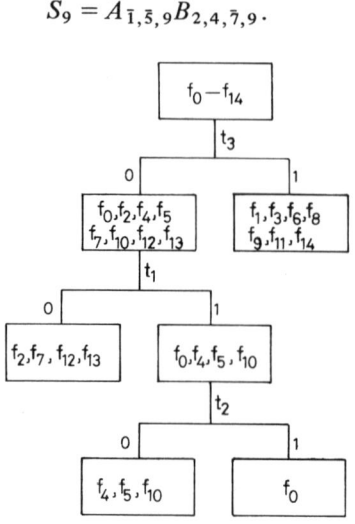

**Figure 5.5.** Partitioning technique.

Note that the path-list subscripts are lead labels (each individual lead in the circuit must be labeled) and may be complemented to allow for inversions in the signal paths.

SPOOF terms may be manipulated according to all of the rules of Boolean algebra, with the exception that terms having *different* path lists are considered as *distinct* algebraic variables. Thus, if R and S are distinct path lists then the following expressions are algebraically irreducible:

$$x_R \bar{x}_S; \, x_R + \bar{x}_S; \, x_R + x_S; \, x_R x_S.$$

In this way the topology of the circuit can be preserved throughout any algebraic manipulations.

In order to illustrate how SPOOF's may be used to generate fault tests consider the SPOOF for the output of the circuit in Fig. 5.3c:

$$S_{11} = A_{1,5,\bar{9},11} \, \bar{B}_{\bar{2},\bar{4},7,\bar{9},11} + \bar{A}_{\bar{1},3,8,\overline{10},11} \, B_{2,6,\overline{10},11}.$$

The effect of a fault can readily be determined from this expression. For example lead 8 s-a-0 causes every term with subscript 8 to be set to zero so that the expression (with subscripts omitted) reduces to

$$S_{11}^{8\text{-at-}0} = A\bar{B}.$$

Similarly, lead 10 s-a-1 yields the expression

$$S_{11}^{10\text{-at-}1} = A\bar{B}.$$

Note that every term with $\overline{10}$ is set to zero.

In order to establish a test for any fault $f$ in a network with output $Z$ on lead $n$ it is necessary to solve the equation

$$Z \oplus S_n{}^f = 1.$$

Thus, a test for lead 8 s-a-0 would be given by

$$(\bar{A}B + A\bar{B}) \oplus A\bar{B} = 1$$

which is satisfied by the condition $A = 1$, $B = 0$. Again, for the fault lead 8 s-a-1 we have

$$S_{11}^{8\text{-at-}1} = A\bar{B} + B = A + B$$

therefore

$$(\bar{A}B + A\bar{B}) \oplus A + B = 1$$

giving the test sequence $A = 1$, $B = 1$. Note that these results are identical to those found earlier in § 5.2.1 using the fault-matrix method.

Though some work has been reported (31) on the use of SPOOF's for fault detection and test generation the method has not as yet been generally accepted. This could be due primarily to the computational costs involved in generating SPOOF's; it has been suggested that the method becomes excessively costly for circuits containing more than 100 gates and 10 logic levels. However, a more efficient computational method for generating SPOOF's has been described by Si and Susskind (32) based on a compatibility relationship between networks. When the subscripts are dropped in the SPOOF representation and subsequent algebraic reductions are prohibited, the SPOOF reduces to an *E-expression*, which has been used to establish multiple fault-detection tests (33).

## 5.3. SEQUENTIAL-CIRCUIT TESTING

The problem of deriving test sequences for sequential circuits is an extremely difficult one, and to date no satisfactory solution has been obtained. There are four possible approaches to the problem.

(a) Formal algorithmic methods, based on state-table analysis and graph theory.

(b) Conversion to combinational models in which the sequential feedback loops are broken to enable combinational techniques to be used. Note that preliminary analysis of the circuit must be performed to detect the feedback loops, a difficult procedure with asynchronous networks.

(c) Heuristic techniques based on fault simulation, such as the sequential analyzer.

(d) Imposing design constraints in which the combinational and sequential logic are physically separated on the printed-circuit board (and hence may be tested independently). This procedure necessitates the inclusion of additional monitor points.

Of all these methods it is really only (a) and (d) which hold any promise of a solution to the problem, particularly when dealing with complex LSI components or at a systems level, since in both these cases it would be possible to integrate the procedures into the initial design process.

Since all the techniques described in § 5.2 have been developed primarily for combinational circuits, they are of limited use when applied to sequential

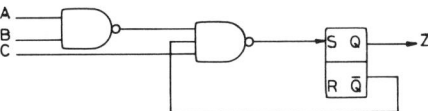

**Figure 5.6.** Feedback in sequential circuits.

circuits owing to the feedback loops inherent in sequential systems. For example, in Fig. 5.6, if the path-sensitization technique is used to set up a path to identify a fault at the output Z, the feedback loop could nullify the sensitive path. Roth's D-algorithm has, however, been applied to sequential circuits (19, 34), identifying and breaking the feedback loops. The circuit is then represented as a cascaded connection of identical combinational circuits, each one representing the sequential circuit at a given instant of time. A possible test sequence for a postulated fault is then derived using an extended D-algorithm which is later verified using simulation techniques. Note that the problem becomes one of multiple fault detection, since a fault in the sequential circuit is replicated in each of the combinational circuits.

Most of the procedures described for sequential-circuit testing are extensions of techniques that were originally developed for combinational circuits. One technique, however, that of state-table analysis, is specifically directed towards finite-state machines and is based on an analysis of the various routes through a state table.

### 5.3.1. State-Table Analysis

The foundations of state-table analysis, or more specifically *machine identification*, are to be found in the work of Moore (35) and, later, of Gill (36). The problem of testing sequential machines is basically one of whether or not it is possible to determine the characteristics of a machine, that is if the state table can be accurately reproduced from its input–output behavior. The type of sequential machine normally considered in this work is the synchronous finite-state machine, which is both strongly connected and fully specified.

Hennie (37, 38) has described a method for testing sequential machines based on the use of *distinguishing sequences*, which are particular input sequences used to identify the initial states of a machine whose state table is known but where there is no information concerning its present state. The method was reasonably successful for machines which possessed well-defined distinguishing sequences and whose implemented circuits contained the same number of states as in the original state table. In many cases, however, the technique required extremely long test sequences—a major problem with this type of approach. The method was investigated further by Kime (39) but with similar results.

The original work by Hennie has also been developed further by Kohavi and co-workers (5, 40, 41), who incorporated the idea of distinguishing sequences into full fault-detection procedures. More important perhaps from the CAD viewpoint is that they also proposed a procedure for designing sequential machines with fault-detection capabilities by introducing extra output variables in such a way as to ensure that the machine always possesses a definable distinguishing sequence (40).

Before proceeding to describe these methods in more detail we must first explain some of the basic terminology used in state-table analysis. An *experiment* on a sequential machine is defined as the application of input sequences to the input terminals of a machine and the recording of the corresponding responses from its output terminals. When the experiment is designed to take the machine through all possible circuit transitions (for instance, to enter all the set–reset states of a counter) in such a way that any faulty operation can be detected at the output terminals, it is said to be a *fault-detection experiment*. Note than an important difference between testing combinational and sequential networks is that, in the case of the sequential machine, both the time and order in which the tests are applied constitutes an essential part of the test procedure. In order to perform a fault-detection experiment decisively it is necessary to know what state the machine is in to start with; most experiments proceed from some *initial state* of the machine which is determined by a *distinguishing* or *homing sequence*.

An input sequence $X_0$ is said to be a distinguishing sequence (DS) if, when applied to a machine $M$ with $n$ internal states, it yields $n$ different output sequences depending on the initial states. By observing the responses of $M$ to $X_0$, the intial state of $M$ at the start of $X_0$ can be determined, assuming that $M$ is functioning correctly. An input sequence which can uniquely determine the final state of a machine, independent of the starting state, is said to be a homing sequence (HS). Every reduced sequential machine possesses a homing sequence (36), but only a limited number of machines have distinguishing sequences; every DS is also a HS but the converse is not true, since in many cases information regarding the initial state is absent.

Distinguishing and homing sequences can be represented graphically by means of a *successor tree* (42), which displays how the states of a machine can be successively resolved by their output states when an input sequence is applied. The successor tree for machine A in Table 5.6 is shown in Fig. 5.7. The tree starts with an *initial uncertainty*, which is the minimal subset of the set of all machine states which is known to contain the initial state (for machine A this is *ABCD* since the machine could start in any one of its states). If an input of 0 is applied we obtain the *uncertainty vector* $(B)(ACD)$ while an input of 1 gives $(B)(BCC)$. The uncertainty vectors are derived by inspecting the state table, noting the next-state outputs, and grouping the states accordingly. The individual uncertainties contained in a vector are called the *components* of the vector. This procedure is repeated at the next, and

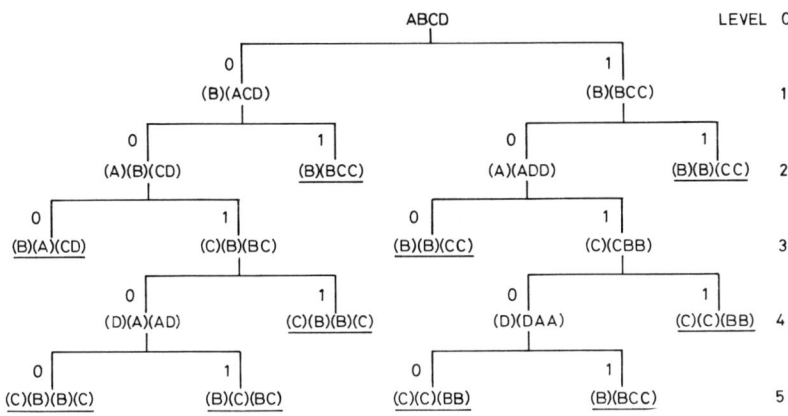

**Figure 5.7.** Successor tree for machine A.

subsequent, levels keeping the states derived from individual components separate and allowing all states to retain their identity (this last condition leads to repeated states in a component). For example, consider the successors at level 1 of $(B)(ACD)$ in Fig. 5.7. The application of a 0 input to machine A when in state $B$ will cause it to go to state $A$, the successor of $(ACD)$, however, depends on the outputs; it is $(CD)$ if the output is 0 and $(B)$ if it is 1; thus the corresponding uncertainty vector is $(A)(B)(CD)$. Similarly the successor for input 1 is $(B)(BCC)$; note that all the next states are included in the vector, and the states grouped together as a component are all derived from the same component at the preceding level.

An uncertainty vector whose components contain a single state only is said to be a *trivial uncertainty vector*; if a vector contains components with either single states or identical repeated states it is called a *homogeneous uncertainty vector*. Thus in Fig. 5.7 $(B)(B)(CC)$ and $(C)(B)(C)(B)$ are homogeneous and trivial respectively. Note that the successor graph terminates when trivial or homogeneous vectors are encountered or a vector which is identical with a successor at a lower level.

**Table 5.6. Machine A**

| Present state | Next state/Output | |
| --- | --- | --- |
| | $x = 0$ | $x = 1$ |
| A | $B/1$ | $C/1$ |
| B | $A/0$ | $B/0$ |
| C | $D/0$ | $C/1$ |
| D | $C/0$ | $B/1$ |

The homing and distinguishing sequences for a given machine can be determined by drawing the successor graph and imposing suitable terminal conditions. The *homing tree* is a successor graph which terminates if any of the following conditions occur.

(a) The node is associated with an uncertainty vector whose non-homogeneous components are associated with some node in a preceding level.
(b) The node is associated with a trivial or homogeneous vector.

In such a tree the branches from the initial node to a node in which the vector is trivial or homogeneous define a homing sequence. Similarly, the *distinguishing tree* terminates for the following conditions.

(a) The node is associated with an uncertainty vector whose non-homogeneous components are associated with some node in a preceding level.
(b) The node is associated with an uncertainty vector containing a homogeneous non-trivial component.
(c) The node is associated with a trivial uncertainty vector.

The branches from the initial node to a node in which each component contains a single state defines a distinguishing sequence. As an example, in Fig. 5.7, applying the termination rules we obtain the homing sequence 11 and the distinguishing sequence 0011. The response of machine A to these sequences and the final states is shown in Tables 5.7 and 5.8 respectively.

Once the state of a machine has been determined by a homing sequence it is necessary to put the machine into a predetermined starting state prior to commencing a fault-detection experiment. This is achieved using a *transfer sequence*, $T(S_i, S_j)$, which is the shortest input sequence that takes a machine from state $S_i$ to state $S_j$. (This is called an *adaptive procedure*, since the transfer sequence is determined by the response to the homing sequence.)

An alternative procedure to using a homing sequence is to use a *synchronizing sequence*. This is an input sequence which takes a machine to a *unique* final state independent of the output or its initial state. Unfortunately

Table 5.7. Response of Machine A
to Homing Sequence 11

| Initial state | Outputs | Final state |
|---|---|---|
| A | 11 | C |
| B | 00 | B |
| C | 11 | C |
| D | 10 | B |

Table 5.8. Response of Machine A to
Distinguishing Sequence 0011

| Initial state | Outputs | Final state |
|---|---|---|
| A | 1011 | C |
| B | 0100 | B |
| C | 0011 | C |
| D | 0010 | B |

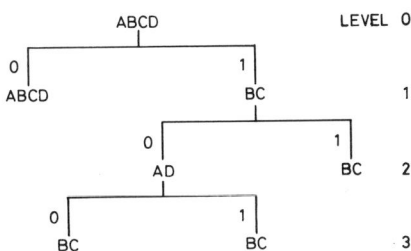

**Figure 5.8.** Synchronizing tree for machine A.

very few machines possess synchronizing sequences, but when they do a preset transfer sequence to a starting state may be employed. In order to derive a synchronizing sequence a modified form of successor graph is used in which the outputs are ignored in the uncertainty vector and repeated states are omitted. Termination occurs when uncertainty vectors that have already occurred at preceding levels are encountered or an uncertainty vector with a *single* element (called a *singleton* uncertainty vector). The synchronizing tree for machine A is shown in Fig. 5.8; note that this machine does not possess a synchronizing sequence.

We are now in a position to design a fault-detection experiment for any strongly connected reduced machine with a distinguishing sequence using the principles outlined above. A fault-detection experiment normally consists of three parts.

**(a)** The application of a homing sequence which identifies the present state of the machine, followed by a transfer sequence to maneuver the machine into some specified initial state (the start of the *preset* test sequence).

**(b)** The application of an input sequence (based on the distinguishing sequence) which causes the machine to visit each of its states and to display its response to the distinguishing sequence.

**(c)** The machine is presented with an input sequence which causes each state transition to be verified for all input conditions.

[It is possible that some transitions will be verified during the part **(b)** procedure.] The experiments assume a correctly operating machine, and that the occurrence of faults will not alter the total number of states.

As an example of designing a fault-detection experiment, let us consider a preset test sequence for machine B, shown in Table 5.9, starting from state *A*. The machine has a homing sequence of 00 and distinguishing sequences 11 and 10; the characteristics of machine B are shown in Fig. 5.9 and Tables 5.10 and 5.11.

In the first part of the experiment applying the homing sequence 00 gives rise to the following possibilities.

### Table 5.9. Machine B

|  | Next state/Output | |
| --- | --- | --- |
| Present state | $x = 0$ | $x = 1$ |
| A | B/0 | D/1 |
| B | C/1 | A/0 |
| C | B/0 | B/0 |
| D | A/1 | C/1 |

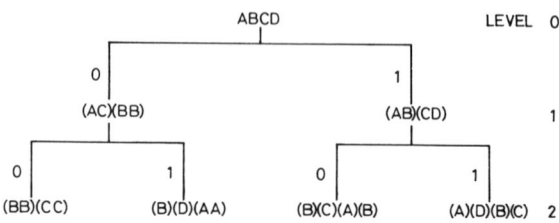

**Figure 5.9.** Distinguishing tree for machine B.

(a) An output response of 01; this indicates that the machine is in state C and therefore a transfer sequence 01 must be applied to set the machine into state A.

(b) An output of 10; this indicates that the machine is in state B and a transfer sequence of 1 is required.

The second part of the experiment (the start of the preset test) begins with the assumption that the machine is operating correctly and is in state A. (This is a major drawback of the method, since a faulty machine could well inhibit the setting of the required initial conditions.) In order to display the response of the starting state A the distinguishing sequence 11 is applied (see Table 5.12a). If the machine has operated correctly up to this point it will be in state C. In order to display the response of state B to the distinguishing sequence, it is necessary to apply a transfer sequence of 0 (to put the machine

### Table 5.10. Response of Machine B to Homing Sequence 00

| Initial state | Outputs | Final state |
| --- | --- | --- |
| A | 01 | C |
| B | 10 | B |
| C | 01 | C |
| D | 10 | B |

### Table 5.11. Response of Machine B to Distinguishing Sequence 11

| Initial state | Outputs | Final state |
| --- | --- | --- |
| A | 11 | C |
| B | 01 | D |
| C | 00 | A |
| D | 10 | B |

# Table 5.12. Fault-Detection Experiments

(a)

| Time | 0 | 1 | 2 | 3 | 4 | 5 | 6 | 7 | 8 | 9 | 10 | 11 | 12 | 13 | 14 | 15 |
|---|---|---|---|---|---|---|---|---|---|---|---|---|---|---|---|---|
| Input | | 1 | 1 | 0 | 1 | 1 | 1 | 1 | 1 | 1 | 1 | 1 | 1 | 1 | 1 | 0 |
| State | A | D | C | B | A | D | C | B | A | D | C | B | A | D | C | B |
| Response | | 1 | 1 | 0 | 0 | 1 | 1 | 0 | 0 | 1 | 1 | 0 | 0 | 1 | 1 | 0 |

(b)

| Time | 0 | 1 | 2 | 3 | 4 | 5 | 6 | 7 | 8 | 9 | 10 | 11 | 12 | 13 | 14 | 15 | 16 | 17 | 18 | 19 | 20 | 21 | 22 | 23 | 24 | 25 | 26 | 27 | 28 | 29 | 30 | 31 | 32 | 33 |
|---|---|---|---|---|---|---|---|---|---|---|---|---|---|---|---|---|---|---|---|---|---|---|---|---|---|---|---|---|---|---|---|---|---|---|
| Input | | 1 | 1 | 1 | 0 | 1 | 1 | 0 | 1 | 1 | 1 | 0 | 0 | 1 | 1 | 1 | 1 | 1 | 0 | 1 | 1 | 1 | 0 | 0 | 0 | 1 | 1 | 1 | 0 | 1 | 1 | 1 | 1 | 0 |
| State | B | C | B | A | D | A | D | C | B | A | D | C | B | C | B | A | D | C | B | A | D | C | B | A | B | A | D | C | B | A | D | C | B | A |
| Response | | 0 | 0 | 1 | 1 | 1 | 0 | 0 | 1 | 1 | 1 | 0 | 1 | 0 | 1 | 0 | 1 | 1 | 0 | 0 | 1 | 1 | 0 | 0 | 0 | 0 | 1 | 1 | 0 | 0 | 1 | 1 | 0 | 0 |

(c)

| Time | 0 | 1 | 2 | 3 | 4 | 5 | 6 | 7 | 8 | 9 | 10 | 11 |
|---|---|---|---|---|---|---|---|---|---|---|---|---|
| Input | | 1 | 1 | 1 | 1 | 0 | 1 | 1 | 1 | 1 | 1 | 1 |
| State | A | D | C | B | A | B | A | D | C | B | A | D |
| Response | | 1 | 1 | 0 | 0 | 0 | 0 | 1 | 1 | 0 | 0 | 1 |

in state $B$) followed by the DS 11. Then to obtain the response of $C$, the sequence 111 is applied, and in a like manner 111 also obtains the response of $D$. At this point the machine is in state $B$. In order to conclude this part of the experiment it is necessary to guarantee the final state of the machine; this is done by putting the machine into state $A$ and applying 110 which has already been established will take the machine from state $A$ to state $B$. The validity of the transition $A \rightarrow B$ is argued on the basis that the homing sequence puts the machine in state $A$ and the response from the distinguishing sequence (after applying the $C \rightarrow B$ transition) indicates that the machine *was* in state $B$. (Note that the states $D$ and $C$ are unverified.) Thus, the second part of the experiment consists of the input sequence 110111111111110. If the expected responses have not been produced by this part of the experiment we can conclude that the machine is faulty. However, at this stage it is impossible to state whether or not the machine has operated correctly, or indeed if the machine is actually in state $C$. Because the machine has produced four different outputs to the DS it verifies that the machine has four states, each of which has been visited once. Consequently, whenever the machine responds to 11 in the same way at different points in the experiment, the machine must have *been* in the same state at each point. Moreover, this part of the experiment also establishes that the sequence 110 takes the machine from states $A \rightarrow B$; similarly the sequence 111 takes the machine from $B \rightarrow C$, $C \rightarrow D$, and $D \rightarrow A$.

In this discussion of fault-detection experiments the example has been treated fairly simply in that the procedures adopted will not yield optimum length-checking sequences (in fact they will approach the upper bound). There are no algorithmic methods for the derivation of optimum length sequences, other than enumerative procedures which are computationally unfeasible. For instance, the second part of the experiment could have been construed more economically by applying the distinguishing sequence 11 which takes the machine to state $C$, followed by 11 again to get to state $A$. Then a transfer sequence of 0 takes the machine to state $B$ followed by two more applications of the DS 11; note that as before the experiment is concluded by applying 11 to take the machine to state $D$ as verified by earlier results—the complete checking sequence is shown in Table 5.12$b$.

The third part of the experiment is used to verify every state transition. The general procedure is to apply a transfer sequence (single input) which causes the desired transition and then to identify it by applying the distinguishing sequence. Since the machine is in state $B$ at the end of the second part of the experiment, the experiment proceeds by checking the 0 – transition out of state $B$. This is done by applying the sequence 011; if the machine is operating correctly it will go to state $A$, as shown in Table 5.12$c$. However, the experiment as constructed so far only verifies that the machine was in state $C$ prior to the application of the distinguishing sequence 11 (determined from the output response), but if a 1 is applied it is now possible to conclude that the machine is in state $D$ since it is known from the earlier part of the experiment that the sequence 111 takes the machine from $C \rightarrow D$. The 0 - transition out of state $D$ is considered next; this is done by applying 011, followed by 0, which ensures the machine is in state $B$. Note that it is necessary to ensure that the state of the machine, both prior to and after the transition, can be specified in terms of previous machine behavior. The remaining transitions can be checked in a similar way; the full checking sequence is shown in Table 5.12c.

In some cases it so happens that a transfer sequence is required to get the machine into the right state to test a transition. The transfer sequences must be applied in such a way that they take the machine through checked sequences only. For example, in time 12 in Table 5.12c the machine is in state $B$ but all the $B$ transitions have already been established; therefore it is necessary to transfer the machine to state $C$, say, in order to test the 0 and 1 transitions. At this stage the transitions $B \rightarrow C$ under 0, $D \rightarrow A$ under 0, and $B \rightarrow A$ under 1 have been verified; therefore the transfer sequence for $B \rightarrow C$ is applied with an input of 0. In this example, for the sake of simplicity, transitional information obtained in the first part of the experiment has mainly been used to verify the transitions in the last part. In general, however, any transition which has been verified at any previous point in the experiment may be used.

The method may be extended to asynchronous circuits providing the following conditions are observed.

(1) The flow table is strongly connected and reduced.
(2) The faulty flow table has no cycles or critical races in its columns.
(3) The number of stable states in any column of a flow table does not increase as a result of a fault.

The derivation of checking sequences proceeds in the normal way with the exception that distinguishing sequences are derived for the set of stable states in each column.

Checking sequences arrived at using these procedures can be very long, and it will be obvious that the lack of an algorithmic procedure will seriously complicate any computer implementation. Moreover, for large-variable machines with multiple inputs the computational requirements very quickly become excessive. Another serious drawback to the method is the validity of the assumption that states do not increase as a result of a fault. This assumption may well be true when the number of states is an integral power of 2 but it could otherwise be unrealistic, particularly for asynchronous circuits.

As we have seen, the state-table technique can be applied to any reduced and strongly connected machine that has at least one distinguishing sequence (which may be determined algorithmically). Unfortunately, machines exist which do not have any distinguishing sequences, in which case the procedure becomes very complicated. This situation is analogous to the problems encountered in the decomposition of finite-state machines in that redundancy must be added to the machine (in this case extra output logic) to effect a non-trivial partitioning of the internal states. The answer lies in the structural properties of the machine, and is another reason why it is better to design a testable machine, rather than attempt to evolve test sequences for an intuitively designed system.

One very important limitation of these techniques is that the test sequence is derived from a symbolic (unassigned) state table and could apply to many different isomorphic machines—that is there are many ways of implementing the machine. Ideally a test set should be based on a description of the circuit which contains information relevant to the actual circuit implementation, for example, the fully assigned state table. In addition it is obviously necessary to translate from an implemented logic circuit into a state table (that is a formal logical description) before the technique can be applied to an intuitively designed circuit.

The generation of test sequences for logic circuits is an extremely important aspect of the CAD process. Various techniques exist for combinational circuits, but the derivation of test sequences for sequential machines is not a simple matter and still remains a relatively unsolved problem. There is a need here for a formal treatment of the problem rather than the usual *a priori* solutions. A major factor is the need for a mathematical model of circuit behavior. Perhaps more important is the diagnosis of faults at systems level, and hence the necessity to consider fault location (and diagnosis to subsystem level) during the initial design process becomes of paramount importance.

## 5.4. DESIGN OF TESTABLE AND SELF-DIAGNOSTIC LOGIC CIRCUITS

Though earlier in this chapter we stressed the need to be able to design logic systems which are easy to test and failure tolerant, at present there are no systematic CAD procedures to perform this function. Notwithstanding this there does exist a considerable number of published papers on this topic and it would be impossible in the space available to endeavor to survey this field in detail. The main area of interest in combinational logic has been the design of circuits which can easily be tested with small and structurally similar test sets. On the other hand, in sequential machine theory, except for a small amount of work on the modification of machines to facilitate fault-detection experiments, attention has been mainly directed towards the design of fail-safe and failure-tolerant machines. In this section an attempt will be made to highlight some of the more important aspects of the work which could form the basis for future innovation.

### 5.4.1. Combinational Logic

At the present time to design a two-level AND–OR network for an arbitrary logic function that requires the minimum number of tests to detect s-a-0 and s-a-1 faults seems only soluble by an exhaustive search over all irredundant two-level realizations of the function. The approach that has been adopted in the work on testable logic is to look for circuit configurations that can be easily tested and then to translate any arbitrary logic function into this form. For example, it is considerably easier to devise a test for an $n$-input parity check circuit if it is configured as a cascaded array of exclusive-OR elements than when it is realized as a two-level AND–OR network.

Reddy (8) has proposed a design technique based on the *Reed–Muller (RM) expansion* (43, 44) which will realize any arbitrary $n$-variable function using a cascaded connection of AND and exclusive-OR gates. The circuit configuration enables the easy detection of single s-a-0 and s-a-1 faults on input and output lines, and has the following properties.

(a) If the primary input leads are fault free then a circuit realization is possible which requires a fault-detection test set with only $(n + 4)$ tests and this test set is *independent* of the function being realized.

(b) If faults can exist on the primary input leads then $(n + 4) + 2n_e$ tests are required where $n_e$ is the number of primary inputs appearing in an even number of product terms in the Reed–Muller expansion for the function being realized. However, by adding an extra AND gate and an observable output to the circuit, the same characteristics as in (a) above will pertain.

Any arbitrary logic function can be described by a Reed–Muller expansion of the form

$$f(x_1, x_2, \ldots, x_n) = C_0 \oplus C_1 \dot{x}_1 \oplus C_2 \dot{x}_2 \oplus \ldots \oplus C_n \dot{x}_n \oplus C_{n+1} \dot{x}_1 \dot{x}_n \oplus$$
$$\ldots \oplus C_{2^n-1} \dot{x}_1 \dot{x}_2 \ldots \dot{x}_n$$

where $\dot{x}_i$ may occur in either true or complemented form, but not both together, $C_i$ is a binary coefficient (0 or 1) and $\oplus$ is the modulo-2 sum (exclusive-OR operation). The product terms associated with each coefficient are determined by only including variables corresponding to those positions in the input vector coincident with 1's in the binary expansion of the coefficient suffix number.

Since the variables $x_i$ may assume all possible binary values there are $2^n$ possible Reed–Muller expansions. A *polarity number* (ranging from $0 \rightarrow 2^n - 1$) is used to identify particular RM forms; the polarity is computed from the binary number formed by writing a 0 or 1 for each variable in the input vector according to whether it is in the true or complemented form respectively. The case where all $\dot{x}_i = x_i$, that is polarity 0, gives the familiar complement-free ring-sum canonical form.

There are two main problems encountered when using Reed–Muller expansions for general logic synthesis. Firstly, the determination of minimum-cost polarity for a given function, and secondly the derivation of the binary coefficients of expansions for the required polarity from the truth table. Though the derivation of the coefficients is relatively straightforward, the determination of minimum-cost polarity is computationally very inefficient, relying chiefly on algorithmic searches. These problems have been investigated by Mukhopadhyay and Schmitz (44, 45) among others, but as yet no satisfactory solutions have been obtained for large-variable systems.

For a three-variable function we have the following RM expansion:

$$f(A, B, C) = C_0 \oplus C_1 A \oplus C_2 B \oplus C_3 C \oplus C_4 AB \oplus C_5 AC \oplus C_6 BC \oplus C_7 ABC$$

which corresponds to the general circuit configuration shown in Fig. 5.10$a$. Note that each AND gate corresponds to a product term in the expansion for which the value of $C_i$ is 1. Now consider the Boolean function

$$Z = \bar{A}\bar{C} + AB.$$

This has the following RM expansion:

$$Z = f(A, B, C) = 1 \oplus A \oplus C \oplus AB \oplus AC$$

the circuit for which is shown in Fig. 5.10$b$. The binary coefficients $C_i$ can either be obtained using the formal procedures given by Mukhopadhyay and Schmitz based on *polarity functions*, or derived empirically from a consideration of the minterms in the truth table. For example, for a three-variable RM expansion the coefficients may be computed using the following rules:

$$C_0 = f_0 \qquad C_4 = f_0 \oplus f_2 \oplus f_4 \oplus f_6$$

$$C_1 = f_0 \oplus f_4 \qquad C_5 = f_0 \oplus f_1 \oplus f_4 \oplus f_5$$

$$C_2 = f_0 \oplus f_2 \qquad C_6 = f_0 \oplus f_1 \oplus f_2 \oplus f_3$$

$$C_3 = f_0 \oplus f_1 \qquad C_7 = f_0 \oplus f_1 \oplus f_2 \oplus f_3 \oplus f_4 \oplus f_5 \oplus f_6 \oplus f_7$$

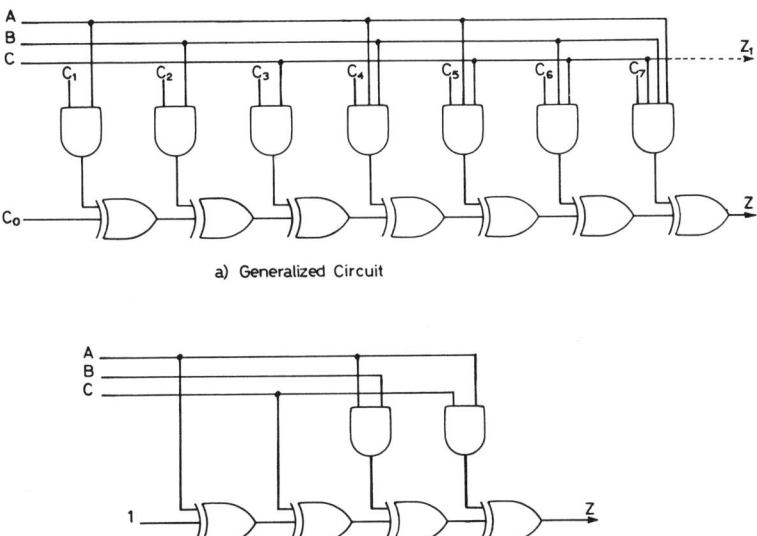

a) Generalized Circuit

b)   $Z = \bar{A}\bar{C} + AB$

**Figure 5.10.** Reed–Muller circuits.

where $f_i$ are the output values of the minterms obtained from the truth table; the procedure can easily be extended for higher-order expansions.

The starting point for the Reddy method is to determine the Reed–Muller expansion for the required switching function and to implement this function directly using the AND-exclusive-OR cascade. Now Kautz (46) has shown that to detect a single faulty gate in a cascade of exclusive-OR gates it is sufficient to apply a set of tests which will exercise all possible input conditions to each gate; such a test for the three-variable circuit shown in Fig. 5.10$b$ is given by

$$
T_1 = \begin{array}{cccc} D & A & B & C \\ \left\{\begin{array}{cccc} 0 & 0 & 0 & 0 \\ 0 & 1 & 1 & 1 \\ 1 & 0 & 0 & 0 \\ 1 & 1 & 1 & 1 \end{array}\right\} \end{array}.
$$

This testing procedure assumes that the primary input terminals, that is the input buses, are fault free and that faults can only occur on the inputs to individual gates. Note that the structure of the test set, and the number of individual tests, is always the same and is independent of the number of input variables. For instance, a four-variable circuit would have the test set

$$T_1' = \begin{Bmatrix} E & A & B & C & D \\ 0 & 0 & 0 & 0 & 0 \\ 0 & 1 & 1 & 1 & 1 \\ 1 & 0 & 0 & 0 & 0 \\ 1 & 1 & 1 & 1 & 1 \end{Bmatrix}$$

In addition Reddy has shown that an s-a-0 fault on the input or output of any AND gate in the AND-exclusive-OR cascade can also be detected by applying either one of the test inputs 0111, 1111. Similarly, an s-a-1 fault on the output of any AND gate can be detected by the test inputs 0000 or 1000. However, an s-a-1 fault at any one of the inputs to the AND gates must be detected separately using the test set

$$T_2 = \begin{Bmatrix} D & A & B & C \\ X & 0 & 1 & 1 \\ X & 1 & 0 & 1 \\ X & 1 & 1 & 0 \end{Bmatrix}$$

where the $X$ entry represents a don't-care condition. The justification for this test set is that, for any input vector of $T_2$, one input is held at 0 while all the other inputs are set to 1. Thus for a particular test an s-a-1 fault on any input will be propagated through the relevant AND and exclusive-OR gates to the output terminal. For an $n$-variable function the full test set will now consist of $T = T_1 + T_2$ and will contain $n + 4$ tests.

In order to detect the presence of primary input faults it is necessary to sensitize an odd number of paths from the faulty input to the output of the circuit. (Note that with the single fault constraint the network is assumed fault free when primary input faults occur.) The requirement for an odd number of sensitized paths arises from the fact that, owing to the modulo-2 addition characteristics of the exclusive-OR gates, any even number of circuit changes would be canceled out. The $n + 4$ tests outlined above will also detect input faults which appear in an odd number of product terms in the original RM expansion. For instance, inputs $A$ and $B$ in our example appear an odd number of times, and hence s-a-0 faults on these lines will be detectable by either one of the test inputs 0111 or 1111; an s-a-1 fault on $A$ will be detected by either 1011 or 0011 and an s-a-1 fault on $B$ by 1101 or 0101.

Reddy has also described a technique to derive tests for input faults which occur for variables appearing in even product terms of the RM expansion. The method increases the number of tests required by $2n_e$, where $n_e$ is the number of input variables that appear an even number of times in the RM expansion. In our example $n_e = 1$ since the variable $C$ occurs twice. However, it is possible to dispense with the additional $2n_e$ tests by incorporating extra logic in the circuit in the form of one or two AND gates and related output terminals. The inputs to the AND gates are those inputs which appear an even number of times; in the case of the circuit of Fig. 5.10*b* this simply means providing an extra output terminal, shown dotted in the figure. With this simple modification the original $n + 4$ set of tests will now detect both primary input and gate faults.

It is interesting to reflect that this technique could easily form the basis for self-checking LSI components. Since the test set is very small and independent of the number of circuit variables it would be feasible to include automatic test generation and checking logic on the chip itself.

One of the major drawbacks to this method is the number of logic levels involved in the circuit realization, which is inherent in any cascaded network. In a subsequent paper Reddy (47) presents an alternative design method employing up to a maximum of three-level AND–OR networks in which single s-a-0 and s-a-1 faults are locatable, subject of course to the usual indistinguishable fault constraints. The technique is based on the theory of *unate functions* (48), which are functions which can be represented as a sum-of-products or product-of-sums expression, but with the proviso that variables can appear in either complemented or uncomplemented form, but not both. (The RM expansion is a special case of a *positive unate function* in which all the variables are in their uncomplemented form.) In practice switching functions are not generally unate, but if a double-rail logic system is employed then any function could be converted to a positive unate one by considering complemented variables to be independent. For example, the function $Z = \overline{A}\overline{C} + AB$ is not unate, but by considering $\overline{A}$ and $\overline{C}$ as independent variables $a$ and $c$ the function could be expressed as $Z = ac + AB$ where $a = \overline{A}$ and $c = \overline{C}$.

An alternative approach to the problem of reducing the number of levels required for the implementation is the use of two-dimensional cellular logic arrays. Saluja and Reddy (49) have described AND-exclusive-OR cellular arrays based on RM canonical forms which will realize any switching function. It has been shown that these arrays are easily testable for the presence of a single faulty cell using $2n + 5$ tests; multiple faults may also be determined by imposing certain constraints on the array configuration.

Another technique for the design of testable logic has been reported by Hayes (50) who has investigated the use of additional control logic to reduce the number of tests and increase the fault-diagnostic capability of a circuit. The basic concept of the method involves controlling the internal circuit conditions using the primary inputs assisted by extra control inputs and gates. The procedure consists of designing a conventional two-input NAND and invertor gate circuit and then transforming this circuit into one employing predominantly exclusive-OR gates. This is achieved by inserting exclusive-OR gates into the input lines of all the NAND gates; where invertors appear these are omitted and also replaced by an exclusive-OR gate. Since only one input of the exclusive-OR gates is required to reproduce the function, the other inputs can be brought out to the primary input terminals and used as control inputs. (Note that, since $x \oplus 0 = x$ and $x \oplus 1 = \bar{x}$, for normal operation the control inputs of the exclusive-OR gates replacing the invertors and those inserted in the NAND-input lines are set to 1 and 0 respectively.)

Fault-detection tests were deduced by considering the basic transformed exclusive-OR module for a two-input NAND gate; this is shown in Fig. 5.11. Hayes showed that only five input test vectors $(x_1, x_2, c_1, c_2)$ were required to ensure full fault cover for the module. Using the same philosophy the method was then extended to a circuit comprising an interconnection of the basic modules, and an algorithm described which enabled the necessary primary and control input conditions for fault detection to be computed. Though the method has the distinct advantage of being able to synthesize circuits which require only five fault tests (the length of the input vectors depending on the number of input variables and control inputs), it does once again lead to multi-level circuits with the usual attendant difficulty of propagation delays. Moreover, an important practical disadvantage of this technique is the number of extra input terminals required; for a complex circuit the number of terminals could easily become prohibitive owing to the problem of pin limitation prevalent in LSI manufacture.

The design of circuits which can be tested using the minimum number of tests has also been investigated by Saluja and Reddy (51) who have proposed a design process that results in circuits which can be fully tested by three test input vectors. The procedure is based upon the fact that any $n$-input AND–OR, NAND–NOR gate can be fully tested for single or multiple s-a-0 or s-a-1 fault conditions by $n + 1$ tests. In a similar way to the Hayes method the design technique consists of translating a two-level AND–OR circuit into a multi-level circuit employing two-input gates throughout; this may be done, for example, using AND–OR–AND constructions. The authors show how, with the addition of extra control inputs and output terminals, it is possible to extend the basic gate-testing idea to any circuit containing only two-input gates; under these conditions three tests would be sufficient for fault detection. Saluja and Reddy also state that the number of extra control inputs required cannot exceed six (thereby overcoming one of the major objections

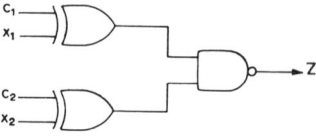

**Figure 5.11.** NAND-exclusive-OR module.

to the Hayes method) and that the additional outputs allow fault location down to a single gate.

Another problem area in test-sequence generation which has been approached from a design viewpoint is that of circuit redundancy, that is the presence of signal lines on which a logical value can exist without affecting the external behavior of the circuit. It is well known that circuits which possess redundancy present great difficulties when deriving test schedules owing to the inherent problems of fault masking. One technique which has been adopted is the identification and removal of redundancies prior to the application of test-generation algorithms. The identification of redundant lines can be carried out fairly simply by considering all possible combinations of signal lines in a circuit and determining whether or not these lines can affect the output. Unfortunately this process can become extremely time consuming owing to the large number of circuit conditions to be investigated.

Dandapani and Reddy (52) have shown that by designing circuits with a structure based on *prime trees* redundancy may be more easily recognized; this form of configuration also allows the generation of simple test sets to detect multiple stuck-at-faults. A *tree network* is a logic circuit in which the output of a gate is allowed to feed the input of only one other gate, that is no fan-out is allowed (except on primary inputs). A *restricted tree network* is defined as a tree network comprised of AND, OR, and invertor gates with the restriction that the invertor gates are fed from external inputs only. A *restricted prime tree* is a restricted-tree network which satisfies the following assumptions.

(a) If the output unit is an OR gate and if

$$Z = T_1 + T_2 + \ldots T_k$$

where $T_i$ is a product term, then $T_i$ is a prime implicant of $Z$ where $1 \leqslant i \leqslant k$.

(b) If the output unit is an AND gate and if

$$Z = S_1 . S_2 . \ldots S_q$$

where $S_i$ is a sum term, then $S_i$ is a prime implicate of $Z$ where $1 \leqslant i \leqslant q$.

A *prime tree* is a tree network containing AND, OR, NAND, NOR, and invertor gates which is either a restricted prime tree or whose test-equivalent network is a restricted prime tree.

The synthesis of prime-tree networks may be accomplished by starting with the sum of prime implicants, or product of prime implicates, for the required function and then applying the following factoring techniques:

$$ab + ac = a(b + c)$$

and

$$(a + b)(a + c) = a + bc.$$

For example, suppose it is required to synthesize a prime tree of the form OR–AND–OR for the function

$$Z = ab + bd + ce + \bar{a}c$$

then factorizing we obtain

$$Z = c(\bar{a} + e) + b(a + d)$$

which represents a three-level prime tree.

In practice of course the factorization process is considerably more complex; in particular, if the function contains prime implicants with a differing number of literals it is essential to group the PI's according to the number of literals and factorize each individual group. Algorithms are presented in the paper for identifying redundant connections and for the synthesis of minimal three-level OR–AND–OR prime trees. The technique, though interesting in its own right, could prove to be extremely difficult to implement on a computer (no indication is given in the paper) owing to the algebraic nature of the algorithm.

All of the methods described in this section are rather academic from the systems designer's point of view, who rarely, if ever, implements large circuits using basic gate elements. However, they could be pertinent to the LSI-component designer, but it will be obvious that computer aids would be essential to buffer the designer from the theoretical methods and to handle large-variable circuits. Unfortunately very few of the algorithms described have actually been programmed, and in many cases it would appear doubtful if efficient computational algorithms for large-variable circuits could be produced. Moreover, in the case of LSI design it would still be necessary to translate the circuits obtained from these techniques into appropriate device characteristics, for example MOS gates. Since a fairly complex function can be realized by a single MOS cell most of the conventional algorithms based on NOR–NAND, OR–AND gates are generally unsuitable for MOS network synthesis. Very little work has been done on the design of logic for direct implementation using LSI, although some progress has been reported by Liu (53) for MOS gates.

### 5.4.2. Sequential Systems

Fault tolerance in digital systems is obtained by incorporating protective redundancy in the system, usually in the form of additional hardware. This can be achieved either by replication of non-redundant elements (as for example in TMR systems) or by including the redundancy as an integral part of the individual basic elements. The underlying principle of *fault-tolerant design* is that machines must be able to tolerate a fault (called *fault masking*) in the sense that the resulting behavior of the machine relates in some specified way to its original behavior. In *fail-safe design*, however, a subsystem module is simply required to operate under fault conditions without adverse effects on the overall system—this is normally achieved by arranging that the circuit produces safe outputs under fault conditions.

This section will deal solely with the design of machines possessing integral redundancy using either error-correcting codes for state assignment or independent self-checking circuitry. It is essential in these designs that any additional logic be kept to a minimum (the reliability is normally inversely proportional to the amount of hardware) and that the tolerated faults can easily be detected in a real-time processing environment. Without fault-detection capability it becomes impossible to determine whether or not a unit is completely fault free or to maintain the reliability of the system by rectifying the tolerated faults as soon as it is conveniently possible.

Russo (54) has shown that using minimum-distance-three state assignments and considering error states when deriving the bistable input equations, it is possible to design synchronous counters which can tolerate single faults and thus automatically correct for one-bit errors. An error occurring in a counter circuit will cause a transition to an error state rather than a required state, providing that the set of required states and the set of error states is disjoint. If all the possible error states for a given transition are known, the counter may be designed to correct automatically for the error by ensuring that a transition is effected to the required state on the next clock pulse; note that the output of the error states must also be assigned a safe condition. The work assumes that only one bistable can be in error at any time with the other bistables sequencing correctly (thus failures will occur if more than one bistable is in error); note that this implies that the input circuitry controls only one bistable. Using a minimum-distance-three state assignment it follows from the theory of error-correcting codes that the failure of any one bistable to change state when it should will result in an error state that will be distance 1 from the correct state and at least distance 2 from any other state. This form of coding will obviously not function correctly for double errors.

Bistable input equations are derived from the assigned state table in the usual way except that error states must now be taken into consideration. For example, in the assigned state table shown in Table 5.13$a$, states are coded such that each state is distance 3 or more from every other state. Consider the transition from state $S_1$ (00000) to state $S_2$ (00111); should a single error occur in a bistable the following error states could result:

## Table 5.13. Error-Tolerant Counters

(a) State table

| | Present state | | | | | Next state | | | | |
|---|---|---|---|---|---|---|---|---|---|---|
| | $A$ | $B$ | $C$ | $D$ | $E$ | $A_+$ | $B_+$ | $C_+$ | $D_+$ | $E_+$ |
| $S_1$ | 0 | 0 | 0 | 0 | 0 | 0 | 0 | 1 | 1 | 1 |
| $S_2$ | 0 | 0 | 1 | 1 | 1 | 1 | 1 | 0 | 1 | 1 |
| $S_3$ | 1 | 1 | 0 | 1 | 1 | 1 | 1 | 1 | 0 | 0 |
| $S_4$ | 1 | 1 | 1 | 0 | 0 | 0 | 0 | 0 | 0 | 0 |

(b) K-maps

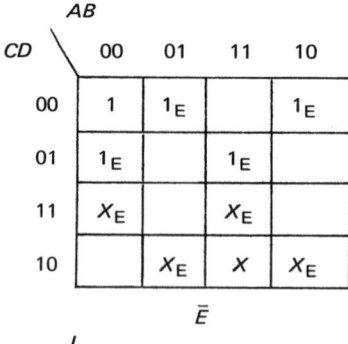

$J_c$ (with $\bar{E}$)

| $CD \backslash AB$ | 00 | 01 | 11 | 10 |
|---|---|---|---|---|
| 00 | 1 | $1_E$ |  | $1_E$ |
| 01 | $1_E$ |  | $1_E$ |  |
| 11 | $X_E$ |  | $X_E$ |  |
| 10 |  | $X_E$ | $X$ | $X_E$ |

(with $E$)

| $CD \backslash AB$ | 00 | 01 | 11 | 10 |
|---|---|---|---|---|
| 00 | $1_E$ |  | $1_E$ |  |
| 01 |  | $1_E$ | 1 | $1_E$ |
| 11 | $X$ | $X_E$ |  | $X_E$ |
| 10 | $X_E$ |  | $X_E$ |  |

$K_c$ (with $\bar{E}$)

| $CD \backslash AB$ | 00 | 01 | 11 | 10 |
|---|---|---|---|---|
| 00 | $X$ | $X_E$ |  | $X_E$ |
| 01 | $X_E$ |  | $X_E$ |  |
| 11 | $1_E$ |  | $1_E$ |  |
| 10 |  | $1_E$ | 1 | $1_E$ |

(with $E$)

| $CD \backslash AB$ | 00 | 01 | 11 | 10 |
|---|---|---|---|---|
| 00 | $X_E$ |  | $X_E$ |  |
| 01 |  | $X_E$ | $X$ | $X_E$ |
| 11 | 1 | $1_E$ |  | $1_E$ |
| 10 | $1_E$ |  | $1_E$ |  |

$$S_{11} = 10111 \qquad S_{14} = 00101$$

$$S_{12} = 01111 \qquad S_{15} = 00110$$

$$S_{13} = 00011$$

Now bistable C is required to be reset ($k_c = 1$) in state $S_2$ (for the condition $\overline{A}\overline{B}CDE$) in order to generate the required transition to state $S_3$. However, if an error has occurred this might not happen, thereby causing erroneous operation. Thus for fault-tolerant operation it is essential to ensure that $k_c = 1$ for the possible error states $S_{11}$, $S_{12}$, $S_{14}$, and $S_{15}$; note that $k_c = 0$ for state $S_{13}$ since there is no change in bistable C for the transition $S_{13} \rightarrow S_3$. The complete set of JK input conditions for bistable C are shown plotted on K-maps in Table 5.13$b$; the entries $1_E$ and $X_E$ indicate the required and don't-care conditions respectively for the error states.

Russo presents an algorithmic technique for extracting the input equations which has been programmed for a digital computer—very few details are given but it was suggested that error-tolerant circuits of this type could be some five or six times the cost of a conventional counter. Thus though the method is conceptually very simple (and consequently of obvious appeal to designers), it suffers from the severe disadvantage of very high implementation costs (higher in fact than using triple-mode redundancy). Moreover, the assignment procedure itself could become very complex for a system with a large number of states; the problem of optimal assignments does not, as yet, appear to have been investigated.

The use of minimum-distance error-correcting codes has been formalized to some extent by Meyer (55), who has also defined and investigated different types of fault masking; the problem of memory redundancy was also considered in this paper and a lower bound on minimum redundancy was proposed.

A general design procedure for fail-safe synchronous machines has been described by Tohma *et al.* (56). This uses $k$-out-of-$n$ codes ($nCk$ codes, where $k$ is the weight and $n$ the number of digits) for the state assignment, with the derivation of the next-state equations employing both the on- and off-set realizations. Note that the resulting circuits would be implemented using D-type bistables. The procedure presented assumes the following conditions.

(a) Failures can only occur in the bistable circuits themselves, that is the input logic and memory elements.
(b) Failure is caused by a single fault in a memory element circuit; multiple faults are not covered.
(c) The fault materializes as a static s-a-0 or s-a-1 on the output of the element only.
(d) Primary inputs to the bistable circuitry are fault free.
(e) The clocking circuits function normally without error.

As with failure-tolerant circuits it is essential that the set of required states and the set of all error states is disjoint, since a failure must cause a transition to an error state rather than a required state. With this proviso a circuit can be designed such that, if a failure occurs, the machine goes into an error-state cycle which generates a safe output condition. Hamming codes may be used for the assignment to effect these conditions, but Tohma has shown that using $nCk$ codes a monotonic function may be derived for the excitation networks (which then requires only uncomplemented variables) thus simplifying the problems of fault detection and realization. This is achieved by arranging that any state variables ($y_i$) in the assignment which has a value $y_i = 0$ has its inverse $\bar{y}_i$ included in a don't-care term. Thus, suppose we choose the 4-tuple 1001 as an assignment code, then 1101 and 1011 would not be used for assignments and consequently included in the don't-care set. In this way the complemented variable $y_i$ can be eliminated from the reduced form of the equation; it is easy to see that this procedure follows naturally from the use of $nCk$ codes. This is shown in Table 5.14 for a synchronous counter assigned using a 2-out-of-4 code; note that the variables in the excitation equations may be derived directly from the assigned state table. For example, the excitation equation

$$Y_2 = y_1 y_4 + y_2 y_4$$

may be generated from the minterms $y_1 \bar{y}_2 \bar{y}_3 y_4$ and $\bar{y}_1 y_2 \bar{y}_3 y_4$ by observing that the variables $y_1 = y_4 = 1$ and $y_2 = y_4 = 1$.

In the general case the *on-set realization* may be defined formally as

$$Y_i = F_i (x, y_1, y_2, \ldots, y_n)$$
$$= \sum_j x_j (M_{j_1} + M_{j_2} + \ldots M_{j_p})$$

and

$$M_{jh} (h = 1 \sim p) = y_{h_1} y_{h_2} \ldots y_{h_k}$$

where $y_{h_1}, y_{h_2}, \ldots, y_{h_k}$ are $k$-state variables having value 1 in a present state $q_h$ that transfers to a state with $Y_i = 1$ under the input $x_j$. Similarly a dual expression can be obtained for the *off-set realization* of the form

$$\bar{Y}_i = \bar{G}_i (x, y_1, y_2, \ldots, y_n)$$
$$= \sum_j x_j (V_{j_1} + V_{j_2} + \ldots V_{j_r})$$

## Table 5.14. nCK State Assignment

(a) Assigned state table

| | Present state | | | | Next state | | | |
|---|---|---|---|---|---|---|---|---|
| | $y_1$ | $y_2$ | $y_3$ | $y_4$ | $y_1'$ | $y_2'$ | $y_3'$ | $y_4'$ |
| $S_1$ | 1 | 0 | 0 | 1 | 0 | 1 | 0 | 1 |
| $S_2$ | 0 | 1 | 0 | 1 | 0 | 1 | 1 | 0 |
| $S_3$ | 0 | 1 | 1 | 0 | 0 | 0 | 1 | 1 |
| $S_4$ | 0 | 0 | 1 | 1 | 1 | 0 | 0 | 1 |

(b) Excitation functions

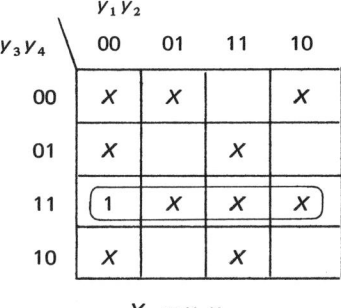

$$Y_1 = y_3 y_4$$

$$Y_2 = y_1 y_4 + y_2 y_4$$

$$Y_3 = y_2 y_4 + y_2 y_3$$

$$Y_4 = y_2 y_3 + y_1 y_4 + y_3 y_4$$

and

$$V_{j_h} (h = 1 \sim r) = \bar{y}_{h_1} \bar{y}_{h_2} \ldots \bar{y}_{h(n-k)}$$

where $\bar{y}_{h_1}, \bar{y}_{h_2} \ldots \bar{y}_{h(n-k)}$ are $n - k$ state variables having value zero in a present state that transfers to a state with $Y_i = 0$ under input $x_j$. By complementing these equations we can obtain the more useful function

$$Y_i = \Pi_j \left( \bar{x}_j + \bar{V}_{j_1} \bar{V}_{j_2} \ldots \bar{V}_{j_r} \right)$$

Using an $nCk$ code, Tohma has shown that two types of fault can result from a single error. These are, firstly, *decreasing faults* which decrease the weight of the state assignment from $k$ to $k-1$ and secondly *increasing faults* which increase the weight to $k+1$. In order to allow for these two types of fault conditions the set of state variables is partitioned into two blocks, $B_1$ and $B_2$, where $B_1$ has $k$ members of state variables and $B_2$ has $n-k$ members. The off-set realization is used for each state variable of $B_1$ and the on-set for $B_2$. Moreover, it is also necessary to treat as a special case assignment codes of the form

$$y_1 = y_2 = .. = y_k = 1$$

and

$$y_{k+1} = y_{k+2} = .. = y_n = 0$$

(called the $k1$ assignment); it is always possible of course to exclude this code from the assignment.

Tohma has shown that if the excitation equations for a circuit are extracted following the procedure outlined above (bearing in mind the constraints of the $k1$ assignment), the equations will also determine state transitions from states having state assignment with weights different from $k$ (the error states). Moreover, the next state of a state with an assignment different to $k$ is also a state with a state assignment different to $k$, thus giving an error-state cycle; this situation also pertains under error conditions.

As an example of this procedure consider machine C shown in Table 5.15 (this is taken from Tohma's paper); then if $B_1$ is the set $\{y_1, y_2\}$ and $B_2$ the

**Table 5.15. Machine C**

(a)

| Present state | Next state | |
|---|---|---|
| | $x = 0$ | $x = 1$ |
| 1 | 1 | 2 |
| 2 | 2 | 3 |
| 3 | 3 | 4 |
| 4 | 4 | 1 |

(b)

| Present state | Next state | |
|---|---|---|
| $y_1 y_2 y_3 y_4$ | $x = 0$ | $x = 1$ |
| 1 0 0 1 | 1001 | 0101 |
| 0 1 0 1 | 0101 | 0110 |
| 0 1 1 0 | 0110 | 0011 |
| 0 0 1 1 | 0011 | 1001 |

set $\{y_3, y_4\}$, using the off-set for $B_1$ and the on-set for $B_2$ we obtain the following excitation equations:

$$Y_1 = \{(y_1 + y_3)(y_1 + y_4)(y_1 + y_2) + x\}\{(y_2 + y_3)(y_1 + y_3)(y_1 + y_4) + \bar{x}\}$$

$$Y_2 = \{(y_2 + y_3)(y_1 + y_2) + x\}\{(y_1 + y_4)(y_1 + y_2) + \bar{x}\}$$

$$Y_3 = y_2 y_3 \bar{x} + y_3 y_4 \bar{x} + y_2 y_4 x + y_2 y_3 x$$

$$Y_4 = y_1 y_4 \bar{x} + y_2 y_4 \bar{x} + y_3 y_4 \bar{x} + y_1 y_4 x + y_2 y_3 x + y_3 y_4 x.$$

From a CAD point of view, Tohma's method would not only appear difficult to program efficiently for a computer, but it has the added disadvantage of requiring a large number of gates to realize the excitation equations. The method has been improved by Diaz et al. (57), who managed to reduce the hardware requirements by placing tighter constraints on the assignment and also to implement the next-state equations with the exclusive use of the on-set form.

A more systematic procedure for deriving fail-safe circuits, which also gives considerable hardware savings over other methods, has been described by Sawin (58). This method is based on partition theory originally developed for the design of asynchronous circuits, but, owing to the similarity of asynchronous- and synchronous-machine models when realized in terms of excitation equations, it is possible to extend the theory to synchronous circuits. As with Tohma's method it is assumed that primary inputs do not fail and that the clocking circuits remain intact. The method only considers static faults of the s-a-0, and s-a-1 type which can occur in the excitation circuitry; multiple faults are not included.

The method consists of deriving a single fail-safe assignment for the specific state table under consideration, using *p-sets* and *r-partitions*, followed by the extraction of monotonic next-state equations. A *p-set* may be defined as follows; the set of predecessors or *p*-set of a state $S_k$ for input column $I_j$ consists of all

$$S_i \in S \mid \delta \ (I_j, S_i) = S_k$$

where $S$ is the set of internal states and $\delta$ the state transition function. For example, for the state table shown in Table 5.16a we have for input $\bar{x}$ the *p*-set of state 2 containing states $\{1,4\}$. The full list of *p*-sets is given below:

$$p_1 = \{1,4\}, \quad p_2 = \{2\}, \quad p_3 = \{3\}, \quad p_4 = \{1,2\}, \quad p_5 = \{4\}.$$

The state assignment may now be generated by associating an $r_i$-partition with each unique $p_i$ in the *p*-set list such that $r_i$ is coded 1 for each state in $p_i$ and

0 for all states not in $p_i$. The full set of $r$-partitions is as follows:

$$r_1 = (\overline{1,4}; \overline{2,3}) \qquad r_3 = (\overline{3}; \overline{1,2,4})$$
$$r_2 = (\overline{2}; \overline{1,3,4}) \qquad r_4 = (\overline{1,2}; \overline{3,4})$$
$$r_5 = (\overline{4}; \overline{1,2,3}).$$

The fully assigned state table for machine D is shown in Table 5.16b. The next step is to extract the next-state equations by considering the *next-state partition* $n_i^p$, which partitions all of the states to be specified 1 for a next-state variable $Y_i$ under input $I_p$ from the states to be specified 0. Hence for machine B we have

for $\bar{x}$: $\;n_1{}^1 = (\overline{2,3}; \overline{1,4}) \qquad$ for $x$: $\;n_1{}^2 = (\overline{4}; \overline{1,2,3})$

$\qquad\quad n_2{}^1 = (\overline{1,4}; \overline{2,3}) \qquad\qquad\quad n_2{}^2 = (\overline{3}; \overline{1,2,4})$

$\qquad\quad n_3{}^1 = (\overline{\phi}; \overline{1,2,3,4}) \qquad\qquad\quad n_3{}^2 = (\overline{1,2}; \overline{3,4})$

$\qquad\quad n_4{}^1 = (\overline{1,3,4}; \overline{2}) \qquad\qquad\quad n_4{}^2 = (\overline{3,4}; \overline{1,2})$

$\qquad\quad n_5{}^1 = (\overline{2}; \overline{1,3,4}) \qquad\qquad\quad n_5{}^2 = (\overline{\phi}; \overline{1,2,3,4})$

Now the next-state equations can be expressed in the following form:

$$Y_1 = f_1{}^1(y_i) I_1 + f_1{}^2(y_i) I_2 + \ldots + f_1{}^m(y_i) I_m$$
$$Y_2 = f_2{}^1(y_i) I_1 + f_2{}^2(y_i) I_2 + \ldots + f_2{}^m(y_i) I_m$$
$$\vdots$$
$$Y_n = f_n{}^1(y_i) I_1 + f_n{}^2(y_i) I_2 + \ldots + f_n{}^m(y_i) I_m$$

**Table 5.16. Machine D**

(a)

| Present state | Next state | |
|---|---|---|
| | $x = 0$ | $x = 1$ |
| 1 | 2 | 3 |
| 2 | 4 | 3 |
| 3 | 1 | 2 |
| 4 | 2 | 1 |

(b)

| Present state | Next state | |
|---|---|---|
| $y_1 y_2 y_3 y_4 y_5$ | $x = 0$ | $x = 1$ |
| 1 0 0 1 0 | 01010 | 00100 |
| 0 1 0 1 0 | 10001 | 00100 |
| 0 0 1 0 0 | 10010 | 01010 |
| 1 0 0 0 1 | 01010 | 10010 |

where $y_i$ are the present-state variables, $Y_1 \ldots Y_n$ are the next-state variables, $I_1 \ldots I_m$ are the input states, and $f_1{}^1 \ldots f_n{}^m$ are functions of the internal-state variables only.

The design equation coefficient $f_i{}^p$ is related to the next-state partition $n_j{}^p$ by the following theorems:

(1)  If $n_j{}^p \leqslant r_i$ then $f_j{}^p = y_i$ or $\bar{y}_i$.

(2)  Let $r_i$ partition $p$-sets $p_i$ of input $I_p$ (where $i = 1, 2, \ldots, x$) then for any

$$n_j{}^p = \overline{(p_1, p_2, \ldots, p_m; \overline{p_{m+1}, \ldots, p})}$$

where $m \leqslant x$ then

$$f_j{}^p = \Sigma\, y_j, y_j \in y_i \qquad \text{where } i = 1, 2, \ldots, m.$$

For example, from machine B we have

$$n_1{}^1 = (\overline{2,3}; \overline{1,4}) = (\overline{p_2 p_3}; \overline{p_1}) \quad \text{with} \quad r_2 = (\overline{2}; \overline{1,3,4})$$

$$\text{and} \quad r_3 = (\overline{3}; \overline{1,2,4}) \quad \text{yielding} \quad f_1{}^1 = y_2 + y_3$$

$$n_2{}^1 = (\overline{1,4}; \overline{2,3}) = r_1 \quad \text{therefore} \quad f_2{}^1 = y_1$$

$$n_3{}^1 = (\bar{\phi}; \overline{1,2,3,4}) \quad \text{therefore} \quad f_3{}^1 = 0.$$

Applying theorems (1) and (2) in this way we obtain the complete set of next-state equations:

$$Y_1 = y_2 \bar{x} + y_3 \bar{x} + y_5 x$$

$$Y_2 = y_1 \bar{x} + y_3 x$$

$$Y_3 = y_4 x$$

$$Y_4 = y_1 \bar{x} + y_3 \bar{x} + y_3 x + y_5 x$$

$$Y_5 = y_2 \bar{x}.$$

Sawin has shown that using this state-assignment procedure and an on-set realization produces a fail-safe design for a synchronous machine. Moreover, the method yields a simple upper bound on the gate requirements of less than or equal to twice the number of $p$-sets. Fault detection may also be simply obtained by examining the parity of the partition set of the present input state of the circuit; if it is even a fault has occurred. The method has considerable advantages over those proposed previously by Tohma and Diaz in that the procedure is more systematic and allows for the simple derivation of next-state equations (and is thus more suitable for CAD) and is economical in hardware requirements.

The design of fault-tolerant asynchronous circuits has proceeded along similar lines, and the two main approaches reported in the literature are the use of a single error-correcting code as the state assignment and assignments based on partition theory. The basic philosophy of fault-tolerant machines remains unchanged: that is the principle of partitioning all possible state codes for a machine into two transition classes, one specified by the normal operation of the machine and the other which is entered under fault conditions. Once the circuit enters a fault class it must continue to dwell in that class until remedial action can be taken to direct it back to the normal operating cycle.

Pradham and Reddy (59) have formally defined an $m$-fault-tolerant asynchronous network as one which will tolerate any kind of fault in the excitation network that results in, at most, $m$ state variables being faulty without adverse effect on its behavior; that is the output sequences, given the input sequences and the initial states, do not change under fault conditions. This may be stated as follows.

An asynchronous sequential network $N$ realizing a sequential machine $M$ is fault tolerant if, and only if, for every pair of state transitions in $M$ (say from $S_i$ to $S_j$ and $S_k$ to $S_l$) $X$ and $Y$ are two states of $N$ that can be reached in the absence of faults during the transitions from the state assignment (SA) of $S_i$ to SA($S_j$) and SA($S_k$) to SA($S_l$) respectively. Then $d_H (X, Y) \geqslant 2_m + 1$ where $d_H (X, Y)$ is the Hamming distance between $X$ and $Y$, $m$ the number of faults, and $i \neq k, l$ and $j \neq k, l$.

The design process described assumes that the asynchronous machine can be specified by a normal-mode flow table and that only single-input-variable changes can occur; the circuit is also assumed to be free of essential hazards. Assignments are based on the STT type of assignment due to Liu and Tracey, but with additional constraints to ensure that the assignment has the characteristics of an error-correcting code. Let $D_{i,j}^{fm}$ be the set of all states of an excitation network $N$ realizing $M$ that can be reached during the transition from SA($S_i$) to SA($S_j$) in the presence of at most $m$ faults. Then for an STT assignment with fault-tolerant properties it is necessary and sufficient to have $D_{i,j}^{fm} \cap D_{k,l}^{fm} = \phi$, $i \neq k, l$ and $j \neq k, l$ for every pair of state transitions under every input if $m$ or fewer of the state variables can be faulty. In addition it is necessary that the state assignment has a $d$-separation with $d \geqslant 2_m + 1$ for the network to be $m$-fault tolerant, where $d$-separation is defined as the number of state variables needed to cover the disjoint subsets of state pairs in the normal STT assignment. For single-fault detection it is only necessary to construct an assignment that will guarantee that any two states that are reached during two different transitions are separated by a Hamming distance of 2.

Design techniques are presented in the paper which show how redundancy may be introduced into the state-assignment procedures of Liu (60) and Friedman (61) to yield fault-tolerant codes; the method is also capable of being extended to include fault detection. The assignment procedure has not been programmed for a computer but there does not appear to be any major problem. However, the technique has the disadvantage of requiring an excessive amount of logic for circuit realization and, more important, it has been suggested (62) that difficulties can arise owing to the existence of masked or undetectable faults in the logic. This comes about as a consequence of not being able to check the added (redundant) circuitry that is used to provide fault detection.

A similar technique for fault detection based on established asynchronous logic design theory has been described by Sawin and Maki (63); the method has been further developed into a general design procedure for single-fault-tolerant circuits (64).

A fault-detecting assignment may be generated by partitioning the destination sets of a flow table such that they have a minimum distance of 2. This requirement satisfies the basic constraint for fault detection that the transition paths of equivalent state classes (that is those states with the same next-state entries for a given input) must not be adjacent. Consider the destination sets (65) $D_i$, $i = 1, 2, \ldots, x$ under input $I_p$; then the set of $r$-partitions $\{r_i\}$ is given by

$$r_i = \{D_i \overset{x}{\underset{j \neq i}{\cup}} D_j\}.$$

For example, in the flow table for a divide-by-two counter shown in Table 5.17a, the destination sets are, for $x = 0$, $D_1 = \{AD\}$ and $D_2 = \{BC\}$ and for $x = 1$, $D_3 = \{AB\}$ and $D_4 = \{CD\}$. The corresponding $r$-partitions are shown below:

$$r_1 = (\overline{A, D}; \overline{B, C})$$
$$r_2 = (\overline{B, C}; \overline{A, D})$$
$$r_3 = (\overline{A, B}; \overline{C, D})$$
$$r_4 = (\overline{C, D}; \overline{A, B})$$

which yields the assignment shown in Table 5.17b.

## Table 5.17. Asynchronous Counter Circuit

(a) Flow table

|   | Input $x$ | | Output $z$ |
|---|---|---|---|
|   | 0 | 1 | |
| A | $\textcircled{A}$ | B | 0 |
| B | C | $\textcircled{B}$ | 0 |
| C | $\textcircled{C}$ | D | 1 |
| D | A | $\textcircled{D}$ | 1 |

(b) Assigned flow table

|   | | Inputs | |
|---|---|---|---|
|   | | $x = 0$ | $x = 1$ |
|   | $y_1 y_2 y_3 y_4$ | $y_1 y_2 y_3 y_4$ | $y_1 y_2 y_3 y_4$ |
| A | 1 0 1 0 | 1 0 1 0 | 0 1 1 0 |
| B | 0 1 1 0 | 0 1 0 1 | 0 1 1 0 |
| C | 0 1 0 1 | 0 1 0 1 | 1 0 0 1 |
| D | 1 0 0 1· | 1 0 1 0 | 1 0 0 1 |

The *partition set* for input $I_p$ is defined as consisting of those state variables which partition the destination sets of input state $I_p$ (called the *partitioning variables*). In our example of Table 5.17b the $r$-partitions $r_1$ and $r_2$ (corresponding to $y_1$ and $y_2$) are the partitioning variables for $x = 0$ and $r_3$ and $r_4$ for $x = 1$; thus the partition sets are $\{r_1, r_2\}$ and $\{r_3, r_4\}$ respectively.

As we have seen earlier the excitation equations for a sequential circuit may be expressed in the general form

$$Y_n = f_n^1 (y_i) I_1 + f_n^2 (y_i) I_2 + \ldots + f_n^m (y_i) I_m.$$

Now in order to ensure that once a circuit enters a fault equivalence class it remains there, the coefficient $f_n^m$ in the equations must be derived using the following theorem.

(a) If the next-state partition $n_j^p \leqslant r_i$ then $f_j^p = y_i$.

(b) If all the elements of $n_j^p$ are in one block of the partition then $f_j^p = 0$ or 1.

(c) Let $r_i$ partition the destination sets $D_i$ of input $I_p$ in the form

$$r_i = \{D_i \overset{x}{\underset{j \neq i}{\cup}} D_j\}$$

then for all $f_j^p$ terms $f_j^p = y_i$ where $i = 1, 2, \ldots, x$. Furthermore, if there exists

$$n_j^p = \{ \bigcup_{i-1}^{m} D_i; \bigcup_{k=m+1}^{x} D_k \} \quad m \leqslant x, j \neq (1, 2, \ldots, x)$$

then $f_j^p = y_1 + y_2 + \ldots y_m$.

(Note that the above rules for deriving the coefficient $f_n{}^m$ represent a formal generalization of the conditions described earlier for the synchronous case.)

It follows from the theorems above that if $y_i$ is a partitioning variable under input $I_p$ then $f_i^p = y_i$. This means that partitioning variables cannot share common logic circuits and fault conditions must therefore be contained within individual circuits. Moreover, it will be seen that each non-partitioning variable is a function solely of the partitioning variables. Furthermore, it can be shown that the next-state equation coefficients $f_i^p$ of any partition set of $I_q$ are realizable using the partition variables of $I_p$ once only. The significance of this theorem is that each partitioning variable is only required to feedback once (or not at all) to realize the $f_i^p$ term of every partition set. It also follows that the next-state equations must be monotonic, that is no invertors are required in the feedback paths.

As an example of deriving the excitation equations consider the counter circuit shown in Table 5.17$b$; from this we obtain

$$n_1{}^1 = (\overline{A, D}; \overline{B, C}) \quad \text{and} \quad f_1{}^1 = y_1 \qquad n_1{}^2 = (\overline{C, D}; \overline{A, B}) \quad \text{and} \quad f_1{}^2 = y_4$$

$$n_2{}^1 = (\overline{B, C}; \overline{A, D}) \qquad\qquad f_2{}^1 = y_2 \qquad n_2{}^2 = (\overline{A, B}; \overline{C, D}) \qquad\qquad f_2{}^2 = y_3$$

$$n_3{}^1 = (\overline{A, D}; \overline{B, C}) \qquad\qquad f_3{}^1 = y_1 \qquad n_3{}^2 = (\overline{A, B}; \overline{C, D}) \qquad\qquad f_3{}^2 = y_3$$

$$n_4{}^1 = (\overline{B, C}; \overline{A, D}) \qquad\qquad f_4{}^1 = y_2 \qquad n_4{}^2 = (\overline{C, D}; \overline{A, B}) \qquad\qquad f_4{}^2 = y_4.$$

The full set of design equations are as follows:

$$Y_1 = y_1 \bar{x} + y_4 x$$

$$Y_2 = y_2 \bar{x} + y_3 x$$

$$Y_3 = y_1 \bar{x} + y_3 x$$

$$Y_4 = y_2 \bar{x} + y_3 x.$$

Fault conditions are easily detected by observing that the parity of the states of the flow table in each partition set is odd. Thus, whenever the circuit assumes a state where the parity of the partitioning variables is even a fault condition exists; tolerated faults can be detected by checking the parity of all partition sets. For the example above faults can be detected by using two parity-check circuits for the conditions $y_1 y_2$ and $y_3 y_4$. The complete circuit is shown in Fig. 5.12; note that the output of the parity-check circuit must be gated with the appropriate input.

Faults can also be detected in the output logic by using the same technique. This is done by forming the equations in a similar way to the next-state equations, treating the output variable as another state variable. An important characteristic of the parity-checking circuits is that they do not need to be assumed fault free (that is the hardcore element normally required in redundant systems). It can be shown that a circuit fault indication will be given even if a parity-check circuit fails (provided of course it was not a tolerated fault).

The fault-detection technique may be used to achieve a single-fault-tolerant system by employing two independent asynchronous circuits, each capable of detecting faults. When one of the circuits experiences a fault it is switched out and the other is allowed to generate the output. Note that this is similar in principle to a triple-mode redundancy system but in this case only two copies of the machine are required. Moreover, the procedure is easily accomplished in a real-time environment with the minimum of hardcore logic. For the method to be effective in operation it is necessary that both the switch and the fault-detection logic be implemented using simple circuitry. In practice the switch consists of a set–reset bistable and a two-level gating circuit consisting of two AND gates and an OR gate; the switch can of course always be designed as a fail-safe circuit. A block schematic of the system is shown in Fig. 5.13. The method shows considerable promise for the design of fault-tolerant systems but would require CAD techniques to facilitate its adoption as an effective procedure for large-variable systems. One obvious

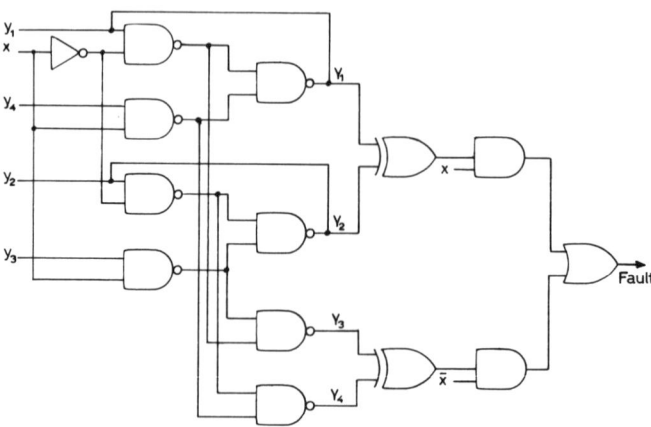

**Figure 5.12.** Fault-tolerant counter.

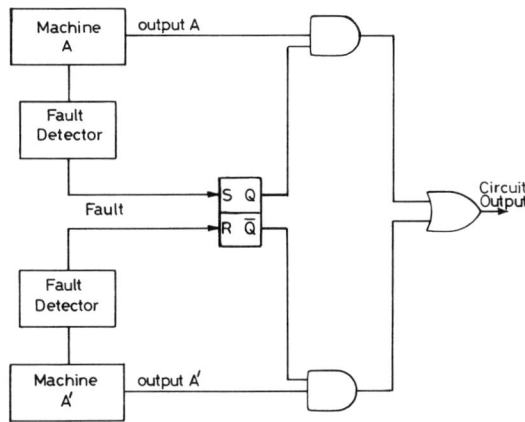

**Figure 5.13.** Single-fault-tolerant circuit.

disadvantage is that protection is only given for single faults; an extension of the method to enable it to handle multiple faults would seem essential for practical applications.

It is interesting to note the similarity in principle between this method and that described by Roberts (65) based on the SPIF concept first proposed by Beizer (66). The *sequential prime implicant function* (SPIF) is an algebraic representation of sequential-circuit behavior which reduces sequential-machine theory to a combinational form. As a consequence it is possible to apply established combinational switching theory to the analysis and synthesis of sequential machines.

The method is based on the similarity between the *transition matrix* of a sequential circuit (derived from the *assigned* state table) and the conventional K-map used in combinational logic. Beizer showed that these matrices and their SPIF representation could be considered as elements of a Boolean algebra. For example, in Table 5.18 the assigned state table can be transformed into a transition matrix which may then be represented by the algebraic function

$$\text{SPIF} = \bar{x}\,(A\bar{B}\bar{A}_+\bar{B}_+ + \bar{A}\bar{B}\bar{A}_+B_+ + AB\bar{A}_+B_+ + \bar{A}BA_+B_+) +$$
$$x\,(AB\bar{A}_+\bar{B}_+ + A\bar{B}\bar{A}_+B_+ + \bar{A}BA_+\bar{B}_+ + \bar{A}BA_+\bar{B}_+) \tag{5.2}$$

These expressions may of course be reduced in the usual way using mapping techniques.

In the transition matrix the rows correspond to the present state of the matrix, and consequently each of the variables $A$, $B$ can be interpreted as specifying the value of its associated circuit node (equivalent to a monitor

## Table 5.18. SPIF Representation for Sequential Circuits

(a) Assigned state table

| Present state | Next state | |
|---|---|---|
| | $x = 0$ | $x = 1$ |
| $AB$ | $A_+B_+$ | $A_+B_+$ |
| 00 | 01 | 10 |
| 01 | 11 | 10 |
| 10 | 00 | 01 |
| 11 | 01 | 00 |

(b) Transition matrix

$A_+B_+x$

| AB \ | 000 | 001 | 011 | 010 | 110 | 111 | 101 | 100 |
|---|---|---|---|---|---|---|---|---|
| 00 | | | | 1 | | | 1 | |
| 01 | | | | | 1 | | 1 | |
| 11 | | 1 | | 1 | | | | |
| 10 | 1 | | 1 | | | | | |

(c)

$A_+B_+$

| AB \ | 00 | 01 | 11 | 10 |
|---|---|---|---|---|
| 00 | | 1 | | |
| 01 | | | 1 | |
| 11 | | 1 | | |
| 10 | 1 | | | |

$x = 0$

$A_+B_+$

| AB \ | 00 | 01 | 11 | 10 |
|---|---|---|---|---|
| 00 | | | | 1 |
| 01 | | | | 1 |
| 11 | 1 | | | |
| 10 | | 1 | | |

$x = 1$

point in the physical realization of the network) prior to the transition. The column headings specify the next state, and similarly the $A_+$, $B_+$ variables can be considered as indicating the value of the node at the end of the transition. Thus the present- and next-state variables can be interpreted as follows.

$A$, $B$ and $A_+$, $B_+$ indicate a transition from a 1 and to a 1 respectively.

$\bar{A}$, $\bar{B}$ and $\bar{A}_+$, $\bar{B}_+$ indicate a transition from a 0 and to a 0.

Using these relationships the SPIF given in Eq. (5.2) may be interpreted for the first term as node $A$ goes from 1 to 0 and node $B$ remains 0 under input $\bar{x}$, similarly for the second term node $A$ remains 0 and node $B$ goes from 0 to 1 under input $\bar{x}$, etc. Following this procedure the SPIF can be used to describe measurements made on an actual circuit and hence a partial behavioral description of the machine, as observed from a particular set of nodes, may be derived.

If the transition matrices for individual inputs are considered (see Table 5.18c), it is possible to define certain characteristics which are possessed by the sequential circuit. For a properly specified machine each row must have one, and only one, entry; Beizer called a transition matrix which violates this rule *unresolved*. An unresolved matrix (or its SPIF representation) that contains a row without an entry is called *ambiguous* since the next state under the input condition is undefined. A SPIF with more than one entry per row is called *contradictory* because of the existence of more than one next state. An ambiguous SPIF has a physical realization; on the other hand a contradictory SPIF would be non-deterministic since the machine would be incompletely specified. Note than an unresolved SPIF can be used to represent any part of a circuit without the necessity of knowing the complete operation of the network.

Beizer used the term *projection* to signify the description of the behavior of a subnetwork of the circuit. Projections can be obtained by replacing all occurrences of the nodes to be projected out (both complemented and uncomplemented forms) in the specified SPIF for the circuit by logic 1 and simplifying. For example, from Eq. (5.2) the projection for node A is given by

$$\bar{x}\,(A\bar{A}_+ + \bar{A}\bar{A}_+ + \bar{A}A_+) + x\,(A\bar{A}_+ + \bar{A}A_+).$$

Alternatively, projections can be established empirically by observation on the actual circuit and then combined, using the AND function, to yield a SPIF description for the circuit. The testing problem consists of tracing projections through a network, resolving ambiguous and contradictory conditions as they occur, until a minimal set of projections representing the network is obtained. The SPIF description derived in this way will subsume the actual SPIF for the network but will not necessarily be equal to it. Thus it is necessary to establish the minimal set of projections whose Boolean product equals the original SPIF for the circuit. A fault-tolerant system can be based on these ideas by considering the sets of projections specified by the sets of prime

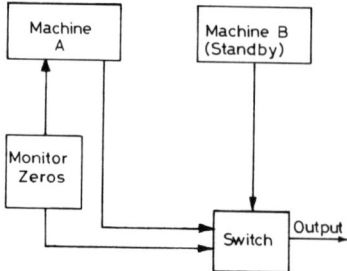

Figure 5.14. Self-repair using SPIF's.

implicants that cover the *inverse* SPIF (that is the zeros of the SPIF). These zero projections are sufficient to specify the SPIF, and thus the correct operation of the circuit can be verified by monitoring the zeros of the set of projections. The zeros represent transitions that *should not occur* during the proper operation of the circuit. However, any changes in the state diagram brought about by fault conditions will give rise to zero transitions.

The method requires two copies of the machine, one acting as standby, and a monitoring and switching circuit. The process operates in a real-time environment and under single-fault conditions the switch need not be considered hardcore; a block diagram of the system is shown in Fig. 5.14. The equations required to design the monitoring circuitry may be generated using the following algorithm.

(a)  Derive the behavioral equations (SPIF) specifying the network.
(b)  Select a projection of the SPIF restricted by single-fault conditions.
(c)  Find the prime implicants of the zeros of the projection.
(d)  Repeat steps (b) and (c) for all necessary projections.
(e)  Find non-redundant coverings for all the prime implicants found in (c), thus covering the entire inverse SPIF.

Note that the method employed for finding the prime implicants of the inverse SPIF can utilize conventional minimization procedures developed for combinational logic. It will be obvious that CAD techniques (with all the attendant difficulties) must be used to enable large-variable systems to be designed.

## REFERENCES AND BIBLIOGRAPHY

1. Bennetts, R. G., and Lewin, D. W. Fault diagnosis of digital systems—a review. *Computer J.* **14**, 199–206, 1971.
2. Chang, H. Y., Manning, E. G., and Metze, G. *Fault Diagnosis of Digital Systems.* John Wiley–Interscience, New York, 1970.
3. Elspas, B., Green, M. W., and Levitt, K. N. Software reliability. *Computer* **4**(1), 22–7, 1971.

4. Ross, D. T., Goodenough, J. B., and Irvine, C. A. Software engineering: process, principle and goals. *Computer* 8(5), 17–27, 1975.

5. Seshu, S., and Freeman, D. N. The diagnosis of asynchronous sequential switching systems. *IRE Trans. Electron. Computers* EC11, 459–65, 1962.

6. Kohavi, Z. *Switching and Finite Automata Theory*, chap. 13. McGraw Hill, New York, 1970.

7. Bennetts, R. G., and Scott, R. V. Recent developments in the theory and practice of testable logic design. *Radio Electron. Eng.* 45, 667–79, 1975. Also *IEEE Computer* 9(6), 47–63, 1976.

8. Reddy, S. M. Easily testable realisations for logic functions. *IEEE Trans. Computers* C21, 1183–8, 1972.

9. Boswell, F. R. Designing testability into complex logic boards. *Electronics* 45, 116–9, 14 Aug. 1972.

10. Schneider, D. Designing logic boards for automatic testing. *Electronics* 47, 100–4, 25 July 1974.

11. Pierce, W. H. *Failure-Tolerant Computer Design*. Academic Press, New York, 1965.

12. Special issue on failure-tolerant computing. *IEEE Trans. Computers* C23(7), 1974.

13. Special issue on failure-tolerant computing. *IEEE Trans. Computers* C24(5), 1975.

14. Wilcox, R. H., and Mann, W. C. (eds.). *Redundancy Techniques for Computing Systems*. Spartan Press, Washington, D.C., 1962.

15. Sellers, F. F., Hsiao, M. Y. and Bearnson, L. W. *Error Detecting Logic for Digital Computers*. McGraw Hill, New York, 1968.

16. Mine, H., and Koga, Y. Basic properties and a construction method for fail-safe logical systems. *IEEE Trans. Electron. Computers* EC16 282–9, 1967.

17. Chang, H. Y. An algorithm for selecting an optimum set of diagnostic tests. *IEEE Trans. Electron. Computers* EC14, 706–11, 1965.

18. Kautz, W. H. Fault testing and diagnosis in combinational digital circuits. *IEEE Trans. Computers* C17, 352–66, 1968.

19. Galey, J. M., Norby, R. E., and Roth, J. P. Techniques for the diagnosis of switching circuit failures *IEEE Trans. Commun. Electron.* 83, 509–14, 1964.

20. Armstrong, D. B. On finding a nearly minimal set of fault detection tests for combinational logic nets. *IEEE Trans. Electron. Computers* EC15, 66–73, 1966.

21. Hackl, F. J., and Shirk, R. W. An integrated approach to automated computer maintenance. *IEEE Conf. Record on Switching Circuit Theory and Logic Design*, pp. 289–300, 1965.

22. Roth, J. P. Diagnosis of automata failures: a calculus and a method. *IBM J. Res. Dev.* 10, 278–91, 1966.

23. Roth, J. P., Bouricius, W. G., and Schneider, P. R. Programmed algorithm to compute tests to detect and distinguish between failures in logic circuits. *IEEE Trans. Electron. Computers* EC16, 567–79, 1967.

24. Friedman, A. D., and Menon, P. R. *Fault Detection in Digital Circuits.* Prentice Hall, Englewood Cliffs, N. J., 1971.
25. Warburton, G. C. Automatic dynamic response system for testing semiconductors. *IERE Conf. on Automatic Test Systems, Conf. Proc. No. 17,* pp. 467-84, April 1970.
26. Sellers, F. F., Hsiao, M. Y., and Bearnson, L. W. Analysing errors with the Boolean difference. *IEEE Trans. Computers* **C17**, 676-83, 1968.
27. Amar, V., and Condulmari, V. Diagnosis of large combinational networks. *IEEE Trans. Electron. Computers* **EC16**, 675-80, 1967.
28. Bennetts, R. G. A realistic approach to detection test set generation for combinational logic circuits. *Computer J.* **15**, 238-46, 1972.
29. Seshu, S. On an improved diagnosis program. *IEEE Trans. Electron. Computers* **EC14**, 69-76, 1965.
30. Clegg, F. W. Use of SPOOF's in the analysis of faulty logic networks. *IEEE Trans. Computers* **C22**, 229-34, 1973.
31. Flomenhoft, M. J., Si, S. C., and Susskind, A. K. Algebraic techniques for finding faults for several fault types. *Digest of Papers Int. Symp. Fault-Tolerant Computing,* pp. 85-90, 1973.
32. Si, S. C., and Susskind, A. K. A method for obtaining SPOOF's. *IEEE Trans. Computers* **C24**, 560-2, 1975.
33. Bossen, D. C., and Hong, S. J. Cause-effect analysis for multiple fault detection in combinational networks. *IEEE Trans. Computers* **C20**, 1252-7, 1971.
34. Kriz, T. A. A path sensitising algorithm for diagnosis of binary sequential logic. *Proc. IEEE Computer Group Conf.,* Vol. 70-C-23-C, pp. 250-9, 1970.
35. Moore, E. F. Gedanken-experiments on sequential machines. *Automata Studies,* pp. 129-53. Princeton University Press, Princeton, N. J., 1956.
36. Gill, A. *Introduction to the Theory of Finite State Machines.* McGraw Hill, New York, 1962.
37. Hennie, F. C. Fault detecting experiments for sequential circuits. *Proc. 5th Ann. Symp. on Switching Theory and Logic Design, Princeton University,* 1964, S.164, pp. 95-110.
38. Hennie, F. C. *Finite State Models for Logical Machines.* John Wiley, New York, 1968.
39. Kime, C. R. An organisation for checking experiments on sequential circuits. *IEEE Trans. Electron. Computers* **EC15**, 113-5, 1966.
40. Kohavi, Z., and Lavellee, P. Design of sequential machines with fault detection capabilities. *IEEE Trans. Computers* **C16**, 473-84, 1967.
41. Kohavi, Z., Rivierre, J. A., and Kohavi, I. Machine distinguishing experiments. *BCS Computer J.* **16**, 141-7, 1973.
42. Poage, J. F., and Mcluskey, E. J. Derivation of optimum test sequences for sequential machines. *Proc. Fifth Ann. Symp. on Switching Circuit Theory and Logical Design, Princeton University,* 1964, S164, pp. 121-32.

43. Muller, D. E. Application of Boolean algebra to switching circuit design and to error detection. *IRE Trans. Electron. Computers* **EC3**, 6–12, 1954.

44. Mukhopadhyay, A., and Schmitz, G. Minimisation of EXCLUSIVE OR and LOGICAL EQUIVALENCE switching circuits. *IEEE Trans. Computers* **C19**, 132–40, 1970.

45. Fisher, L. T. Unateness properties of AND-exclusive-OR logic circuits. *IEEE Trans. Computers* **C23**, 166–72, 1974.

46. Kautz, W. H. Testing faults in combinational cellular logic arrays. *Proc. 8th Ann. Symp. Switching and Automata Theory*, Oct. 1971, pp. 161–74.

47. Reddy, S. M. A design procedure for fault-locatable switching circuits. *IEEE Trans. Computers* **C21**, 1421–6, 1972.

48. McNaughton, R. Unate truth functions. *IRE Trans. Electron. Computers* **EC10**, 1–6, 1961.

49. Saluja, K. K., and Reddy, S. M. Easily testable two-dimensional cellular logic arrays. *IEEE Trans. Computers* **C23**, 1204–7, 1974.

50. Hayes, J. P. On modifying logic networks to improve their diagnosability. *IEEE Trans. Computers* **C23**, 56–62, 1974.

51. Saluja, K. K., and Reddy, S. M. On minimally testable logic networks. *IEEE Trans. Computers* **C23**, 552–4, 1974.

52. Dandapani, R., and Reddy, S. M. On the design of logic networks with redundancy and testability considerations. *IEEE Trans. Computers* **C23**, 1139–49, 1974.

53. Liu, T. K. Synthesis algorithm for 2-level MOS networks. *IEEE Trans. Computers* **C24**, 72–9, 1975.

54. Russo, R. L. Synthesis of error-tolerant counters using minimum distance three state assignments. *IEEE Trans. Electron. Computers* **EC14**, 359–66, 1965.

55. Meyer, J. F. Fault tolerant sequential machines. *IEEE Trans. Computers* **C20**, 1167–77, 1971.

56. Tohma, Y., Ohyama, Y., and Sakai, R. Realisation of fail-safe sequential machines by using a *K*-out-of-*n* code. *IEEE Trans. Computers* **C20**, 1270–5, 1971.

57. Diaz, M., Geffroy, J. C., and Courvoisier, M. On-set realisation of fail-safe sequential machines. *IEEE Trans. Computers* **C23**, 133–8, 1974.

58. Sawin, D. H., III. Design of reliable synchronous sequential circuits. *IEEE Trans. Computers* **C24**, 567–9, 1975.

59. Pradhan, D. K., and Reddy, S. M. Fault-tolerant asynchronous networks. *IEEE Trans. Computers* **C22**, 662–8, 1973.

60. Liu, C. N. A state variable assignment method for sequential switching circuits. *J. A.C.M.* **10**, 209–16, 1963.

61. Friedman, A. D., Graham, R. L., and Ullman, J. D. Universal single transition time asynchronous state assignment. *IEEE Trans. Computers* **C18**, 541–7, 1969.

62. Sawin, D. H., III, and Maki, G. K. Comments on "fault-tolerant asynchronous networks". *IEEE Trans. Computers* **C24**, 756–8, 1975.

63. Sawin, D. H., III, and Maki, G. K. Asynchronous sequential machines designed for fault detection. *IEEE Trans. Computers* **C23**, 239–49, 1974.

64. Maki, G. K., and Sawin, D. H., III. Fault-tolerant asynchronous sequential machines. *IEEE Trans. Computers* **C23**, 651–7, 1974.

65. Roberts, D. C. A processor for implementing SPIF techniques for self-repair. *Computer Des.* Dec. 1969, pp. 59–64; Jan. 1970, pp. 63–9.

66. Beizer, B. Towards a new theory of sequential switching circuits. *IEEE Trans. Computers* **C19**, 939–55, 1970.

67. Susskind, A. K. Diagnostics for logic networks. *IEEE Spectrum* **10**, Oct. 1973, pp. 40–7.

# Index of Names

# Index of Subjects